D0235449

Trading in children:
a study of private fostering

International Library of Social Policy

General Editor   Kathleen Jones
Professor of Social Administration
University of York

Arbor Scientiæ
Arbor Vitæ

A catalogue of the books available in the **International Library of Social Policy** and other series of Social Science books published by Routledge & Kegan Paul will be found at the end of this volume

Trading in Children

a study of private fostering

Robert Holman

Department of Social Administration and
Social Work
University of Glasgow

Routledge & Kegan Paul
London and Boston

First published in 1973
by Routledge & Kegan Paul Ltd
Broadway House, 68–74 Carter Lane,
London EC4 5EL and
9 Park Street,
Boston, Mass. 02108, U.S.A.
Printed in Great Britain by
C. Tinling & Co. Ltd,
London and Prescot
© Robert Holman 1973

ISBN 0 7100 7538 3

To my mother
and in memory
of my father

Contents

vii

Tables

Acknowledgments

The research study upon which this publication is based was financed by grants from the Home Office Research Unit and the Research Committee of the Faculty of Commerce and Social Science of the University of Birmingham. Miss Valerie Bartlett, Miss Susan Levett, Mrs Hazel Couch, Mrs Rosamund Thorpe, Mrs Diana Newton and Miss Gilda Peterson rendered much valuable help, particularly in the time-consuming tasks of judging, categorising, coding and data analysis. Professor François Lafitte, the head of the Department of Social Administration of Birmingham University, allowed me to spend much time away from the department while undertaking the field work. Mrs Marian Batten gave her usual encouragement and efficient secretarial services, ably supported by other members of the clerical staff. Gratitude must also be expressed to the officials of the two children's departments, the foster parents and natural parents, for without their co-operation the study could not have been made. Above all, my thanks are due to my family. My wife, Annette, participated at all stages. My children, Ruth and David, were a constant source of delightful distraction which served to refresh me for further application to the research.

This volume is a rewritten and shortened version of a Ph.D. thesis. Inevitably much has had to be left out. In particular, lack of space forbade the inclusion of all but one of the interview recording schedules, the letters used in the research and the 'Instructions and Guide to the File Recorder, Interviewers, Coders and Categorisers'. The omission is unfortunate as a major part of the research was taken up in schedule design, question formation, testing, the defining of terms and of categories. However, those with specialist research interests can consult the full work in the library of the University of Birmingham.

1   Background to the research

The boarding-out with foster parents of children separated from their own parents is now generally regarded as the form of care most likely to promote their emotional, social and physical well-being. The Curtis Report (Home Office, 1946) declared that boarding-out, or fostering, to adopt the word now in common use, was 'the best method, short of adoption, of providing the child with a substitute for his own home' (Home Office, 1946, para. 460). The ensuing Children Act (1948) no less clearly made the same point, giving local authorities a duty to board out children in their care unless it proved 'not practicable for the time being' (para. 13). The same Act required local authorities to appoint children's committees who, through children's departments, would be responsible for children taken into or committed to the care of the local authorities.[1] The departments responded by making strenuous efforts to foster children so that on 31 March 1970, according to the Home Office (1970b, p. 5) there were 71,210 children in the care of local authorities in England and Wales, of whom 30,210 were boarded out.

It has not been widely realised that alongside local authority and voluntary society fostering – which involves these organisations selecting foster homes for children in their care – exist several thousand foster children placed in foster homes selected by their parents or guardians. Such children are known as child protection cases or private foster children. They are not in the care of the local authorities, although the children's departments do possess some supervisory duties and powers in regard to them. The lack of knowledge about private fostering is best illustrated, amusingly, by the Prime Minister who, in November 1968, on receiving a question in the House of Commons about private foster children, answered in terms applicable only to children in the care of public bodies.[2] None the less, private foster children have been the subject of a number of pieces of legislation, and the very question directed to the Prime Minister was an indication of growing public concern about them.

1

Private fostering in the past

Until the second half of the nineteenth century, children placed privately with foster parents received no more protection or supervision from the law or statutory agencies than children remaining in their own homes. Mary Hopkirk has documented a number of cases, from Victorian times and before, of parents, particularly unmarried mothers, farming-out, giving away and even selling their infants to other adults who subsequently neglected them. Contemporary public opinion did not appear unduly perturbed, even when informed, until well past the middle of the century. The founding of the Infant Life Protection Society in 1870, however, marked a growing concern with the high mortality rate amongst children, particularly illegitimate children. The mortality rate amongst infants under one year old farmed-out in large cities was estimated at between 70 and 90 per cent.[3] During the same period, a number of inquests and prosecutions made it obvious that some private foster mothers (and natural parents) were murdering their children for financial gain. The children, their lives having been insured with several burial clubs, would be murdered by an excessive use of opiates – commonly used to keep babies quiet – by burning or scalding, by suffocating or by neglect. The case of the notorious foster mother, Mrs Waters, who was tried and executed for the murder of several foster children in 1870, was one of the influences leading to the establishment of the Select Committee on the Protection of Infant Life. Its report, published in 1871, uncovered a widespread system of private fostering, or 'baby-farming' as it was then called.

The report led to the first Infant Life Protection Act (1872). Under its provisions, private foster mothers who took two or more children for reward, that is for some source of income whether in cash or kind, were required to register with the local authority. The local authority for its part could refuse to register any house it thought unsuitable and strike off the register any person incapable of providing proper food and attention or guilty of serious neglect. The death of any foster child had to be reported to a coroner. As in all following enactments, it was made clear that persons fostering relatives or taking children from public institutions were exempted from the provisions. The Act, for all its fine intentions, was never fully implemented, not least because it failed to lay its duties and powers upon any specific department or committee. The horror stories continued, culminating in the trial of another foster mother, Mrs Dyer, in 1896 for murder. The following year another Infant Life Protection Act (1897) gave the local authorities greater powers of inspection and removal of foster children, defined the meaning of 'improper care', and indicated that inspection should be carried out by committee members or officials of the Poor Law rather than by the police. The children's upper age-limit to which the powers applied was set at five years. The 1897 Act was to be the last piece of legislation solely concerned with child protection until the Children Act (1958). In the intervening years, enactments relating to private fostering were tacked on to other pieces of child legislation.

The Children Act (1908), although mainly concerned with juvenile offenders, did raise the age-limit to seven years, made child protection legislation applicable to homes taking only one child, and put the responsibility for inspection definitely with the Poor Law. For the next twenty-eight years, no legislation directly affected the care of private foster children, although the age-limit was raised by two more years in 1932. However, during these years the Poor Law machinery was being gradually dismantled and the supervision of private foster homes began to fall within the scope of local health departments. Thus it is in the Ministry of Health's *Eighth Annual Report* of 1926–7 that it is claimed that the worst abuses of 'baby-farming' had been eradicated. The movement of foster child protection into the health field was confirmed by the Public Health Act (1936) and the Public Health (London) Act (1936). The Acts stipulated that persons intending to take children under nine years of age to nurse and maintain for reward had to inform the welfare authorities before the placement commenced. The authorities, who began to discharge their duties through health visitors, had to visit the children 'from time to time' and to satisfy themselves as to their well-being.

Information on foster children coming under the terms of the 1936 Acts is, as Middleton (1971, pp. 225–6) points out in his history of the care of children in the first half of the present century, 'non-existent'. He could only imagine that 'ample opportunity for indifferent child care existed, for local authority staffs were small'. Not until the Curtis Report of 1946 did the quality of care given private foster children come under published public surveillance, although even here it formed but a fragment of a document mainly concerned with children in the care of public bodies. The Children Act (1948), which implemented many of the recommendations of the Curtis Report, raised the age at which children placed in private foster homes were subject to the legislation to the upper level of 'compulsory school age' (once placed before this age the child remained subject to the provisions until he was eighteen). At the same time the newly-formed children's departments became responsible for implementing statutory responsibilities towards private fostering.

In the ten years following the Children Act (1948), little attention was directed towards private foster children as the new departments grappled with the problems of children entrusted to their care. In 1949, the Home Office knew of 7,411 private foster children in England and Wales. In addition, it reported another 25,640 children in independent residential schools, whom the Home Office considered came within the terms of child protection legislation as defined by the Acts of 1936 and 1948. In fact, a Chancery Court ruling held that such children were not 'living apart' from their parents and hence not liable to inspection by children's departments. It became clear that the legislation relating to private foster children required re-stating and there followed an enactment specifically concerned with private fostering, the Children Act (1958).

The Children Act (1958) was the legislation applicable to private fostering at the time the research for the present study was conducted.[4] It stipulated the private foster parents' responsibilities towards the local authority as well as the local authorities' duties and powers in regard to private fostering. These provisions will be discussed in detail in a later chapter. It defined private foster children as being those 'below the upper limit of compulsory school age, whose care and maintenance are undertaken for reward for a period exceeding one month by a person who is not a relative or guardian of the child' (Section 2).

Children falling within the scope of the above definition are the subject of the study. To avoid confusion, it is as well to spell out which children are not included. Obviously, children received into the care of local authority children's departments or of voluntary children's societies are excluded. Voluntary bodies sometimes arrange for children to be fostered out either as foster children or pending a placement to an adoptive home. These too are excluded, for the research is concerned with children placed with private foster parents by their own parents (or guardians) and not by an agency. Also excluded are children sent by their parents to private nurseries, children's homes or other institutions. Children placed directly by their parents or any other party for adoption are not included, for the subject matter is fostering, not adoption.[5] Lastly, the study is one of notified private foster children, that is, of private fostering known to the children's departments. No doubt many private fosterings occur without the children's departments being informed, but it is impossible even to hazard a guess at their numbers.

Knowledge and opinion about private fostering

The rapid growth in local authority fostering has been accompanied by a number of pieces of research and a considerable literature, both in the form of child care text books and articles in social work journals. However, almost no research has concentrated on private fostering. Jean Packman, in her comprehensive study of children in public care (1968) gives more attention than any other researcher to the subject – a total of eight pages (pp. 127–33 and 227). She thought that children's departments saw private foster children as a 'fringe responsibility' and postulated that illegitimacy would account for many of the children with their parents being of 'a higher social class than those of children in public care'. But mainly Packman bewailed the lack of facts, saying, 'there are no published statistics which indicate the circumstances which lead to private placement in foster homes.' The lack of basic facts may explain why a study of the child care text books recommended by social work training courses revealed that none gave more than two pages to the child care officers' work with private foster homes.

The only concrete fact to emerge about private fostering in the last decade is that the number of notified fosterings has increased. The returns of local authority children's departments in England and Wales, as published by the Home Office, give the following figures:

1961	6,780	1966	10,600
1963	8,038	1969	10,907

The increase has been one factor leading to a renewal of concern about private fostering. The lack of established knowledge has not inhibited individual writers and official bodies expressing opinions about it. A review was made of as much of this opinion as possible. These sources, which provided the hypotheses for the present research, included reports issued by the Home Office, annual reports of local authority children's departments, statements by the Association of Children's Officers and the Association of Child Care Officers, articles in the press and statements made in parliament. In addition, some starting points were culled from the *Report on the Care of Pre-School Children*, otherwise known as the Yudkin Report, and a voluntary society report, *Racial Integration and Barnardo's* (Dr Barnardo's Homes, 1966).

The sources concurred on a number of points.[6] It was thought that in the south-east, private foster children were frequently placed by coloured students. David Waddington MP added that children could be placed with ease, and considered that there was then a tendency for natural parents to lose touch.[7] The private foster parents, it was agreed, were sometimes of poor quality, and the late Sir Cyril Osborne MP, in speaking of 'the increase of foster homes, many of which are dirty, unhealthy and dangerous', recalled the term 'baby-farming' implying that overcrowded conditions led to financial profit.[8] Private foster children were thus, in the words of one children's department, 'at risk physically and emotionally' and liable to be 'passed by a harassed parent from one unsatisfactory home to another'.[9] Whatever the risks, it was suggested that the children's departments could do little to help. In 1967, the Home Office's *Report on the Work of the Children's Department, 1964–6*, attributed this to 'problems arising from the legal limitations on the exercise of the powers of local authorities to impose requirements about numbers of children, standards of accommodation, etc.' (p. 16).

The danger of opinions is that they can give rise to false generalisations. Thus a few cases of badly treated private foster children have prompted some persons to speak as though all were so treated. Research functions to give a knowledge-base which is more reliable than opinions. Yet the opinions, taken in conjunction with a pilot survey in a London borough, did serve as a source from which the objectives and hypotheses of the study could be formulated.

The primary objective was to provide the first description and analysis of private fostering, private fostering being taken to include the foster parents, the foster children, the natural parents and the children's departments. Within this it was hoped to test the general hypothesis that, within the local authority areas chosen for study, the private foster children would reveal conditions and difficulties at least similar to those of such children in local authority foster homes, without receiving a similar level of service and help from the children's departments. Following this, the hypotheses covered eight main sections concerning the following: the identity of the private foster parents; the identity of the private foster children; the suitability of the private foster parents; the treatment of the private foster children; the condition of the private foster children; the identity of the natural parents and their reasons for using private foster homes; the relationship between the natural parents and the private foster homes; and the role of the children's departments. Within each section were a number of hypotheses, which will be stated in each chapter.

An approach to the study

Completed or ongoing fosterings?

The objectives having been defined, an approach towards them was necessary. It was decided that the only way to obtain the necessary information was by selecting a sample of private foster children and closely studying them and their foster parents. This determined, the next question was whether to examine completed fosterings, that is, past ones, or current, ongoing fosterings. The following reasons decided for the latter. First, the information available from child care officers and foster mothers about current cases would be less susceptible to memory-failure than with old cases. Second, the cases would be operating at all junctures and stages of fostering, and not just at the end. Third, it would have proved extremely difficult to compile a sample of completed fosterings for the local authority does not record the later movements of the foster parents or the children. The research would thus have had to resort to the methods of Kornitzer (in adoption research) who advertised for adopters (1968, pp. 21–2). Respondents of this kind are self-selected and hence make up a very biased or one-sided sample. In Kornitzer's case it seemed that 'successful' adopters rather than 'non-successful' responded.

Measurement

The inclusion of terms such as 'suitable' in the statement of hypotheses implies ways of measurement or assessment. If one foster mother may be considered suitable and another unsuitable, then clearly some means has to exist whereby they are distinguished. The research thus had to devise or adopt instruments of measurement. The various ones used will be explained in the relevant chapters. They ranged from straightforward enumeration, such as the number of persons living in the foster homes, to devices adapted from other research such as the father participation measure of the Newsons (1963, ch. 14), to attitude scales based on foster parents' replies, to assessments made by child care officers.

Measurement in itself is not enough. To say that a foster father participated on six child-rearing items out of ten does not indicate whether he should be considered 'fully' participant or 'non' participant (to use the Newson terms) unless it has been established which number of items is equivalent to which grades of participation. In other words, standards are required. In the social sciences, standards can rarely be attributed to any absolute base, they usually involve some form of subjective judgment. Often these judgments are generally accepted and can be incorporated into research. Thus persons living in a density of over one and a half persons per room are usually considered to be in overcrowded conditions. Another approach is to compare one group in society with another. In the present research the attempt was made to compare the conditions or behaviour of private foster parents and children with, first, those of the normal population and, second, with local authority foster parents and children.

Comparisons were made, where appropriate and possible, with research findings relating to 'normal' populations, that is, with parents who do not take foster children and children who are not foster children. Comparisons of this nature deter the researcher from deducing that certain characteristics are peculiar to his sample when they are, in fact, common to a larger population. To give one example, it was possible to compare the conditions of overcrowding amongst private foster homes with other sections of the population, and thus to conclude whether they were any more likely to experience this particular disadvantage.

A second important source of comparison was with local authority foster homes. Both private and local authority foster children are separated from their own parents and can be expected to show some differences in behaviour or development compared with children remaining at home. However, if strong differences were found in the treatment of, condition of, or services given to the two groups, then there would be grounds for believing that they were caused by the different types of fostering. Already the research of Parker, Trasler, Gray and Parr and others provided valuable material for local authority fosterings. However, research amongst neither normal nor local authority fostering populations contained comparative material for all the factors which it was desired to explore. Therefore consideration was given to drawing two contrast groups, one of children living with their natural parents and one of children in local authoity foster homes. The limits of finance and time meant that only one group could be used, and the choice fell upon the local authority group for two main reasons. First, a central part of the research was to assess the services given by the children's departments to private foster homes. As little work of this nature existed in respect of local authority fosterings it was not possible to find a source of comparison in previous research. Second, the work of the Newsons, the National Cohort Study, the census, to mention but three sources, indicated that comparative material would be more readily available for normal than for foster homes.

The contrast group could have consisted of local authority foster parents (accompanied by their foster children), or of local authority children (accompanied by their parents). It was decided to select via children, as it was their treatment and condition which provided a major focus of the research. The private foster children, as will be explained, comprised a total population, that is they consisted of all the private foster children in two local authorities. However, the two authorities in the areas chosen for the study had far more local authority foster children, so some means of matching was required. Simultaneously, it was felt important to control variables which are known to influence the course of fostering. Significantly, Goode and Hatt in their well-known *Methods in Social Research* claim the control of known variables to be one of the key points in research design (1952, pp. 78–91). No doubt there are variables of which the researcher has no knowledge, and the only possible action is to ascertain from previous studies which variables have been established, and from the pilot study which ones are likely to influence the course and outcome of the subject. The factors were the child's age, his age at placement, the time he had been in the placement, his sex and his nationality. Interestingly, after the research design was completed, the publication of George's research confirmed that the age of the child was particularly influential and that studies could falsely record two other factors as casually related when the real link was age (1970, pp. 214–15). If these variables were controlled or held constant, then differences between the two groups of foster children could, with more confidence, be attributed to the influence of the different kinds of fostering. To achieve this, a local authority contrast group was drawn by precision-matching the private foster children for the aforementioned factors. The manner and difficulties of the matching will be explained in a later paragraph, but here two important points must be made. First, by matching certain factors the investigator may overlook differences in the overall distribution of those same factors amongst the groups as a whole. For instance, the researcher could have found that all the private foster children were under five years old and then have matched them for age from the much larger local authority group, but overlooking the important point that, say, 50 per cent of the latter were over ten years of age. It is therefore necessary also to make comparisons with local authority children as a whole. Second, although the foster children were matched pairs, their foster parents are not matched for their qualities or attributes. Therefore when the two groups of children are statistically compared a matched-pairs technique must be used, but the same does not apply to comparisons of foster parents.[10]

The location of the private foster children

Having determined to study a group of private foster children, the researcher had to decide how to obtain a sample from the thousands of private fosterings known to local authority children's departments. One method would have been to take a one in every hundred random sample from the thousands. However, the resultant sample would have been spread over a very large number of local authorities, making for difficulties of time and distance as well as that of obtaining the co-operation of all the children's departments concerned.[11] Practical reasons thus made it necessary to select private children from a geographically concentrated area. In choosing the location, four factors were taken into consideration: the area had to provide enough cases to allow statistical work to be carried out on them; it had to be reasonably accessible to the researcher who was residing in the Midlands; it had to be not abnormally different from the child populations and children's departments of most other local authorities; and, if possible, the area should include a city and a county in order that comparisons could be made between the two. All four conditions were found in a city and its surrounding county in the Midlands.

The city chosen for the study was a prosperous manufacturing area, its industry characterised by engineering which was succeeding the traditional hosiery and footwear trades as the main single source of work. Opportunities for female labour were plentiful, with an estimated 40 per cent of women in employment. The county, which surrounds the city, was a rural area with a number of small towns with light industries.

To what extent do the children's departments of the city and county differ from others in England and Wales? In 1968 the city had 665 children in its care, being 8·5 per thousand of its population under eighteen years: 59·3 per cent of the children in care were in foster homes. The county had 482 children in its care, this being 3·7 per thousand of its population under eighteen, with 58 per cent boarded out in foster homes. These figures compare with the figures for England and Wales of 5·2 per thousand population in care and 49·5 per cent in foster homes. A study of the statistics relating to children in the care of local authorities shows that cities tend to have a higher percentage in care than counties, a point confirmed by Packman's research (1968, p. 19). Thus the city and county in this study are not untypical of children's departments as a whole. The percentage of children fostered is somewhat above average, although both departments fall within the great cluster of children's departments whose boarding-out percentage is between 45 and 65 per cent. Thus of thirty-one children's departments in the Midlands region, only four were above and two below this range. The Home Office returns also allow an examination of the age structure of children in care and of methods of accommodation other than fostering. Again, the city and county do not reveal any outstanding divergences from the national pattern. Further, there is little difference between reasons for receptions into care. It is fair to conclude that the two children's departments are not unrepresentative of children's departments as a whole.

Turning to the staffing of the children's departments, it is possible to make comparisons between the number of child care officers who are (i) professionally qualified, which entails having the Home Office Letter of Recognition; (ii) partially qualified, which entails having some other qualification in the social sciences; and (iii) non-qualified (see Table 1.1 for figures supplied by the Association of Child Care

Table 1.1   Qualifications of child care officers in the study areas and in England and Wales

	City	County	All county borough councils in England and Wales	All county councils in England and Wales
	%	%	%	%
Professionally qualified	42·1	50·1	28·6	45·5
Partially qualified	53·2	5·6	22·8	18·0
Non-qualified	4·7	44·4	48·6	36·5
Totals*	100·0	100·0	100·0	100·0

*As figures are rounded to the nearest figure after the decimal point, the totals will not always total 100 per cent.

Officers for the year 1967). This Table shows that both the city and county have somewhat more trained staff than is available for county boroughs and county councils. It is therefore to be expected that the standards of child care help offered to both children in public care and to private foster children would not be lower than in most other places.

It is also possible to calculate the numbers of child care officers per 1,000 population. In the city the figure was 0·066, for the county 0·045. By comparing this with similar calculations made for eighteen other local authorities it can be seen that the two study areas were neither extremely well off nor extremely poorly off (Holman, 1970b, Appendix A, Table 11).

Turning to the numbers of private foster children in the city and county, what comparisons can be made with other local authority areas? The Home Office does not publish numbers per 1,000 of populations under eighteen as they do for children in public care, but it is possible to calculate this. Using the figures for 1968, the city had 0·77 and the county 0·66 children per 1,000 population under eighteen supervised under the Children Act (1958). The average figure for all county boroughs in England and Wales was 0·80 and for county councils 0·58 (London boroughs are excluded from these calculations). The city and county are thus near average.

The subject of immigrants is often linked with private fostering, so it is as well to consider the percentage of immigrants in the two study areas. The 1966 sample census (Great Britain) Immigrant Tables give the number of residents born in new Commonwealth countries.[12] The city had 10,500, a high number compared with most other local authorities, but not sufficient to put it amongst the cities with the highest percentage. A number of London boroughs and other industrial and university towns in the Midlands and the South have more. The county had 2,440, a not abnormal number for a county council.

The present research does not claim to be representative of all private fosterings. None the less, it is of importance that the local authorities in which the study occurred were not abnormally different from other authorities in their child care and other social features.

It may be interjected at this point that, in fact, the research found few differences between the private foster children and parents of the city and county. Where differences were found they will be commented upon but otherwise the children from the two areas will be taken together as one group.

Drawing the sample

An earlier section made it clear that the research was not concerned with children in private nurseries and private children's homes. Neither was it concerned with independent boarding schools caring for children for over one month in the school holidays who do come within the terms of the Children Act (1958). As it happened, at the time there were no children of this kind notified to the two local authorities but had there been they would have been excluded from the sample. The sample of private foster children could therefore be found in the very straightforward manner of taking every child notified to the two children's departments under the terms of the Children Act (1958) on a certain date in 1968.

As mentioned, a contrast group of local authority foster children was needed. A list was drawn up of all children in public care and fostered out by the two children's departments. The few boarded out with relatives were removed in order to delete one variable, for a child fostered privately with a relative would not come within the meaning of the Children Act (1958). The local authority children were then matched against the private ones for sex, age, age when placed in the foster home and the nationality of the children's parents. Matching for the first three factors proved comparatively straightforward, but not for the last. It became obvious that the children of West African parents were in large numbers within the private fostering group but not amongst the local authority one. On the other hand, children of mixed racial parentage were frequently found amongst the local authority children but not amongst the private ones. Obviously this was a major difference to be further examined, but matching proceeded on the basis of pairing together children having at least one parent of non-United Kingdom origin. For instance, a child of West African parents was matched with a child of a West Indian man and a British girl. It was felt that the colour element might well produce similar problems, whatever the nationalities. On this basis the city sample could be matched, but nearly half of the county children still were not. Consequently, in the subsequent analysis of the research every item was tested with and without the children matched for nationality, and the differences noted. The overall result of the sampling was that 143 private foster children were matched with 143 local authority children, this giving 100 private foster mothers (an embarrassingly convenient number) and 122 local authority foster mothers.

Sources of information

The previous sections have shown why the research required a sample of private foster children and a local authority contrast group. The next stage was to determine what kind of material was required in order to discuss the hypotheses and then how it should be obtained.

The sample, or study population, consisted of ongoing or live cases, that is, they were foster children in existing foster homes on a selected date in 1968. The question arose whether relevant information could be best found by creating some means whereby the fosterings could actually be observed in action by the researcher or whether to rely solely on the children's departments' records and the verbal comments of the fostering participants. The direct observation approach had been used by Heinicke and Westheimer (1966) in their study of the reactions of children placed in day and residential nurseries. Its main advantage consists in the data being immediately and directly available to the researcher instead of coming via the memory of others. Its disadvantages, as far as the present research was concerned, were three-fold. First, if the child care officers and foster parents had known the children were being observed they might well have changed their behaviour towards them. In other words, the research effect would have become a new influence in the fostering situation. Second, the practical difficulties of watching a foster home are great, far more so than watching children in nurseries. Third, research observation techniques, even when backed by large resources, can usually be sustained for very limited time periods and therefore cover few children. Heinicke and Westheimer's study dealt with but a handful of children and then only for a few weeks. The hypotheses of the present study required information not just over a few weeks but stretching from the beginning of the fosterings up to the point the research was undertaken. The reliance on file reports and the comments of the fostering participants obviated the above disadvantages. Material could be collected which related to the past and present, but none was taken from the children's departments' records after the date the child care officers were informed which cases were to be studied. Hence any changed behaviour towards the children would not have been incorporated into the research. The potential disadvantage of this particular means revolved around its partial dependence upon people's memories. However, memory fallibility became less of a threat for the following reasons:

a much of the material required was 'concrete' fact systematically recorded in set places on official forms. Examples are the nationality of the children and the dates on which officers visited the foster homes.

b much of the material was hardly liable to memory slip, for instance the foster mother giving her marital status or her age.

c as far as possible information was geared to the present or immediate past. Instead of asking if the natural parents had visited the child regularly in the past, the foster parent was asked how often they had visited in the last year.

d questions relating to past events concerned matters which were so major as to leave little room for error, for instance whether a child had had pneumonia. Stott's experiment (1957) shows that mothers tend to be reliable informers of such information. He also argues that parents' memories concerning their children's previous experiences are remarkably reliable, provided a skilled interviewer is used.

e much of the information was obtained from files consisting of reports written by child care officers soon after their visit to a foster home. They were not therefore asked to cast their minds back over events which happened many years before.

f some of the information could be obtained from more than one source, and thus checked. Some data taken from the foster mothers could be compared with that on official records or received from the child care officers. Reliability of information is discussed in the Appendix.

Before starting the research in the Midlands some weeks were spent looking at private fostering in a London borough. Here, a pilot survey was carried out. This experience showed that there were five main sources of material relating to private fosterings – the file records or reports kept by the children's departments, the foster mothers, the child care officers, the natural parents, and, to a lesser extent, the schools attended by the children (if of school age). The children themselves are omitted from the sources. It was anticipated that some would not be aware of their fostering status and that hence their foster parents would not agree to their participation in the project.

Children's departments' file records or reports

The use of case histories or case records as a basis on which to make generalisations about social phenomenon has been subject to strong criticism. In the worst examples, as Simon points out concerning some American studies, '[they are] statements of belief presented as theory, documented with cases. Or else certain points are made and illustrated to enlighten the reader without measure or estimates as to validity or reliability.'[13] Such studies, usually presented by case-workers or psychiatrists drawing upon their own caseloads and reports, have two further weaknesses. Being therapeutic interviews they have not used recording schedules, hence the case records considered are not always comparing the same material. Second, the cases are not selected in a random way but are chosen to illustrate a preconceived point. Not surprisingly, the cases are not matched with controls, the information is not categorised or coded, no statistical analysis is made.

However, the above failings can be overcome so that case records can be employed to provide reliable data. For instance, Parker (1966) in his research on local authority fostering relied almost entirely on case records. But he was not using his own cases. He drew a sample and collected similar material from each record. In this way the material obtained can be confidently used to test hypotheses, instead of being taken as a proof of a predetermined doctrine.

The files kept by children's departments are case studies or reports in the sense that they present a picture of the past history and process of a child. Yet they are also records which collect certain items of information concerning every child. Some of these items are pre-scribed by legislation. Both departments kept files on every private and local authority foster child as well as separate records concerning persons who had applied to be local authority foster parents. The files contained a wealth of information. Every visit, every telephone call, every caller to the office was recorded. Duplicates of letters were kept; certain basic information was recorded on sheets at the front of the file, such as the date of birth or dates of moves. In addition the child care officers recorded their visits to the homes, their assessments of the fostering situation and of the individual participants. Obviously these are subjective assessments, but they are none the less valuable. Social workers are trained to be aware of their own motives and needs which may influence their perceptions; hence their records are probably more reliable than most. It can be seen that the file informa-tion was central to the research. It was collected on a file recording schedule previously tested during the pilot survey.

Foster mother interview

The research of Parker and Trasler relied heavily on file information but not on interviews with foster mothers. In this study it was felt there was information which only foster mothers could give, for instance concerning their attitudes towards the child care officer. Information was collected by a recording schedule. The interviews were also tape-recorded. The playing back of a tape reduces the chances of the interviewer missing what the respondent is saying because he is so busy scribbling down the previous sentence or because the answers do not fit in with what he expects to hear. A further advantage of the tape recording is that it makes available the respondents' own words to give life to quantitative data. To this end it was considered important to record as many interviews as possible. The Newsons in their first study tape-recorded under a third of their interviews with mothers, namely those conducted by their university interviewers, while not using tapes with those interviewed by health visitors (1963, p. 26). This approach may induce bias in that the most voluminous material and the examples given were taken from a minority of the cases. In the present study very few foster mothers objected to the use of the tape recorder. Occasionally a baby, and once a dog, bit the microphone but, as other researchers have found, generally the presence of the recorder did not appear to inhibit the foster mothers, who were given assurances that their identity would remain anonymous.

Child care officers

Children's departments allocate their cases or clients to particular child care officers, who usually retain them for as long as they remain. The officers thus build up considerable knowledge about their clients. All the officers responsible for the private and local authority foster children in the study were interviewed using a recording schedule. The methods employed to construct the schedule and obtain the information were similar to those for the foster mothers but, in addition, senior child care officers who supervised the officers' cases were asked to answer some identical questions relating to the assessment of the foster homes. It thus became possible to calculate the degree of agreement between their assessments.

Schools

Some of the hypotheses involved the children's progress and behaviour at school. The information required was comparatively straightforward; it did not, for instance, involve an assessment of attitudes, and could be collected by a postal questionnaire to schools to be completed by head teachers and class teachers. The limitations of such questionnaires are well-known. The response rate is usually low and the researcher has no chance to clarify dubious points with the respondent. George, using the postal method, had response rates of 61·4 per cent and 80·3 per cent from foster parents in two areas (1970, p. 43). The question raised is to what extent are non-respondents different from respondents. It follows that postal questionnaires should only be used when a high response rate is likely, or there is some way of comparing respondents and non-respondents. In the present study, the support of the two local authority education departments ensured a good response.

Natural parents

It had been intended to interview all the natural parents of the foster children. However, the children's departments concerned and the Home Office felt that contact with some parents could lead to complications. For instance, some natural parents who had almost dropped out of a fostering situation might have been stirred to return, so causing distress to the foster parents and foster children. These points were accepted, and instead it was agreed to try to contact natural parents only where the children's department thought it advisable and where foster parents gave permission for an approach. It became clear that the number obtained would be so small as to make any statistical work of little value. However, it was decided to interview some natural parents with a recording schedule as a kind of addendum to the main research. Of course, a good deal of information about the natural parents was collected from the files and is used for a fuller analysis.

Excluding the natural parents, four major sources of information were available. The material required was sought from them, using recording schedules, and based on three major principles or guidelines:

a that where possible information should be sought from more than one source. Kornitzer's method of relying heavily on data from adoptive parents is open to the criticism that her research presents adoption only through the eyes of one party. The practice in the present research of drawing on more than one source enabled information to be checked and gave a more comprehensive study of each fostering.

b that information would be collected by persons independent of the children's departments. Fanshel used child welfare officers to interview and gain research information from other fostering participants (1966, p. 18–19). As they asked them questions concerning the agency and its officers, it seems likely that the interviewees would be inhibited in their replies, not wishing to criticise the agency which employed the interviewers. In the present study, the researcher was himself able to carry out virtually all the work on the file records, interviews with the private foster parents and child care officers. A research assistant did some of the interviewing of the local authority foster parents.

c that, as far as possible, the information would be sought in a form which could be quantified.

An account of the construction of the recording schedules, of the construction of the questions, of the reliability and truthfulness of responses, and one of the recording schedules, are contained in the Appendix. The other schedules, the letters used in the research, the instructions and guide used by the file recorder and the methods of categorising and coding can be found in my thesis in the library of the University of Birmingham (1971).

The response

All the careful construction of recording schedules and the drawing of samples would be of little avail unless the givers of information were willing to co-operate. The active backing of the children's and education departments meant that all the child care officers participated in interviews and all the schools returned their questionnaires. The active support of the foster parents had also to be won. The procedure for interviewing the foster mothers was that initially a letter from the children's officers informed them that the researcher was acting with their approval. I then wrote explaining the project, stressing the confidentiality of the interview, and emphasising that I was not employed by the local authority. A suggested interview date and time was inserted along with a stamped addressed card to allow the foster mother to decline or change the date. Only one of the private foster mothers and four of the local authority foster mothers declined to be interviewed. As far as could be ascertained those who refused did not differ in any other way from those who accepted. They were then asked if they would complete a postal questionnaire, and to this they agreed. The co-operation of the research population was extremely high by any standards. The reason probably rests in the foster parents' own belief that they were providing a worthwhile social service about which they were pleased to talk.

The information obtained from the file records and interviews by the methods described above was categorised and coded and then put on IBM punch cards ready for analysis. The findings can now be discussed in the chapters which follow.

2　The private foster parents

In the absence of any research whatsoever on the subject, the identification of the characteristics of the private foster parents became a major objective of the study. It was hypothesised that the private foster parents would show different characteristics from local authority foster parents. Previous research, particularly that by Parker and Trasler, had demonstrated certain attributes or characteristics of local authority foster parents which had contributed to the success or failure – measured by how long fosterings lasted – of foster homes. Assuming that such factors could be equally influential on private fosterings, it was important to include them in the study. Therefore, information was sought on the foster parents' total number of natural children, the number of natural children still living with them, and their (i.e. the foster parents') age. A second hypothesis was that the private foster mothers would be characterised by a record of continually taking foster children, by taking large numbers at any one time, and by taking young children for short periods. In addition, data were sought on birthplace, social class and marital status, factors which Parker and Adamson had found useful in describing local authority foster mothers.

Characteristics of the private foster parents

Birthplace

The birthplaces of the private and local authority contrast groups (see Table 2.1)[1] reveal a general similarity. In both, over half the mothers were fostering in their region of birth while nearly 70 per cent were from the Midlands. Adamson's study of local authority foster parents in Monmouthshire found that 52 per cent had lived there since birth so 'confirming the impression that foster parents tend to belong to the less mobile sections of the community' (1968, p. 433).

The government sample census of 1966 estimates the birthplaces of all females in the city and county studied. It gives birthplace

Table 2.1   Birthplace of the foster mothers

	Private foster mothers		Local authority foster mothers	
	No.	%	No.	%
The study area (city or county)	64	64	67	54·9
Elsewhere in the Midlands	15	15	18	14·8
Elsewhere in the United Kingdom	18	18	34	27·9
Eire	2	2	1	0·8
West Indies	0	0	1	0·8
Europe	1	1	1	0·8
Totals	100	100	122	100·0

according to the Registrar General's regions and not counties and cities, but it is possible to observe that 78·9 per cent of these females were born in the Midlands, compared with 79 per cent of the private foster mothers. It can be concluded that according to birthplace the private foster mothers do not differ greatly from the local authority group or the general population. Certainly there was no evidence that they were predominantly from coloured commonwealth countries. According to the sample census only 1·6 per cent of the females in the city and county had been born in the Commonwealth, colonies or protectorates, compared with none of the private foster mothers.

Marital status

Eighty-five of the private foster mothers were married at the time of the research, seven were co-habiting, three were widowed, two were divorced, two single and one separated. The local authority foster mothers showed a similar distribution except that only one was co-habiting. However, co-habitation does provide a male figure, and only 8 per cent of the private fosterings and 8·1 per cent of the local ones were without a foster father. The sample census figures for all women of twenty years and over in the two local authorities do not take into account co-habitations and separations, but it is worth noting that over 70 per cent were married, 13 per cent widowed, over 12 per cent single, and under 1 per cent divorced.

Social class

The social class of local authority foster parents has attracted the interest of researchers. Wakeford (1963) argues that downward social mobility is itself related to motivation, the women compensating for lost status by becoming foster mothers. However, this argument has not taken into reckoning the general finding, for instance by Parker and by Gray and Parr, that local authority foster parents are under-represented in the lowest social class as well as the highest when compared with the general populace. What of private foster parents? The assessment of their social class was made according to the Registrar General's *Classification of Occupations, 1966*. This system facilitates comparison with previous research and fitted into the recording schedule approach of the study.[2] The findings are presented in Table 2.2. A comparison with the city and county 1966 census

Table 2.2   Socio-economic class of the foster parents

	Private foster parents		Local authority foster parents	
	No.	%	No.	%
I Professional	2	2	5	4·1
II Intermediate	14	14	19	15·6
III Skilled	38	38	60	49·2
IV Partly skilled	27	27	26	21·3
V Unskilled	19	19	12	9·8
Totals	100	100	122	100·0

population showed the private foster parents to be drawn dispropor-tionately from the lower social classes. As the census included persons as young as fifteen, a more meaningful comparison can be made with the fathers of children of primary school age according to material given in the Plowden Report. This recorded 4 per cent in social class I, 14 per cent in II, 59 per cent in III, 16 per cent in IV, and 6 per cent in V, with 1 per cent unclassified (Central Advisory Council for Educa-tion, 1967, vol. 2, pp. 99–100). Again, the private foster parents are seen to be much more heavily weighted towards the two lowest social classes.

The contrast group of local authority foster parents gave a social class distribution very similar to that of Parker's sample of foster parents in Kent. Interestingly, however, the private foster parents tended to be of lower social groupings than even them. The difference was statistically significant (dividing the classes I–III/IV–V, $\chi^2 = 5\cdot5140$, $P = <0\cdot025$).[3] Thus private foster parents were marked not only by being drawn from lower social groupings than the population as a whole, but even lower than the local authority foster parents.

The social class of private foster parents has implications for the condition and treatment of children placed with them. Heraud's review of sociological research (1970) suggests that social classes can be distinguished by differing means of communication, child-rearing practices and behaviour patterns, as well as by differing attitudes and material conditions. Thus problems arising from differences of opinion and difficulties in communication may occur between private foster parents of one class and natural parents (or social workers) of a higher one. Foster children, too, may experience problems when taken from one set of child-rearing practices and attitudes – which would have shaped their intellectual, social and emotional aspirations and ways of functioning – and placed in an entirely different environment.

Number of natural children

The private foster mothers' number of natural children did not differ significantly from that of the local authority contrast group. Like most married women of over twenty years in the normal population, over half had two, three or four children.[4] Interestingly, only 14 per cent were childless, a proportion much less than that of the census population. On the other hand, 15 per cent had five or more children compared with a census figure of 8·5 per cent. Wakeford and Fanshel have argued that childlessness motivates some women to foster. These findings suggest that childfullness must also be taken into consideration, some women possibly wishing to continue the satisfactions gained from their successes in the mothering role.

The foster parents' number of natural children is not necessarily the same as the number still living with them. Twenty-three of the private foster parents had no natural children at home, twenty-two had one child, twenty-seven had two, and twenty-eight had three or more. In Table 2.3 the numbers are compared with local authority foster parents in the contrast group and with two other samples.

Few differences can be discerned between the numbers of natural children at home of the private foster parents and the local authority contrast group. Yet the local authority foster parents in the Parker and Gray and Parr samples had far fewer children at home. Why should such differences occur between the local authority groups? The contrast group was derived via a matching with private foster children. The foster parents can therefore be expected to take on

Table 2.3   The number of natural children living at home with various samples of foster mothers

No.	Private foster mothers %	Local authority foster mothers %	Local authority foster mothers (Parker) %	Local authority foster mothers (Gray and Parr) %
0	23	22·2	41·2	49
1	22	25·4	37·3	27
2	27	27·0	15·8	16
3 and more	28	25·4	5·7	8
Totals	100	100·0	100·0	100

some of the features of the private foster parents. The private foster children were characterised, as will be shown, by being under five years of age, by being in the foster homes for a short period and by having foster mothers in young age-bands. Young mothers themselves tend to have more children at home, for their own youngsters have not grown up and left. The local authority foster children were matched for age and time in the placement and, not surprisingly, their foster mothers therefore reflected the youth and number of children at home of the private ones.

It must be stressed that while the private foster parents comprised the total population of such persons in the study areas, and may or may not be typical of private foster parents as a whole, the local authority contrast group was not a total population and is certainly not typical. The two tentative conclusions reached are, first, that the number of natural children at home of private foster parents and of the contrast group of local authority ones selected via a matching of the foster children, shows little difference. Second, compared with random samples of local authority foster parents, the private ones tended to have more children at home. The findings take on particular interest when put beside Parker's claim that foster home breakdowns are least likely to occur where no natural children are present, and most likely where three or more are at home (1966, p. 64).

The age of the private foster mothers

At the time of the study, 81 per cent of the private foster mothers were in the age-range of thirty-one to sixty years. Comparison with the local authority contrast group and with all married women in the areas revealed few differences save that the latter tended to have more in the over-sixties range.

An examination of the age of the two groups of foster mothers at the time the foster child was placed with them again revealed no statistically significant differences. However, it was implied above that where a feature of the local authority foster parent group appeared to stem from the factors involved in matching, then comparisons should be made with other local authority samples. The local authority children were matched with the young age and short placements of the private foster children, features which tended to be associated with younger women. Comparison was therefore made with the samples used by Trasler and Gray and Parr (see Table 2.4). This Table shows

Table 2.4   *Age groupings of foster mothers at time placement was made, compared with similar data from other research*

Years	Private foster mothers %	Local authority foster mothers %	Local authority foster mothers (Trasler) %	Local authority foster mothers (Gray and Parr) %
Under 30	22	27·0	1·8	8
31–40	36	40·2	27·5	25
41–50	29	21·3	35·9	40
51–60	10	9·8	28·8	23
61 and over	3	1·6	6·0	4
Totals	100	100·0	100·0	100

that the private foster mothers tended to be younger at the time of placement than local authority foster mothers in general. In particular, proportionately far more were under thirty years of age. The importance of the finding is increased by Trasler's demonstration that children placed with women who were under forty years of age at the time had less chance of fostering success than those put with older foster mothers (1960, p. 219). To sum up a complicated analysis: the private foster mothers and those of the contrast group of local authority foster mothers had very similar age structures: but a comparison of the total population of private foster mothers in the study areas with random samples of local authority foster mothers suggested that the former were characterised by being younger at the time of taking their foster children.

Although additional features will be introduced as the study proceeds, a profile of private foster mothers has emerged. Notwithstanding the many exceptions, they tend to be from the lower social groupings, to be married, residing in the area of their birth, with two to four children, and having started to foster before they were forty. Their social characteristics do not easily distinguish them from other women in the community, or from the contrast group. Indeed, apart from the greater likelihood of private foster mothers being from social classes IV and V, the hypothesis that they would reveal different characteristics from the local authority contrast group must be considered undermined. However, a comparison not with local authority foster parents matched via the foster children, but with samples more representative of local authority foster parents as a whole, revealed the private foster parents as having more natural children at home and being younger at the time they commenced fostering.

The private foster mothers' experience of child care

Numbers of present foster children

The second hypothesis of the present chapter stated that the private foster mothers would be characterised by a record of continually taking foster children, by taking large numbers at any one time, and by taking young children for short periods. At the time of the study, eight of the private foster mothers had three foster children, while the remainder had only one or two. The local authority foster mothers tended to have more, with nineteen, 15·5 per cent, looking after three or more. The fees charged for the foster children will be discussed later, but on the basis of numbers taken there was little evidence that the private foster mothers were 'baby-farming' by crowding in large numbers of children at any one time. The degree of overcrowding depends on two additional factors: the number of rooms available (which will be discussed in chapter 6) and the number of other children present. Table 2.5 includes all the children who either slept in the home or who were daily-minded there. Comparable figures are given not only for the contrast group but also for a sample of households of primary school children used in research for the Plowden Report. In order to save space, percentages only are given in Table 2.5. From this Table it can be seen that the private foster homes tend to care for more children than the sample drawn from households with a child

Table 2.5   Total number of children cared for by foster mothers and sample of households with a child at primary school

No.	Private foster mothers %	Local authority foster mothers %	Plowden sample %
1	11	9·8	9·2
2	22	23·8	36·2
3–4	43	39·3	40·6
5 and more	24	27·0	14·0
Totals	100	100·0	100·0

at primary school, but not more than the local authority homes. Presumably the numbers in the latter did not cause undue problems of overcrowding or mean that the mother could not give sufficient care to the foster child, or else the children's department would not have approved the placement.

The nature of previous private fosterings

The sections of the hypothesis relating to the private foster mothers continually taking foster children and taking young children for short periods meant that data was required on their previous foster children, that is, on completed fosterings. The research had been orientated towards present, ongoing placements, but the digression to the past gave the opportunity to obtain information only available from completed fosterings.

All but 23 per cent of the private foster mothers had previously cared for other people's children. The types of care included daily-minding, taking relatives' children, and fostering without payment as well as fostering within the definition of the Children Act (1958). The local authority foster mothers also displayed a propensity to take

Table 2.6   The number of private foster children previously cared for by private foster mothers

No.	Private foster mothers
0	56
1–2	17
3–5	10
6–10	7
11–20	6
21 and more	4
Total	100

other people's children, although not to the same extent. The number of actual private foster children taken by the private foster mothers is presented in Table 2.6. The aggregate number of private children previously cared for amounted to 320 of whom 228 were coloured or half-caste. The average number of previous foster children per foster mother works out at 3·2. However, 56 mothers had had no previous foster children, so the average for the remainder was 7·3. Even amongst these, most had had only one or two children, while a minority had abnormally high numbers, some with over 50 children. Thus 27 of the mothers accounted for 297 of the previous children, an average of 11 each. It can be concluded that although the majority of private foster mothers had not taken large numbers, a sizeable minority, over a quarter, had done so.

Few studies have looked at the fostering record of local authority foster mothers. Gray and Parr did so and, in comparison with the private mothers, show somewhat lower proportions taking large numbers: 7 per cent had taken six or more children, compared with 17 per cent of the private mothers (1957, p. 46). They considered that a record of two or more foster children entitled a woman to be termed a 'professional'. Twenty-four per cent of their sample was thus designated, but they could find few other differences between them and the non-professionals save that the former were more likely to have had more natural children. I feel that if professional implies foster mothers whose way of life included the taking of foster children, then two children (who may have been taken together and for a very short period) is hardly an adequate criterion. It is doubtful if a number constitutes the best means of definition, but at least six previous children would indicate a persistent attempt to foster on a continuous basis. Seventeen per cent of the private mothers could be termed professionals by this criterion.

It was also postulated that the private foster mothers would take young children and for short periods. Young was taken to mean in the pre-school years, but what is a short placement? Gray and Parr calculated that their sample of children had spent an average of 4·7 years in public care.[5] Trasler and Parker used placement lengths of three and five years as the minimum length of a successful fostering. Thus it would appear reasonable to regard one year as a short period for a placement.

Of the 320 private foster children previously cared for, it was found that 183 were under one year old when placed, 127 were between the ages of one and under five, while only ten were five years or older. Further, the majority stayed for less than a year, 172 left before one year was completed, 103 stayed between one and under two years, 37 between two years and under five years, and 8 for five years or more.[6] As they stayed for comparatively short periods, it becomes of interest to ask why their placements did end. The reasons the private foster mothers gave can be seen in Table 2.7.

Table 2.7   Reasons why previous private foster children left the private foster homes

		No.	%
Natural parent(s) resumed care after:			
	completing studies	132	
	hospitalisation or confinement of mother ended	24	
	finding accommodation	22	
	being reunited	19	
	mother got married	15	
		212	66·2
Foster parents sent child back after:			
	child's behavioural problems	34	
	child became ill	8	
	natural parents criticised foster parents or visited too often	31	
	natural parents did not pay	12	
		85	26·6
Other		23	7·2
Totals		320	100·0

It is reasonable to conclude, first, that the private foster children were characterised by short placements and, second, that over a quarter had been ended not amicably but due to friction between the fostering participants.

To sum up: the section of the second hypothesis asserting that the private foster mothers would take large numbers of children at one time was not upheld; the section relating to them continually taking foster children was only partially upheld, for although three-quarters of the private foster mothers had some previous experience of caring for other people's children, only 17 per cent had taken six or more previous foster children: the section hypothesising that the children they took would be young and subject to short placements was upheld. But the foster parents' previous children are not the focus of the research. It is to the private foster children present with them that attention is now turned.

3   The private foster children

Much has been said about private foster children but little is known about them. Therefore – as with the private foster mothers – an initial objective of the research was to identify the private foster children. Five hypotheses helped to shape the direction of the identification, namely that the private foster children would be characterised by (i) being largely the children of West African parents; (ii) being largely the children of students wishing to be free to study; (iii) being frequently illegitimate; (iv) being predominantly in the under-five age-grouping; (v) being subject to numerous changes of foster homes. In addition, attention was paid to the considerable range of research on local authority foster children – which is listed by Dinnage and Pringle in their *Foster Home Care: Facts and Fallacies* – in order to pinpoint factors known to influence the course and outcome of fosterings. These included the age of the children, the age at placement, the reasons for their reception into care, their legitimacy, sex and number of previous foster homes. Most of the information, such as that 46·2 per cent of the private foster children were male and 53·8 per cent female, was readily available in the files of the children's departments and could be checked by questions to the foster mothers. Similar data was collected for the local authority contrast group.

Nationality

Over 60 per cent of the private foster children (see Table 3.1) had both parents of foreign nationality.[1] However, none of these was Asian, a fact which may lend weight to the view that Asians tend to insulate their family problems, making few demands on outside help. The proportion of those with two West Indian parents, 4·2 per cent, may also appear low when put beside the contention of writers, such as Fitzherbert, that they are particularly liable to be separated from their parents (1967, pp. 40–6). Undoubtedly, the outstanding finding is the high proportion, 60·8 per cent, of children whose parents were West African. It had been hypothesised that large numbers would be of this nationality, but not that they would make up over half the

Table 3.1　Numbers of foster children according to the nationality of their parents

	Private foster children		Local authority foster children	
	No.	%	No.	%
United Kingdom (both parents)	45	31·5	76	53·1
West Indian (both parents)	6	4·2	11	7·7
West African (both parents)	87	60·8	2	1·4
Asian (both parents)	0	0·0	3	2·1
European and non-European (mixed parentage)	2	1·4	49	34·3
Other	3	2·1	2	1·4
Totals	143	100·0	143	100·0

total. Prior to the present research, the Home Office had observed numbers of West African children but had thought them mainly confined to authorities in London and the south-east. The above figures show that they also predominate the private fostering scene in a large part of the Midlands.[2] If the research population is typical of private fostering as a whole, then it would be true to say that West African children make up the majority of private foster children in England and Wales.

The County Immigration Tables of the sample census of 1966 show that the population of the city and county which was born abroad was proportionately far below that found in the private fostering population. Clearly, the high incidence of West African children, by comparison with the census population, is a marked feature of private fostering. But how do the figures compare with those for children in the care of voluntary children's societies and children's departments? The Home Office does not publish figures of children in care according to nationality, but the present researcher received reports issued by Dr Barnardo's, the National Children's Home and seventeen local authority children's departments. From their figures three points can be made.[3] First, the numbers of children with one or both parents from abroad in the care of voluntary bodies and children's departments has increased in recent years. Second, of these the greatest proportion are of racially mixed parentage, with the next largest those with two West Indian parents.[4] Third, that the number with two West African parents is small. For instance, in 1968 Birmingham had only two and Sheffield no children in care whose both parents were West African. These findings are very different from those for private fostering. Despite the increase, children with one or both parents from abroad remain a minority in local authority care but were a majority amongst the private foster children. The children in public care included comparatively many whose parents were of two nationalities, the private foster children very few. Children whose both parents were West African were a rarity in the children's departments, but comprised a majority in the private fostering population.

Further evidence of the contrast between the nationalities of children in local authority care and private foster homes was found in the efforts to form a local authority contrast group. As explained in chapter 1, an attempt was made to match them for nationality with the private foster children, but only two West African foster children could be found in the care of the city and county children's departments. Consequently, as far as was possible they were matched on the basis of having one parent who was not from the United Kingdom. The results, seen in Table 3.1, show that of such children in the local authority group the majority was of nationally mixed parentage. In fact, 34·3 per cent were in this position, nearly all having mothers from the United Kingdom and fathers from either Asia or the West Indies.

There can be no doubt that a major nationality difference was established between the composition of the private and local authority foster children. The hypothesis that the private foster children would be largely of West African parents was upheld. Certain questions follow on. Why were the West African children so predominant in private fostering while so few were in the care of children's departments? Does the fostering of such children pose particular problems for foster parents who are virtually all from the United Kingdom? Is their treatment and condition worse than that given to other foster children? These questions will be taken up in later chapters.

Legal status

The likelihood that illegitimate children lack the support of two parents and two sets of grandparents led Packman to postulate that 'illegitimacy must account for a high proportion of the children maintained in private foster homes' (1968, p. 128), and to the hypothesis that the private foster children would frequently be illegitimate. The importance of illegitimacy in contributing to the use of private foster homes is underlined by the finding that thirty-two, 22·4 per cent, of the private foster children were of this status. The incidence of illegitimacy is much higher than in the population as a whole, and is enough to uphold the stated hypothesis.[5] However, a comparison between the private and local authority foster children brings out an interesting finding, as illustrated in Table 3.2.

The local authority foster children were significantly more likely to be illegitimate than the private ones ($\chi^2 = 46 \cdot 711$, d.f. $= 1$, P $= <0 \cdot 001$).[6] Other studies of local authority children agree that they consist of proportionately more illegitimate children. Gray and Parr's sample showed that $35 \cdot 3$ per cent of children in public care were illegitimate, with 51 per cent of the illegitimate being boarded out (1957, p. 16). In Trasler's sample of local authority foster children, over 50 per cent were illegitimate (1960, p. 12).

Table 3.2   Legal status of foster children

	Private foster children		Local authority foster children	
	No.	%	No.	%
Legitimate	111	77·6	48	33·6
Illegitimate	32	22·4	95	66·4
Totals	143	100·0	143	100·0

The high proportion of legitimate children in the private sector as against the local authority one is related to the preponderance of West Africans. Children of West African parents were significantly more likely to be legitimate than those of United Kingdom or other parents ($\chi^2 = 7 \cdot 010$, d.f. $= 2$, P $= <0 \cdot 050$). It will be remembered that West Africans occurred hardly at all amongst the local authority group. The finding has further important child care implications. As legitimate children are more likely to possess two interested parents, they can expect more parental visiting than the illegitimate. Again, it would seem that a return to the parental home is more probable than where a child has only one parent. However, the position of the thirty-two illegitimate private foster children must not be overlooked. Although both Trasler (1960, p. 12) and Parker (1966, p. 41) agree that legal status is not statistically related to the breakdown of foster homes, there is evidence to suggest that illegitimate foster children experience difficulties in understanding and accepting the fact of their legal status (Baylor and Monachesi, 1939, pp. 156–7). The question thus arises whether the private foster parents are as capable as local authority ones in helping the children with this difficulty, and whether the child care officers give them the same degree of service as they do to local authority illegitimate foster children. Further, if illegitimacy is such a strong feature of children in public care, why do some illegitimate foster children go to foster homes outside the local authority system? These questions will be explored in later chapters.

Age of the foster children

At the time the research was undertaken, 42 of the private foster children, that is 29·4 per cent, were under two years of age; another 55, 38·5 per cent, were between two years and under five years; 40, 28·0 per cent, were between five years and under fifteen years, while 6, 4·2 per cent, were fifteen years and over. The sample census for 1966 for the city and county showed that only 30 per cent of the child population was under five years. Clearly, the private foster children were heavily weighted towards younger children by comparison. But what of the local authority foster children? The contrast group was matched for age, but instead comparison could be made with other studies. Gray and Parr's sample of local authority foster children revealed 22·4 per cent of the boys and 20·3 per cent of the girls in the under-five age-range (1957, pp. 13–14). The Home Office figures for 1968 relating to all children in care (not just foster children) have 21·1 per cent in the under-five age-range, 58·8 per cent in the five to fifteen age-range, and 20·2 per cent above this. Beside the local authority children, the private ones showed a far higher proportion amongst the under-fives and far smaller ones in the other age groups.

Research in child care has been less concerned with current age, more concerned with the children's age when placed in their foster homes. Of the private foster children 91 were placed when under one year of age, while 63 of these were under six months. A further 18 were between one and two years of age, and 20 between two and five. Only 14 were placed when older than five. The local authority contrast group was matched for age at placement, but comparison can be made with the samples of Trasler and Parker in Table 3.3.

Table 3.3 leaves no doubt that one of the most striking features of private fostering compared with local authority is the young age at which its children were placed: 63·6 per cent were in their foster homes before they were one year old, compared with 5·8 and 8·1 per cent in the local authority samples. It needs to be pointed out that 'age at placement' pertains to the foster home in which they resided at the time the research was undertaken. The private foster children may have earlier been in a previous foster home. Similarly, the age for the local authority ones is not necessarily that when they were

Table 3.3   Foster children's age at placement in foster homes

Years	Private foster children %	Trasler's local authority foster children %	Parker's local authority foster children %
Under 1	63·6	5·8	8·1
1–under 5	26·6	44·2	46·9
5–under 11	9·8	31·9*	36·8
11 and over	0·0	18·1	8·1
Totals	100·0	100·0	100·0

*Trasler used an age division at 10 not 11 years.

received into public care. They may have first been to a reception centre or another local authority foster home. However, the Home Office figures for 1968 do give also the ages at which children were received into care. Of the children received in the year preceding 31 March 1968, 24·4 per cent were under two, 28·5 per cent were in the two to five range, 43·1 per cent were five to fifteen, and 4 per cent were over fifteen years. By any comparison, the private foster children remain significantly weighted towards the under-fives.

Table 3.4 shows that a third of the private foster children had been in their foster homes for under one year, 50·4 per cent for one to under-five years, and 16·1 per cent for five years or more. The local authority contrast group was matched for duration of placement,

Table 3.4   Length of time private foster children had been in their foster homes

Years	No.	%
Under 6 months	26	18·2
6 months–1	22	15·4
1–2	21	14·7
2–5	51	35·7
5–11	14	9·8
11 and over	9	6·3
Totals	143	100·0

but comparison could be made with Gray and Parr's sample although it measured the time children had been in care at the time of their research, not the time in a foster home: 20·2 per cent had been in care for under one year, 38·2 per cent for one to five years, and over 40 per cent for longer periods (1957, p. 10). Clearly, the local authority children tended to have far longer periods in care than the private foster children did in foster homes. Of course, neither Gray and Parr's figures nor Table 3.4 indicate how much longer the placements would have lasted, but the study made in chapter 2 of completed private fosterings suggests that the private ones are of shorter duration than local authority ones. Indeed, the short duration of many of the placements is another distinctive feature of private fostering.

The age structure of the private foster children has been demonstrated as not only different from a cross-section of the child population, but from local authority foster children as well. Is this likely to matter? Evidence from earlier research suggests that the age factor has an influential bearing on the development of children separated from their own parents. The famous work of Bowlby and his successors has served to popularise maternal deprivation theories which generally claim that after six months the younger the child at separation the more damaging are the likely effects on his emotional development (1951, pp. 46–51). On the other hand, Parker argues that the earlier a child is placed in a foster home the greater the chances that it will succeed (1966, p. 42). Yet again, it is argued that the later a child is placed the more likely he is to accept that he is a foster not a natural child – a subject which will be taken up in a subsequent chapter.

The hypothesis that the private foster children would be predominantly in the under-five age-grouping was upheld. But why were they so young, placed before they were five and experiencing short placements? Obviously, children under five present more problems of caring than those who spend much of their time at school. However, this does not explain why private fostering should receive a far greater proportion of this age-range than local authority ones. Although final answers will not be presented here, some indications can be provided by examining which types of private foster children were predominantly in the under-five age-range.

First, the legal status of the private foster children showed some interesting correlations with the age structures. Taking five years as the dividing line, the legitimate were statistically more likely to be younger than the illegitimate ($\chi^2 = 13 \cdot 981$, d.f. $= 1$, P $= <0 \cdot 001$), and to have had a shorter placement ($\chi^2 = 28 \cdot 952$, d.f. $= 1$, P $= <0 \cdot 001$). The relationship between legal status and age of placement was not statistically significant. A previous section has explained that legitimacy itself was closely related to the nationality of the children. Therefore, second, it is not surprising to find that the West African children were significantly more likely than the non-West Africans to be younger ($\chi^2 = 48.489$, d.f. $= 1$, P $= <0.001$), to be placed earlier ($\chi^2 = 14.117$, d.f. $= 1$, P $= <0.001$), and to have experienced shorter placements ($\chi^2 = 26.281$, d.f. $= 1$, P $= <0.001$). It can be concluded that the predominance of children in the younger age-structures is due to the high number of legitimate West African children in the private fostering sector but not in the local authority one. The reasons why these particular children required early placements and why they were not found in local authority care will be discussed in a later chapter.

With regard to length of placement, the legal status of the children was important irrespective of nationality. Thus if the West African children are removed from the private fostering population, the illegitimate were still significantly likely to have had longer placements (dividing at five years, $\chi^2 = 6.715$, d.f. $= 1$, P $= <0.010$). The illegitimates tended to be the children of unmarried mothers who, after placing their children, struggled for a number of years to support themselves and pay the fostering dues, and thus found it difficult to reach a stage where they could resume care. It will be remembered that the local authority samples studied showed a higher proportion of illegitimate children than the private fostering one.

Finally, the local authority children's departments appear obliged to cater for two types of older children whom the private foster homes do not. First, delinquent children. Local authorities have no choice but to take children committed into their hands by juvenile courts. Obviously courts do not commit offenders to private foster parents who, in any case, might well be wary of taking older children displaying delinquent tendencies. Second, maladjusted children. Children so emotionally disturbed as to be officially deemed maladjusted are sometimes referred to and taken into care by children's departments who may place them in foster homes, children's homes or in schools for the maladjusted. Such children are rarely so deemed before the age of five, indeed their problems often do not come to light until they are at school. Private foster parents are unlikely to want to take children known officially as maladjusted. Hence another body of older children is directed towards the local authority but not the private fostering sector.

Changes of foster homes

The child care literature asserts that changes of foster homes are damaging to the emotional development of children. First, it is argued that moving confuses the children, making it more difficult for them to understand their own position and identity. Dinnage and Pringle would apply the term 'fosterization' to the confusion arising from a succession of significant mother figures (1967a, p. 21). Second, the opinion is expressed, for instance by the Yudkin Report, that 'recurrent moves in themselves are likely to make a child more and more difficult in behaviour and less likely to be fostered successfully' (1967, p. 41). In the USA Eisenberg, comparing foster children referred to child guidance clinics with those not referred, found the former to have experienced far more foster homes. The children's behaviour caused them to be moved from foster homes, while the very moves made the children more difficult in behaviour.[7] However, the relationship between previous foster homes and fostering success is not that straightforward, and Parker actually found that the experience of *one* previous foster home, provided it was successful in that it did not end 'because of a breakdown in personal relationships', actually promoted the success of a succeeding fostering (1966, p. 55).

Table 3.5 tabulates the number of previous foster homes of the private and local authority foster children.[8] Seventy-four, that is 51·8 per cent, of the private foster children had experienced at least one previous fostering. The number of local authority foster children, 66, 46·21 per cent, in the same position was smaller but not significantly so.[9]

Table 3.5   Foster children's number of previous foster homes

No.	Private foster children		Local authority foster children	
	No.	%	No.	%
0	69	48·3	77	53·8
1	36	25·2	36	25·2
2	16	11·2	22	15·4
3	11	7·7	5	3·5
4	3	2·1	1	0·7
5 and over	8	5·6	2	1·4
Totals	143	100·0	143	100·0

The significant difference comes with those having three or more previous foster homes, 15·4 per cent of the private foster children as against only 5·6 per cent of the local authority ones ($\chi^2 = 7·00$, d.f. $= 1$, $P = <0·010$). A comparison with Parker's work also shows the private foster children as having more fosterings, even although his sample, being older, had had more time in which to move. Nearly 11 per cent of Parker's children had had two or more foster homes, compared with 26·6 per cent of the private foster ones (1966, p. 54). Dinnage and Pringle, in their review of the literature, express great concern at the number of moves experienced by local authority foster children (1967a, pp. 6–7). Yet private foster children were subject to even more movement. Particular concern must be felt for the 5·6 per cent who had been moved upwards of five times. Later, such multiplicity of changes will be tested against their emotional and physical development. None the less, the statement of the hypothesis that the private foster children would be subject to numerous changes is only partially upheld, for 73·5 per cent had at most only one previous foster home. Further, despite the fears that have been expressed about West African children, they were not significantly more liable to change than any others.

Reasons children were separated from their parents

It is a platitude to say that no child is separated from his parents for a single reason. Yet for purposes of comparison and clarification a primary reason must be singled out. The Home Office, in its annual publications of returns from local authority children's departments, has employed a fourteen-fold classification of the main reasons for which children are received into public care under Section 1 of the Children Act (1948). Their classification was adopted with some modifications in order to facilitate comparison between the private foster children and the local authority groups. The files were examined and the children allocated to a category,[10] a task made straightforward by the practice of child care officers of usually specifying a category themselves.

Table 3.6 establishes a predominant characteristic of private fostering. With 86, that is 60·1 per cent, being the children of students, the hypothesis that this would occur is convincingly upheld. Also notable are the 18, 12·6 per cent, separated by reason of their mothers working, the father never having been present, and the 11, 7·7 per cent, separated because their father had deserted and their mother worked.

The distinctions between private and local authority systems are revealed when comparison is made first with the contrast group of foster children and then with a sample of all children in care. The local authority contrast group contained no children separated because the parents were students, and fewer where the mother worked following the father's desertion. On the other hand, it showed far greater numbers where separation resulted from the mothers'

Table 3.6 Reasons the foster children were separated from their parents

	Private foster children		Local authority foster children	
	No.	%	No.	%
No parent	1	0·7	0	0·0
Abandoned or lost	1	0·7	10	7·0
Death of mother, father unable to care	3	2·1	6	4·2
Deserted by mother, father unable to care	10	7·0	13	9·1
Mother works because father deserted	11	7·7	5	3·5
Mother works because father never present	18	12·6	34	23·8
Students	86	60·1	0	0·0
Accommodation difficulties	2	1·4	18	12·6
Illness of mother	3	2·1	31	21·7
Other	8	5·6	26	18·2
child rejected by mother	2		7	
mother not cope with children	4		6	
child not accepted by mother's new husband	0		6	
other	2		7	
Totals	143	100·0	143	100·0

illness, from mothers working where the fathers had never been present, from accommodation difficulties and from the children being abandoned.

Turning to Gray and Parr's sample of children in public care, one point becomes immediately evident, namely that its 4 per cent of juvenile offenders committed under a Fit Person Order appear to have no counterparts in the private fostering section. Nor would there seem to be much overlap with the 21·7 per cent who were non-offenders but entrusted to local authority care under Fit Person Orders mainly for being in need of care and protection. Fit Person Orders can remove children from their parents without the latters' consent. Private foster placements are made voluntarily, so it is appropriate to make comparison with the local authority children in Gray and Parr's sample who were voluntarily received into care under Section 1 of the 1948 Act. These made up nearly three-quarters of all the children in care at the time of their research. An examination confirms the findings in respect of the contrast group, that is that amongst the local authority children were proportionately considerably more separated because of accommodation difficulties, abandonment, and fathers being deserted by their spouses. On the other hand, they had few if any children of students, and proportionately considerably fewer whose mothers had been deserted by their husbands (1957, p. 9).

Although the kinds of children coming to private and local authority fostering show some overlap in the reasons for separation from their parents, it is clear that they also draw upon very different types of child populations. Obviously children without any effective parents, such as the abandoned, and those committed by the courts, will be directed towards public care. But explanations must be sought why the children of students and of mothers bereft of husbands were proportionately more prominent in the private field. The question thus becomes not just why were the children separated from their parents, but why were they put into private foster homes instead of some other form of care?

Groupings of the private foster children

A multiple analysis of the legal status, nationality and reasons for separation of the private foster children allowed certain groupings to be established as follows (the numbers of children are given in brackets):

a   Both parents West African, legitimate, separated because parents were students (83).

b   Both parents United Kingdom, illegitimate, separated from mother because father was never present (15).

c   Both parents United Kingdom, legitimate, separated because father had been deserted by mother (9).

d   Both parents United Kingdom, legitimate or illegitimate, separated because mother had been deserted by father (8).

e   Other (28).

A similar analysis was made for the local authority children in the contrast group:

a   Both parents United Kingdom or mixed nationality, illegitimate, separated from mother because father never present (29).

b   Both parents United Kingdom or mixed nationality, legitimate or illegitimate, separated because of mother's illness (25).

c Both parents United Kingdom or mixed nationality, mainly legitimate, separated because of accommodation difficulties (17).

d Both parents United Kingdom, mainly legitimate, separated because father had been deserted by mother (10).

e Various nationalities, illegitimate, separated because abandoned (9).

f Both parents United Kingdom, legitimate, miscellaneous reasons for separation (13).

g Mixed nationality, illegitimate, miscellaneous reasons for separation (13).

h Both parents West Indian, illegitimate, miscellaneous reasons for separation (8).

i Other (19).

Comparing the private and local authority groupings, some similarity can be observed in the grouping consisting of United Kingdom children, legitimate, separated because the father had been deserted by the mother, and the illegitimate United Kingdom children whose fathers had never been present. However, the differences are more outstanding than the similarities. In particular, the local authority children did not include the major private grouping, that of legitimate children of West African students, neither did it have a separate grouping for United Kingdom children whose mothers had been deserted by the fathers. The groupings, now established, can be used throughout the study.

To summarise: it proved possible to identify the composition of the private foster children. With over 60 per cent the legitimate offspring of West African students, most under five years of age and placed before they were one year old, they could be sharply distinguished both from children in the normal population and those in local authority care. Other noteworthy minority findings were that 22·4 per cent were illegitimate, 31·1 per cent had United Kingdom parents, 15·4 per cent had experienced three or more foster homes and some were placed because their father had deserted or was never present or because their mother had left. Generally speaking, the private foster children were separated for reasons different from the local authority ones, were frequently different in nationality and experience, and had found themselves in paths directed towards different kinds of fosterings. The next chapter will discuss whether these fosterings gave them foster parents of different suitability.

4 The suitability of the private foster parents

Publicity in the mass media, parliament and professional journals having cast doubt upon the capacities of private foster parents, a major objective became the examination of their suitability. Focus was provided by the hypothesis that many private foster parents would be considered unsuitable to act in the fostering role.

What is suitability? By what standards are the private foster parents to be judged? Clearly, those persons whose opinions cast doubts upon private foster parents were using the practice of local authority foster homes as their standard. They were assuming that private foster children would require from their foster parents the qualities and capacities required for children in public care. This assumption was accepted and I proceeded to devise means of evaluating the foster parents according to criteria laid down for local authority foster parents.

Before continuing it is necessary to explain at what stage children's departments make their assessment of applicants wishing to become local authority foster parents. They do so, in most cases, before a child is placed with them, and usually before they have any particular child in mind. Thus the study of suitability will be concerned with factors which were ascertained or which existed before the fosterings commenced. It will not be concerned with factors which only came to light as a result of the fosterings.

What is a suitable foster parent?

Guidance for child care officers as to what constitutes suitability for local authority foster parents is found in two main sources, official guidance from the Home Office and the opinions of experts as published in child care literature.

Official guidance

In 1955 the Home Office published its *The Boarding-Out of Children Regulations*. They state that a child may only be fostered with a husband and wife jointly, a woman only, a male relative, or a 'man who is acting jointly with his wife as a foster parent but whose wife has died or left the home' (Regulation 2). They indicate that material standards should be satisfactory (Regulation 17). The factors an officer should then investigate before making a decision about suitability are then listed as:

a 'the reputation and religious persuasion[1] of the foster parents and their suitability in age, character, temperament and health to have charge of the child';

b 'whether any member of the foster parents' household is believed to be suffering from any physical or mental illness which might adversely affect the child or to have been convicted of any offence which would render it undesirable that the child should associate with him';

c 'the number, sex and approximate age of the persons in that household' (Regulation 17).

Child care officers do not select private foster parents, hence they receive no official guidance on the matter. However, the Children Act (1958) does specify certain persons as being so unsuitable that they are open to the designation of 'disqualified person', that is disqualified from acting as a private foster parent. Section 6 of that Act lists such persons as those who have had a child removed having been found to be in need of care and protection; who have had their rights over a child taken away by a resolution passed under Section 2 of the Children Act (1948); who have had a child removed under the provisions of the Children Act (1958); who have been convicted of any offence specified in the First Schedule of the Children and Young Persons Act (1933); and who have been refused registration, or have had such registration cancelled by the local health authority, to act as a child-minder.

Child care texts

Literature in the child care field has devoted a great deal of space to the criteria by which social workers should select or reject foster parent applications. A review was made of the literature, especially of the work of Hutchinson (1943), Charnley (1955), Glickman (1957), Balls (1958), Trasler (1960), Dyson (1962), Kastell (1962), Timms (1962), Stroud (1965), Jenkins (1965), Kay (1966) and Pugh (1968). From this review[2], it was possible to identify eight main points which, it was generally agreed, contributed to suitability to act as foster parents. Interestingly, the eight points bear a close similarity to the nine items of 'Basic requirements for foster families' compiled by the Child Welfare League of America and presented by Wolins (1963, p. 100). The points are:

   a   The capacity to feel and express love and warmth towards a foster child.

   b   Emotional stability in the applicants' own past experiences, in their present marital relationship and in their personality as a whole.

   c   The 'right' motivation or need which impels them to want to foster, the fulfilment of which would be satisfying both to foster parents and child.

   d   The existence of a 'normal' family life in which relationships between members are emotionally satisfactory.

   e   An acceptance of the fact of fostering, that is, that the applicants would not regard it as adoption but would be prepared to co-operate with the children's department and with the natural parents.

   f   The capacity to provide for a child's material and physical needs.

   g   An age-level which is not too elderly.

   h   The presence of a male able to play a full part as foster father.

Assessing the foster parents

From the official guidance and child care literature emerges a picture, or rather a list of items, relating to suitability or unsuitability in prospective foster parents. My task then became to translate this into a way of evaluating the private and local authority foster parents in the study. Three main approaches were used. First, the file records were examined to ascertain the number of foster parents with the unsuitability factors outlined by the Boarding-Out Regulations. Second, the child care officers' judgments were employed as to whether they would have approved of the private foster parents to act for the local authority. Third, information was compiled on how many of the private foster parents had actually applied to take local authority children and with what result.

Unsuitability factors from the file records

The file records of the fosterings were examined for the unsuitability factors mentioned by the Boarding-Out Regulations and the Children Act (1958). The practice of the children's departments of keeping their assessments of applicants to foster and their initial assessments of private foster parents in files separate from the main files made easier the policy of using only factors ascertained before or in the very early stages of the fosterings.[3]

In order to achieve uniformity of assessment between the many cases, definitions of the factors were made for use by the file recorder. These were as follows:

a 'Physical or mental illness which might adversely affect a foster child.' No illness was accepted as constituting an unsuitability factor unless certified by a doctor or psychiatrist. A physical illness was counted only if it might prevent a person carrying out normal parental functions.

b 'Conviction for a serious offence.' Regarded only if the person was convicted for an offence against a child.

c 'Own children in care under Section 2 Resolution of the Children Act (1948), or found to be in need of care and protection.' The finding of being in need of care and protection had to be made by a court.

d 'Factors about other members of the household which might adversely affect a foster child.' This was taken to refer, first, to other adult members who might have committed a serious offence or be mentally ill as defined above. Second, to the children of the household. Here a factor was counted only if a child was officially deemed maladjusted; if convicted for an offence which resulted in a supervision or probation order; if the school complained of the child's prolonged absenteeism or behaviour; or if the child was officially regarded as mentally ill.

f 'Age.' As with the other factors, the Home Office does not define what it means when it regards age as possibly constituting an unsuitability factor. However, an upper age-limit to foster parents has received some public discussion, and two decisions are worth mentioning. One of the children's departments in the study had opposed the adoption of a child of four years by a woman of fifty-seven on the grounds that she would be too old when the child reached adolescence. The court accepted the department's arguments and would not allow the adoption. Next, in London, after the death of a foster child in a fire, the evidence disclosed that the foster parents were over seventy years old, and the coroner declared that there should be an upper age-limit for foster parents. The children's department concerned responded by banning the over-sixties from receiving new foster children.[4] Taken in conjunction with the com-

C

monly expressed view that elderly foster parents find difficulty in coping with adolescents, it was taken that if it seemed likely that a child would reach his teens when one or both of the foster parents was over sixty-five, their age was considered to constitute an unsuitability factor. One exception was made: if the intention of the foster parents was clearly that of short-term foster parents, so that the expectation was that the child would not be in the home when he reached his teens, then age was ruled out as an unsuitability factor.

g 'Character or temperament.' These extremely vague terms were interpreted cautiously, and again noted only where some distinct trait of the foster parents or an aspect of their relationship was recorded on the file as almost certain to adversely affect a child. Examples are foster parents subject to violent outbursts of temper accompanied by physical assault, excessive withdrawal, or very poor marriage relationships.

h 'Other factors.'

i. Timms (1962) and Leeding (1966) point out that children's departments take up references in regard to the Boarding-Out Regulations term 'reputation'. As both children's departments in the study also took up references for private foster parents, comparison could be made and a note was made where a reference was very much against the applicant.

ii. A note was also made of any person counting as a disqualified person under the Children Act (1958), except when already referred to in (b) and (c) above.

iii. Any other factor which might adversely affect the child was left to the researcher's discretion to select from the file reports. However, as with all categories, a tendency to caution rather than a ready selection of factors was observed.

Child care officer assessments

The review of child care literature revealed a wide range of factors or criteria which are held to show that applicants are suitable or unsuitable to foster. It was assumed that the child care officers would use similar criteria in assessing applicants, a not unreasonable assumption as the literature was drawn from that recommended by social work training courses. Hence the officers were asked to evaluate the private foster parents by saying whether they would have accepted them to act as foster parents for the local authorities. They were thus asked to make the kind of total or holistic judgment which they did in practice when they had to recommend that fostering applicants be accepted or rejected. As a check on whether they were using the recommended criteria, the officers were further asked to give reasons for their decisions. Their responses are not presented here and it must suffice to report that their criteria showed a remarkable similarity to that of the literature.[5]

Lastly, as a check on the reliability of the child care officers' judgments, a senior officer was asked to make a similar judgment. The senior would have supervised the officer's handling of the cases and would so be familiar with them. The reliability procedure is explained in the Appendix, it suffices here to say that a product–moment correlation of $+0.78$ was found.

Actual applications to foster

The third approach was to discover which private foster mothers actually had applied to the children's department (or to a voluntary

Table 4.1 Unsuitability factors in foster parents (file material)

	Private foster parents		Local authority foster parents	
	No.	%	No.	%
Physical or mental illness which might adversely affect a foster child	13	13	3	2·5
Conviction for a serious offence against a child	6	6	1	0·8
Own children in care under Section 2 resolution or in need of care and protection	8	8	0	0·0
Factors about other members of household which might adversely affect a foster child	14	14	3	2·5
Age	14	14	9	7·4
Character and temperament	14	14	3	2·5
Other factors:				
reputation 7				
co-habiting irregularly 2				
disqualified person 3				
material standards 6				
other 12	30	30	8	6·6
Totals*	99	—	27	—
Number of foster parents with no unsuitability factor	45	45	97	79·5

*Totals do not make 100 private and 122 local authority foster parents as more than one factor could be recorded against each.

body) and how many had been accepted or rejected. The foster mothers were asked directly for this information while a check was made from the records of the children's department concerning the accuracy of their replies.

The unsuitable foster parents

The number of unsuitability factors found in the file records are given in Table 4.1. For purposes of comparison the findings for the local authority foster parents are presented in the same Table.

Ninety-nine unsuitability factors were recorded against the hundred private foster parents, an average of 0·99 per foster parent. Fifty-five of the private foster parents revealed at least one unsuitability factor while forty-five had none. Although not the most numerous, particularly noticeable were the eight who had had their parental powers over natural children removed by Section 2 resolutions passed under the Children Act (1948) or by courts finding them in need of care and protection and the six convicted for a serious offence. It must be remembered that the Table gives the number of foster parents not foster children. In fact, eighty-six, that is 60·1 per cent, of the private foster children were with foster parents displaying at least one one unsuitability factor.

Twenty-seven unsuitability factors were found against the 122 local authority foster parents, an average of 0·22 per foster parent.[6] Twenty-eight, 19·6 per cent, of the local authority foster children were with the unsuitable ones. Only twenty-five, 20·5 per cent, of the local authority foster parents showed at least one unsuitability factor as against 55 per cent of the private foster parents. Thus according to the file material, the latter were significantly more likely to be unsuitable ($\chi^2 = 28·41$, d.f. $= 1$, $P = <0·001$). For the assessments by

Table 4.2   Child care officers' assessment of whether they would have approved the private foster parents to be local authority foster parents*

	No.	%
Approved	25	26·3
Probably approve	18	18·9
Doubtful	17	17·9
Not approve	35	36·9
Totals	95	100·0

*The officers felt unable to form a definite decision in five cases which are therefore not included. The number of officers participating was thirty-six.

the child care officers themselves of the foster parents, see Table 4.2.

The child care officers would have disapproved of or been doubtful about allowing fifty-two, 54·8 per cent, of the private foster parents to look after local authority foster children.[7] These were caring for 55·2 per cent of the private children. As children's departments are likely to give final approval to applicants in whom officers feel great confidence, it is probable that only twenty-five, 26·2 per cent, of the private foster parents would have been accepted had they applied. The senior child care officers reached very similar conclusions.

The third approach used to assess the suitability of the private foster parents was to detect the results of their actual applications to become official foster parents (see Table 4.3).

Table 4.3   Applications by private foster parents to foster for local authorities or voluntary agencies

	No.
Applied and accepted	24
Applied and rejected	19
Not applied	55
Other (application pending)	2
Total	100

Nineteen, 42·2 per cent, of those who made applications were rejected as unsuitable. Nevertheless they were still caring for thirty-five private foster children. It is fair to point out that the number of rejections is not a true reflection of the picture. A study of the files showed that a number of private foster parents 'sounded out' the child care officer about applying, but were discouraged or 'headed off', and hence never made an official application. In addition, amongst those counted as approved were some about whom the local authority later changed its mind and decided not to use further.

Case studies of unsuitable private foster parents

The definition and assessment of unsuitability, being a complicated subject, required three different approaches to tackle it. They revealed, respectively, that 55 per cent of the private foster parents had at least one unsuitability factor against them on the file records, that 54·8 per cent of those on whom the officers gave decisions would not be approved to act for the local authority, and that 42·2 per cent of those who had actually applied to official bodies had been rejected.

Overall, sixty-three of the one hundred private foster parents were unsuitable by at least one of the means of assessment.

The findings presented have been in statistical terms. Now illustrations will be given from the cases studied. The danger of case studies is that generalisations are made from non-random selection. Hence this chapter has stressed the use of numerical data. The following examples are provided to give some flesh to the numerical skeleton, but they must not be taken as typical cases. They are examples of the unsuitable, but many of the private foster parents, it must be remembered, were considered suitable:

a   In her late fifties at the time of the interview, the foster mother had had fourteen previous private foster children. The file recorded a number of factors which could be counted as constituting unsuitability factors. Extremely deaf, she had lived with a number of men, having five illegitimate children. She had been with her present cohabitee for some five years. The condition of her own children was especially noted by the child care officer writing the file. One son was serving a long prison sentence, while the foster mother had been fined for the persistent truancy of her daughter. The health visitor had expressed concern about the care given, and it was established that she was leaving a one-year-old daily-minded child alone in the house while she did a paid job. The present foster child was a ten-year-old girl of a British mother. The child care officer would not have approved the foster parents to act for the local authority, saying, 'The foster father is too old and they have not the accommodation. The foster mother cannot accept natural parents, and would not help foster children to accept them. She couldn't cope with any real problems such as teenage.'

b   The foster mother had been in her early twenties when she took the foster child, a girl of one year. Previous to this she had had an illegal abortion before 'marrying' an older man. His children, by a former marriage, were in public care, and he had been fined for neglecting them, and imprisoned for failure to pay. Both foster parents were mentally unstable, the foster mother being graded a 'feeble-minded defective' at one point, and spending a period in a mental hospital.

c   Caring for three Nigerian children at the time of the research, this foster mother – who was separated from her husband – had been involved in a controversy over a previous child. A Nigerian foster child had been removed by his dissatisfied parents to other foster parents, who discovered severe scars on the child's back. A doctor confirmed he had been badly burned, and suspicion fell on the first foster mother.

Her own children had been in care while she was in hospital. Of her six children one was a mentally handicapped four-year-old (at the time of the research), while two older boys had been bound over by the court for minor delinquency. The health visitor and general practitioner thought she had too many natural children to cope adequately; in fact, at the time of the research, twelve persons shared the six-roomed dwelling.

d This foster mother, who had taken sixteen previous foster children, had had a colourful career. Her first natural children – twins – were by her brother. She then married, having five further children. Her husband deserted her because of her 'promiscuity'. The NSPCC made investigations and a medical report on the twins stated they were 'anaemic and under-sized, suffering from nutritional deficiency'. The children's department received four of her children into care, passing Section 2 resolutions on grounds of her being unfit owing to her mode of life. A fifth child had gone with the father, but was also later received into care. She became pregnant again before starting a co-habitation in which another child had since been born.

e The foster parents, according to the file, were kindly and affectionate people but too old. The woman was sixty-nine and the man sixty-seven when the foster child, a few-months-old boy, was taken on a long-term basis.

f The foster mother was in her fifties when she took a two-year-old girl, a few months after her husband's death. Prior to this the probation officer was helping their marital relationship, and commented that she had a bad temper, 'instability and an inability to stand up to the difficulties within the home'. The same officer was involved with the adolescent son who had been rejected by her.

g The foster mother was in her fifties when she separated from her husband because of his violence and drinking habits. Of her two teenage sons, one was on probation and the other had sexually assaulted his younger sister. He continued under the supervision of the mental health department, was deemed an 'aggressive psychopath', was violent to his mother and sister, and 'makes few social contacts as he is unable to make relationships'. Following press publicity when the assault on the sister was taken to court, the family moved to a completely new district and here took a six-year-old Nigerian girl. The woman's application to foster for the children's department had been rejected because of the 'son's violent temper'.

Which foster parents are unsuitable?

Statistical calculations established few significant correlations between different types of private foster parents and unsuitability or between particular kinds of private foster children being in unsuitable placements. Trends were detected suggesting that 'professional' foster mothers were more likely to be unsuitable and that children with two or more previous foster homes were more likely to be with unsatisfactory foster parents but the findings were not quite statistically significant. Thus the legal status, nationality, age, or age at placement of the private foster children was not related with being with unsuitable foster parents. Only one factor appeared consistently to be of importance. Private foster parents from social class V were significantly more likely than those from other classes to (i) have a factor of unsuitability recorded against them in the file material ($\chi^2 = 11 \cdot 236$, d.f. $= 1$, P $= <0 \cdot 001$) and (ii) to have the officers assess them as not approved or doubtful about being local authority foster parents ($\chi^2 = 13 \cdot 685$, d.f. $= 1$, P $= <0 \cdot 001$).[8]

Although private foster parents in social class V were significantly more likely to be assessed as unsuitable, it should not be concluded that the lower the social class the greater the chance of being unsuitable. On the contrary, the findings did not reveal social class IV to be more unsuitable than social class III, social class III more than social class II and so on. Nor, in the local authority sample, were foster parents in the lowest class likely to be more unsuitable than any others. Further, Parker's research indicated fostering success to be related to the lower the class of the foster parents (1966, pp. 67–70). The explanation would appear to be that in private fostering there are a number of foster parents with records of offences against children, visits from the NSPCC, mental illness, and the removal of their parental rights over their own children. In many ways they resemble the multi-problem families which were the subject of Wilson's research (1962). The foster fathers in these families tended to be in unskilled occupations and so weighted social class V foster parents towards unsuitability. Such persons were not acceptable to the local authority children's departments and so did not form a significant grouping within their foster parents.

In this, the first study of the suitability of private foster parents, the hypothesis, that many would be considered unsuitable to act in the fostering role, has been upheld. Clearly, the private foster children were more at risk of being put with unsuitable foster parents than the local authority children. As children's departments possess some powers over private fostering, the question is raised, why were they prepared to tolerate lower standards in the private fostering world? Why did they not exercise their power to disqualify persons, such as those with criminal records or whose natural children had been removed from them, who obviously came with the definition of a disqualified person according to the Children Act (1958)? Answers to these crucial queries will be attempted in a later chapter. At this point it suffices to say that dual standards of fostering are allowed to exist with more unsuitable foster parents being tolerated in the private fostering sector than in the local authority one. This might appear justifiable if the two systems catered for different types of children, that is with children whose differing needs and conditions required different forms of care or help. Again, a later chapter will assess the condition of the private and local authority foster children.

5 The treatment of the private foster children (1)

The assessment of the private foster parents' suitability was not designed to examine the ways in which they actually treated the children, nor to describe the children's condition. As attention will now be focused on these subjects, a distinction must be made between treatment and condition. The task is not a straightforward one, for doubtless the way a child is treated affects his condition, while the same condition, in turn, influences the manner in which his foster parents treat him. None the less, for the purposes of study and discussion the distinction must be made. Treatment is taken to involve the activities stemming from the foster parents to the foster children, the attitudes and practices expressed towards them, the things they do for or to the children, the amenities or facilities they provide for them. Treatment will be examined in the present and the following chapter. Condition involves the current position of the children, their emotional and physical health, their educational attainments; in short, the ways in which they function, whether as a result of the treatment received from their foster parents or not. Their condition will be investigated in chapter 7.

How can treatment be measured? One approach would have been for the researcher or the child care officers to make an overall subjective judgment of the treatment on a ranked scale, for instance 'very satisfactory', 'satisfactory', down to 'very unsatisfactory'. Spence used medical personnel to make such overall assessments of the way in which natural mothers treated their children (1954, p. 121), and Raynor made a similar judgment about the treatment given to adopted children (1970, pp. 158–60). At times such assessments are a legitimate research tool. They can be used when it is desirable to repeat the same kind of judgments which professional workers make in practice. For instance, a child care officer actually does make overall subjective assessments about fostering applicants, and accepts or rejects according to his judgment. At other times they are used because time, resources or a lack of knowledge leave no alternative. They can be used too as a balance to methods which are not so all-embracing and subjective in their nature. However, when used as the sole means of assessment they are prone to a number of limitations. Thus Spence's method can be criticised on the following grounds. First, it was a subjective not an objective measurement. The judgments of health visitors and doctors as to what constituted satisfactory treatment may have reflected their own social class background, biases and prejudices. In other words, the meaning of 'satisfactory' was not clearly defined. Second, the lack of definition meant that different judges may have judged according to different criteria. Third, the global aspect of the judgment meant that no attempt was made to break down 'satisfactory' mothering into its various parts (except that there was some reference to satisfactory mothers safeguarding the health of their children). Yet it seems reasonable to assume that some mothers would provide satisfactory care in some aspects of treatment, say in providing food, but unsatisfactory care in, say, providing affection.

An alternative to the overall assessment approach involved identifying the various components of treatment. An examination of publicly voiced fears about private fostering enabled five main activities to be located – the manner in which the foster parents conducted the reception and placement of the children into their homes; the attitudes of the foster mothers towards the children; the foster child-rearing methods employed; the degree of involvement of the foster fathers; and the housing conditions provided for the foster children. Of course, the five by no means fully cover the ways in which foster children are treated, but they were chosen for three main reasons. First, as mentioned, public statements had mentioned them. Second, previous research and child care text books suggested they were of importance to development of foster and natural children. Third, they were amenable to study and measurement.

Thus, within the major objective to examine the way in which the private foster children were treated in their fostering situation, attention was focused on five hypotheses:

a that the placement arrangements for many of the private foster children would be made in a haphazard manner which is not in the best interests of their welfare;

b that the private foster mothers' attitudes to the children would frequently not be conducive to their welfare and would frequently be dependent upon making financial gain;

c that   the   foster   child-rearing   practices   advocated

by the private foster mothers would be unsatisfactory;
   d that the private foster fathers would be little involved with the foster children;
   e that the private foster children would be in housing conditions marked by overcrowding and a lack of amenities.

The first three hypotheses will be discussed in the present chapter, the remaining two in chapter 6.

The placement arrangements

The private foster parents' treatment of the foster children begins with the way in which they obtain them and the manner in which they arrange for them to be received into their homes.

Selecting child and foster home

The child care literature places great store on the need for local authorities to 'match' the right child with the right foster parents. Pugh (1968, p. 45), discussing the nature of 'matching', or 'assessment' as it is sometimes called, says:

> It is not only of the child but also of his situation; it is an assessment of the child within the network of his past and present relationships . . . an assessment not only of the present but also of the future; an attempt to estimate how long the child will remain in care and how the people in his life are going to act and feel in relation to him and to each other.

Such assessments, Pugh continues, require information about the 'child's development, physical condition, behaviour, feelings, relationships and interests' (ibid., p. 46). Stroud develops the subject by describing how, when a child is received into public care, he can be kept in a reception centre so that staff can initially decide which kind of care is needed – a children's home, boarding school or a foster home – before, if selecting the latter, considering which set of foster parents would best meet his particular needs. Possibly the children's department may have few available foster homes but at least officers are aware of the value of careful selection and regard the process as an integral part of the treatment of a foster child.

Turning to private fostering, the selection of children for foster homes is outside the scope of the children's departments. The 'matching' process is the responsibility of the natural parents and the foster parents. Clearly, they lack the facilities of reception centres and the choice of different forms of care; equally clearly there are not available lists of private foster parents from whom the parents select one. How then do they come into contact with each other? The answers are given in Table 5.1. Over a third of the private foster children were

Table 5.1   *Manner by which private foster children and foster parents came into contact*

		No.	%
Foster parents answered an advertisement		51	35·7
Foster parents inserted an advertisement		1	0·7
Introduced via a friend or relative		43	30·1
Foster parents knew natural parents beforehand		15	10·5
Other		33	23·1
	via child care officer	10	
	via other social worker	6	
	chance meeting	13	
	via priest	2	
	other	2	
Totals		143	100·0

placed via advertisements, usually in local papers or magazines. The advertisement market was significantly more likely to concern children from grouping (*a*) that is the legitimate children of West African students (dividing this grouping/other, and advertisements/ other, $\chi^2 = 19.238$, d.f. = 1, P = < 0.001). Such children were also found homes through contacts passed on by friends and relatives, indeed it appeared that a considerable 'grapevine' operated to bring foster parents and children into touch. As only a minority of natural parents could be interviewed it is not possible to say with certainty how carefully they selected the foster parents. But the fact that natural parents rather than foster parents had to advertise, combined with the finding, to be given later, that many parents travelled from London and the south-east to make the placements, suggests that foster homes were in short supply. In some cases it was obvious that the parents were so desperate to find a foster home that they would have placed with almost anyone. The foster parents, for their part, seemed equally unaware of the desirability of 'matching' child and home. From the interviews with them it appeared that some might select which advertisements or contact to follow up according to the sex or age of child they wished to have, but few considered what kind of child would best fit into their family.

Fifteen children came in touch with their foster parents because their parent already knew the foster parents. Typical would be the father recently widowed or deserted by his wife, who prevailed upon friends to take his child. In such cases the foster parents may never even have considered taking a foster child, let alone given thought as to the kind of child they could best help. Even more sudden and unconsidered were contacts made by a chance meeting. The following examples serve to underline the sudden and unexpected nature of such placements:

> 'We'd gone to town and his [foster child's] daddy and mummy were standing at the bus stop with him in his arms – he was eight weeks old – going to a foster home. She dropped her dolly and ran to the baby. The parents found the foster home was too grubby, so he wrote to me and came the next Saturday.'

> 'My daughter wanted a coloured child and I applied to the children's department, but they did not have any coloureds. In a coffee shop I met a girl who was sobbing. I bought her a cup of tea and she got talking and told me that she had five children and was fed up; she had recently had another baby which she had in her arms and she was considering committing suicide. I comforted her and quietened her down, and she said would I like the baby. I weighed her up – she looked reasonably well educated – so I offered to take the child, who was a half-caste, to the seaside for a few weeks to see how it went. I discovered later that the child had already been in five foster homes, and although he was fifteen months old could not speak or walk. I took him on holiday and kept him for three months, and at the end the mother said "You can keep the little b . . .".'

> In one case the contact was made and the placement arranged without the (future) foster mother being informed. Her husband was visiting his sister-in-law, the foster mother of a West African child, when the natural parents also chanced to call. When they explained that they were seeking a foster home for their second child, the husband offered and agreed to take him.

Although some individual foster parents may have given careful consideration to the type of child to take, the manner in which most contacts were made – especially through advertisements, referrals from friends and relatives, and chance meetings – combined with the descriptions of placements offered by some foster mothers, suggests that generally little attempt was made to assess whether the children were likely to 'fit' happily into the new homes.

Preparation for reception of the child

Child care literature is unanimous in stressing the wisdom of carefully preparing children for their move to a foster home. Trasler (1960, p. 150) considered a lack of preparation as pertaining to the 'bad' old days of child care when:

> a child might be brought to her [foster mother] with little or no warning. . . . There was an almost total absence of the careful planning and discussion which normally precedes a modern placement, and it was rare for the foster mother to get to know the foster child in any real sense before the placement was made.

Charnley (1955) even claims that preparation is 'the keynote of success in all child placements'.

Research concerning the effects of preparation is not as prolific as the exhortations given by the child care literature. Nevertheless, what there is supports their claims. Dinnage and Pringle cite a project in the USA concerning Negro children which reported that those prepared for their placement later more fully understood the reasons for their move than those not prepared (1967a, p. 113). Parker detected a trend showing that children who had five or more contacts with their foster parents before they were placed had more successful fostering outcomes (1966, pp. 56–7).

Thus both texts and research concur on the value of careful preparation, but a closer examination is needed to discover why they think it is so. A common reason put forward is that a gradual placement is less frightening to the child and, at the same time, allows the foster mother to get to know his habits, eating fads and behaviour patterns so that she can enable him to settle down more easily. Another reason is that a prepared move is more likely to allow the child to accept the reasons for leaving his parents and to lessen the pain of separation. Moss (1966, p. 153), an experienced psychiatric social worker, believes that children of nearly all ages must resolve the 'conflict of separation' and adds, 'I have also observed how difficult this process becomes when children have not been well prepared in advance for the separation and placement.'

Having established the value of preparation, its meaning had to be defined and a means found by which to quantify it. Three elements seemed to be involved. First, the number of contacts or meetings between the foster parents and the child before the latter actually moved into the foster home. In his study of local authority fosterings, Parker ascertained the number of contacts from the file records of the children's department. The same method could not be used in the present research for the files of the private foster children did not record contacts made before the placement started and hence before the children's department was concerned with the case. Instead, the private foster parents were directly asked how many times they met the child before the placement. Second, preparation involves the information about the child given to the foster parents before the placement. Parker's research, involving only file material, could not ascertain this, but in the present study the interviews with foster parents facilitated relevant questions. The pilot study identified five main subjects of information – feeding, sleeping, behaviour, previous experience away from parents and child-rearing methods used. The foster parents were asked an open question about information received and their answers coded into the appropriate classifications. It was assumed that information covering none or one item could be regarded as 'barest details'. In the case of the local authority children, information could also have come by the child care officer, so for purposes of comparison local authority foster parents were also questioned.

The results showed that ninety-five, 66·4 per cent, of the private foster children had no contacts before placement, twenty-two, 15·4 per cent, had one contact, six, 4·2 per cent, had two to five contacts, and twenty, 14 per cent, had more than five. But what do these numbers mean? Parker's research indicated that five or more contacts were needed before the success of the placement was influenced. Only twenty-one, 14·7 per cent, of the private children had this type of experience. However, a comparison with the local authority foster children revealed that although they had seen their foster parents on more pre-placement occasions, the difference was not statistically significant (the amount of information about the foster children given to the foster parents can be seen in Table 5.2).

Table 5.2   Information given about foster children to foster parents

	Private foster children		Local authority foster children	
	No.	%	No.	%
Barest details (0–1 items)	120	83·9	89	62·2
More details (2 or more items)	23	16·1	54	37·8
Totals	143	100·0	143	100·0

Although a majority of both kinds of foster parents said they were given only the barest details of information about the children, the private foster children were significantly less likely to be accompanied by more than one item of information ($\chi^2 = 18.221$, d.f. $= 1$, P $= <0\cdot001$). The result is hardly surprising for the local authority foster parents were in touch with the child care officers at the time of the placement and, presumably, the officers were more aware of the need to pass on information than the natural parents who handled the private placements.

Private fostering is clearly open to the practice of children being handed from one person to another with very little accompanying knowledge about them. In one case, a woman indicated to a friend, who was fostering a child, that she might be interested in taking his sibling. She continued:

'The parents came suddenly. The mother didn't bother to look at the house, just put her down in my arms and said, "You've brought your own up, do the same for mine." Then she left without saying anything to the child.'

Similarly, another woman half agreed to take the child of a nurse whom she met while in hospital for an operation. Afterwards the nurse came round with the baby:

'I couldn't resist her. I shouldn't have taken her but I did. I knew nothing about her, she just came and all she said was, 'I give her Carnation".'

At times natural parents failed to reveal factors which were obviously important such as the case where a foster mother took a child without being told that he had had a turbulent history including at least six previous placements. More regularly, they failed to pass on, and the foster parents did not seek, information on the child's eating, sleeping and behaviour patterns which, if given, might have eased the child's transition from one home to another.

A statistical analysis of the data reveals three further main points. First, the children who experienced few contacts prior to placement are likely to be the same ones about whom little information is given (dividing at 0–1 contacts/2 or more contacts and barest details/ more, $\chi^2 = 27\cdot083$, d.f. $= 1$, P $= <0\cdot001$). Second, such children were significantly more likely to have found their foster homes through the advertising medium rather than any other way. (Thus for children with one or fewer contacts the statistical relationship with advertising was $\chi^2 = 10.836$, d.f. $= 1$, P $= <0.001$.) Third, these relationships are, in turn, a function of the grouping which made most use of the advertising market, namely the children of West African students. They were significantly more likely than other private foster children to have had only one or less contacts ($\chi^2 = 19.655$, d.f. $= 1$, P $= <0.001$) and to be associated with only the barest of details being passed on ($\chi^2 = 11.492$, d.f. $= 1$, P $= <0.001$). It appears that the West African students, often desperate to find foster homes, advertised widely. As the only possible placements were some distance away involving considerable distances to travel, they had less time and opportunity, even if they and the foster mothers possessed the inclination, to ease the children's transition by a number of preparatory visits and the passing on of information. On the other hand, the remaining children, usually the children of United Kingdom parents who were deserted spouses or unmarried mothers, appeared to be placed within the area of residence of their parents so that the opportunities to make contacts, and the possibilities of knowing the foster parents beforehand, were greater.

To conclude: the evidence suggests that many private foster children had had their foster homes found for them through the haphazard means of advertisements, casual referrals and chance meetings. Further, the majority of private foster children did not meet their foster parents until the day they went to live with them, and most changed hands without adequate information being passed on. The private foster parents apparently were not aware of the desirability of making contact before the placements occurred, and were not prepared to seek out extra information about the children. The hypothesis that the placement arrangements for many of the private foster children would be made in a haphazard manner which is not in the best interests of their welfare can be considered upheld.

The attitudes of the private foster mothers

Psychological theory and research has laid great store on mothers' attitudes as a major means through which children's personalities are formed.[1] To mention but two long-established studies, Davis and Havighurst (1947) and Spinley (1954) explain the development of an effective conscience as dependent upon the loving, consistent attitudes of parents, especially of mothers. Similarly, it is argued that the attitudes of foster mothers play an important part in the development of foster children and so are a central part of treatment. The belief that private foster mothers were deficient in this sphere led to the hypothesis that their attitudes would not be conducive to the welfare of the private foster children, and that they would frequently be dependent upon making financial gain.

Which attitudes are conducive to welfare? A review of the child care literature identified two attitudes (or clusters of attitudes) which it was considered essential for foster parents to possess and express.[2] First, attitudes which convey affection and security. Charnley and Kastell, for instance, are two authors who stress the need for affection. By this they mean the expression, by the foster parents, of such warmth and concern that the foster child is convinced they want him. They link affection closely with 'security' which means that they have assured the child that their affection will be continued. In the USA, Fanshel (1966, pp. 118–19) includes affection within the term 'warmth' which is found in the person who 'genuinely likes and enjoys the child, finds contact with him rewarding and pleasant, is appreciative and approving of the child's personality'. Of all the writers, it is Trasler who devotes most space to the expression of affection. From his research he deduces that it helps foster children cope with their rejection experiences and enables them to develop the emotional capacities to relate not only to the foster parents but to persons outside the foster home. He concludes (1960, p. 147) that the foster mother's capacity to express affection 'is a source of reassurance against fears of being abandoned once more; it gives the child that sense of security, of being a loved and valued person, which is most important to his emotional development'. This affection, or love, he makes clear is demonstrated both actively by verbal reassurance and passively by the acceptance of the foster children's sullenness, destructiveness, and other difficult behaviour.

Attitudes relating to affection and security are, hopefully, found in most families. Paradoxically, the second cluster can be displayed only by foster parents, namely that they should convey a realistic accept-ance of the concept of fostering. Trasler emphasises the vital importance of foster mothers recognising 'that the child is not entirely their own' (1960, p. 139), while Charnley and other writers argue that they should not even show attitudes appropriate to adoptive parents.

The two clusters of attitudes are in some ways in conflict. The foster mothers are expected to love the children but not to regard them as their own. Yet the necessity for the 'realistic' attitudes springs from four strong arguments. First, research studies, particularly that of

Weinstein (1960), demonstrate that foster children 'adjust' more easily to a foster home when they understand the true nature of their position. Second, it is argued that the children will only gain this understanding as the foster parents display in their attitudes that the children are foster children. Third, foster children frequently return to their own parents, and difficulties may occur if the foster parents have emotionally weaned them away from them. Fourth, it is argued that foster parents whose basic attitude is (natural) parental will be unwilling to co-operate with child care officers whose visits are a reminder of the true status of the child.

The assessment of attitudes

Having established which attitudes are needed by foster parents, there remained the problem of assessing the attitudes of the foster mothers in the study. It was assumed that questions about the foster mothers' reasons for fostering, their consideration of the gains they made from it, and their conception of the duty of foster parents, would reveal something of their attitudes. More specifically, attention was focused on how they regarded their foster children, how strong was their intention to keep them, and their desire to change the foster children's status to that of adoptive children (for which no payments can be made).

Once the areas of study were determined, there remained the notoriously difficult task of devising questions to assess attitudes. The difficulties of this task and the construction of the questions are discussed in the Appendix. Here it suffices to say that various types of questions were employed in order to approach the subject in different ways. If they provided a general consistency in the type of responses, then it could be assumed that they were indeed identifying the respondents' attitudes. The four main types of questions were as follows:

a Open-ended opinion questions which simply encourage the respondent to express their views in their own words. Their responses were taken down in full and later categorised and coded by judges. Thus the foster mothers were asked, 'What made you and your husband think you would like to have foster children?' 'What do you gain from having a foster child?' 'What do you regard as your duty to give to your foster child?' and 'If his parents consented, would you adopt this foster child?'

b Thurstone's method of forming attitude questions was used to select attitude statements which represented the way in which the foster mother regarded the foster child. The method provides a measure of the intensity of feeling within a framework of attitudinal statements chosen by more objective means than the judgment of the researcher. An explanation of the formation of the question can be found in the Appendix.

c   Guttman's method was employed to develop a scale for quantifying the foster mother's 'keeping' score, that is, her determination to keep the foster child. Instead of just asking 'Are you determined to keep the child?' the Guttman method allows the construction of a cumulative scale which scores the differing conditions under which the foster mother would or would not keep a child. The method is discussed in the Appendix, as is a test of reproductability which had the satisfactory result of showing that the responses to the questions had been consistently cumulative.

d   Four straightforward factual questions elicited the amount and type of payments received by the foster parents.

Motive, gains and duty

Before presenting the findings, it is necessary to explain the form in which they are presented. The findings relating to the foster parents' motive, gains and duty refer to their attitude to fostering in general as well as to a specific foster child. Thus the question regarding why the foster parents started to foster need not refer to the foster child they had with them at the time of the research. The tables quantifying these responses will be given in terms of the number of foster parents. However, the questions relating to the statement representing their attitude, their views on adoption and the keeping score, applied to the particular foster children with them at the time of the study, and hence the Tables will give the number of foster children as well as the number of foster parents. Percentages are not presented in these tables for reasons of space. Lastly, the Table presenting the amount paid for each child is given in terms of the numbers of children only.

The private foster mothers' stated reasons for fostering as presented in Table 5.3 are categorised into four major reasons and 'other'. Within each, further sub-reasons are itemised. A third gave as their primary reason an answer related to their desire to have a family of their own or to create a family. Such women could confidently be expected to regard their foster child in a natural child relationship to themselves. Twenty-three per cent explained their main motive as a

Table 5.3   Foster mothers' stated reasons for fostering

	Private foster mothers		Local authority foster mothers	
	No.	%	No.	%
Desire to have or enlarge family				
(a) lost own child	9		7	
(b) could not have own or more of own	20		21	
(c) substitute for adoption	0		10	
(d) wanted more	1		10	
(e) wanted child of particular sex	3		5	
	33	33	53	43·4
Circumstances				
(a) knew child's parents	3		9	
(b) knew the child	12		8	
(c) developed from daily minding or other temporary arrangement	7		4	
	22	22	21	17·2
Fondness and concern for children				
(a) fond of children	13		13	
(b) wants to help children	7		13	
(c) related to own happy or unhappy childhood	3		1	
	23	23	27	22·1
Need to fill vacuum in foster mother's life				
(a) need to work	1		5	
(b) loneliness	7		3	
(c) fill place of own grown up children	7		4	
	15	15	12	9·8
Other				
(a) financial	3		2	
(b) company for or needs of own child	3		5	
(c) influenced by another foster mother	1		2	
	7	7	9	7·4
Totals	100	100	122	100·0

fondness or concern to help children. Often this was expressed as a desire to help deprived or unfortunate children. Although the foster parents in the above group often expressed affection and concern for the children they wanted as part of their own family, here the over-riding motive was concern without any conditions about the child's relationship to them. Twenty-two per cent indicated that they commenced to foster because they found themselves in circumstances where they felt constrained to do so. An example concerns the husband who asked his life-long friends to take his child following the death of his wife. Obviously some such foster parents acted from a sense of duty rather than of affection for the child or a desire to add to their own family. Indeed, a minority was prepared to state that they had not felt affection and had taken the child in a grudging manner. Fifteen per cent of the private foster mothers said they fostered to satisfy some need or vacuum in their own lives, the tenor of their words stressing concern for themselves rather than for children. Only 3 per cent stated that financial profit was a major reason inducing them to foster.

Table 5.3 shows the primary reasons rendered by the foster mothers. Many explained their decision to foster by a number of different reasons. The Table of supplementary reasons is not given, but it is worth noting that 66 per cent of the private foster parents stated as a primary or supplementary reason that their motive was to extend their family, or that it sprang from a concern for children. In other words, 34 per cent of the foster mothers did not mention at all their concern for children or a desire to extend their family life.

The local authority foster parents revealed almost the same percentage giving as their primary reason a fondness and concern for children. However, a greater proportion, 43.4 per cent, fostered from a desire to have or extend their family, while fewer did so having found themselves in circumstances which constrained them or to satisfy a vacuum in their own lives. As with the private foster parents, very few were concerned with financial gain, and, again in similar fashion, when supplementary reasons were included only a minority expressed neither concern for children nor a desire to add them to their families.

The attitudes associated with the reasons for commencing to foster are not necessarily the same as those felt once the fostering is established. These are shown in the foster mothers' opinions of what they considered to be their duty towards the foster children.

Table 5.4 shows that over half the private foster mothers specifically

Table 5.4   The foster mothers' duty towards their foster children*

| | Private foster mothers | | Local authority foster mothers | |
	No.	%	No.	%
Love	51	51	64	52·5
Security	9	9	19	15·6
'Same as own children'	38	38	56	45·9
A normal family life	15	15	21	17·2
Meet their physical needs	9	9	14	11·6
Other	17	17	17	13·9
understanding	4		3	
firm discipline	1		4	
'everything'	6		2	
other	6		8	

*The foster mothers could give more than one duty so totals are more than the total number of foster mothers and percentages total more than 100.
No. private foster mothers = 100.
No. local authority foster mothers = 122.

stated that it was their duty to give love to the foster children. The tabulation gives all the responses made by the private foster mothers and not just their primary ones. However, a further analysis revealed that all but two of them expressed their duty in at least one of the following ways – love, security, a normal family life, treating the children the same as their own. All these categories have the ring of affection and concern. Only two private foster mothers defined their duty solely in terms of meeting the children's physical needs for food, clothing and shelter. The responses of the local authority foster mothers were in a similar vein and with a similar distribution.

The foster mothers having said why they started to foster and how they perceived their duty once the fostering was under way, were then asked to look back and evaluate what they had gained from the experience.

It can be seen from Table 5.5 that the private foster mothers considered that they made positive emotional and social gains from fostering. Their answers were mainly in terms of love, happiness, satisfaction, and the completion of family life. Once again their responses are given in multiple not primary form, but a further analysis revealed 80 per cent of them expressing their gain in terms of at least one of the following – love, happiness, satisfaction or completion of family life. Not one private foster mother thought she made financial gain although several made the point that they did not.

Table 5.5   The foster mothers' gains from fostering*

	Private foster mothers		Local authority foster mothers	
	No.	%	No.	%
Love of the child	27	27	19	15·6
General happiness	35	35	49	40·2
Satisfaction of helping others	22	22	26	21·3
Companionship	15	15	9	7·4
Completion of family	13	13	31	25·4
Other	27	27	25	20·5
broadens experiences	8		7	
gives purpose to life	4		2	
provides a job	3		2	
problems and anxieties	3		2	
no financial gain	4		9	
other	5		3	

*The foster mothers could give more than one gain so totals are more than
the total number of foster mothers and percentages total more than 100.
 No. private foster mothers = 100.
 No. local authority foster mothers = 122.

Only three private foster mothers expressed their answers in negative
terms saying that fostering had given them extra problems and
anxieties. Thus the majority considered themselves well satisfied with
fostering. Again, the responses of the local authority mothers were
not markedly different either in content or distribution.

The preceding three tabulations have been based upon the private
foster mothers' own opinion of themselves. As such they are subjective statements in which they may have portrayed themselves in
the manner in which they thought would win the approval of the
interviewer. However, three points give some grounds for confidence
in their responses. First, the content of responses was consistent
among the three questions. Second, the responses of different foster
mothers was consistent in pattern for each individual question.
Third, there was consistency between the content and distribution of
the responses of the private and local authority foster mothers.
Assuming, then, that the answers did reveal the way in which the
private foster mothers felt, it can be concluded that they were typified
by attitudes of affection for the foster children, a desire to win their
love, and a wish to involve them fully in their own family life. In
addition, the overriding impression is of a well-meaning, sincere
attempt to help children and of a high valuation of affection, security
and family life. These attitudes and feelings occur despite the racial

background of the children and despite, as will be shown, the insecurity of some foster mothers about how long the children would stay. The stereotype of the affectionless woman 'baby-farming' unloved children for financial gain had little place in the minds of the foster mothers themselves. It is true that some foster mothers may have loved the children not as foster children but as natural children, it is true that affection in itself does not make a suitable foster home. But, at least, the private foster mothers were aware of the need to give affection to foster children. In this respect they were little different from the local authority foster mothers.

Statistical tabulations can convey little of the feeling the foster mothers expressed. Therefore some examples will be given, in the foster mothers' own words, of how they valued affection, security and family life. To the question concerning why the foster parents started to foster, some extracts are as follows:

'I love children, you have to because it's hard work. I'm gifted with being able to love, not just taking into a home.'

'I was in a foster home myself, pushed from home to home. I thought if I was a foster mother I'd never give them up, they are not parcels to be shoved from house to house.'

'We both come from big families and are fond of children. We like to give a good home, to give help where needed.'

'I can't have any more of my own. I keep thinking about children who've no home of their own – we have room so we take them.'

To the question concerning their duties towards the foster children, some private foster mothers said:

'Everything I have got. The same as I give to my own. When I was in a foster home I used to long for the foster mother to put her arm around me and I prayed she would cuddle me. You must treat them like one of your own.'

'Affection and love, your whole life. Equality with other children in the house so she feels she is wanted. Everything a child needs. A happy and contented life.'

'I love him, I worship him.'

'Love, understanding and trust. Trust beyond everything else. Don't count the change in front of them. Trust them when they go out. If you love them they trust you. Clothes and riches are not the answer – it's to know that mother's always there.'

To the question concerning the gains they made from fostering, some foster mothers replied, in part, as follows:

'When they sit and talk to you, kiss you goodnight and tell you they love you. The greatest gain is to know that they love you.'

'A child's trust. To know she has absolute trust in me: she believes anything I say is truth. The love they give back. You have the first baby smile, the baby snuggling up to you – the mother misses that.'

'Peace of mind. Being useful in life. The love of a young child, especially at my age when the family are grown up. These last five years have been wonderful. All through the summer we go out a lot and she's so dependent upon us. It's a wonderful feeling to know that she loves us so much.'

'Lots of love. What would I do with my life, my husband is gone? I need the love of children.'

'Something I always thought I'd been cheated out of, a little boy. I don't gain money. It annoys me when neighbours say he was lucky to fall into a home – well it was me that was lucky.'

Foster mothers' attitudes towards the study children

As explained, the use of Thurstone's method allowed the compilation of attitude statements from which the foster mothers selected the

Table 5.6   Foster mothers' attitudes towards the foster children

	Private fostering		Local authority fostering	
	Foster parents	Foster children	Foster parents	Foster children
'I regard him as my own child'	53	71	77	88
'I know he's not mine but I treat him the same'	45	68	44	53
'He is a means of making money while at the same time doing something worthwhile'	2	4	1	2
Totals	100	143	122	143

one which represented their attitude towards the children in the study. Tables 5.6 and 5.7 now present findings in terms of the children and foster parents.

Remembering that the child care literature and research advocated that foster children should not be regarded as natural children, it is of importance that seventy-one of the private foster children, 49·7 per cent, were regarded in this way by their fifty-three foster parents. Sixty-eight, that is 47·6 per cent, had forty-five foster parents whose attitude was represented by 'I know he's not mine but I treat him the same'. This attitude, which implies a recognition of the child's true status combined with affection for him, is the one which child care experts deem most desirable. Only four private foster children were regarded by their two foster parents as a means of financial profit, even when it was acknowledged that a mercenary attitude did not preclude the children benefiting from their care. The local authority foster children tended to be regarded in the same ways, with no significant differences between the two groups.

Strength of 'keeping' feeling

The cumulative conditions under which foster parents would give up their foster children were devised as: if payments stopped altogether; if the parents were a nuisance; if the child's behaviour was very difficult; and if he was a bad influence on their own children. A point was awarded for each condition under which the foster parents would retain care. Thus a score of four means they would have kept him whatever the conditions. A score of three means, because the scale and system was designed to be cumulative, that the foster

Table 5.7   Intensity of the foster parents' determination to keep their foster children

Keeping score	Private fostering		Local authority fostering	
	Foster parents	Foster children	Foster parents	Foster children
0	13	22	1	1
1	7	7	6	11
2	15	23	9	9
3	14	22	23	27
4	51	69	83	95
Totals	100	143	122	143

parent would have kept him under the first three conditions but not the fourth. And so on.

Sixty-nine, 48·3 per cent, of the private foster children would have been kept by the fifty-one foster mothers in all the conditions. The finding suggests that many considered themselves to possess very intense feelings towards their foster children, feelings that would prompt them to retain care in the most trying circumstances. On the other hand, there were twenty-two private foster children, 15·4 per cent of the total, whose thirteen foster mothers would have given up their care if any of the circumstances had occurred. Presumably these were the children most vulnerable to sudden removals from foster homes. Such low keeping scores existed hardly at all amongst the local authority fosterings. Indeed, the local authority fosterings were significantly more likely to have a higher keeping score. Dividing the score at two and under/over two, the difference was significant for the foster children, $\chi^2 = 16·970$, d.f. $= 1$, P $= <0·001$, and for the foster parents, $\chi^2 = 14·874$, d.f. $= 1$, P $= <0·001$. Thus the private foster children were more at risk of losing their foster homes in given conditions.

Attitudes to adoption

The nearest relationship to that of a natural parent is that of adoption. Thus to ask foster parents if they would adopt their foster child is to ask for a committal to a permanent relationship for which no income is received from the child's real parents or the children's department.

Ninety-three, 65·0 per cent, of the private foster children would have been adopted by their seventy foster parents if circumstances had allowed. This is not to say that all who professed a wish to adopt failed to regard and treat their charges as foster children. Thirty-seven, 25·9 per cent, of the private foster children would not have been adopted even if their twenty-two foster parents had been free to do so. In the case of thirteen children, the private foster parents were undecided as to what action they would take if circumstances changed. The response distribution for the local authority children and foster parents was similar to that of the private fosterings, and there were no statistically significant differences. Certainly, a picture did not emerge of private foster parents who differed from their local authority counterparts by being more interested in the financial gains of fostering than in the relationship with the children.

Payments for foster children

Although the receipt of high fees for private foster children would not constitute proof that financial gain was a main motive of the private foster mothers, a finding that they received low income from this source would indicate that their attitudes were not primarily shaped by mercenary considerations. The financial income from all sources received for the foster children is given in Table 5.8. Table 5.8 shows

Table 5.8 Weekly financial payments made for the foster children to the foster parents

	Private foster children		Local authority foster children	
	No.	%	No.	%
Under 30 shillings	27	18·9	0	0·0
Thirty shillings and under £2	35	24·5	46	32·2
£2 and under £3	75	52·4	82	57·3
£3 and under £4	3	2·1	15	10·5
£4 and under £5	3	2·1	0	0·0
£5 and over	0	0·0	0	0·0
Totals	143	100·0	143	100·0

that the weekly payment made for twenty-seven of the private foster children, that is 18·9 per cent, was under thirty shillings while for a further thirty-five, 24·5 per cent, it was between thirty shillings and under two pounds. Should these amounts be considered low? At the time of the research, a guardian's allowance, which is paid by the Ministry of Social Security amounted to £2 5s. 6d. per week.[3] This amount is certainly not considered excessive but at least 43·4 per cent of the private foster children were paid for at rates below it.

Another form of comparison is with the rates paid by the children's departments in the study areas. At the time of the research, the basic rate varied from £2 15s. to £4 5s. per week according to the child's age, a clothing allowance of up to 17s. 6d. being included.[4] However, the departments had discretion to add extra allowances to the weekly rates so comparison was made not with the stated standard rates but with the actual incomes in respect of the local authority foster children in the contrast group. The Table shows that although no local authority payments reached the £4 and below £5 which was paid for three private foster children, generally speaking the higher rates were paid in the local authority sector. Certainly, none of the local authority children were below the thirty shillings which applied to

18·9 per cent of the private children. Taking under £2 as the dividing line, payments for the private foster children were significantly lower than for the local authority ones ($\chi^2 = 14\cdot220$, d.f. $= 1$, P $= <0\cdot001$).

The comparison between the private and children's departments' rates is not a completely accurate one as sometimes the natural parents of the private foster children gave clothing in addition to payments whereas the clothing allowance paid for the local authority foster children is included in the figures stated above. Clothing was given regularly (at least once every three months) for thirty-eight of the private foster children, occasionally (less than once every three months) for fifty, and never for fifty-five. On the other hand, the private foster parents were financially disadvantaged in two directions. First, children's departments usually pay supplementary allowances as well as weekly rates. The departments studied paid allowances for Christmas and birthday presents, for holidays, an extra clothing grant on starting school (or leaving school), extra grants for enuretics, for sports equipment, for fares to hospital and school, and so on. Private foster parents were unlikely to receive such bonuses. Second, the regularity of income guaranteed to local authority foster parents could be denied the private foster parents. Payment was regular (natural parents always paid or did not miss more than twice every three months) in respect of ninety-six of the children, but irregular (missed three times or more every three months) for forty-seven. Neither was low pay compensated by regularity; indeed, those receiving under thirty shillings were significantly more likely to be irregularly paid ($\chi^2 = 17\cdot233$, d.f. $= 1$, P $= <0.001$).

How important were financial factors in private fostering? No doubt many private foster parents could not have cared for the children without the money they received from the natural parents, but a number of reasons suggest that financial profit was not a major inducement to fostering. First, very few private foster parents could have been making a profit. It is usually concluded, for instance by Stroud (1965, pp. 117–18) and George (1970, pp. 225–7), that local authority foster parents are underpaid in the sense that they may well be out of pocket as a result of looking after a foster child. Yet the private foster parents tended to receive lower sums even than them. No wonder that, when asked, sixty-four of the one hundred private foster mothers said that the payments they received did not cover the costs of keeping the child. Second, even those foster mothers who might have been expected to charge the highest rates did not do so. The 'professional' foster mothers did not receive significantly more than less experienced women. Neither was there any indication that they made their profit by taking in large numbers of children at one time. Third, the private foster parents did not appear to take advantage of a situation of being in demand to put up their fees. Fourth, the foster mothers almost certainly could have used their skills to earn more money. Most were in reach of a city with a great demand for female labour but, if desiring to stay in their own homes, could have taken advantage of the demand for child or daily-minders. Oddly enough, although daily-minding involves children staying for only part of the day – they are usually brought and collected by parents who go out to work – the research of Gregory suggests that their fees are higher than for private foster children (1969, pp. 235–9). Further, daily-minders often can handle several children at a time, as they do not require sleeping space and amenities, and hence can receive a number of weekly incomes. Yet private foster parents opt to work longer hours for lower incomes. Thus it can be safely concluded that the prospect of financial gain was not a major influence shaping the foster parents' attitudes. Of course, the foster parents' previous experiences revealed that sometimes the lack of payments by natural parents forced them to hand the children back. At the same time it is evident that many foster parents endured low and irregular payments. Finance was not the factor that tied them to the children.

The present chapter has focused on the desirability of the foster mothers showing affection for their foster children, accepting them as foster rather than as natural children and not being dominated by attitudes relating to financial gain. A consistent finding was that the private foster mothers did regard themselves as possessing deep love and affection for their charges. Such was their affection that nearly half indicated that they were prepared to keep the foster children in all the adverse circumstances which were suggested, while the majority would have liked to adopt them. Any stereotype of the unloving or unfeeling private foster mother is therefore refuted. However, as hinted earlier, affection in itself, although necessary to the development of a foster child, is not enough.

The attitude of over half the private foster mothers was to regard the foster child as their own child. The child care literature is agreed that such an attitude does not enable a child to understand his own background and position, makes the foster parents unwilling to give him understanding of this, makes it more difficult for him to rejoin happily his natural parents, and makes the foster parents less amenable to co-operating with the children's department. The potential difficulties can best be summed up in the words of the woman who said: 'Accept it [foster child] as your own, keep it away from the parents.' She had undoubted affection for her foster child, but was actively opposing the growth of a relationship between him and his parents.

A further implication for foster parents who regard the child as their own is that they reinforce problems of role conflict and role confusion. Banton points out that attitudes and roles are interrelated, certain attitudes are appropriate to particular roles, roles are partially formed by prevailing attitudes (1965, pp. 146–9). On the one hand these private foster parents develop the attitudes and behaviour appropriate to a natural parent. They give great affection, may be determined to keep the child whatever happens, integrate him into the family. On the other hand their actions and attitudes are not compatible with natural parenthood; they take payment for the child, and in many cases, as will be shown, accept – even encourage – visits from the natural parents, which implies the eventual return home of the child. The foster parents are thus trying to act in two conflicting roles, that of a parent and of a foster parent. A part of the problem is that not only do these roles conflict but there is confusion as to just what is the role of a foster parent. The child care texts may define how a foster parent should regard and treat a foster child, but such clear-cut assertions probably do not reach private foster parents and, if they do, they are not told how to put them into operation. The fostering role is not one commonly met within the family. It is rarely if ever discussed by neighbours or by the mass media. Hence, no common body of expectation is built up about it. Moreover, it would seem from the present study that foster parents do not live near each other, they are not concentrated in a certain number of streets, so there are few opportunities for mutual discussion. Being uncertain, the private foster parents will sometimes be perplexed and confused as to how to treat their foster children. For instance, what attitude should they adopt towards the foster child when, during a visit from his natural parents, both he and the foster mother's natural child misbehave? Wolins would even go so far as to say that the resultant confusion within the foster mother is a cause why some decide to resolve their problem by opting out, that is by ceasing to be foster parents (1963, p. 141).

The conflict and confusion of the foster parents' attitudes and roles

D

presumably will be conveyed to their foster children. Children usually have their own expected pattern of behaviour made clear to them by the way in which parents treat them. This will not occur if the foster parents are unsure how to perform their treatment task. It seems likely, for instance, that the foster children will not have a clear directive on how to regard their foster parents, what their attitude should be towards the foster parents' own children, or how they should relate to their own parents. Of course, local authority foster children and foster parents are open to the same confusions and conflicts. But at least, as will be shown, they enjoy the closer attention of the child care officers to help them clarify their positions.

By no means all the private foster parents treated the foster children as their own natural child. Forty-five were able to accept the paradox of fostering, by which they recognised their charge as a foster child but could still offer affection to him. Probably the private foster mothers' own words can best describe how they put this attitude into operation. One said, 'You must love them, yet be prepared to give them up.' Another: 'Take the child in as your own, although you know in your heart he is not, and give him love and security; make him feel wanted.' Perhaps the following advice only makes sense coming from a foster mother, 'Love them, but you can't love them as your own.' Or as another put it, 'Don't be too possessive. The child is just borrowed. You have the privilege of loving them.'

Nearly all the private foster parents saw the foster child either as a natural child or as a foster child whom they could yet treat in the same way as they did their own children. The attitudes of very few foster mothers were related to financial motives. Monetary gain emerged as a factor of small importance to the private foster mothers, although, no doubt, some experienced difficulties due to the low amounts paid to them.

Finally, it is of interest to inquire whether any particular types of children were associated with the private foster mothers' attitudes. Their affection was extended to all, but the children in the West African grouping were significantly less likely to be regarded as natural children (dividing grouping a/other groupings, and testing by the two main attitudes, $\chi^2 = 6 \cdot 4384$, d.f. $= 1$, P $= <0 \cdot 010$). The same children were significantly less likely to have the higher keeping scores expressed by their foster parents (dividing keeping scores at 2 and under/more, $\chi^2 = 4 \cdot 8029$, d.f. $= 1$, P $= <0 \cdot 050$). Children placed for reasons connected with having only one interested parent were significantly more likely to be regarded as natural children ($\chi^2 =$

5·661, d.f. = 1, P = <0.025). Possibly the racial difference between foster child and foster parents, combined with – as will be shown later – the more frequent visits of their parents, made it harder for the foster parents to treat the West Africans as natural children. On the other hand, children with only one parent, being less likely to receive visits and having greater prospects of staying permanently in the foster home, were more open to being treated as natural children.

The subject of attitudes is a complex one, and not surprisingly no straightforward conclusions may be made about the hypothesis which commenced this chapter. Most private foster mothers expressed the attitude of affection which is essential to the welfare of foster children. However, over half regarded them as natural children. At least, the claim that they were unduly influenced by financial motives can be refuted.

Foster child-rearing practices

The distinction between the attitudes of foster mothers and the practices they would advocate in regard to foster children is a fine one, but for the sake of discussion it must be made. Practices are taken to involve the ways in which the foster mothers would react to specific situations in the fostering process.[5] In order to ascertain their responses the foster mothers were asked three open questions about a short case history of a foster girl, which touched upon points the child care literature identified as being of importance, namely the reasons for the child's behaviour, the way in which she should have been treated, and the child's knowledge of her past.

In order to evaluate the foster mothers' responses it was necessary to know how they should or ought to have answered. Therefore the child care officers were asked the same questions, and their recommendations taken as yardsticks. At the same time, responses could be compared with those of the local authority foster parents. The case history about which the questions were asked is as follows:

Mrs X was an experienced foster mother looking after two boys and her own daughter. Annette, aged seven and a half, was placed with her. She was illegitimate, and had already been in a nursery and a previous foster home.

Mrs X was very firm with Annette and quickly suppressed her cheekiness. She proved useful in the home, although rather a cry-baby. At school she was competent in her work but a nuisance in class because she was always seeking attention.

After two years the two boys left to get employment. Annette was very lonely. Mrs X did not encourage her to make friends, and would not allow her to bring other children home to play, so she spent most of her time alone in her bedroom.

Annette asked Mrs X questions about her own mother, but the foster mother thought it best to avoid them and said, 'They are no good to you – don't bother your head about them.'

Annette had occasional bouts of screaming and temper tantrums. Mrs X punished her by corporal punishment.

Understanding the foster child's behaviour

It was assumed that the foster mothers' treatment of the foster children would be related to their understanding of behaviour. Thus the child care officers and foster parents were asked to give explanations for the behaviour of the child in the case record. The officers agreed in identifying four areas of explanation. As the private and local authority foster parents did not differ greatly from each other, the findings will be presented briefly and not in tabular form. First, the officers agreed that the foster child's behaviour was partly attributable to the poor treatment given her by the foster mother.[6] In particular they stressed that the foster mother did not make a loving and individualistic relationship with the girl. Most of the private and local authority foster mothers gave similar explanations. Just as an earlier finding suggested that they possessed feelings of affection for their foster children, so also they perceived its value in any fostering situation. As one foster mother explained:

'The foster mother probably did not show that she loved her.
All children need love as well as firmness. The foster mother
did not give her attention, therefore she had temper tantrums.'

Second, the officers also saw the foster child's behaviour in terms of her reaction to the treatment given her. Thus they explained that she responded by being insecure and by testing out the extent of the foster mother's love by behaving badly. Only 21 per cent of the private and 22·1 per cent of the local authority foster mothers described the situation in these ways, but there was no statistically significant difference between the two groups of foster parents.

Third, the officers specified the lack of stimulation in the foster child's environment, in particular noting her lack of friends. Her behaviour, they thought, was partly protest against her isolation. Again, most foster parents of both kinds made similar points, especially highlighting the girl's loneliness.

Fourth, the officers argued that the child's previous separation experiences would result in behavioural problems, and create confusion about her own mother which would promote anxiety. Over one-third of the local authority foster mothers made a similar analysis but only 15 per cent of the private foster mothers (the difference was statistically significant, $\chi^2 = 8 \cdot 5947$, d.f. $= 1$, P $= <0 \cdot 010$). The need for foster children to possess a true understanding of their relationship to their past and to their natural parents has been established by the research of Weinstein. Later, the present research will assess what knowledge the foster children actually possessed. Here it suffices to say that foster parents who did not discern the significance of a child's previous experiences in a case where it was made obvious, may be unlikely to do so in their own foster children.

Dealing with the foster child

A second question concerned the way in which the foster mother should have dealt with the foster girl's behaviour. The officers advised four main ways of treating her. Not surprisingly, they are closely related to their perceptions of the causes of her behaviour. First, they recommended a number of items which are all part of promoting an affective relationship between foster mother and foster child. These included factors such as showing love, understanding the child, allowing her to express her feelings. Second, they recommended that she be encouraged to have more friends and outside interests. Third, it was felt that emphasis should be given to explaining to her the position of her mother. The meaning here is that the foster mother should take the initiative in raising the matter. She should provide explanations as to why the foster child did not live with her mother, and explain who her mother was. Fourth, the officers came out strongly against the use of corporal punishment, which they felt would probably make her worse. The responses of the foster parents are presented in Table 5.9. As they could give more than one answer the responses are multiple. Findings are in terms of percentages in order to facilitate comparison within a confined space.

The numbers of private and local authority foster mothers advocating the promotion of a relationship, the child having more

Table 5.9   Foster mothers' opinions on how to deal with the foster child*

	Private foster mothers %	Local authority foster mothers %
Foster mother should promote an affective relationship	59	42·6
Child should have more friends	43	53·3
Foster mother should explain to child about her mother	17	30·3
Corporal punishment not to be used	22	21·3

*As the respondents could give more than one opinion the percentage totals make more than 100.
No. of private foster mothers = 100.
No. of local authority foster mothers = 122.

friends, and the non-use of corporal punishment were not significantly different. However, the private ones were significantly less likely to recommend helping the foster child by explaining about her mother ($\chi^2 = 7·1654$, d.f. $= 1$, P $= <0·010$). The local authority foster mothers were much more alive to the child's need to have information about her mother and the reasons for the separation.

Answering the foster child's questions

Finally, information was sought on the way in which the foster mother in the case should have answered the girl's questions about her mother. The responses were categorised and coded in a primary way with three main alternative answers. However, the child care officers were divided between two of these. Over half, 52·8 per cent, considered the foster mother should have answered fully, telling the whole truth about the girl's mother, her illegitimacy and her past, although presenting it in as positive a light as possible. One officer explained: 'The questions should be answered as frankly as possible. ... Help the child to see some positive aspects of the mother's behaviour, i.e. that she cared in some ways and did what she thought best – thus helping the child to feel valued and wanted.' The remaining officers advised the telling of partial truth, holding back facts which were too painful: 'These questions should not be avoided. They should be answered not by telling lies though not necessarily by telling the whole truth. Some painful information may need to be withheld.' Clearly a split existed between officers who would place disagreeable

The treatment of the private foster children (1) 85

facts before a foster child, but compensating with some positive aspects, and those who would shield the child more fully. However, no officer recommended withholding all information or telling direct lies.

Two ways of tackling the foster child's questions thus gained some approval from the child care 'experts'. The responses of the local authority foster mothers were almost identical with those of the officers: 54·9 per cent recommended telling the whole truth, and 37·7 per cent the partial truth (with the remaining few classified as 'other'). The private foster mothers differed. A smaller proportion, 40 per cent, advised the whole truth, a larger proportion, 46 per cent, the partial truth (with 4 per cent 'other'). But the most striking difference was the appearance of 10 per cent who advocated telling nothing at all. For instance, some said:

'Say nothing at all, or the child will think you want her to go.'

'Leave it alone, it raises trouble. She may grow like the parent.'

'Say the mother has passed away and nothing more. The child then has a clean break. Or else the foster child has to choose between the mother and the foster mother. It's not worth letting them know.'

If these foster mothers reacted to questions from their own foster children in the way they advocated, then it is likely that the children would be deprived of knowledge about their own parents. As pointed out, the child care literature states that a lack of such knowledge is likely to handicap a child's adaptation to his foster home. Of course, even those who advised telling the truth may not have done so in practice. The child's actual knowledge will be ascertained in a later chapter.

To sum up: in general, both in terms of understanding the causes of a foster child's behaviour and in recommending ways to help, the private foster mothers' views concurred with those of the child care officers – and of the local authority foster parents. They perceived how a foster mother could fail a child, how a foster child would react to such a foster mother, how loneliness and isolation could affect the child's behaviour. Thus the private foster mothers did not emerge as punitive, unthinking creatures with no understanding of the fostering needs of children. But in one important sphere they fell short of the child care practices advocated by the experts, and so lent weight to the hypothesis that their fostering child-rearing practices would be unsatisfactory. Few appreciated how a foster child's previous child care experiences could adversely affect her later behaviour. Few realised how unhappy, confusing experiences with a natural parent could similarly harm the child. Lacking this understanding, the private foster mothers tended not to recommend the help of clarifying to the foster child the events of the past, of dispelling fear and ignorance by explaining who her mother was, and of reducing anxiety by discussing the reasons why she was separated from her parents. Indeed, a number of the private foster mothers went to the extreme of saying that a foster child should be told nothing, even when she directly asked questions about her own mother. Not only did they fall short of the practices recommended by the officers, the private foster mothers differed here from their local authority counterparts. Probably the greater contact between the officers and the local authority foster mothers enabled the latter to assimilate the views and practices of the former.

6 The treatment of the private foster children (2)

In the preceding chapter the treatment given by the private foster parents to the private foster children was discussed by focusing on their preparations for the children's placement, their attitudes, and their foster child-rearing practices. The two remaining areas of treatment, the involvement of the foster fathers and the quality of accommodation provided by the foster parents, will now be examined. Both areas are regarded as part of treatment in that they come within the activities, attitudes and provisions stemming from the foster parents to the children.

Involvement of the foster fathers

It is a commonplace assertion that children are profoundly influenced by their fathers. Children separated from their natural fathers will be open to the influence of their father substitutes. Doubts concerning the manner in which private foster fathers fulfil the part of substitute father led to the hypothesis that they would be little involved with their foster children.

The importance of the involvement of the foster fathers with their foster children can be shown in two ways. First, by discussing how a natural father influences his child and, second, by examining the specific contribution of the foster father. Having discussed the manner of the influence of such involvement, an attempt will be made to establish means whereby that of the private foster fathers can be assessed.

The part of the natural father

Explanations of how and why fathers influence their children partially depend on which psychological school is accepted as valid. Psychoanalytic theory postulates how the father affects his children during certain stages or phases. In particular, Freudians have stressed the significance of the father in the formation and resolution of the Oedipus complex and in the development of the super-ego. Other work emphasises the role of the father as a model by which both sons and daughters perceive and adopt the behavioural patterns of male figures. Sociologists have stressed the part of the father as a socialising agent who prepares his children for the roles they can fulfil in society. Despite the varied approaches there is fundamental agreement that the father is a determining influence on the emotional and social growth of his children. It follows that fathers can have a positive or negative effect on the development of the children's personalities and on the way in which they relate to society as a whole.

If broad theories portray the general relationship between fathers and their children, it is research projects which more precisely show their outcomes. Four pieces of research can be briefly mentioned, that of Andry, Balbernie, the Schaffers and the Newsons. Andry's research compared delinquent and non-delinquent boys aged eleven to fifteen years.[1] He established that the former had had less contact with their fathers, had inferior environmental communication (which involved doing hobbies together, going out together) and less emotional communication (as measured by a readiness to turn to fathers for advice or help). Boys subjected to such treatment, Andry argued, were liable both to over-protection from their mothers and to feelings of hostility to their fathers, which were eventually projected on to society in the form of delinquency. Similarly, Andry argued that fathers who communicated poorly and participated rarely with their sons constituted inadequate models, so that the boys had no satisfactory and positive father figure with whom they could identify. In this situation the boys did not feel they could act out their problems within the homes with such unsatisfactory figures, but did so in the wider society.

Balbernie's study of children aged seven to seventeen who were referred to a child guidance clinic, detected a statistically significant correlation between cases which did not improve and the inactivity of the fathers. Many were 'cold', 'neurotic' or 'rejecting', and he concluded that the 'omission of the father in child guidance treatment' was an important factor in the children's lack of progress (1966, p. 146).

The Schaffers compared children received into the short-term care of a children's department with a control group not received into care whose mothers were likewise hospitalised for a confinement. They examined the part played by the father in the home, establishing a significant relationship between fathers who helped 'a lot' with household tasks and the care of the children, with not coming into care (1968, pp. 65–6). The terms on their scales such as 'help a lot', 'never helps', were not defined, as the authors admit, but the differences between the amount of participation between the two groups of fathers was very striking. The authors suggest that the lack of participation was typical of the fathers' whole involvement pattern which constituted an important factor contributing to the fact that they could not cope with the children when their wives were absent, even for a short period.

The Newsons, in their study of the fathers of one-year-old, and later of four-year-old, children, were concerned simply to establish the extent to which they participated in the care of their children, rather than assessing whether participation correlated with any particular outcome. From interviews with the mothers they obtained information on the amount the fathers helped in changing the nappy, bathing the child, and other child care activities. From this they graded 52 per cent of the fathers as highly participant, 27 per cent as moderately so, and 21 per cent as non-participant. Within this there was some tendency for participation to decrease as the fathers' social class became lower. The Newsons concluded that 'the willingness of so many fathers to participate actively in looking after such young children is, we believe, a very distinctive feature of modern family life in England' (1963, p. 139).

Finally, before leaving the outline of research findings, mention must be made of educational research concerning the fathers' part in motivating their children towards learning. The Plowden Report discusses the relevant studies and indicates that the presence of interested fathers contributes positively to their children's educational attainments.

Research of the type summarised above serves to establish that fathers are as decisive an influence on family life as are mothers. Assuming that private foster fathers are expected to take on many of the functions of natural fathers, it becomes important to assess how adequately they perform. The above projects help towards this end in two main ways. First, they identify some of the means or ways by which fathers are involved with their children – by communication, by participation, and simply by being present. Second, they provide standards or yardsticks by which the performances of the private foster fathers can be evaluated.

The part of the foster father

Child care texts have given less attention to foster fathers than foster mothers. None the less, a review of the literature reveals a general agreement that they should be as committed towards the fosterings as are their wives. By 'committed' is meant the positive determination to become a foster parent and to do the job well. Unless he is so committed, it is felt that the foster child would soon perceive that he was not wanted. Stroud adds that 'the foster father must be brought into active involvement from a very early stage and kept that way' (1965, p. 97), while Adamson concludes that his participation 'is of the greatest importance to the success of the placement' (1968, p. 34). They claim that unless this occurs the foster father's rejection of or even rivalry with the child will not only hinder his development but will bring the fostering to a close.

Child care research has little to say about foster fathers. The review of fostering research by Dinnage and Pringle hardly mentions them. Roberts, in a write-up of foster parent group meetings (1962), notes that some foster fathers voiced feelings of jealousy and resentment about their foster children. Parker and Trasler give them little space, and even American research is unusually sparse. The exception is Fanshel (1966), but he concentrates on a description of agency foster fathers accompanied by a discussion of their role perceptions, their perceived inconveniences from fostering, and their reactions to agency staff. He does not examine the extent and manner of foster father involvement.

Taking the literature on natural and foster fathers together, five areas of involvement can be identified. These are: whether a foster father exists at all; the degree of commitment of the foster father towards the fostering; the extent to which he is present; his participation with the foster child; and his communication with the child. They will be examined in turn in relation to private foster fathers and private foster children. Use will again be made of local authority fosterings and, where possible, of non-foster homes for comparative yardstick purposes. The methodology of each area will be discussed as the chapter proceeds.

Is there a private foster father?

At the time of the research, thirteen, 9·1 per cent, of the private foster children were without foster fathers. The comparative figure for the local authority foster children was twelve, 8·4 per cent, there being no statistically significant difference between the two groups. In most of the local authority cases there had been a foster father at the start of the fostering, but the foster mother had been widowed. Local authorities are reluctant to place with single women unless they have a particular qualification – for instance, a nurse to help with a handicapped child. The private foster group included mothers who were widowed or separated *before* they commenced their present fosterings, but the numbers involved are too small to draw any general conclusions. However, it is true to say that although local authorities are reluctant to use homes without father figures, there is nothing to stop single women taking in private foster children.

How do the above figures compare with previous studies? Parker found only 6 per cent of the local authority foster homes in his study to lack a foster father (1966, p. 73). The Plowden Report provides figures for children of primary school age, most of whom were living with their natural parents. Only 4 per cent were living in houses without a father or father substitute (Central Advisory Council for Education, 1967, vol. 2, p. 105).

Commitment of the foster fathers

Foster fathers' sense of commitment was assessed in two ways. One question asked the foster mother with whom the idea of the fostering started, a second enquired whether the foster father had tried to persuade her to stop the fostering once it had started. The results for the first question, comparing with the local authority group, are given in Table 6.1: 117 of the private fosterings were initiated by

Table 6.1   Foster parents with whom idea of fostering started

	Private fostering		Local authority fostering	
	Foster parents	Foster children	Foster parents	Foster children
Foster mother	80	117	62	77
Foster father	1	1	11	13
Both	11	13	44	48
Totals	92	131	117	138

Note: 8 private foster homes and 5 local authority ones were excluded as there was not a foster father present when the decision to foster was taken.

eighty, that is 87 per cent, of the private foster mothers on their own. Only thirteen of the fosterings, taking in 12 per cent of the private foster fathers, jointly involved both foster parents in the decision. In one case the private foster father initiated the move. The local authority situation shows the foster fathers much more fully involved. Forty-eight of the fosterings, taking in forty-four, that is 37·6 per cent, of the foster fathers, were the result of joint decisions. Eleven foster fathers, that is 9·4 per cent, had actually taken the initiative in thirteen of the local authority fosterings (the difference was statistically highly significant, $\chi^2 = 27·822$, d.f. $= 2$, P $= <0·001$). Certainly, if a lack of initial involvement indicates a lack of commitment, then over three-quarters of the private foster fathers were found wanting.

The question whether the foster father later tried to persuade his wife against fostering is explored in Table 6.2. If it is assumed that the

Table 6.2   Foster fathers' efforts to persuade foster mothers to cease fostering

| | Private fostering | | Local authority fostering | |
	Foster parents	Foster children	Foster parents	Foster children
Tried to persuade	14	22	5	6
No attempt	77	107	109	129
Totals	91	129	114	135

Note: 14 private and 8 local authority fosterings were excluded because of the absence of a foster father. The numbers are not exactly the same as in the previous Table as in some cases the foster father died soon after the fostering began and was thus excluded. In other cases, foster mothers who began to foster when alone later remarried or co-habited, and these are now included.

more committed foster fathers would not attempt to persuade their wives to end the fostering, then Table 6.2 lends further support to the claim that private foster fathers were less committed than the local authority ones. Fourteen, that is 15·4 per cent, of the private foster fathers had tried persuasion to stop twenty-two fosterings. Only five, 4·3 per cent, of local authority foster fathers had done so, the difference being statistically significant ($\chi^2 = 7·2796$, d.f. $= 1$, P $= <0·010$). The comments of the foster mothers indicated that pressure was most commonly applied when they were ill – and the husbands were required to do more with the children – and when natural parents 'made a nuisance of themselves'. Other foster fathers tried to persuade their wives when the latter were tired or, in one case, because he disliked 'coloureds'. In these circumstances, husbands were likely to reveal their lack of commitment.

It should be noted at this juncture that some foster fathers had not endeavoured to persuade their wives (and hence are not counted in the Table) to stop fostering but had tried to get them to change the type of fostering. Most obviously, some wanted their wives to do short-term, not long-term fostering.

A clear case exists for asserting that the majority of private foster fathers had not been initially committed to fostering, while a number definitely were known to have tried to end their fosterings. What effect is this likely to have on the foster children concerned? First, the child care text books suggest that foster fathers not initially committed will not involve themselves with the children as the fostering proceeds. Second, it seems likely that they will be more prepared to end a placement. Especially in times of strain with the children or natural parents, they will lack the desire and determination to continue. In one case, the private foster mother said her husband had been opposed to her wish to foster, but gave way after she cried. It is not a surprise to discover from the file that later, when neighbours complained about the behaviour of the foster child, there was a rift between the foster parents as the foster father put pressure on his wife to be rid of the child. Third, the disagreements between the foster parents, the resentment of the foster fathers, and the latters' desire to end the placement could be conveyed to the children. Obviously the foster fathers had not succeeded in ending the fosterings by the time the research took place, but children who knew the matter was under discussion could only feel insecure.

Extent to which foster fathers were present

The fact that a natural father is the enumerated head of his household does not necessarily mean that he spends a major part of his time there with his family. Andry assessed the amount of time fathers were absent by asking the boys in his study whether their fathers had been often on shift, overtime or night work (1960, pp. 41–3). He did not clarify such terms as 'very often', and the Newsons' method of asking specifically how many nights per week the husbands were away seemed more reliable. But even the Newson method is open to improvement. The fact that fathers were away for a night would not necessarily mean that they missed time with their children. They could see their children to bed, depart for the night shift, and return in the morning before the children arose. Information was therefore sought on how many evenings (from 5 p.m. onwards) they were away per week, the assumption being that such an absence would involve missing some time with their children. Perhaps even more important to family life than the evenings is the weekend, when parents and children can usually expect to be together. Therefore information was sought from the private foster mothers on the number of weekends per month that their husbands were away.

Twenty-eight, that is 30·8 per cent, of the private foster fathers were absent from their forty-one foster children for at least two evenings a week.[2] The local authority foster fathers were away less – twenty-five, that is 22·5 per cent, from twenty-nine children – but the difference was not statistically significant. Table 6.3 adds to the

Table 6.3   Number of weekends foster fathers were absent per month

	Private fostering		Local authority fostering	
	Foster fathers	Foster children	Foster fathers	Foster children
0	64	90	106	125
1	19	26	2	2
2–4	8	13	3	3
Totals	91	129	111	130

information about the private foster fathers' absences by showing that twenty-seven, 29·7 per cent, were away from their thirty-nine foster children for at least one weekend per month. Of these, eight deprived their foster children of their presence for at least half the weekends in a month. Moreover, private foster children who missed their foster fathers in the evenings were also significantly likely to miss them at weekends (dividing evenings 0–1/2–4/5–7 and weekends 0/more, $\chi^2 = 27·617$, d.f. $= 2$, P $= <0·001$). By contrast, only five, 4·5 per cent, of the local authority foster fathers were away from their five foster children for at least one weekend per month. Thus the private foster fathers were significantly more likely to spend weekends away ($\chi^2 = 23·754$, d.f. $= 1$, P $= <0·001$).

The numbers of private foster fathers away at least two evenings a week and/or away at least one weekend a month – around 30 per cent in each case – seems remarkably high. But is it so in comparison with natural fathers? The Newsons' study found that 17 per cent of the natural fathers of one-year-old children spent an average of at least two nights a week away from home. Research completed for the Plowden Report lumped together whether fathers were on shift work, permanent night work or working away at least two nights a week. The results which apply to fathers of children of primary school age showed 22 per cent so absent (Central Advisory Council for Education, 1967, vol. 2, p. 117).[3]

It can be concluded that private foster fathers spend more evenings (or nights) away from home than do natural fathers, as well as more weekends away than local authority foster fathers. One explanation could be that private foster parents are predominantly drawn from social classes III, IV and V, where occupations are more likely to be of the type which involve evening, shift or weekend work. Certainly, both the Newsons' and Plowden's results confirm that social classes III and IV (but not V) had fathers who were absent more often than those from social classes I and II. However, when a further analysis was made it was found that the private foster fathers in all the social classes were absent more than those in their corresponding classes in the Newsons' and Plowden research. Another possible explanation is that the tendency of such men to spend much time out of the home was a factor contributing to their wives' decision to take up fostering. Consequently, a disproportionate number of 'absent' men would be located in the private fostering group by comparison with the samples of natural parents. Further, the local authority children's departments would be wary of accepting as foster parents men who were frequently absent from their homes, hence the difference between the two fostering groups. Certainly, a few private foster mothers did say that they fostered because their husbands were out a lot and more indicated that there was a vacuum in their life which needed to be filled.

Whatever the explanation, the important finding is that significant numbers of private foster fathers were not involved in their homes for a considerable part of the week. Such foster fathers who are often away may not provide adequate treatment for their children. They may not provide the opportunities or the time for communicating with their foster children, for stimulating intellectual interests, for acting as a model for the children's own development. Thus some private foster children, already separated from their natural fathers, were being, in effect, also separated from their substitute fathers. For the older foster child put in this situation, not only must he try to cope with wondering why he is without his natural father but he will also question if and why his foster father is rejecting him. Lastly, it is worth pointing out that the Newsons thought that men who were frequently away built up a social life away from home leaving their wives and children to form routines and habits which excluded the male figure. Thus the father was excluded from family life and participated less in child-centred activities in the home. It is to the subject of participation that attention is now turned.

The private foster fathers' participation

As mentioned previously, the natural father's participation in the everyday life of his family has been examined by the Newsons. Participation in child-centred tasks and activities is regarded as a major means of involvement with children. It involves the father in undertaking alone or jointly with his wife tasks focused on the children, such as bathing them, and activities which are for and with the children, such as playing with them.

Having decided on the meaning of participation, some means of assessing it had to be devised. The Schaffers' method of simply assessing, on a three point scale, the fathers' participation in the care of children, failed to break down participation into its component items (1968, p. 66). The Newsons more carefully identified the various items – changing the nappy, putting to bed, etc. – and then graded, by information received from the natural mothers, on a three point scale the fathers' participation on each. This approach was adopted for the present study partly because of its methodology, partly because its use would enable the findings for foster fathers to be compared with natural fathers. The Newsons' work, however, was mainly devised for the fathers of children of one year of age. Most of their items could be applied to children up to five years old, with the exception of that concerned with nappy changing, but what of foster fathers with children over five years old? Andry's work suggested that the participation of such fathers centred less round the tasks side of participation, more on the activities for and with the children. Therefore, questions were devised to assess the foster fathers' participation in taking the older children out alone, talking with them, and playing or doing hobbies with them.[4]

Participation having been broken down into parts, some method was needed to put it back again. A foster father might be highly participant on one item but non-participant on all others. A method of overall assessment was required. Again, use was made of the tried methods of the Newsons who classified fathers into highly participant, moderately participant, and non-participant. Obviously, the exact methods of the Newsons could not be applied as the present study had extra items to fit older children but the general form was the same. Thus the Newsons defined a highly participant father as one who will 'do anything for the children' with at least three of the activities marked 'often' and the rest 'sometimes'. The present study required the same for children up to five years. However, for children over that age, where only three items were recorded, a highly participant father required at least one marked 'often' and the other two 'sometimes'. The Newsons defined a moderately participant father as one 'who in general is prepared to help with the children if he is asked or in an emergency, but who doesn't do a great deal as a matter of course', with most of the items checked 'sometimes' and usually one job marked 'never'. Again this definition was accepted with reference to children up to five. For older children, at least two items had to be scored 'sometimes' with one marked 'never'. A non-participant father, according to the Newsons, thinks that 'dealing with young children is definitely not a man's job' and will have most items rated 'never'. For the older children, the present study rated as non-participant fathers scoring at least two 'nevers' alongside one 'sometimes'. The Newson method did leave some loopholes, especially with fathers scoring extremes such as three 'often' and four 'never'. In these cases the interviewer was expected to make the overall assessment in conjunction with the content and tone of the mothers' replies. However, in eventuality the method proved very workable with nearly all scores fitting within the definitions. Table 6.4 presents the findings for the private foster fathers of children aged under five. Figures for the number of foster children concerned are given alongside. For reason of lack of space, percentages only are presented.

Table 6.4 Degree of participation of private foster fathers in child-centred tasks and activities with foster children under five years of age

	Nappy changing PFF* %	PFC† %	Feeding PFF %	PFC %	Bathing PFF %	PFC %	Getting to sleep PFF %	PFC %	Attending at night PFF %	PFC %	Playing PFF %	PFC %	Taking out alone PFF %	PFC %
Often	12·0	10·5	8·9	9·2	1·8	1·1	5·3	4·6	3·6	2·3	25·0	23·0	8·9	10·3
Sometimes	44·0	39·9	67·9	69·0	44·7	46·0	58·9	57·5	50·0	50·6	57·1	59·8	60·7	62·1
Never	44·0	49·6	23·2	21·8	53·4	52·9	35·7	37·9	46·4	47·1	17·9	17·2	30·4	27·6
Totals	100·0	100·0	100·0	100·0	100·0	100·0	100·0	100·0	100·0	100·0	100·0	100·0	100·0	100·0

*PFF=private foster fathers.
†PFC=private foster children.
No. of private foster fathers=56.
No. of private foster children=87 (with exception of nappy changing where item applied to only 38 of the private foster children).

It can be observed that generally the private foster fathers did not participate extensively in tasks and activities with foster children under five. Only in one item, that of playing, did the percentage engaging often in the activity reach twenty-five. Over 50 per cent never bathed their child, 44 per cent never changed the nappy, and

17·9 per cent never even played with their private foster child. Substantial numbers of the under-fives had little involvement with their private foster fathers but what of older children? (See Table 6.5.)

Table 6.5   Degree of participation of private foster fathers in child-centred activities with foster children of five years and over

	Taking out alone		Playing or doing (or taking interest in) hobbies		Talking	
	PFF %	PFC %	PFF %	PFC %	PFF %	PFC %
Often	25·7	21·4	28·5	23·8	37·1	30·9
Sometimes	34·3	35·7	45·7	45·2	60·0	64·3
Never	40·0	42·9	25·7	31·0	2·9	4·8
Totals	100·0	100·0	100·0	100·0	100·0	100·0

No. of private foster fathers=35.
No. of private foster children=42.

Approximately between a quarter and a third of the private foster fathers often took their older children out alone with them, talked to them, played with them or took an interest in their hobbies. None the less, some 40 per cent never went out accompanied just by their foster child while 25·7 per cent took no interest in their play or hobbies. Perhaps even more concern should be felt for the minority of 4·8 per cent of the private foster children whose foster fathers never spoke to them.[5]

The impression is created that the private foster fathers were not

Table 6.6   Degree of participation of local authority foster fathers in child-centred tasks and activities with foster children under five years of age

	Nappy changing LFF* LFC† % %	Feeding LFF LFC % %	Bathing LFF LFC % %	Getting to sleep LFF LFC % %	Attending at night LFF LFC % %	Playing LFF LFC % %	Taking out alone LFF LFC % %
Often	38·1 41·7	45·1 45·3	35·2 34·9	45·1 51·2	35·2 38·4	63·4 63·9	50·7 48·8
Sometimes	23·8 22·9	40·8 41·9	26·8 29·1	33·7 31·4	42·3 39·5	35·2 34·9	38·0 41·9
Never	38·1 35·4	14·1 12·8	38·0 36·0	21·2 17·4	22·5 22·1	1·4 1·2	11·3 9·3
Totals	100·0 100·0	100·0 100·0	100·0 100·0	100·0 100·0	100·0 100·0	100·0 100·0	100·0 100·0

*LFF=Local authority foster fathers.
†LFC=Local authority foster children.
No. of local authority foster fathers=71.
No. of local authority foster children=84 (with the exception of nappy changing which applied to only 48 of the local authority foster children).

characterised by full and active participation in the lives of their foster children. Possibly, however, such a lack of participation is a feature of other types of fostering. Attention is now focused, by way of comparison, on the foster fathers in the local authority contrast group.

Table 6.7 Degree of participation of local authority foster fathers in child-centred activities with foster children of five years and over

	Taking out alone		Playing or doing (or taking interest in) hobbies		Talking	
	LFF %	LFC %	LFF %	LFC %	LFF %	LFC %
Often	30·0	30·4	60·0	60·9	70·0	71·7
Sometimes	47·5	47·8	40·0	39·1	30·0	28·3
Never	22·5	21·8	0·0	0·0	0·0	0·0
Totals	100·0	100·0	100·0	100·0	100·0	100·0

No. of local authority foster fathers=40.
No. of local authority foster children=46.

Tables 6.6 and 6.7 reveal that on all items, with the exception of taking out the older children alone, over a third of the local authority foster fathers were assessed as participating 'often'. Clearly they undertook the tasks and activities with their foster children far more frequently than their private counterparts. Indeed, on every item except one they were significantly more likely to show greater participation than the private foster fathers.[6] Most marked were the following. Only 25 per cent of the private foster fathers played often with the younger foster children compared with 63·4 per cent of the local authority ones: on the other hand, 17·9 per cent never played compared with only 1·4 per cent of the local authority males. Only 8·9 per cent of the private foster fathers often took out the younger children on their own compared with 50·7 per cent of the local authority fathers: contrariwise, 30·4 per cent of the private men never took out their foster children while only 11·3 per cent of the local authority ones were in this grade. Similarly, whereas 25·7 per cent of the private foster fathers never played with or contributed to their foster children's hobbies, not one local authority father was so graded. Only 37·1 per cent of the private males often spoke to their foster children but as many as 70 per cent of the local authority foster fathers. These differences in participation by the two types of foster fathers mark one of the most outstanding contrasts found between private and local authority fostering.

Amalgamating the individual items and scoring for an overall assessment, as explained earlier, allowed the formulation shown in Table 6.8.

Table 6.8   The degree of participation of private foster fathers (overall assessment)

	Private foster fathers	%	Private foster children	%
Highly participant	12	13·2	13	10·1
Moderately participant	53	58·2	79	61·2
Non-participant	26	28·6	37	28·7
Totals	91	100·0	129	100·0

From Table 6.8 it can be noted that only a minority of the private foster fathers, 13·2 per cent, were graded as highly participant. Hence only a minority of the private foster children, 10·1 per cent, were benefiting from father substitutes who actively and fully involved themselves in the child-centred tasks and activities of their households. However, a yardstick is needed against which the proportions can be evaluated. This is found again in the local authority contrast group but also in the natural fathers used in the Newson research.

Table 6.9   The degree of participation of private and local authority foster fathers and natural fathers (overall assessment)

	Private foster fathers %	Local authority foster fathers %	Natural fathers (Newsons' sample) %
Highly participant	13·2	50·5	52
Moderately participant	58·2	43·2	27
Non-participant	28·6	6·3	21
Totals	100·0	100·0	100

No. of private foster fathers=91.
No. of local authority foster fathers=111.
No. of natural parents (Newsons' sample)=709.

The findings given in Table 6.9 confirm, on an overall assessment, the difference in participation degree between the private and local authority foster fathers. Only 13·2 per cent of the former were graded as highly participant as against over 50 per cent of the latter: 28·6 per cent of the private foster fathers were non-participant as against

6·3 per cent of the local authority ones. The private ones were significantly more likely to be less participant ($\chi^2 = 38\cdot050$, d.f. $= 2$, $P = <0\cdot001$).

Turning to the natural fathers studied by the Newsons, it is at once apparent that although the private foster fathers participated less than the natural fathers, the same is not true of the local authority ones. Indeed, fewer local authority fathers were graded non-participant, although more natural fathers were highly participant. However, comparisons with the Newsons' sample are not altogether valid, for two forms of bias were operating. First, the foster fathers had children covering all ages, the natural fathers had only one-year-old children.[7] Second, the foster fathers, as was shown, were drawn disproportionately from the lower social classes who, the Newsons point out, tend to participate less in child care tasks and activities. To eliminate the bias an analysis was made of those foster parents with a child under one year and of those in the three lower social classes. It was found that the same trend still held good, the private foster fathers participated least, the local authority men had the fewest non-participants, and the natural fathers the greatest proportion of highly-participant.

Over a quarter of the private foster children had non-participant foster fathers. They would therefore miss much of the enjoyment that derives from a close relationship with a father figure. Whether deprived of splashing around in the bath with him, or of playing in the park with him, such children missed an interaction which most other children can expect. A concerned foster father can provide intellectual stimulus, promote communication, convince the child he is valued, as well as acting as a model on which the foster child can base his own behaviour. Undoubtedly, the private foster children were less likely to receive these benefits than either natural children or local authority foster children. The following two examples are presented not as typical of worst cases, but to show what actually could occur:

a The private foster father appeared to do almost nothing with a foster child aged four. The foster mother complained, 'He doesn't do a thing with him [the foster child]. He won't make anything for him like fathers do, children always prefer the things you make.' She added, however, that 'He has a rheumatic knee, so he can't do a great deal. He is too active for him.' Both the foster parents were elderly, and one consequence of an elderly foster father (this one was in his seventies) is an expected inability to be involved with young children.

This man, wanting rest and quiet more than anything, could not be bothered with the affairs of a foster child. When the boy's natural mother visited he invariably went out in order to avoid involvement. The foster parents' own daughter visited regularly and saw more of the child than the foster father. Clearly, the latter could not serve as an adequate male role model for the boy, and the file recorded the poignant fact that he always played 'mothers and aunts, not mothers and fathers'. In addition he proved to be a highly tense child, very aggressive and difficult to handle.

   b   A private foster father, with an eleven-year-old male and nine-year-old female foster child, scored 'never' on every item of participation. Both children were presenting problems. The girl had been found in the streets begging and making advances to strangers and was a persistent soiler. The boy likewise soiled and was enuretic. He stuck very closely to his foster mother, who said, 'My husband doesn't do much with them – he doesn't go looking for them, he has to work hard. He is a bit strict and he [foster boy] is a bit wary of him – he's always sticking up for me. If there is anything wrong in the house Dad always blames me, but he always blames Dad.' The boy also displayed tremendous anxiety as to whether he was going to have to leave the foster home. The child care officer commented on the marital problems in the home, and it was clear that the foster parents were using the foster children as ammunition for their own battles. By ignoring the boy the husband was able to hurt his wife.

Communication

The final aspect of involvement to be studied concerned emotional communication between children of eleven years and over and their foster fathers. Using the methods devised by Andry, an assessment was made of the older foster children's readiness to turn to them. However, it happened that only twelve private foster children were in the upper age-range. Thus it suffices to report that not one spent most of his time indoors with his foster father, consulted him if in trouble, or turned to him for advice. The local authority foster children were much more communicative with their foster fathers.[8]

   Five areas of foster father involvement have been examined. In three of these substantial numbers of private foster children were discovered to be treated in an unsatisfactory manner. In all, 102, that is 71·4 per cent, of the private foster children, covering 78 of the foster homes, were not satisfactorily involved with their foster fathers in at least one of the following ways: having no foster father; the foster father trying to persuade his wife to end the fostering; the foster father being absent for two or more evenings per week or two or more weekends per month; having a non-participant or non-communicative foster father. Of course, some of these children were experiencing different forms of non-involvement at the same time. Thus the hypothesis that private foster fathers would be little involved with their foster children can be considered upheld. The comparable local authority figures were 51, that is 35·7 per cent, covering 45 foster homes.

Two cautionary notes must be added. First, there is a danger of assuming that *all* private foster fathers are rarely involved with their foster children. Examples of private foster fathers enthusiastically and fully involved did occur. Some of the foster mothers made glowing comments:

'He idolises her [West African foster child]. He even takes her to his club on Sundays. There has never been a night on which she has been separated from us.'

'If anyone asks him how many children he's got, he says three; he never thinks of explaining.'

Second, the results do not prove that the private foster children would have received more father involvement if they had stayed with their natural fathers. Possibly the latter had been little involved themselves, a factor which may even have contributed to the reasons why the children left home in the first place. What can be said is that previous research suggests that in general natural fathers participate more in child-centred activities than did the private foster fathers and that the private foster children would have received more adult male interest and stimulation had they been in local authority foster homes.

Throughout this section frequent reference has been made to the effects of the foster fathers' lack of involvement with the children. The extent of the effects no doubt will depend on a number of other factors – the children's stage of development when they came to the foster home, the quality of their previous experiences with their natural parents, their length of stay in the foster home, the quantity and quality of their contacts with the natural parents, the degree to which the foster mothers can compensate for the inadequacy of the foster fathers. Even so, it must be said that the children concerned were in environments which failed to provide three conditions usually regarded as essential for normal child development: namely, an adult male figure, who is usually present and who expresses his wish for the child to stay, who is prepared to communicate and who is willing to participate in child-centred tasks and activities. But lastly, leaving aside the effects on the child, it is worth noting that the physical or psychological absence of the foster father will throw even greater strains on the foster mothers.

The accommodation of the private foster children

In turning to the housing situation of the private foster children, it is not intended to condemn those foster parents whose accommodation is inadequate. Probably they wish to have better houses and they cannot be blamed if they are unable to afford them. Yet the housing environment provided by the foster parents is an important influence on children and hence fits into a chapter dealing with treatment.

The influence of housing conditions

The connection between housing conditions and the development of children is not in doubt. Schorr, after a cautious review of the literature, concludes, 'in one direction the evidence is overwhelming: extremely poor housing conditions perceptibly influence behaviour and attitudes' (1964, p. 2). However, before briefly reviewing research to establish which kinds of conditions are influential, it is worth pointing out that a relationship between inadequate housing and a particular social malaise is not always a direct or straightforward one. For instance, there is a well-established link between poor housing and delinquency. Yet the relationship may come via the attitudes of a particular kind of parents who can only afford, or for some reason choose, a certain type of housing. Other relationships, as Schorr points out, are clearly much more direct, for instance the relationship between overcrowding and certain diseases.

A number of research projects have made a link between poor housing, especially overcrowding, and bronchitis, pneumonia, whooping-cough, skin diseases, home accidents and infant mortality. Spencer (1970, p. 108) sums up his review of the research with:

Thus stress and nervous conditions can be brought about by poor housing conditions, while dwellings which are damp, inadequately heated and lacking sufficient ventilation can give rise to various diseases, or exacerbate such illnesses where they are existing in embryo form within a particular person. Health can thus deteriorate as a result of bad housing conditions. Bad conditions of housing can also be a hazard because of potential accidents, inadequate means of escape in case of fire, steep and poorly lighted stairways, and so on.

Equally well established is the relationship between bad housing and adverse educational functioning. Among a number of studies the best known are those of Douglas and the research undertaken for the Plowden Report. Overcrowding, sharing of amenities, and living in neighbourhoods characterised by a lack of play space and privately rented tenacies were shown to be particularly associated with low educational performance. Douglas (1964, p. 38) summarises his results thus:

> For any given level of measured ability, children living on
> council estates have better chances of going to grammar school
> than those who live in privately rented dwellings. This appears
> to be explained by the better provision of grammar school
> places in these new areas rather than by any special qualities of
> the children, or the sharpened aspirations of their parents. When
> housing conditions are unsatisfactory, children make relatively
> low scores in the tests. This is so in each social class, but
> whereas the middle class children, as they get older, reduce this
> handicap, the manual working class children from unsatisfactory
> homes fall even further behind; for them, overcrowding and
> other deficiencies at home have a progressive and depressive
> influence on their test performance.

Research on the effects on the emotional and social development of children is less well documented. However, Schorr points to studies which suggest that a lack of space leads to fatigue and irritability in the parents, inhibits discussion within the family, and encourages members to stay out of the home (1964, pp. 13–14). The Newsons detected a connection between overcrowding and a tendency for mothers to smack their children (1968, p. 424). In general it is agreed that poor housing conditions adversely affect the behaviour of parents which, in turn, influences the functioning of the children.

The above effects have mainly, although not exclusively, resulted from overcrowding and a lack of basic housing amenities. Therefore the hypothesis formulated was that the private foster children would be in housing conditions marked by overcrowding and a lack of amenities. However, it is well established, for instance by Cullingworth, that these defects are closely related to the 'tenure type' and age of houses (1965, pp. 21, 38). Similarly, Spencer points out that private rented housing is likely to be older than other types, while older housing is likely to possess more defects (1970, pp. 61–2 and 79). Thus the present research also studies these aspects of housing deprivation.[9] The accommodation of the foster children was therefore examined in respect of the four specific aspects, so avoiding the more general approach of, say, George who classified housing physical standards into 'above average', 'average', and 'below', without specifying what was being evaluated.

Tenure type

Remembering that owner-occupied houses are associated with the best and private rented tenancies with the worst aspects of accommodation, the 'tenure type' of the private foster parents and their children is shown in Table 6.10.

Table 6.10 Tenure type of dwellings of private foster parents and children

| | Private foster parents | | Private foster children | |
	No.	%	No.	%
Owner-occupied house	31	31	40	28·0
Local authority house	39	39	61	42·6
Local authority flat	2	2	2	1·4
Private rented house	16	16	23	16·1
Private rented flat	2	2	2	1·4
Other	10	10	15	10·5
Totals	100	100	143	100·0

Forty, that is 28 per cent, of the private foster children resided in owner-occupied dwellings. Sixty-three, that is 44 per cent, were in council tenancies. Twenty-five, 17·5 per cent, lived in privately rented houses or flats. None lived in privately rented rooms. The remaining fifteen, 10·5 per cent, were in various forms of tied or free accommodation which was owned by the foster father's employer.

How does the distribution of tenure type amongst the private foster children compare with other sections of the community? Taking the local authority foster children, a similar number, fifty-four, that is 37·8 per cent, were in council dwellings. However, seventy, 49 per cent, were in owner-occupied dwellings. They were therefore significantly more likely to be so housed than the private foster children ($\chi^2 = 11\cdot842$, d.f. $= 1$, P $= <0\cdot001$). Only eleven, 7·7 per cent, of the local authority children resided in privately rented tenancies. Thus the private foster children were significantly more likely to be in that sector of housing which displays the most adverse housing features ($\chi^2 = 5\cdot765$, d.f. $= 1$, P $= <0\cdot025$).

A comparison with other children in the community is not possible as most housing research gives findings in numbers of dwellings, occupants, or, most frequently, households rather than in numbers of children. Within the present research no foster family was part of another household so the numbers of foster parents were equivalent to the number of households. Hence comparisons can be made through this means.

Thirty-one per cent of the private foster parents were in owner-occupied dwellings, 41 per cent in council accommodation, and 18 per cent in privately rented houses or flats. Cullingworth (1965) shows that in England in 1962 the tenure distribution of households was 43 per cent in owner-occupied, 21 per cent in council dwellings, 34 per cent in private rented, and 2 per cent in other forms. The sample census for 1966 allows percentages to be given for all households in the two local authorities which were studied: 53·8 per cent were in owner-occupied dwellings, 22·3 in council dwellings, 20·1 in privately rented, and 3·9 per cent in other forms. These figures do include households which had no children so it is useful to add the findings of the government survey, *Circumstances of Families*, published in 1966, whose sample consisted of *families* with at least two children. Its figures were 44 per cent in owner-occupied dwellings, 33 per cent in council tenancies, 14 per cent in privately rented ones, and 9 per cent in other forms. Thus in terms of households or families, the proportions in privately rented tenancies did not differ much between private fostering and the population as a whole. However, a larger proportion of the private foster households were in council tenancies and a smaller proportion in owner-occupied dwellings, the tenure type which appears to give most advantages.

Age of dwellings

Older housing is not only associated with a lack of basic amenities and a greater likelihood of structural defects, it is also frequently located in neighbourhoods which lack social amenities such as play space and modern educational institutions. Thus private foster children who live in older dwellings may – although not necessarily – be experiencing social handicaps other than those of their dwelling itself (see Table 6.11).

Table 6.11   Age of dwellings of private foster parents and children

	Private foster parents		Private foster children	
	No.	%	No.	%
Up to 1914	36	36	48	33·6
1914–39	29	29	43	30·1
Post-1939	35	35	52	36·4
Totals	100	100	143	100·0

Forty-eight, that is a third of the private foster children were found in dwellings constructed before 1914. Although no systematic attempt was made to grade neighbourhoods, the researcher's impression was that a large proportion of these children lived in the decaying 'inner ring' part of the city. At one dwelling, the front door was boarded up, the hall had no lights, the rooms were barely furnished and unheated, while a notice on the front wall declared that it had been condemned by the local authority and was due for demolition. Turning to the local authority foster children, only fifteen, 10·5 per cent, were in pre-1914 property. The private foster children were thus significantly more likely to be located in the oldest dwellings ($\chi^2 = 24\cdot200$, d.f. = 1, P = <0·001). The number of local authority children, forty-four, 30·8 per cent, in dwellings from the inter-war years was virtually the same as that of their private counterparts. However, the eighty-four, 58·7 per cent, in modern dwellings made them significantly more likely to be so housed than the private children ($\chi^2 = 14\cdot629$, d.f. = 1, P = <0·001).

Comparison with the age of dwellings inhabited by other children in the population as a whole is difficult as housing surveys which record age usually do so in numbers of dwellings or accommodation units rather than persons. However, it is possible to compare the distribution of the private foster parents according to the age of their dwelling with that of the ages of dwellings as given by Woolf for England and Wales in 1964.[10] In fact, the proportions of private foster parents in each age-band were found to be similar to the distribution of all accommodation units. None the less, as older people, who tend not to have young children, are found disproportionately in older dwellings, and younger persons, who tend to have young children, in more modern property, it is probably true to say that the 33·6 per cent of private foster children in the oldest property is proportionately greater than that of all children in the population.

Overcrowding

Three measures of overcrowding were taken. The first discovered that only five private foster children and eight local authority children were sharing their beds with others. The finding concurs with that of the Newsons for children living with their natural parents that bed sharing, even amongst young children, is 'negligible' (1963, p. 79).

The second measure adopted was the one most frequently found in housing surveys, the average number of persons per room (see Table 6.12). An average of over 1·5 persons per room is usually

Table 6.12   The average number of persons per room in dwellings of private foster parents and children

Per room	Private foster parents No.	Private foster parents %	Private foster children No.	Private foster children %
0 to 1·5	88	88	118	82·5
Over 1·5 and up to 2	9 ⎫ 12	9 ⎫ 12	20 ⎫ 25	14·0 ⎫ 17·5
Over 2	3 ⎭	3 ⎭	5 ⎭	3·5 ⎭
Totals	100	100	143	100·0

taken by research projects to constitute overcrowding. Twenty-five, that is 17·5 per cent, of the private foster children were in this position. Only five, 3·5 per cent, of the local authority were in dwellings with an average of over 1·5 (and none in rooms with an average of over 2). Thus the private foster children were significantly more likely to be overcrowded ($\chi^2 = 14\cdot286$, d.f. $= 1$, P $= <0\cdot001$). Further, the proportion of private foster children so situated was higher than the 11·2 per cent of children of primary school age which the Plowden Report found in overcrowded conditions (Central Advisory Council for Education, 1967, vol. 2, Table 42).

Twelve per cent of the private foster parents were in dwellings with an average number of persons per room over 1·5. If they are taken to represent households then comparison can be made with other housing research. The sample census of 1966 recorded that only 1·2 per cent of households in England and Wales and 0·8 per cent of those in the city and county areas of the present study were similarly over-crowded.

Other fostering research projects have not assessed overcrowding in the above terms. As Gray and Parr did examine the average number of persons per bedroom of a large number of local authority foster children, it was appropriate to do the same for the private foster children. They found that 13 per cent of the local authority children were in homes with an average of over two persons per bedroom which they took to constitute overcrowding (1957, p. 38). For the local authority children in the present study the figure was forty-seven, that is 32·9 per cent, but for the private foster children eighty-two, that is 60·8 per cent. It will be remembered that, in contrast to Gray and Parr's findings, the study samples contained a high proportion of children under five years of age who could be expected to have more chance of sharing a room, but the discrepancies between the private and local authority children are still large. Again, the differences between the private and local authority children in the present study was statistically significant ($\chi^2=22\cdot857$, d.f.$=1$, P$=<0\cdot001$).

Basic amenities

An assessment was made of the foster homes' degree of availability of hot and cold piped water, cooking stove, sink, internal water toilet, fixed bath and a garden or yard. Thirty-four of the private foster children, that is 23·8 per cent, were in dwellings which lacked the exclusive use of at least one amenity. They were significantly more likely to be so handicapped than the local authority foster children, of whom only fourteen, that is 9·8 per cent, so lacked ($\chi^2=5\cdot921$, d.f.$=1$, P$=<0\cdot025$). No children lacked the use of a garden or yard, and the most common lack was that of an indoor toilet.

How does the position of the private foster homes compare with the rest of society in regard to missing exclusive use of basic housing amenities? Again, taking the numbers of private foster parents to be the same as their number of households, 20 per cent lacked at least one of the six listed amenities. The national home conditions survey, 1967, found that 25 per cent of dwellings in England and Wales lacked exclusive use of at least one of four amenities (quoted in Spencer, 1970, p. 78). The sample census of 1966 identified 32·3 per cent of households in the city and county areas as lacking exclusive use of at least one of three amenities. Thus the private fostering households did not appear in a worse position than these more general populations. Again, however, as children tend to be with younger people in more modern properties which do not lack amenities, it is likely that the proportion of private foster children so handicapped is higher than for children as a whole.

The experience of adverse accommodation, it was explained, can influence children over a variety of areas. Poor physical health, accidents, under-achievement at school, are known to be associated with housing deprivations. In addition, there are strong grounds for thinking that communication between children and their parent figures and the capacity of children to develop personal relationships within the home are hindered in overcrowded environments. Therefore it is a serious finding that many of the private foster children experienced the shortcomings outlined in the preceding sections. In all, ninety-six, that is 67·1 per cent, of the private foster children experienced at least one of the following – room overcrowding, bedroom overcrowding, or lack of exclusive use of a basic amenity. Fifty-three, 37·1 per cent, of the local authority children were similarly placed. There is no doubt that not only were the private children more prone to accommodation handicaps than their local authority counterparts but also than the populace at large. Thus the hypothesis that the private foster children would be in housing marked by overcrowding and a lack of amenities could be considered upheld.

Why were so many private foster children found in inadequate accommodation? One explanation is that the private foster parents were disproportionately drawn from the lower social classes, which themselves are more poorly housed than others. Hence the private foster parents could not provide adequate housing for themselves, let alone their foster children. It was interesting, however, that amongst the private foster parents there was established no statistically significant relationship between class and housing standards. Another possible explanation is that accommodation is a factor likely to be considered by child care officers in vetting prospective foster parents, so that those with poor conditions are less likely to find their way into the local authority field but are allowed to undertake private fostering. Thus the private foster parents whom the officers would not have approved, or were dubious about, to act for the local authority, or who possessed unsuitability factors according to the file material, were statistically more likely to be in dwellings with adverse housing features. For instance, those with unsuitability factors were significantly more likely to have overcrowded bedrooms

E

than those without such factors ($\chi^2 = 5 \cdot 7239$, d.f. $= 1$, P $= < 0 \cdot 025$). Those whom the officers would not have approved, or were dubious about, to be local authority foster parents were significantly more likely to be in dwellings built before 1914 ($\chi^2 = 8 \cdot 5478$, d.f. $= 1$, P $= < 0 \cdot 010$).

Whatever the reasons, the housing environment of the private foster children is a matter of some concern. It is ironic that the work of Packman demonstrates that poor housing, particularly over-crowding, is among the most important factors leading to children coming into care (1968, pp. 58–61). On the one hand local authority children's departments take children from their parents because of environmental inadequacies, and usually insist on their foster parents having sufficient space and amenities. On the other hand, private foster children are frequently placed in housing conditions which seem to count against their social, physical and emotional development.

The treatment of the private foster children

The exploration of the private foster parents' treatment of their foster children required the definition of treatment, the identification of activities in which treatment occurred, and means of measuring and evaluating it. The wide-ranging and complex nature of the subject meant that no simplistic conclusion could be reached but, at least, sweeping condemnations of the treatment given by private foster parents were brought into question. Generally, the private foster mothers expressed affection and concern for their charges similar to that of the local authority foster mothers. Few appeared to possess motives or attitudes that were cruel, indifferent or geared to mercenary gain.

It was on matters relating specifically to the fostering aspects concerned in raising foster children that the treatment rendered by the private foster mothers was found to be lacking. Many of the placements were arranged and made by them with little attempt to match the children with the foster parents, and with little understanding of the advisability of introducing children gradually into their new homes. Indeed, the private foster mothers did not arrange to meet two-thirds of the children until the actual day when they were handed over. The great majority were placed with very little information about their backgrounds, habits, needs and behaviour being passed from the parents to the foster parents. The local authority foster mothers were much more liable to receive such information. Further, nearly half of the private foster children were regarded by their foster parents as natural children, an attitude which, although springing from the best of intentions, could entail problems for children who had to resolve the fact of their fostering status and who might well return to their own parents in the future. In addition, the private foster mothers were significantly more likely than the local authority ones not to understand how a foster child's previous experiences could affect her behaviour, while some even advocated that a foster child should not be told anything about her natural parents and background.

At least, nearly all the private foster mothers appeared highly motivated towards fostering and concerned about the children. The same could not be said for many of their husbands. Over 15 per cent of the private foster fathers had tried to end the fosterings, over 30 per cent were absent at least two evenings a week, nearly 30 per cent absent at least one weekend per month. Perhaps most telling of all, over 28 per cent were assessed as non-participant in regard to the private foster children, and only 10 per cent as highly participant. By contrast, the local authority foster fathers were significantly more likely to spend more time in the foster homes, to be more committed towards the fostering, and to be more participant in it.

For children separated from their own parents, some with foster fathers who took little interest in them, the circumstances and standards of their physical environment becomes even more important. Yet over two-thirds of the private foster children experienced at least one form of housing deprivation. Thus the accommodation provided by the private foster parents was inferior not only to that of the local authority foster children but also to that of the populace as a whole.

In at least three of the five activities, the treatment received by the private foster children was generally unsatisfactory according to the yardsticks employed. If, as the last two chapters have emphasised, the private foster parents' treatment affects the functioning and development of the children, then no doubt the adverse features identified by the present study will leave an imprint on their lives.

7   The condition of the private foster children

The treatment methods used by the private foster parents can be expected to influence the condition of their children. However, the two are not necessarily causally related. The aggressive behaviour of a foster child may be a consequence of his earlier treatment at the hands of his natural parents rather than of his relationship with his foster mother. None the less, the condition of the foster child, whatever the cause, will affect the progress of the fostering and is an essential point of focus in a study of private fostering.

The condition (or conditions) of the private foster children is taken to be their present way of functioning, their modes of behaviour, their position or situation in regard to such matters as health and education. But which of the many conditions of a foster child should be examined, should the size of his feet, his I.Q., his functioning as an athlete? The child care literature and research has long indicated that separation from their natural parents is likely to adversely affect the condition of children in three major areas: emotional, physical and educational. More recently, attention has been directed to a fourth condition, namely the children's knowledge about their own position as foster children. These four conditions, then, were selected for study. It was further considered that the treatment given by the foster parents and the conditions displayed by the children could be brought together by asking whether the former were meeting the latter's needs. With the broad areas of study named, specific hypotheses could be formulated as follows:

That substantial numbers of the private foster children would display signs of emotional deprivation.

That they would be likely to experience poor health.

That they would function poorly at school.

That in many cases the private foster children would not possess accurate knowledge about their relationships with their foster parents.

That substantial numbers would not have their material,
emotional and intellectual needs adequately met by their foster
parents.

The various conditions will now be examined in turn. Within each
the same approach will be adopted. The meaning of each condition
will be discussed, the means of measurement and evaluation discussed and the results presented.

Emotional condition

Separation and emotional deprivation

Since the 1930s a large number of studies have claimed that children
separated from their natural parents are prone to display abnormal
emotional conditions or emotional deprivation. Many of the early
works were lacking in research methodology and liable to sweeping
generalisations. There followed a number of cautious reviews of the
research – for instance, those by Yarrow, Dinnage and Pringle,
Jehu and Ainsworth – which have attempted to separate the chaff
from the wheat and to state acceptable conclusions. In a publication
by the Child Welfare League of America (1962, p. 3), Yarrow
decides that the evidence 'adds up with an impressive consistency in
its general conclusions: deviating conditions of maternal care in early
life tend to be associated with later disturbances in intellectual and
personal-social functioning.'
    Jehu comes to a similar deduction from his survey of 1966, adding
'Certain processes are more affected, interpersonal relationships,
language and abstraction being especially vulnerable; motor behaviour less so.'
    The reviews all add qualifications to their general conclusions. In
particular they warn that disturbances are by no means the inevitable
result, that they can occur without separation, that the effects are not
necessarily irreversible, and that the quality of the substitute home can
modify or even prevent the disturbances.
    Enough has been explained to establish that children separated
from their natural parents are vulnerable to adverse effects. Private
foster children obviously fall within the category of separated
children, and it can be anticipated that their condition might differ
from that of children not subjected to their experiences. But which
conditions are to be examined? The research shows that children can

be affected in a variety of ways, physically, educationally, socially and so on. But most attention has been directed towards their emotional condition. By this is meant the condition of the children's personality, in particular their ways of relating to themselves and others. Where the children's development in this sphere has been hindered or abnormal, it has usually been referred to as emotional deprivation or as adverse emotional condition.

The next task in the study was to establish in what ways emotional deprivation is expressed by children. The research worker worked through previous studies, particularly those dealing with children separated and then placed in foster homes, and categorised four main expressions. Here a question of terminology is raised. What is the correct term to be given to the effects? It has been decided to follow Vernon (1964) in calling them 'traits', which he defines as a person's 'more enduring characteristics – abilities, habits, and more general dispositions'. He adds that it is assumed that most traits are bi-polar, with most people falling in the middle. Thus most people are expected to get irritable at some time, but irritability would not be considered their trait unless consistently displayed.[1] The four traits identified by a wide number of researchers as symptomatic of emotional deprivation were aggression, anxiety, difficulty in making relationships, and withdrawal. This division excludes delinquency, physical development and educational malfunctioning, which are considered separately.

a Aggression

The display of aggression or hostility is a consistent finding amongst children separated from their parents. Goldfarb (1943) attributes it to a lack of normal ego and super-ego growth, which has been impeded by the separation and which is expressed as a pattern of impulsive behaviour lacking normal inhibitory controls, the children lacking both normal guilt about their aggression and possessing a low frustration tolerance. It is reported amongst children in adoptive homes (Witmer, 1963), those treated by child guidance clinics (Hewitt and Jenkins, 1946), those in institutions (Goldfarb, 1943; Lewis, 1954) and those in foster homes (Trasler, 1960). Heinicke and Westheimer (1966) found it a marked characteristic in children separated for comparatively short periods and placed in a residential nursery. The aggression is in many forms, among them being acts of violence, cruelty, starting fights and attacking other children, open defiance of authority, malicious mischief, temper tantrums, screaming fits, deliberate destructiveness, verbal aggression and persistent untruthfulness. Trasler, in discussing the aggression of foster children, explains that it can be directed against the natural parents for rejecting them, against the foster parents who may be held equally responsible for the separation, or against the children themselves.

b Anxiety

Anxiety, like all the traits mentioned, is experienced by all children. What is meant here is anxiety consistently above the normal, a tendency to be unduly worried, even fearful, out of all proportion to the threat. It is shown as restlessness, over-sensitivity, poor sleep and bad dreams, excessive nail-biting, thumb-sucking, fidgeting, tics, unwillingness to take up challenges because frightened of failure, and an inability to concentrate on anything that demands sustained attention (enuresis could be added, but is considered separately in the section dealing with physical health and development). Amongst the researchers who have detailed anxiety as an effect of separation are Lewis, Trasler, Goldfarb, Douglas and Blomfield, and Pringle.

Trasler, in discussing the anxiety of foster children, regards it as stemming from three main sources. First, as an 'attempt to repress otherwise inhibited hostile feelings towards the parents or substitute parents which conflict with feelings of affection for them'. Second, from fears 'of being unable to survive without his parents'. Third, from fears 'of being again rejected' (1960, p. 53).

c Difficulty in making relationships

Bowlby's early study of juvenile thieves concluded that maternal separation could result in 'a lack of affection or feeling for anyone'. Numerous subsequent studies, including those by Goldfarb, Levy, Lewis, Pringle and Trasler, have also observed the reluctance of some children who have experienced separation to be drawn into personal relationships. Lewis points out the almost converse way in which this is displayed when bids for attention are so demanding that eventually they provoke rejection. On the other hand the children might refuse to make any advances at all.

Trasler's work, of particular interest because it concentrates on fostering, stated that 'the most striking characteristic of children who have suffered rejection by their parents (or parent-substitutes) is that they lack security in their relationship with others.' In severe cases the child 'withdraws from all but the most superficial relationship with others', while in less severe cases he shows 'great reluctance to make emotional relationships with his foster parents. He may be very slow to show his affection for them' (1960, pp. 58–9).

d Withdrawal

Freud and Burlingham (1954) reported this trait as early as 1944. Sometimes referred to as social apathy, it is, as Leon Yarrow (Child Welfare League of America, 1962) points out, a consistent and major finding of the research studies and is exhibited as an apparent indifference to or dislike of social attachments, a lack of responsiveness, an apathetic response to social approaches and an absence of social initiative. Obviously, the trait of withdrawal has close links with difficulty in making relationships. The difference is that trait (c) applies specifically to individual personal relationships. The present one refers to a more general withdrawal from all kinds of activities, and not just personal relationships. For example, an insistence on playing alone at an age when children usually play in groups.

Assessing emotional deprivation

The expressions or traits of emotional deprivation having been identified, it was then necessary to devise means of ascertaining their existence amongst the private foster children. Consideration was given to applying psychological tests with particular attention paid to Stott's Bristol social adjustment guide. Eventually, however, it was decided not to use them. Their administration would have posed practical problems. The Bristol social adjustment guide is usually completed by teachers and a request for this service might well have endangered the chances of securing the co-operation of the local authority education departments and individual schools for the purposes of providing even more essential educational data. Permission would also have been required from the foster parents. Tests applied directly to the children would have posed not only administrative problems but would have caused the children to wonder about the purpose of it all. No doubt these problems could have been overcome if there was complete certainty about the validity of the tests but the lack of this was the strongest reason for not using them. M. Kellmer Pringle, a renowned psychologist, in discussing the question of measuring emotional adjustment, concludes: 'The difficulties of obtaining a reliable and valid measure of adjustment are very considerable; much less progress has been made by psychologists in this field than, for example, in measuring intellectual abilities and attainments' (1966, p. 160). Trasler came to the same conclusion after, in particular, experimenting with the Levy scale of adjustment (1955, Appendix 4).

The lack of useful tests was less serious because the foster parents and child care officers constituted two sets of persons well qualified to comment on the behaviour of the children. The former, in most cases, had had continuous contact with them, had often had previous foster children, and usually had raised or were raising their own children. The latter were experienced or trained, or both, in observing and noting the very subject under investigation. Vernon (1964), following his critical review of tests, states that the observation of experienced persons has much in its favour, while Pringle placed confidence in the information provided by houseparents about the emotional condition of children in institutions. Thus it was decided to collect the information from the foster parents and the officers, a decision which aptly fitted in with the methods used for collecting information for much of the rest of the study.

Like other questions in the research, the ones to obtain information about emotional deprivation had to meet two requirements. First, they needed to avoid the expression of generalised, global judgments. A question such as, 'Is the child emotionally deprived?' would prompt a response which did not distinguish between the various components of the subject. Thus the questions were directed towards the four traits already identified. Second, they needed to promote replies which distinguished between varying intensities of the traits. It was not enough to say that a child was or was not aggressive. Therefore, the respondents were asked to give their judgments on a four point scale, 'persistently', 'often', 'occasionally', and 'never or normal'.

Obtaining information about the foster children's emotional traits involved further problems. There was a possibility that the foster parents would be reluctant to admit abnormal behaviour by their foster children. How would they judge the difference between abnormal behaviour and what was, say, the kind of outburst seen, at some stage, in every child? These problems were met in the following ways:

a The base for judgment of the trait was taken as the interviewee's view of normality. Thus they were asked not 'Does he display aggression?' but 'To what extent does he display more than normal aggression?' At the same time they were handed a card with the four point scale on it. A person indicating 'never or normal' was not saying the child never showed aggression but that he never showed it above what they considered to be normal.[2]

Presumably the foster parents' perception of normality would spring from their own experiences within their culture or subculture. The officers would have similar influences shaping their view of normality, although probably fewer would have raised their own children, plus that of their professional training and experience. Both foster parents and officers are what Vernon calls 'involved' people whose judgment can be trusted because they evaluate something about which they have actual experience and knowledge.

b The questions concerning traits were put to the foster parents, the child care officers and the senior child care officers. If the foster parents had been reluctant to admit the existence of traits or if they had been evaluating from a different concept of normality than that of the officers, then little agreement could have been expected between their replies. However, a product – moment correlation was worked out for the replies of the foster parents against those of the child care officers and of the officers against their seniors. The results were satisfactory, showing an acceptable level of agreement.

c As Buckle and Lebovici point out: 'All children show signs of disturbed behaviour at some time or another, and professional intervention is justified if the disorder persists' (World Health Organisation, 1960, p. 87). It was just possible that at the time of the interviews the children were displaying behaviour which at that time the foster parents interpreted as abnormal but which in fact was not going to last with the result that in retrospect they would have regarded it as normal. Therefore, in order to err on the side of caution the research accepted as evidence of emotional traits only those indicated to be 'persistently' or 'often' above normal.

In addition to the question on traits, information was sought from the foster parents and files on whether the children had been advised to attend a child guidance clinic. As throughout the research, similar information was obtained for the local authority fosterings.

The findings

The emotional condition of the private foster children, as displayed in their possession of certain traits, will now be presented (see Table 7.1). Although material was collected from the officers and the foster parents, the assessments given by the latter will be used in order to retain consistency with most of the other tabulations in this chapter.

Table 7.1   Traits displayed by private foster children of two years and over

	Aggression No. %		Anxiety No. %		Difficulties in relating No. %		Withdrawal No. %	
Persistently Often	2⎫ 27⎭	28·7	9⎫ 35⎭	43·6	1⎫ 10⎭	10·9	2⎫ 10⎭	11·9
Occasionally Never	15⎫ 57⎭	71·3	21⎫ 36⎭	56·4	5⎫ 85⎭	89·1	5⎫ 84⎭	88·1
Totals	101	100·0	101	100·0	101	100·0	101	100·0

Twenty-nine, that is 28·7 per cent, of the private children were assessed as being aggressive 'persistently' or 'often'. Forty-four, that is 43·6 per cent, were anxious to this degree. Eleven, that is 10·9 per cent, showed difficulties in relating to this extreme extent and twelve, 11·9 per cent, were persistently or often withdrawn. Thus considerable numbers of foster children were assessed to possess emotional traits above what the foster parents (and child care officers) considered as normal behaviour.

It must be remembered that other children in the community, including those living with their own parents, will show abnormal traits. How do the private foster children compare with them? If private foster children who possess traits persistently or often are assumed to need psychiatric help, such as from a child guidance clinic then, in all, 63·4 per cent required such aid. Clearly this percentage is much higher than the 5·4 to 7·9 per cent of the child population as a whole which the Underwood Committee calculated to want psychiatric guidance (see Ministry of Education, 1955).

Another form of comparison is with the local authority foster children, far fewer of whom displayed traits persistently or often. Only 9·5 per cent did so in regard to aggression, 10·5 per cent for anxiety, 7·6 per cent for difficulties in relating, and 6·7 per cent for withdrawal. The private foster children were thus significantly more likely than their local authority counterparts to be persistently or often aggressive ($\chi^2 = 9·143$, d.f. $= 1$, P $= < 0·010$) and to display anxiety in this extreme form ($\chi^2 = 21·560$, d.f. $= 1$, P $= < 0·001$).

Some children displayed extremities in more than one trait, as can be seen in Table 7.2, which gives the private and local authority children side by side. This Table reveals that far more private than

Table 7.2   Number of traits displayed persistently or often by private and local authority foster children of two years and over

Traits	Private foster children		Local authority foster children	
	No.	%	No.	%
Four	1	1·0	1	1·0
Three	6	5·9	0	0·0
Two	18	17·8	6	5·7
One	39	38·6	19	18·1
None	37	36·6	79	75·2
Totals	101	100·0	105	100·0

local authority foster children were emotionally deprived in the sense of having at least one trait in an extreme form. Sixty-four, 63·4 per cent, of the former were in this position as against twenty-six, 24·7 per cent, of the latter. The difference was statistically significant ($\chi^2 = 12·565$, d.f. $= 1$, P $= <0·001$).

As more private foster children were reported with extreme traits, it might be expected that more would be referred to child guidance clinics. Yet only seven private as against eight local authority children were so referred. As percentages, 6·9 per cent and 7·6 per cent, they are slightly above the 5·5 per cent of the school population which Douglas (1964) found attended a clinic.[3] Notably the referred children were all displaying traits 'persistently' or 'often', a finding which lends weight to the suggestion that such children need psychiatric guidance. If this is so, then of the children in this position approximately one in three of the local authority children were referred to child guidance, but only one in nine of the private foster children. It seems that the latter do not have the same access to the service as the children in local authority care.

The tabulated findings are ample evidence to uphold the hypothesis that substantial numbers of the private foster children would display signs of emotional deprivation. Statistical material, however, although essential, does not give the 'feel' of the traits, does not show their force as perceived by the foster mothers. Therefore there follows a number of illustrations taken directly from the words of the private foster mothers.

Aggression was expressed in violence towards objects such as the destruction of toys, the smashing of household goods, 'tearing sheets into strips', or towards persons as shown in swearing, refusals to obey, temper tantrums, and even bodily violence. A four-year-old Nigerian boy was reported by his foster mother as being unable to hold his temper in check, and when upset, swiping around him, knocking things off the table.

Of a nine-year-old girl who had been with the foster mother three years it was said:

'She is very bad tempered and draws a lot of attention to herself by showing her paddy . . . she wants all your attention and if you don't give it to her she'll do anything to get it, to the point of being deliberately naughty. And when you give it to her she demands more than you've got strength to give her. She can't lead a steady life. . . . I brought her and [foster mother's natural daughter] some dolls. She put all [natural daughter's] dolls down the toilet and cut their hair off, because she had to have a bit more than her.'

A five-year-old girl had been in her foster home for nearly four years, but the foster mother reported, still

'goes frantic, goes spare, throws herself around. She has a terribly strong temper. . . . She goes frantic and throws herself around.'

Aggression, though less frequent than anxiety traits, probably worried the foster mothers more. Not only was it more frightening, not only was it difficult to control, but it was less easy to explain. Thus the foster mothers resorted to explanations like 'bad blood'. With regard to anxiety traits, they often made a connection with the child's feelings of insecurity about leaving the foster home, being taken by his parents, etc. Of course, in many cases the foster mothers may well have been projecting their own fears, but this does not mean that the children's anxieties were any less real. Some illustrations follow:

'He's always worried about the possibility of leaving. If we [foster parents] lark about and pretend to fight he gets worried. He's worried that his parents will take him away. He's scared of strangers.'

'She worries about her two brothers who are away from her.

They don't correspond and it's in her mind. Sometimes she's not with you, like she's drying the pots and drops the teatowel but she doesn't realise it for a few seconds. I think she's probably been thinking all day about the boys.'

'He sees all but says nothing. He worries about everything – if I'm not well, if he can't do his school work, if any of the others are late home. Right now he's worried in case he has to leave me. His mum promised that she'd have them once she got settled and he wants to go to her, but at the same time he wants to know that I'm there.'

Other foster mothers did not relate the anxiety to any one particular cause but to a variety of subjects:

'She worries about everything. Going to school, going home, she cries and says she doesn't want to go and rubs her hands together.'

The illustrations about anxiety have been selected to show how foster mothers saw a relationship between such traits and a specific cause. Thus less space has been given to describing the actual expression of anxiety in nail-biting, lack of concentration, nervousness, or, as one foster mother complained, 'She picks wall paper off the wall, she picks away at anything, the hole in her jumper. . . .'

Children with difficulties in relating, although less numerous than those showing anxiety, posed considerable problems for the foster parents. The difficulty was sometimes in relating to the foster parent, like the little girl who 'has no feelings at all. You can get cross and smack her and she doesn't cry. She doesn't want affection, doesn't even want to be touched.' In other cases it was in regard to friends:

'She does not make friends outside. If friends do come in she doesn't want them to stay. She has left the G.L.B. [Girls' Life Brigade] and will only go to church with me. She has always been like this. Even as a baby she would cry when taken out in the pram and wanted to return home. If anyone came she wanted them to go.'

Finally, the withdrawn children were characterised by a general retreat from life:

'He is lacking in will power, just apathetic. Give him a ball and he'll just hold it, not throw it. He'll just stand in the garden for hours. At meals you have to tell him to drink, he won't think to do it for himself.'

'He sits on the floor for long periods. He sleeps a lot. The doctor says he is withdrawing from life.'

Physical health and development

Early studies of maternal separation concentrated on its effects on children's personality and psychological functioning. Later studies began to assert that separation leading to depriving experiences could also adversely affect physical health. Thus Pringle wrote: 'People working with young deprived children have noted that separation from the mother is often followed by indifferent physical health' (1965, p. 76). But what is indifferent or poor health, and which aspects of it should be considered? A review of previous research of the health of both separated and non-separated children showed a concentration on three main areas, proneness to illness, incidence of handicaps and progress in developmental stages.

The assessment of physical health

The location of three areas of health is but the initial step towards collecting information about the private foster children. Each area had to be further broken down and means of assessing and evaluating the data devised. In the case of proneness to illness, it was decided to concentrate on respiratory illnesses for three reasons. First, as Spence and his colleagues point out, they are 'still in this country the most important cause of death and illness in early childhood' (1954, p. 45). Second, the work of Spence and of Douglas and Blomfield – although not specifically with children separated from their parents – suggests a correlation between depriving home circumstances and respiratory illnesses. Third, coloured immigrant children are alleged to be particularly vulnerable to such illnesses. The Barnardo's report of 1966 (p. 23) made this point particularly strongly.

The main respiratory diseases, according to Spence, are bronchitis, asthma, pneumonia and whooping-cough. The foster parents were therefore asked whether the children had had them while they were in the foster home. It was decided not to accept second-hand information about the occurrence of such illnesses in previous foster homes, or when with the natural parents. In addition, colds are a form of respiratory disease but, as Spence and his colleagues explain, are considered serious only if occurring frequently. Therefore, a question sought frequency by asking how many colds the children had had in the preceding three months – a period short enough to allow reliance on the foster mothers' memories.

Foster children with physical or mental handicaps will pose problems for themselves and the foster parents. It was therefore desirable to identify the number of private foster children with handicaps. The first stage was to categorise handicaps. Using Gesell's classification (1954), nine areas of handicap were identified. The foster parents were then asked whether, while in the foster home, the children had any handicap for which they received, or had received, medical treatment. Thus, if they replied just that the child lisped it would not be recorded. But if the child received speech therapy it was counted. As a check on replies the files were also examined to see if the child care officers had recorded any handicaps.

The rate at which children achieve developmental stages in walking, talking and speaking has received close attention in recent years. Gardner (1964) has explained how motor functioning is related to the promotion of aesthetic skills, such as painting, which in turn, help to shape personality. On the other hand, backwardness in sphincter control can inhibit children from social participation. Research has noted a tendency for children separated from their parents to be slow developers. Spitz (1954) reported backwardness in walking. Both Pringle (1965) and Gay (1969) observed retardation in language development, Lewis (1954) detected a lack of sphincter control (wetting and soiling). Clearly, it was necessary to discover the position for private foster children.

In order to assess whether the foster children had developed normally it was necessary, first, to define what is meant by the terms 'walking' and 'talking', and, second, to decide at what age children normally achieve the developmental stages. Both Gesell and Pringle in their authoritative works make it clear that by 'walking' they mean not just a tottering step but movement for several yards unsupported by other persons or things. By 'talking' is meant not the utterance of one word like 'dada', but the use of a simple sentence, that is the ability to arrange words in an order. Wetting and soiling are, of course, self-evident, but the research accepted as a lack of sphincter control only when wetting or soiling occurred consistently, occasional mishaps were not counted.

A number of studies, based on observation and research, have laid down ages at which certain developmental stages should be reached.

Amongst the best known are those of Gesell (1954) and Sheridan (1960). The extensive longitudinal study by Pringle *et al.* (1966) of over 11,000 children in the first seven years of their lives serves to lay down the ages at which most children actually do reach the stages. Erring, if anything, on the side of caution, it can be said that most children walk by the age of one-and-a-half years, talk by two years, achieve daytime bladder control by three years, night control by five years, and daytime bowel control by four years.

Information concerning the above was sought during the foster parent interview. Of course, the approach adopted by no means attained to, say, the comprehensive methods used in the Pringle national study to test speech development. But it was hoped the methods used would identify the children who had not reached the very basic developmental stages in certain areas. Finally, two further limitations had to be imposed. First, some children would not have been in the present foster homes when they reached the stages of development. Rather than accept what knowledge the foster mothers had gained from the natural parents on these subjects, it was decided to exclude these children. Second, for children who had been in the foster homes for some years, the naming of the year in which a developmental stage was reached would require considerable powers of recall. It was thus decided to exclude children aged over seven years from the questions. This age also brought the research into line with the upper age-range used in the Pringle study.

The findings

Sixty-six, 46·2 per cent, of the private foster children had experienced bronchitis in their present foster homes. Fifty-four, 37·8 per cent, had suffered at least two colds in the preceding three months. Although the percentages with asthma, pneumonia and whooping-cough were lower – 4·2, 5·6, and 8·4 per cent – it would seem that the private foster children did have a high incidence of respiratory illnesses. However, comparison must be made with other groups of children.

Philp's study of children from very adverse home circumstances but living with their own parents showed only 4·6 per cent having had respiratory illnesses (1963, Table 14). This very low figure is partly explicable by the higher age-range of his sample for respiratory illness is most prevalent in young children so that illnesses experienced in early childhood may not have come to the notice of the researchers. In fact large-scale research amongst both pre-school and school-age children establishes that such diseases, especially bronchitis, are very common. Spence's Newcastle study concerned only children under one year of age – the most vulnerable group – finding that 23 per cent had suffered from severe colds, 22 per cent from bronchitis, 10 per cent from whooping-cough, and 5 per cent from pneumonia (1954, p. 43). The Plowden Report points out that as many as 37 per cent of children at some time have attacks of bronchitis, that asthma and bronchitis are the commonest conditions for which children are admitted to special schools for the delicate, and that in 1963 respiratory diseases occurred at a prevalence of 17·3 per 1,000 children up to the age of fourteen. Of course, comparisons are not straightforward because with the private foster children the measurement was of illnesses experienced in the foster home (which might be a short period) not over the whole of their lives. However, this would result in underscoring the illnesses of the private foster children so it can be concluded that they had a much higher incidence of bronchitis, and probably of other respiratory illnesses as well (Central Advisory Council for Education, 1967, vol. 2, pp. 63–5).

Turning to the contrast group of local authority children, it was found that they had less experience of respiratory illnesses than the private foster children. Only 17·5 per cent had had bronchitis and only 19 per cent more than one cold (the differences were statistically significant: for bronchitis, $\chi^2 = 23·030$, d.f. $= 1$, P $= <0·001$; for colds, $\chi^2 = 23·151$, d.f. $= 1$, P $= <0·001$). Fewer local authority children also experienced the other illnesses, but the difference was not statistically significant.

The influence of other factors on the condition of the private foster children will be discussed in a later section, but it is appropriate to consider here the comparatively high incidence of bronchitis and colds. The fact that they were significantly more likely to experience them than the local authority children suggests that the high incidence was not just due to parental separation alone. It was found that amongst the private foster children those from the West African grouping were significantly more likely to experience persistent colds ($\chi^2 = 4·3817$, d.f. $= 1$, P $= <0·050$), and a definite trend towards significance occurred concerning bronchitis. The local authority group had hardly any children from this grouping. However, this does not necessarily mean that such children are constitutionally more liable to these illnesses. It may be that they are more likely to be found in environments which promote illness. The influence of over-crowding, house-type, etc., on health conditions will be considered at a later stage.

The handicaps of the private foster children can be seen in Table 7.3.

Table 7.3 Physical and mental handicaps amongst private foster children

	No.	%
Visual	2	1·4
Epilepsy	0	0·0
Motor	4	2·8
Cardiac	0	0·0
T.B.	0	0·0
Speech	8	5·6
Deafness	0	0·0
Mental	2	1·4
Other	6	4·2
None	128	89·5

Totals will not be 143 and 100 per cent because some children had more than one handicap.
No. of handicaps=22.
No. of children with at least one handicap=15.
Total number of private foster children=143.

Twenty-two handicaps were borne by fifteen private foster children, that is 10·5 per cent of the total. Excluding two with mental handicaps, 9·1 per cent had a physical handicap.

The Seebohm Report (Home Department, 1968) estimated that one in twelve of the child population had a physical handicap (Appendix Q). The incidence amongst the private foster children was not much above this, although it is worth noting that the number with speech defects was well above what would be expected when comparing what the Plowden Report estimates as the national incidence of this particular handicap (Central Advisory Council for Education, 1967, vol. 2, Appendix 2).

Turning to local authority foster children, the contrast group had forty-five handicaps amongst twenty-five children, that is 17·5 per cent of the local authority foster children. The difference with the private children was not statistically significant, but it is worth considering why the incidence was higher amongst the local authority children. First, the research enumerated only handicaps for which medical treatment had been given. This stipulation was necessary as a means of defining the handicap, but it is possible that some private foster parents did not observe or take for treatment certain handicaps. On the other hand, the closer attention given by child care officers to children in care would ensure that disabilities were noticed and treated. Second, it may be that physical or mental handicap is a factor which contributes to local authority willingness to receive a child into care. They may argue that a handicapped child places too great a strain upon certain parents, where they might refuse to take their non-handicapped children who might, therefore, be placed by the parents in a private foster home. None the less, some 10 per cent of the private foster children were handicapped in some form and they prompt the questions as to what kind of problem this posed for the private foster parents, and whether the children received help comparable to that given to handicapped children in local authority foster homes.

Of the private foster children aged between two and seven on whom information was known, fourteen, that is 22·2 per cent, were not walking at the age of eighteen months. Of the fourteen, two were still not walking although over two years old, four had commenced to do so between two and three years, and the others between eighteen months and two years. Gesell says that the average age of walking is fifteen months. If it is added that Sheridan claims that at eighteen months most children are walking 'well', then the figure of 22·2 per cent seems large. This is confirmed by the national study of seven-year-olds, which found that only 4·3 per cent had not been walking at eighteen months (1966, p. 194). The incidence of non-walkers was also high amongst the local authority children amounting to sixteen, that is 29·1 per cent. The findings certainly lend supporting evidence to the view that separation and the conditions associated with it tend to retard motor development.

Similar trends emerged concerning talking. Seventeen, 25·3 per cent, of the private foster children for whom information was available could not say a simple sentence at two years of age. Eight had eventually reached this stage between two-and-a-half and three years, five between three and four years, while four, all between two and three years, were still not speaking at the time of the research. The national study of 11,000 seven-year-olds reported that only 6·2 per cent could not talk at two (1966, p. 194). As the figure for the contrast group of local authority children was twenty, 33·8 per cent, the conclusion is not that private foster children are worse off than local authority children in this connection. Both compare very unfavourably with the 'normal' population and it would seem that they both experience the adverse results of separation.

Turning to bed-wetting and soiling, it was found, first, that twenty-two, that is 35·5 per cent, of the sixty-two private foster children for whom information was available were daily enuretic after three years of age. Second, that five, that is 10·9 per cent, of the forty-six on whom information was available had been soiling daily after four years of age. Third, that twelve, that is 33 per cent, of thirty-six had experienced nocturnal enuresis after five years of age.

How do these figures compare with other populations? Douglas and Blomfield (1958, pp. 129–30) in their large-scale study of children born on a certain date, discovered that at the age of four, 12·2 per cent were either occasional or regular bed-wetters, at the age of six it was 10·3 per cent, and at seven years 7·3 per cent. They add that bed-wetting was highest amongst the children of manual workers (1958, p. 130). The Newsons' study of four-year-old children in Nottingham recorded that 11 per cent wet their beds most nights, while 2 per cent were persistent daily soilers (1968, p. 319). Pringle *et al.* (1966, pp. 74–5) found in their sample of seven-year-olds that 4·4 per cent wet by day after three years of age, 1·2 per cent soiled daily after four years and 10·9 per cent wet nightly after five years.

Clearly, the private foster children had a greater incidence of enuresis and soiling than children of a 'normal' population. But what of other deprived or separated children? According to Philp, 34·5 per cent of the children of 'problem families' were wetting their beds occasionally or regularly at four years, and 21·5 per cent at six years (1963, Table 15). These percentages are higher than those given for the normal populations, but not more than those for the private foster children. Amongst the local authority foster children, 11 per cent were wetting daily after three years, none soiling daily after four years, and 20·6 per cent wetting nightly after six years. Thus the private children were significantly more likely to wet daily ($\chi^2 =$ 9·844, d.f. $=1$, P $= <0·010$). Trends showing them as more likely to soil daily and to wet nightly were not quite statistically significant.

The private foster children suffered from bed wetting and soiling proportionately far more than children living with their natural parents. The difference held good even when the incidence amongst children living with foster parents in social classes III, IV and V was compared with children of natural parents from the same classes. The private foster children also wetted and soiled proportionately more than other groups of deprived and separated children. Lewis has pointed out that these symptoms are expressions of children's fears and anxieties (1954, p. 37). The actual implications for the children and their foster parents will be discussed at a later stage.

To summarise

The private foster children did not appear to have unusually high proportions experiencing handicaps. But well over a third had suffered from some form of respiratory illness even in the time they had been in their present foster homes while the proportions who wetted and soiled beyond normal development stages were greater than for other groups of children. High numbers were backward in developing the capacity to walk and talk. Thus the hypothesis that many private foster children would experience poor health can be considered upheld.

Educational condition

What is involved in educational functioning? The present study's focus on education cannot compare in width or depth with research exclusively concentrated on education, and it must suffice to look at four main areas which previous research has identified as of prime importance – the type of school attended, ability and attainment, social functioning at school and parental interest in the schooling. Further, a review of the literature,[4] especially of the research of Pringle, Gay, Douglas, Lewis, Ferguson, Wilson and that completed for the Plowden Committee, suggested that children separated from their natural parents would be vulnerable in these areas.

Most of the desired educational information was obtained from a postal questionnaire completed by the foster children's head and class teachers. The education departments supplied the name and type of the children's school while the headmasters indicated if they would have benefited from attendance at a special school. The assessment of ability and attainment proved more difficult. It was not within the scope of the research to apply educational tests and, as was discovered, few schools possessed the results of any intelligence tests completed by the children. Therefore recourse was made to Ferguson's method of examining actual class performance, according to teacher's assessments, within a three point scale. However, Ferguson had assessed only overall scholastic ability while the present research distinguished between subjects. Further, it was not clear whether his ratings compared the child with all those of his age, of his school, or of his class. Instead, in the present study teachers were asked to grade the children as above average, average and below average by comparison with others in their class in the three subjects of reading, writing and arithmetic. In addition they gave the children's overall performance in class by the same comparison and the same scale.

Turning to the assessment of social functioning at school, a number of studies have defined and described what they meant by unusual or unacceptable social behaviour within an educational context. They itemised abnormal aggression, pilfering, abnormal attention demanding, being a 'nuisance', withdrawal and displaying a high degree of absenteeism. Therefore in the present study, teachers were asked whether they had 'experienced any particular problems with the child's behaviour?' and, if so, were requested to describe them. Absences from school could easily be measured by obtaining the necessary information from the school.

Lastly, some means was required of assessing the interest taken by the private foster parents in the children's education. The Plowden Committee, which claimed that it was the most important single factor, apart from native ability, influencing a child's progress, drew on research which measured parental interest by the number of times parents visited school (Central Advisory Council for Education, 1967, vol. 2, pp. 55 and 106–7). The same method was employed in this study and the information obtained via the questionnaire.

The educational spheres to be studied have now been defined and means of assessing them set out. Before the results are presented, it is necessary to point out that it ensued that only forty-one of the private foster children were at school, the majority being of pre-school age. In addition it should be mentioned that the nationality structure of the school group was different from that of the study group as a whole. Thus of the forty-one, twenty-six had both parents from the United Kingdom, four had both from the West Indies, nine had both from West Africa, one was of mixed parentage, and there was one who did not fit into these categories.

Type of school attended

All the school-age private and local authority foster children attended day schools (see Table 7.4). With the exception of one private foster girl at a fee paying denominational establishment, all were at local authority schools. Three, that is 7·3 per cent, of the private foster children were at special schools. Of these two attended schools for the educationally subnormal and one for the maladjusted. The small numbers involved mean that no general conclusions can be drawn

Table 7.4   Type of school attended by foster children

| | Private foster children | | Local authority foster children | |
	No.	%	No.	%
Primary	32	78·0	39	83·0
Secondary	6	14·6	7	14·9
Special	3	7·3	1	2·1
Totals	41	100·0	47	100·0

but it is interesting to note that only one, that is 2·1 per cent, of the local authority children were at special schools while the national study of seven-year-olds found only 1 per cent at day special schools.

The headmasters considered that another six of the private foster children required a special school. Of these they thought that three should go to maladjusted day schools where their behavioural problems could be coped with and that three should attend boarding schools as, in their opinion, the foster parents were not suitable to care for them. Thus altogether, twelve, that is 29·3 per cent, of the private foster children were at or were thought to require special forms of education. The headmasters did not consider that any more of the local authority children wanted such help. In addition it is worth noting the finding of the Plowden Report that 2 per cent of children at primary schools were thought to be in need of special schooling. Although the numbers of children in the private fostering group attending school were small, the high proportion at or needing extra educational care must be considered an important finding, one which poses problems for the schools, the foster parents, and, not least, the children themselves.

Ability and attainment

The performances in individual subjects, as assessed by the teachers, for private foster children are shown in Table 7.5. In each subject nearly half the private foster children were assessed as below average. Only in reading were more than a quarter graded as above average. Thus the private foster children tended to fare worse than most other children – presumably mostly children living with their natural parents – in their class. Although 26·8 per cent were above average in reading, the fact that 48·8 per cent were below average may cause some concern for, as Pringle explains, reading 'is the most basic educational skill . . . backwardness in reading has an adverse effect on

Table 7.5 Private foster children's subject grading by comparison with classmates

	Reading		Writing		Arithmetic	
	No.	%	No.	%	No.	%
Above average	11	26·8	8	19·5	4	9·8
Average	10	24·4	13	31·7	17	41·4
Below average	20	48·8	20	48·8	20	48·8
Totals	41	100·0	41	100·0	41	100·0

a child's progress in most other work' (1965, p. 175).

Because the children were assessed in comparison with their classmates it is difficult to consider them against other samples. For instance, a local authority child assessed as average within her class may in fact have similar abilities as a private child assessed as above average in her class. With this caution the results for the contrast group are given in Table 7.6. The local authority children were

Table 7.6 Local authority children's subject grading by comparison with classmates

	Reading		Writing		Arithmetic	
	No.	%	No.	%	No.	%
Above average	8	17·0	3	6·4	2	4·2
Average	24	51·1	23	48·9	28	59·6
Below average	15	31·9	21	44·7	17	36·2
Totals	47	100·0	47	100·0	47	100·0

predominantly placed as average in each subject whereas the private ones had been predominantly below average. However, fewer local authority children appeared in the above average ranking although fewer were below average.

As well as the individual subject assessments the teachers made an overall assessment of the children's academic performance in comparison with their classmates. The results for the private foster children are presented against those of the local authority children (see Table 7.7). This Table reveals a similar trend as was found for the individual subjects. The local authority children were most heavily grouped in the average ranking. The private children had proportionately more graded as above average yet also had more graded as below average although the differences were not quite statistically significant.

Table 7.7   Foster children's overall grading by comparison with class-mates

| | Private foster children | | Local authority foster children | |
	No.	%	No.	%
Above average	10	24·4	4	8·5
Average	12	29·3	26	55·3
Below average	19	46·3	17	36·2
Totals	41	100·0	47	100·0

If on a normal distribution of scholastic attainment 15 per cent of children are expected to be above average, 70 per cent average and 15 per cent below average,[5] then the private foster children, by comparison with their classmates on both subject and overall assessments, were over-represented at the lower end of the scale. The finding appears to lend support to that of previous research that separation from parents does retard educational attainment. But the low level of functioning may also reflect the greater distribution of private foster children amongst persons from low social groupings whose children tend to achieve educationally less well than those from higher social classes. Whatever the cause, the significant conclusion is that children placed with foster parents are more likely than their classmates to be graded educationally below average. Obviously, the educational development of the children will affect their futures but, in addition, some natural parents may be disappointed at lack of academic success. The potential therefore exists for disagreements between them and the foster parents.

Social functioning at school

The schoolteachers reported that twenty-one, that is 51·2 per cent, of the private foster children posed problems within the school setting. An analysis of their replies showed five main categories of problems. First, and most common, were children displaying anxiety or worry symptoms severe enough to impede their progress. A typical statement was, 'He is, I feel, emotionally upset . . . he has fits of crying and needs extra fuss.' Others mention the children being extremely restless, unable to concentrate, and nervous. Second, there was a group of children marked by their aggressiveness towards teachers and pupils. Consistent extreme bad temper, persistent lying and petty theft were mentioned. Of a fourteen-year-old girl the teacher commented that she 'has always been of an aggressive nature, is quick to resent criticism, and an inveterate smoker since the second year'. She added that the girl had an unsatisfactory attendance record, was frequently late, and used 'domestic problems' as reasons for early departures in the afternoons. Third, other children were extremely attention-seeking, like the five-year-old coloured child who often 'attaches herself with tremendous intensity to one particular child, regardless of whether the attraction is mutual. She tends to monopolise the child in question and is over-possessive, thus producing unhappy situations'. Fourth, and by contrast, a few were marked by their withdrawal from teachers and fellow pupils. A five-year-old boy was described as 'artistic and imaginative . . . and of undoubted ability'. Yet he was so reluctant in 'attempting things for himself' that he was graded as below average in performance on all subjects. An eight-year-old girl with similar gradings showed 'acute embarrassment when spoken to by adults' which, combined with 'an abrupt way of speaking' made it difficult for teachers to relate to her at all. Fifth, although many had poor attendance records, only two cases of persistent truancy were cited as problems.

The incidence of school misbehaviour must be seen in the light of that of other kinds of children. The Newsom Report (Central Advisory Council for Education, 1963), referring to older children at secondary modern schools, estimated that about 5 per cent of pupils present serious behavioural problems. Stott (1965) asserts that some 8 per cent of girls and 11–15 per cent of boys show behavioural disturbances at school. Obviously, separated children can be expected to show more disturbance than the cross-sections of the school population referred to in these studies. But the private foster children displayed significantly more problems than the local authority ones, of whom one-third caused their teachers to note disturbances ($\chi^2 = 4\cdot263$, d.f. $= 1$, P $= <0\cdot050$). The fact that the $51\cdot2$ per cent of private children compares unfavourably even with the $35\cdot7$ per cent found in Wilson's study (1962, pp. 73–4), whose sample was deliberately drawn from families displaying social problems, makes one of the most disturbing findings of this research.

The high incidence of behavioural problems leads to an expectation of frequent absences from school. The method of measuring attendances was one used in previous research, consisting of ascertaining the number of mornings and afternoons a child could have attended in the term, noting his absences, and thereby working out a percentage of actual attendances. Results are given in Table 7.8. As

Table 7.8   Private foster children's percentage of attendances during school term

Percentage of possible attendances	No.	%
95–100	17	41·5
90–94	8	19·5
20–89	14	34·1
0–19	2	4·9
Totals	41	100·0

can be seen, 41·5 per cent of the private foster children were in the range of highest possible attendances, but what is satisfactory attendance? Wilson argues that 90 per cent and above attendance is a satisfactory level (1962, p. 70). By this criteria 39 per cent of the private foster children were unsatisfactory attenders. Compared with Wilson's finding that 78 per cent of socially deprived children were poor attenders this figure may not seem high. But Wilson's sample contained proportionately more children of secondary school age and she observes that secondary school attendance is usually worse than primary school attendance (1962, p. 70). The figure for the private foster children is higher than the 30 per cent which the Plowden Committee reported for primary school children and the 17 per cent of local authority foster children. The difference between the private and local authority foster children was not quite statistically significant.

Foster parent interest

As explained, the private foster parents' interest in their children's education was assessed by obtaining information on the number of times they had taken the initiative to contact their schools. The findings now present the number of foster parents as well as the children.

Table 7.9   Contacts with private foster children's school at foster parents' initiative

	Private foster parents	%	No. of private foster children	%
Made contact	19	54·3	22	53·7
No contact	16	45·7	19	46·3
Totals	35	100·0	41	100·0

Just over half the private foster parents, covering 53·7 per cent of the children, had taken the initiative in approaching the schools. How does this figure compare with other foster and natural parents? Over three-quarters of the local authority foster parents, covering 74·4 per cent of the children, had done so. Thus the private foster children were significantly less likely than their local authority counterparts to have their schools contacted ($\chi^2 = 3·8417$, d.f. $= 1$, $P = <0·050$).

Turning to natural parents for comparative material, the Plowden Committee examined parental contact with schools in two main directions: whether the parents approached the schools before their children started, and whether they met staff once they were there. Their findings, that some 62 per cent of parents of primary school children make the first kind of approach, and over 80 per cent the second type, are not dissimilar from the figure for the local authority foster parents, but well above those for the private ones. Further, when the Plowden sample is broken down by social class, even the number of contacts by parents from social class V are above those for the private foster parents as a whole (Central Advisory Council for Education, 1967, vol. 2, p. 139).

The results indicate that, compared with other groups, the private foster parents display a lack of interest in their children's schooling. Previous research has demonstrated the relationship between such interest and children's educational attainment, confirmatory evidence for which was found in the present research. At this point, however, another effect must be mentioned, namely that lack of foster parent interest can result in the teachers having insufficient knowledge about the foster children. Consequently, schools may even possess wrong information. In one case the staff thought the private foster child was legally adopted; in others they had no idea of the pressures children were experiencing due to insecurities about their natural parents. No doubt many of the behavioural problems shown at school were closely related to the fostering situation, yet only in a minority of cases did teachers appear well informed.

With over a quarter of the private foster children who were at school considered to require special education, with their predominant attainment grading in comparison with their classmates as below average, with over half showing behavioural problems at school, with well over a third being unsatisfactory attenders, and with nearly a half having foster parents assessed as showing little interest in their schooling, there is little doubt that the hypothesis that private foster children would tend to function poorly at school can be considered upheld. Indeed, their educational condition, which tended to be inferior to that of the local authority foster children and of children with natural parents, must provoke serious concern.

Self-knowledge and the private foster children

The desirability of foster children possessing self-knowledge – that is, accurate knowledge about their relationship to their foster parents – has been the subject of a growing number of studies. Tarachow, in an early and influential clinical study (1937), argued that the concealing of the facts about the relationship increased a foster child's personal difficulties and hindered his adjustment to the foster home. Cowan and Stout developed Tarachow's ideas by applying them to a sample of foster children concluding that 'unless the child is able to satisfy himself about his past experiences, and to relate them to his present situation, he cannot achieve a satisfactory degree of security' (quoted in Trasler, 1955, p. 5). Trasler came to similar conclusions. He asserted the foster children's need to possess accurate knowledge about themselves adding, 'it appears that experiences which give rise to severe anxiety are usually those which are inadequately understood' (ibid., p. 107). The most extensive research on self-knowledge, however, was completed in the USA by Weinstein (1960). Amongst his many findings perhaps the most important was that the children's knowledge and understanding of their fostering circumstances was positively related to their position of 'well-being' as assessed by child welfare workers. Adapting some of Weinstein's methods for use with children in British foster homes I also concluded that adaptation to fostering, as assessed by child care officers, was related to their degree of self-knowledge (Holman, 1966, pp. 295–8).

All the studies agree that a lack of knowledge promotes anxieties and insecurities in the children which in turn hinders their adaptation to and progress in their foster homes. They also agree that foster children are affected not just by what they know, or do not know, but how they know it. In other words, they claim that the truth about a child and his background should be told in a sympathetic and positive manner. They explain that if the reasons for the child not being with his own parents are conveyed in a manner which implied total condemnation of the parents or rejection of the child then the child's own image of himself as a person of worth is damaged. They argue, further, that if the explanation is presented positively, putting it in terms of circumstances which could not be helped and emphasising the positive characteristics of the parents, then the child would develop more confidence in himself as a person who could be loved.

None of the above studies have applied to private foster children and the exploration of their condition required two main pieces of information. The first, concerning whether the children knew their true relationship to the foster parents, could be obtained by a direct question to the latter. The second, for those who did know their relationship, concerned the manner in which it had been conveyed to them. Thus the foster parents were asked to explain how the children received the knowledge and their responses categorised and coded.[6]

Knowledge about the fostering relationship

Of the 101 private foster children aged two and over, eighty-seven, that is 86·1 per cent, were aware that they were not the natural children of the persons with whom they lived. Fourteen, 13·9 per cent, had been told or given the impression that they were the natural children of the home. Amongst the 105 local authority foster children only seventy-six, 72·4 per cent, were aware of their true relationship, while twenty-nine, 27·6 per cent, held a false impression. The fact that the local authority children were significantly more likely not to know the truth of their relationship ($\chi^2 = 5\cdot8906$, d.f. $= 1$, P $= <0\cdot010$) may come as a surprise but there is a ready explanation. If the children of the West African students are removed from the sample, then there is no significant difference between the private and local authority children concerning knowledge about their real relationship. The students, of course, made up a large portion of the private fostering group, but were not represented in the local authority group. What was it about them that caused the difference? First, as will be shown, students tended to visit more regularly than other parents, hence their children had more chance of learning the truth via contact. Second, they were more likely to make it clear to the foster parents that the placement was a temporary one – unlike single parents whose future was more uncertain – so that foster parents were less inclined to pretend that they were the natural parents.

The finding that 13·9 per cent of the private foster children had not been told the truth of their position is still a serious one. The research already quoted implies that such children would experience anxieties and fears and find it difficult to adapt to their foster homes. It appears from adoption studies, such as that by McWhinnie, that troubles and fears can beset even those children who have no parental contact (1967, ch. 4). But amongst the private foster children were some whose confusions were increased by having contact with their relatives yet at the same time having foster parents who strove to keep the truth from them. The following case examples will make the point more vividly:

a   The unmarried mother of a five-year-old girl visited her irregularly but when she came offered great affection, was ready to discipline her, and spoke of taking her away for a holiday. The girl, who had always been taught to refer to the visitor as auntie, was completely bewildered by her behaviour, so much so that it affected her school work so that her headmistress commented, 'The child is quite terrified of the thought of her mother, even though she thinks of her as aunt. Letters arriving upset her.'

b   An eight-year-old girl was the illegitimate daughter of the daughter of the foster mother's brother. Although the whole extended family knew of the relationship, the attempt was still made to preserve the fiction that she was the natural child of the foster mother. The girl was puzzled and probably had guessed or half guessed the truth. It is worth adding that she had an I.Q. of 70, attended a school for the maladjusted where her educational performance was poor, and that she persistently stole from other children's desks and clothes.

The manner in which they received the knowledge

As explained, the actual fact of whether the children are told the truth

Table 7.10   *Manner in which the foster children received knowledge about their fostering situation*

	Private foster children		Local authority foster children	
	No.	%	No.	%
Foster parents explained:				
reasonable	20 ⎫		25 ⎫	
mixed	10 ⎬ 36	41·4	3 ⎬ 30	39·5
hurtful	6 ⎭		2 ⎭	
'Picked up' the knowledge	36	41·4	9	11·8
Child knew at time of placement	13	14·7	33	43·4
Other	2	2·5	4	5·3
Totals	87	100·0	76	100·0

is but one aspect of self-knowledge. Equally important is the manner in which the knowledge was conveyed to them. From Table 7.10 it can be seen that thirty-six of the private foster children, that is 41·4 per cent, learned of their relationship directly from their foster parents. Of these, twenty were deemed to have been given reasonable explanations which were characterised by answers stressing the circumstances which made it necessary for the natural parents to place their children, combined with the conveyance that not only did the foster parents want them but that so did the natural parents. Thus one foster mother explained:

'You stay with me because your mother can't manage to
keep you. When you're old enough you'll be able to go home,
but you'll still be able to come back and see me.'

Six of the private foster mothers' explanations were classed as harmful or hurtful to the child. Half of these gave outright condemnation of the child's parent(s), for instance:

'I explained that she [natural mother] is a loose woman. I told
her about the nine illegitimate children.'

The others implied a lack of love and concern for the child, as though that was the main reason for the separation:

'I say the parents didn't have room and didn't love you.'

Similarly, another told the foster child that her parents were 'too busy' to have her. The remainder of the thirty-six foster mothers who rendered an explanation gave a mixture of positive and negative factors.

Amongst the private foster children who were aware that they were not related to the foster parents, another 41·4 per cent 'just picked up the knowledge'. This group is to be distinguished from those who had no knowledge at all. The latter's foster parents not only volunteered no information but denied the truth, so directly misleading them. The former's foster parents made no direct denials, they implicitly acknowledged that they were not the natural parents but they avoided talking about the subject. The children were thus left to garner what they could, a method to be regarded as almost as unsatisfactory as having no knowledge at all. The children concerned were put in a position causing them to question why the subject was avoided, with overtones that something had to be hidden. The reaction of the child could be increased anxiety to seek out more details, or, and this seemed more common, a collusion with the foster parents so that they

F

too were reluctant to broach the matter directly for fear of what they would find out. In other cases the resulting confusion was not unlike that of children with no knowledge. One half-caste, illegitimate girl of fifteen had always known she was a foster child, as her foster mother put it, 'She grew up with it.' But the foster mother had never explained to her why she had left her own parents. Not surprisingly the girl was showing anxieties, disliked any mention of the term 'foster', and kept asking if 'having an illegitimate baby is hereditary'. Not least, there is the danger that the foster children will 'pick up' the wrong information. A boy of seven believed – and told others – that his real father was dead, whereas in fact the putative father was very much alive, and it was not impossible that they would meet in the future.

Turning to the local authority foster children, 39·5 per cent – a similar proportion to that for their private counterparts – received their information from their foster parents. However, proportionately more received a reasonable explanation. Only nine, 11·8 per cent, 'picked up' the knowledge, a far smaller proportion than for the private foster children. On the other hand 43·4 per cent knew at the time of the placement compared with 14·7 per cent. The remaining four had learned directly from their child care officers. Undoubtedly, the local authority foster children received more full, more reasonable and more satisfactory explanations than their private counterparts, and were less likely to rely on 'picked up' information. Their more advantageous situation appears closely linked with the activities of the child care officers. First, the officers had frequently worked with the local authority children before they came into care and had enabled the natural parents to explain to the children, even young ones, about forthcoming changes. Second, the officers had often worked closely with the local authority foster parents, enabling them to see the value of giving explanations to the children. In some cases the potential to do this was a factor involved in choosing local authority foster parents. It will be recalled that in chapter 5 the local authority foster parents were shown to be much more aware of the need to explain past events, and more ready to pass on the truth to the children than the private foster mothers. Third, as mentioned, in four cases the officers themselves had taken on the task of telling the local authority children. With regard to private fostering, the officers usually had no contact before the placement was made and, as will be shown, tended to have infrequent contact with private foster parents and children.

The inclusion of the manner in which knowledge was conveyed puts a different complexion on the comparison between the private and local authority foster children. If foster children who have just 'picked up' knowledge, received a hurtful explanation, or received no explanation, are considered to be in an unsatisfactory condition then the total private foster children so placed is fifty-six, that is 55·4 per cent. The comparable local authority figure was forty, 37·1 per cent. Thus the private foster children were significantly more likely to possess unsatisfactory self-knowledge ($\chi^2 = 4·129$, d.f. $= 1$, P $= <0·050$). The hypothesis that substantial numbers would not possess accurate knowledge about their real relationships with their natural parents can be considered upheld. According to the research already mentioned, such children will find extra difficulties in adjusting to the fostering situation and experience more anxieties and fears within it.

Multiplicity of adverse conditions

The study has now established how many individual private foster children experienced certain conditions which could be considered adverse or unsatisfactory. In all, 117, that is 81·8 per cent, of them suffered at least one of the following – an emotional trait graded as 'often' or 'persistent', a respiratory illness in their present placement, a physical or mental handicap, retardation in physical development, 'below average' grading on a subject at school, social problems at school, unsatisfactory self-knowledge. Large as the percentage is, it tells nothing of the multiplicity of conditions borne by some children. An important observation was that the adverse conditions rarely occurred singly, children often experienced more than one.[7] Two case studies can be given to illustrate children with multiple conditions:

a The private foster girl was thirteen at the time of the research. Her father was in prison when she was born and her parents never reunited. Her mother left her in the daily care of lodgers, and she had at least one other private foster home before being placed in her present home in her second year. The children's department was concerned about her, but the foster parents' continual mobility and unwillingness to co-operate kept official contacts to a minimum. At seven years of age the police took her back to her foster home after finding her out late at night in the streets. Later an accident in the home caused a severe burn requiring intensive hospital treatment. At junior school she displayed consistent aggression, when she was present, and at one time the teachers refused to take her, describing her school behaviour as 'violent tempers and uncontrolled'. Secondary school brought little improvement. She was referred to a child guidance clinic, but the foster parents refused to co-operate. She showed many signs of sexual precociousness, and when twelve disappeared with a lodger from whom the police rescued her in another town. At the time of the research the girl was displaying extreme symptoms of anxiety and aggression. The foster mother complained of her violent temper, saying the girl had physically attacked her simply because she had got her up early for school. She was still nocturnally and sometimes daily enuretic. Hospital examination could find no physical explanation. Lastly, it is worth noting that although, according to a Terman Merrill test, she had an above average I.Q., her school performance was below average on all the subjects assessed.

   b   The condition of a five-year-old Nigerian boy, fostered for two years, gave cause for note in the areas of emotional traits, health and education. Extremely withdrawn and unable to relate to adults, his foster mother explained:

> '[He] will not speak to adults in authority. He speaks to our children but not to us. There is a complete lack of communication with adults. If he is hit, he stands there. He used to sulk for hours. He will not respond. He'll sit for hours on a chair until we tell him to get down. He will not eat until told to. He is slow to learn. It took hours of patient repetition before he could do a jig-saw – although he is not unintelligent. He'll hold his water until the very last minute rather than move to the toilet. He is the delinquent of tomorrow.'

In addition, the boy walked with difficulty due to a shortening of the muscles in the back of a leg, and stuttered badly. Although the foster parents, who showed tremendous concern for the child, had arranged pre-school education for him, he still did not function at school in a way comparable with other children.

Factors associated with the adverse conditions

The adverse conditions experienced by many of the private foster children clearly have implications for their present and future happiness and functioning. It is important, therefore, to detect whether there are any factors in the private fostering situation which are associated with the conditions. The matter has been approached in two ways; first, by examining factors which previous studies suggest are important; second, by relating other factors which the present research has thrown up. To avoid a multiplicity of figures, the tests of significance are given as an Appendix at the end of this chapter.

Age of separation from mother

A great number of research studies – including those by Goldfarb, Freud and Burlingham, Bowlby and Pringle – agree that age of separation has a direct effect on the extent and degree of deprivation. The present research did not record the age at which the private foster children were first separated but the age at which they entered the present foster home. However, as many children had not had previous separation experiences, the ages are probably synonymous in these cases. In fact, age appeared influential at only three points. Children placed before they were six months were less likely to display extreme aggressive traits, while those placed before one year had a greater chance of having foster parents who demonstrated their educational interest by visiting their school. On the other hand, children placed before two years had less prospect of receiving a satisfactory explanation as to why they were foster children. Possibly the younger the child when received, the closer the relationship developed with the foster parents as seen in the educational interest. Yet its very closeness may have inhibited some from giving a full explanation of the child's status from fear of diminishing the child's nearness to them.

Changes of foster home

No statistically significant correlations were found between number of moves and the children's condition. However, at two points definite trends were perceived. They indicated that private foster children with two or more moves were likely to display at least one extreme trait, yet had more chance of knowing the truth about their fostering position. This is not an altogether unexpected result, for child care writers have often asserted the ill-effects on personality of multiple moves, while children undergoing such moves are hardly likely to have illusions about their relationships with foster parents.

Quality of the substitute mother

The present study had not worked upon an assessment of the term 'quality' of the foster parents, but it was worth examining the condition of the children in relation to the foster parents' 'suitability' as derived from the file material and from the judgments of the child care officers. As expected, private foster parents showing unsuitable factors were associated with a number of adverse conditions amongst the children. The most highly significant relationships were with physical health, such as having had respiratory illnesses, and poor school attendance.

Presence of a sibling

The presence of a sibling in the foster home produced an advantage in two ways. First, children fostered with a sibling were less likely to show the trait of aggression. Second, they received more satisfactory explanations of why they were fostered. Probably it is harder to conceal the truth from siblings, and the one can act as an informant to the other.

Turning from factors which previous research suggests may influence the condition of foster children, attention is now directed to other factors.

Accommodation

All the measures of poor educational subject performance showed a trend towards correlating with overcrowding, a lack of basic amenities and residence in private rented property. Consistent and statistically significant findings appeared most strongly between these indices of housing deprivation and unsatisfactory school attendance and the display of behavioural problems at school.

There were also some significant findings showing that children living in private rented property were more prone to respiratory illnesses. Those children in overcrowded conditions were more likely to have foster parents who did not visit their schools and to have an unsatisfactory record of school attendance.

Legal status

Illegitimate children were far more likely to be in complete ignorance about the truth of their relationship with the foster parents than the legitimate. Further, amongst those who were aware that the foster parents were not their real parents, the illegitimate were more likely to possess an unsatisfactory explanation. As mentioned, the legitimate children, being mainly the offspring of West African students, were visited more frequently by their natural parents and were expected to return to them. The illegitimate ones, having at most only one interested parent, were more likely to stay for longer periods. Hence the foster parents could be tempted to maintain the pretence that they were natural members of the family.

Participation of the foster fathers

The extent to which the private foster fathers participated in the upbringing of and involved themselves with the foster children emerged as a major influence on their condition. Children whose foster father had a 'non-participant' grading were significantly more prone to extreme withdrawal, while there were definite trends towards the traits of aggression, anxiety and difficulties in relating. Similarly, such children were more likely to be poor attenders at school and to display behavioural problems there.

Nationality

Amongst the private foster children nearly all the coloured children were the offspring of West African students. The relationship between them and the experience of respiratory illnesses has already been discussed. As far as other illnesses or handicaps were concerned, the West African children were no more liable than the other children. Further, they did not fare any worse at school than the other private foster children. Indeed, they were less likely to show behavioural problems there. Of course, the private foster children as a whole did not function well at school, but the above findings suggest this was due to factors other than those of race. Small as the number of children at school were, the results do concur with larger studies such as that of the ILEA (1969), which find that immigrant children, once they have settled, can do as well as non-immigrant children in their schools.

Number of natural children at home

Only concerning health did the number of children present seem important. Private foster children living with three or more of the foster parents' natural children had a greater chance of suffering from bronchitis and persistent colds.

The unsatisfactory conditions of the private foster children can not be attributed to a single factor within private fostering. They can not, for example, be simply related solely to the trauma of separation from natural parents. Rather, they result from the whole complex of factors which make up private fostering. Their conditions were more depriving than those of the local authority children because, to mention some reasons, their foster parents were more unsuitable, their foster fathers participated less in their lives, and their standards of accommodation were not as high. But whatever the reasons, the adverse nature of their conditions will have implications for all the participants in private fostering.

Adverse conditions – implications for the fostering participants

Generally speaking, the position of the private foster children can be regarded as unsatisfactory: 63·4 per cent of those aged two and over had at least one emotional trait in an extreme form: nearly a half suffered from bronchitis and over 30 per cent from persistent colds in their present placements: 22·2 per cent had been backward in learning to walk and 25·3 per cent in learning to talk: 35·5 per cent were daily enuretic after three years of age, 10·9 per cent soiled daily after four years, and a third experienced continuing nocturnal enuresis after five years of age: of the children at school, 29·3 per cent were considered to need special forms of education, over a third were assessed as performing below average in comparison with their classmates, 51·2 per cent posed school behavioural problems, 39 per cent had unsatisfactory attendance records and 46·3 per cent had foster parents assessed to take little interest in their education: lastly, over a half were considered to have been inadequately informed about their relationships to their foster parents. On most of these conditions, the private foster children were significantly likely to be more disadvantageously placed than their local authority counterparts.

The existence of these conditions has severe implications for the private foster parents and children. To deal with a child displaying an extreme emotional trait, in constant ill-health, or who soils daily, or who possesses a multiplication of the conditions outlined, can impose very severe strains on the foster mothers. The strains manifested themselves in two main directions. First, they could create physical burdens. Children who regularly soiled or wetted for many years led to extra physical labour as well as extra cost in washing and replacing clothes, sheets and blankets. Elderly foster mothers were particularly vulnerable to physical strain. In one case, a woman in her late sixties, herself badly crippled and with a husband who had been forced to retire from work because of bronchitis and a weak heart, was caring for a five-year-old boy unable to walk due to poliomyelitis. The foster mother had to carry him everywhere, including a weekly visit to hospital for treatment. Second, the foster mothers could be bewildered by the foster children's behaviour and baffled as to how to cope with it. For instance, the question of getting children 'clean' loomed large in some homes. Foster mothers who had managed the matter in a straightforward manner with their own children found that normal methods did not work with anxiety-ridden older children. One child not only continued to wet nightly after she was five but was consistently 'dirty', was always in drains, had drunk 'water she had passed' and eaten her own faeces. Not surprisingly, the foster mother was disgusted and quite unable to think how she should handle the girl. In like manner, the extreme aggression or withdrawal of some children and, at times, their lack of progress in walking and talking could cause the foster mothers great anxiety and possibly give their husbands grounds for encouraging them to give up the arduous task of fostering.

The implications for the foster children were as severe as those for the foster mothers. Their daily pattern of life was constantly influenced by their adverse conditions. The older children who still wetted or soiled faced the sneers of their classmates at school and the condemnation of their foster parents at home for actions which they could not control. Some children were daily enduring the emotional pain of doubting whether they really were the natural children of the persons with whom they lived.

Thus the day-to-day life of the private foster children could be made wretched by their adverse conditions. But what of the long term effects? Some research suggests that early signs of abnormal aggression and school misbehaviour can be pointers to future delinquency. A substantial number of the private foster children were graded as showing aggression in an extreme form and assessed as displaying behavioural problems at school. Leaving delinquency aside, there is the matter of their future adult emotional life. Will they function as normal persons able to love and be loved? What kind of parents will they make? Although research is sparse, it is safe to assert that children showing severe personal problems at an early stage are starting with severe disadvantages. Of course, adult emotional ill-health is not the inevitable result of unsatisfactory childhood conditions and experiences. Much will depend on the compensatory relationships and services given to the children.

As many private foster children experienced unsatisfactory conditions, it might have been expected that the social services would be especially orientated towards them. However, the reverse appeared to operate. They had less chance than the local authority children of being referred to child guidance and special education. Their teachers were not always aware that they were foster children.[8] Medical practitioners were sometimes reported as being unsympathetic to their needs. At least three foster mothers, all in desperate need of counsel, said that their doctor's only advice was to send the children back. A not uncommon occurrence was for private foster children's medical treatment to be withheld or delayed until the signed consent of a natural parent could be obtained – a process which could take a considerable amount of time. Of course, these points do not necessarily constitute a criticism of the services. Child guidance clinics cannot be blamed for not having children referred to them. Teachers cannot know a child is fostered unless the information is passed to them. The difference between the services given the private and local authority foster children turned on the part played by the child care officers. They were prepared to ensure that children in public care obtained appointments and attended clinics and hospitals and were more ready to attend to their educational needs. They even sought out foster parents with nursing qualifications for handicapped children in care. The same did not apply to the private foster children. The actual service given by the children's departments to the two types of foster children is the subject of a later chapter and it is enough here to state that it appeared that the children showing the most adverse conditions had the least chance of receiving professional help.

Meeting the needs of private foster children

The last three chapters have examined the treatment given to and the condition of the private foster children. To round off the subjects, it is necessary to evaluate the foster parents' treatment in relation to the needs of their foster children.

The child care literature specifies three main areas of foster child need – the material, the emotional and the intellectual. Consequently, some means was required of assessing to what extent the private foster parents met these needs of their foster children. The meaning of each need was carefully defined and the child care officers asked to grade, on a five point scale, the position of each child (see Table 7.11).[9] Child care officers are trained or experienced in regard to these needs but as a check their senior officers did the same exercise. A satisfactory correlation between their responses was obtained as is explained in the Appendix (see page 294). The officers were satisfied that the

Table 7.11 Extent to which private foster children's needs were met by private foster parents

	Material needs		Emotional needs		Intellectual needs	
	No.	%	No.	%	No.	%
Definitely	83	58·0	41	28·7	39	27·2
Probably	41	28·7	48	33·6	46	32·2
Partly	13	9·1	19	13·2	20	14·0
Doubtful	6	4·2	22	15·4	31	21·7
Not	0	0·0	13	9·1	7	4·9
Totals	143	100·0	143	100·0	143	100·0

material needs of most private foster children were being met. However, they considered it doubtful or certain that 24·5 per cent and 26·6 per cent were not having their emotional and intellectual needs met. Further, several added that although they considered the present position satisfactory, they did not think the foster parents would cope as the children grew older. The officers were not asked for comments but some gave extra material which can be used for illustration. Thus one said:

'John seems to be retarded both physically and mentally. The obvious frustrations that he experiences make him very naughty and difficult. Mrs . . . [foster mother] herself, while good with babies, cannot cope with the activity and emotional problems of toddlers. John's awareness of his foster mother's inability to cope undoubtedly adds to his problems.'

Another explained:

'This is a good home but the children get bored because the foster mother does not give them enough toys or activity. The children are too intelligent for this foster mother. They are well cared for physically but Mrs . . . has not the imagination to give them any interests and the parents will not supply toys.'

Table 7.12 shows the figures for the local authority children. The

Table 7.12   Extent to which local authority foster children's needs were met by local authority foster parents

| | Material needs | | Emotional needs | | Intellectual needs | |
	No.	%	No.	%	No.	%
Definitely	119	83·2	80	55·9	76	53·1
Probably	22	15·4	37	25·9	47	32·9
Partly	1	0·7	12	8·4	13	9·1
Doubtful	1	0·7	7	4·9	6	4·2
Not	0	0·0	7	4·9	1	0·7
Totals	143	100·0	143	100·0	143	100·0

percentages of local authority children whose needs were 'doubtful' or not met were as low as 0·7, 9·8 and 4·9. Thus the private foster children were significantly more likely to have their emotional needs unmet (dividing definitely, probably, partly/doubtful, not, $\chi^2 = 10·260$, d.f. = 1, P = <0·010). Again they were significantly more likely to have their intellectual needs unmet ($\chi^2 = 23·441$, d.f. = 1, P = <0·001).[10] Thus there appears a good case for upholding the hypothesis that substantial numbers of the private foster children would not have their needs adequately met in regard to their emotional and intellectual needs but for rejecting it in regard to material needs.

Appendix

	χ^2	d.f.	P
Aggression displayed persistently or often, other/placed before six months of age, not	3·8503	1	<0·050
Foster parents contacted school, not/placed before 1 year of age, not	4·468	1	<0·050
Unsatisfactory explanation of fostering, not/placed before 2 years of age, not	6·1452	1	<0·025
School attendance below 90 per cent, not/foster parents with unsuitable factors, not	13·405	1	<0·001
Experienced pneumonia, not/foster parents with unsuitable factors, not	5·8042	1	<0·025
Experienced whooping cough, not/foster parents with unsuitable factors, not	4·3429	1	<0·050
Experienced persistent colds, not/foster parents with unsuitable factors, not	5·3813	1	<0·025
School attendance below 90 per cent, not/foster parents not approved by officers, other	11·893	1	<0·001
Aggression not displayed persistently or often, other/presence of a sibling, not	4·4567	1	<0·050

	χ^2	d.f.	P
Satisfactory explanation of fostering, not/ presence of a sibling, not	4·1212	1	<0·050
School attendance below 90 per cent, not/ dwelling lacked basic amenity, not	9·2276	1	<0·010
School attendance below 90 per cent, not/living in private rented property, not	4·2273	1	<0·010
School attendance below 90 per cent, not/room density over one and a half persons, not	6·4071	1	<0·025
School behavioural problems, not/bedroom density over two persons, not	4·1084	1	<0·050
Experienced asthma, not/living in private rented property, not	4·5904	1	<0·050
Experienced pneumonia, not/living in private rented property, not	6·2112	1	<0·025
Foster parents not visit school, visited/bedroom density over two persons, not	7·7973	1	<0·010
Foster parents not visit school, visited/room density over one and a half persons, not	3·8671	1	<0·050
Not know truth about relationship, other/ illegitimate, legitimate	5·5623	1	<0·025
Unsatisfactory explanation of fostering, other/ illegitimate, legitimate	5·6820	1	<0·025
Withdrawal displayed persistently or often, not/non-participant foster father, other	8·3266	1	<0·010
School attendance below 90 per cent, not/non-participant foster father, other	8·0658	1	<0·010
School behavioural problems, not/non-participant foster father, other	4·0394	1	<0·050
School behavioural problems, not/West African children, other	8·9125	1	<0·010
Experienced bronchitis, not/living with three or more of the natural children, not	4·5734	1	<0·050
Experienced persistent colds, not/living with three or more of the natural children, not	4·5804	1	<0·050
Unsatisfactory explanation of fostering, other/ foster father wanted wife to stop fostering, other	3·886	1	<0·050
Unsatisfactory explanation of fostering, other/ foster mother regards child 'as my own', other	6·8809	1	<0·010

8   Natural parents and their use of private foster homes

The paucity of opinion, let alone knowledge, about the natural parents of private foster children allowed the formation of only two hypotheses. First, that numbers would be West African students wishing to study and unable to provide other forms of care except private fostering. Second, that numbers would be unmarried mothers wanting to work and unable to provide other care. Already the study has shown that many were West African students and unmarried mothers but it has not explained the circumstances causing them to place their children, neither has it explained why they chose private fostering. In order to pursue these items, a two-fold approach is adopted. First, a quantitative analysis will be made of the incidence amongst the natural parents of circumstances known to be associated with children being separated from their homes. Second, an account, drawing upon case material, will be given of why the different types of private natural parents placed their children and why they used the private fostering system.

The 143 private foster children belonged to 118 pairs of parents, the 143 local authority ones to 127 pairs. Much of the data required about them could be obtained from children's departments files, but some necessitated interviews with the parents themselves. As explained, it proved possible to interview only twenty-nine of the private natural parents.[1]

It follows that the information used is of two kinds, the file data which applied to all natural parents both private and local authority and the interview data which concerned but a minority of the former. Clearly the twenty-nine interviewed parents constitute a biased sample so any findings are treated with caution. None the less, they provided valuable 'live' material which did contribute to an understanding of private fostering.

Circumstances of the natural parents

In chapter 3 the categories devised by the Home Office for analysing the reasons children were received into public care were applied to

156

the private foster children. This system is limited in that it attributes a single cause whereas in reality a number of factors are involved. Packman's research remedies this defect by detecting a variety of 'at risk' circumstances which tended – although not invariably – to be associated with reception into care. Here mention will be briefly made of eight factors identified by Packman (1968) and others as characterising parents of children in public care before determining whether the same were found amongst the parents of private foster children.

First, Packman and the Schaffers both found the natural parents to be disproportionately drawn from the lower social classes. Such parents, they argued, were not only more likely to lack the financial and accommodation resources needed to cope with children, but are more inclined to approach the statutory services when in need. Second, Packman recorded that 46 and 28 per cent of the mothers and fathers studied were under thirty years of age when their children entered care. She considered that younger couples were more vulnerable in times of crisis as they had had less time to build up economic resources. Third, she found that over 10 per cent of the parents were from outside the British Isles compared with 3·5 per cent for the population as a whole. She concluded that they had fewer relatives to sustain them when care was needed for their children. It must be interjected that, in addition, coloured parents would have greater difficulties in finding accommodation suitable for children.[2] Fourth, Packman drew attention to the status and location of the placing parents: 41 per cent were without the support of the other parent. This 'at risk' element in lone parenthood was confirmed by George's finding that even amongst legitimate children in care only a quarter had parents living together. Fifth, the Schaffers' work established that the parents of children received into short term care were significantly more likely to have been in their residence for under two years and to have moved more frequently than a control group who continued caring for their children. In Packman's study 16 and 14 per cent of the mothers and fathers respectively had been living in their local authority for under two years. As their geographical mobility seems higher than for the population as a whole (Packman, 1968, p. 57) it is suggested that mobile families were 'at risk' in that they did not have time to form supportive relationships in the community.

Sixth, Packman's finding that the natural parents were in housing conditions far inferior to the population as a whole confirms that inadequate housing or difficulties in finding accommodation contributes to the break-up of families. She reported that at the time of reception into care, 8 per cent were living in one room (compared with 2 per cent in the general population) and 6 per cent in two rooms (compared with 5 per cent). Their overcrowding, she thought, was explained by the fact that 31 per cent depended on private rented accommodation the weakest section of the housing market.

Seventh, Dinnage and Pringle have pointed out the risks associated with low income (1967a, p. 34). Parents in poverty lack the resources to purchase adequate housing or day care. Lastly, the large amount of research on the functions of kinship ties has led to the belief that parents of children received into public care have lacked ties with and therefore help from their families.[3] The Schaffers reported that the mothers of children received into care were less likely to have their mother still living than those in the control group. Those with live mothers were more likely to live further away and see less of them. In addition both mothers and fathers tended not to live near relatives. Only 28 per cent saw a relative daily compared with 49 per cent of the controls. Heinicke and Westheimer also found the availability of relatives an important factor in keeping children out of a residential nursery (1966, pp. 77–8).

The research outlined above establishes that 'at risk' factors, experienced singly or in combination, can place parents in circumstances where the only course of action is to place their children with the children's department. The question then arises as whether the parents of children placed privately were subject to similar factors and circumstances.

Social class

Sixty-three, that is 56·2 per cent, of the 112 parents whose occupations were known, were classified as students.[4] Clearly the natural parents of the private foster children were characterised by being students whereas the local authority contrast group had none. In order to facilitate comparison, the social class distribution is presented in Table 8.1 with the students excluded.[5]

The private natural parents were significantly more likely than their local authority counterparts to be in the higher social classes (dividing I–II/III/IV–V, $\chi^2 = 8·8138$, d.f. = 2, P = <0·025). This finding is partially attributable to numbers of unmarried mothers in nursing and secretarial posts who were not so marked in the contrast group. However, the bulk of parents in both groups were from the lower

Table 8.1 Social class of natural parents, where known, and excluding students

	Private No.	Private %	Local authority No.	Local authority %
I	2	4·1	0	0·0
II	6	12·2	3	4·2
III	18	36·7	18	25·0
IV	8	16·4	18	25·0
V	15	30·6	33	45·8
Totals	49	100·0	72	100·0

three classes while comparison with census material showed social class V to be particularly over-represented. Certainly, the evidence did not support Packman's beliefs that users of private foster homes would tend to come from the higher and richer classes (1968, p. 51). They, like the local authority parents, would tend to experience the 'at risk' factors associated with the lower social groupings.

Age of parents

Table 8.2 Age of natural parents of private foster children when child placed in foster home*

	Mothers No.	Mothers %	Fathers No.	Fathers %
Under 21 years	7	7·3	1	1·1
21 and under 25	50	52·1	27	29·0
25 and under 30	29	30·2	47	50·5
30 and under 40	10	10·4	16	17·2
40 and over	0	0·0	2	2·2
Totals	96	100·0	93	100·0
Dead	5	—	0	—
Not known	17	—	25	—

*It will be observed that the age-ranges employed for the natural parents differ slightly from those for foster parents. For instance, for the former it was '30 and under 40 years', for the latter, '31 to 40 years'. The explanation is that the research used the measures at each stage which facilitated comparison with previous research work.

It can be seen from Table 8.2 that of the parents of the private foster children whose ages were known, 89·6 per cent of the mothers and 80·6 per cent of the fathers were under thirty years of age at the time they made the placements. They therefore tended to be younger even than Packman's sample and were predominantly in the age groups which can be considered most vulnerable. The local authority natural parents, whose tabulation is not presented, were also predominantly under thirty. However, they were significantly more likely to be older than their private counterparts (dividing ages at under 30/31–40/41 and over, for the mothers, $\chi^2 = 8 \cdot 9705$, d.f. $= 2$, P $= <0 \cdot 025$, and for the fathers, $\chi^2 = 16 \cdot 405$, d.f. $= 2$, P $= <0 \cdot 001$).

Country of origin

The third 'at risk' factor concerned natural parents' country of origin. The nationality (which was their country of origin) of the pairs of parents of the private foster children is given in Table 8.3. Well

Table 8.3   Nationality of natural parents of private foster children

	No.	%
Both parents from United Kingdom	42	35·6
Both from West Indies	5	4·2
Both from West Africa	66	55·9
Both from Asia	0	0·0
One from Europe, one from elsewhere	2	1·7
Other	3	2·5
Totals	118	100·0

over half the natural parents were of West African, West Indian or mixed nationality and were hence likely to experience the disadvantages just outlined. Most strikingly, the proportion was far higher than that found in Packman's local authority sample. As pointed out, an attempt to match the private and local authority fosterings met with failure, a failure which underlines the far greater proportion of natural parents from abroad and in the private sector.

Status and location

Two pieces of information were relevant to assessing whether the natural parents were without the support of a partner. First, the legal relationship between the mother and father (see Table 8.4).

Table 8.4 Legal relationship between natural parents of the private foster children

	No.	%
Parents married to each other	84	71·8
Mother single, father married	9	7·7
Both parents single	13	11·1
Other (one parent divorced, the other widowed, married, single: father single, mother married, widowed, etc.)	11	9·4
Totals	117	100·0
Not known	1	—

Legal status does not reveal if the parents were actually together at the time the child was placed. So, second, it is necessary to supplement Table 8.4 with the information that of the 118 placing parents, forty, that is 33·9 per cent, were without the support of a partner when their child was put in the foster home. They were single women living alone or married persons whose partner had died, deserted or divorced. If the natural parents in the two areas studied are typical of those of private foster children elsewhere in the country, it is reasonable to conclude that they are much more likely than the population as a whole to suffer the disadvantages of lone parenthood. The natural parents in the local authority contrast group showed eighty-one out of 127 placing parents as being alone. They were thus significantly more likely to be in this position ($\chi^2 = 20·718$, d.f. $= 1$, $P = <0·001$).

So far, circumstances have been examined in which there was material available for nearly all the natural parents in the study. Information about the remaining factors could only be determined in respect of the twenty-nine parents of private foster children who were interviewed. Of these, twenty-one were students born in West Africa while the remaining eight were born in Britain or Eire (with the exception of one couple from Australasia). Because of the differences between these two sets of parents, results will be presented separately.

Mobility

The twenty-nine placing natural parents were questioned as to their length of residence and number of moves (see Tables 8.5 and 8.6). Over a third of the interviewed parents had lived for only two years or less in their area, a figure even higher than that for Packman's

Table 8.5   Length of time interviewed natural parents of private foster children had lived in their town or district when their child was placed

Years	West Africans	Other	Total
Up to 2	8	3	11
2–5	11	3	14
Over 5	2	2	4
Totals	21	8	29

Table 8.6   Number of moves experienced by interviewed natural parents of private foster children since the birth of their first child

Moves	West Africans	Other	Total
None	0	0	0
1–3	15	4	19
4–10	6	3	9
11 or more	0	1	1
Totals	21	8	29

parents, while only a minority had resided there for over five years. Remembering that they tended to be the parents of very young children so that the time in which they had made their moves was short, it can be seen that they also had a high rate of moving. Indeed, over a third had moved four or more times. Thus amongst the twenty-nine parents there was a definite record of frequent moves and newness to areas so that probably in time of need they were unlikely to have made local contacts which would prove helpful in relation to caring for children.

Housing conditions

The interview schedule for the natural parents of the private foster children was designed to collect material on the tenure, age and density of occupation of the conditions of the natural parents. A problem, however, was whether people who tended to be mobile could be expected to remember accurately the conditions under which they lived at the time their children were placed. It was decided therefore to collect information on their present conditions for not only would this be readily available, but, in view of the fact that their children were no longer with them and some had higher incomes because they were free to work, was not likely to be worse than at the time of separation.

Table 8.7   Tenure type of dwellings of interviewed natural parents of private foster children

	West African	Other	Total
Owner-occupied house	3	1	4
Private rented flat	2	5	7
Private rented rooms	15	0	15
Local authority house	0	1	1
Other	1	1	2
Totals	21	8	29

With over three-quarters of the parents in private rented accommodation (see Table 8.7), it is no surprise that twenty-six, that is over 88 per cent, were in dwellings built before 1914, 55·2 per cent in room densities of over 1½ per room, and 69 per cent in bedroom densities of over two persons (Tables not given). Comparison with figures given earlier confirms that not only did their conditions tend to be worse than the population as a whole but also than the parents of local authority children in Packman's study.

Financial income

Low income, it was explained, was a factor associated with parents ceding their children to public care. But what is low income? In 1967 the average male wage in manufacturing industries was under £22 per week.[6] In the same year it was stated that 90·6 per cent of male manual workers earned £15 and over, the figure including payments for overtime and being recorded before deductions.[7] A mother with a child under five and a rent of £2 10s. would have received a minimum of £8 1s. from social security benefits. The income of the natural parents can be compared with these levels. As with accommodation, income was assessed as at the time of the interview.

The figures shown in Table 8.8 require some explanation. For eighteen of the West African parents the income represents the joint income of two working parents. In one of the eight 'other' cases it was also a joint income. It can be seen that nine, that is almost a third of the natural parents, were in receipt of under £15 per week. Amongst the West Africans, seventeen were receiving £15 or more but these were couples with two incomes. Had the woman cared for the child and not worked the majority would have received under £15. Even so, most of the parents received less than the average manufacturing wage.

Table 8.8   Weekly income (net) of interviewed natural parents of private foster children

	West African	Other	Total
Under £5	1	1	2
£5 and under £10	2	0	2
£10 and under £15	1	4	5
£15 and under £20	11	1	12
£20 and over	6	1	7
Not known	0	1	1
Totals	21	8	29

Availability of relatives

The relationship between the natural parents and their relatives was examined in relation to their own parents and their siblings, that is the relatives most likely to offer help. The questions established whether they did possess these relatives, how near they lived at the time their child was put in a foster home, and how often they had contact with them at the time of the interview. They were formulated around approaches used in former kinship research in order to facilitate comparability (see Table 8.9).

Table 8.9   Contact between interviewed natural parents of the private foster children and their own parents

When last seen	Mother			Father		
	West African	Other	Total	West African	Other	Total
0–1 month	0	3	3	0	1	1
1–6 months	0	0	0	0	0	0
6–12 months	1	3	4	1	0	1
More	17	2	19	16	0	16
Parent dead	3	0	3	4	7	11
Totals	21	8	29	21	8	29

Although dealing with very small numbers, it is worth noting the tendency for little contact with parents when compared with the generally frequent contact found in studies of normal populations. Amongst the West Africans contact was negligible and even amongst the 'others', only three had seen their mothers within the previous six months while only one still had a father alive.

An even more striking lack of contact is found with parental in-laws. Amongst the West Africans none had seen either in-law for at least twelve months. Amongst the eight 'others', again none had seen in-laws. This is partially explained by the fact that three of the mothers-in-law and six of the eight fathers-in-law were dead.

It has emerged that death of a parent or in-law is one reason why there could be no help from that quarter in time of need. The general lack of contact is further explained by how far away the living relatives resided. All the parents and parental in-laws of the West Africans lived abroad. Interestingly, in the eight 'other' cases distance was also a general problem. Taking both parents and in-laws into account there were only two examples (both mothers) where they lived in the same town or district as the placing parents at the time the child was put in a foster home.

Contacts with siblings are conveyed in Table 8.10. It can be seen

Table 8.10   Contact between interviewed natural parents of the private foster children and their own siblings

When a sibling last seen	West African	Other	Total
0–1 month	6	3	9
1–6 months	2	0	2
6–12 months	1	2	3
More	11	2	13
Has no siblings	1	1	2
Totals	21	8	29

that at the time of the interviews, less than half of the placing parents had seen a sibling within six months. Again the explanation partly rests on distance. For thirteen of the West Africans their nearest sibling was abroad with only four having a sibling in the same town or district. Amongst the eight 'others', four had a nearest sibling who lived over a hundred miles away and only two had one in their town or district.

Similarly, only a third of the West Africans and only one of the 'others' had seen a sibling-in-law within the previous twelve months. Again this is partially explicable by a lack of siblings-in-law and the distance they lived away. Amongst the West Africans, for thirteen the nearest sibling-in-law was abroad while only five had one in the same town or district. Amongst the 'others' half had no relatives of this kind and of the remainder only one had a sibling-in-law within a hundred miles.

To sum up. The twenty-nine interviewed natural parents showed little of the close kinship ties, as expressed in amount of contact and nearness of residence, which earlier studies have reported in well established and stable communities. It follows that when in need of help in regard to their children they would be unlikely to receive it from within their families and would have to turn outside to the social services or to non-relatives.

The investigation has made it possible to establish some of the circumstances and characteristics of the natural parents of private foster children. They tended to be West African students or parents from the lower social classes, mostly under thirty years of age at the time of placement, and with numbers without the support of a partner. Further, some evidence suggested they were geographically mobile, in poor housing conditions, in receipt of low incomes and with few contacts with relatives. These circumstances served to sharply distinguish them from parents in the population as a whole. In addition, these natural parents, it is clear, had as few resources when in time of need, as many pressures, and as many 'at risk' circumstances as the natural parents of children received into the care of local authorities. The question that follows is why were their children put in private foster homes instead of some other form of care, in particular why were they not received into care by the children's departments? Some answers will be sought in an examination of the various types of natural parents.

Classification of natural parents

The collection of data, especially that relating to nationality, occupation and reasons for separation, enabled the parents of the private foster children to be classified into four main groupings. Their numbers along with comparable figures for the parents of the local authority children are shown in Table 8.11. A close examination will be made of each grouping.

Over half the private parents were West African students. The extent of their domination of the private fostering field is shown by the fact that the next largest grouping, unmarried mothers, totalled only 15·3 per cent. Amongst the sixteen 'others' were two who placed their children because they could not find accommodation and three fathers who did so when their wives were absent due to illness.

The local authority figures serve to show the dissimilarities and

Table 8.11   Classification of natural parents of the foster children

	Private		Local authority	
	No.	%	No.	%
West African students	64	54·2	0	0·0
Unmarried mothers	18	15·3	32	25·2
Deserted mothers	10	8·5	5	3·9
Deserted fathers	10	8·5	17	13·4
Other	16	13·6	73	57·5
Totals	118	100·0	127	100·0

similarities between the two types of parents. They included no West African students and fewer deserted mothers. Unmarried mothers and deserted fathers appeared in both types of fostering (although in greater proportions in the local authority section) and again the question is raised why were some helped by the local authority and others not? Finally, the large category 'other' needs breaking down. It consisted of seven parents who abandoned their children, fourteen who were without accommodation, twenty-seven where the mother was ill and the father unable to care and twenty-five parents who fell into a number of smaller categories such as rejecting mothers (those who completely rejected their children), rejecting husbands (especially where they reject stepchildren), and parents who could not cope with children.

West African students

The West African students made up the largest proportion of the parents. The word students as used here means that their child was placed in order to allow the parents to study. Not all were full-time students. Some had taken jobs to finance their studies. Frequently the wives were in paid employment so freeing their husbands to attend college all day, while the wives went to evening classes.

It is common to hear the assertion that West Africans place their children in foster homes because they want to study while their cultural background makes fostering acceptable to them. Of their high motivation towards education and qualifications there can be little doubt. The West Africans interviewed in the present study revealed a determination to succeed whatever the cost, reinforced by a fear of returning to Africa without a qualification. As one student put it, 'To some it seems impossible that we should put study before children. But we Nigerians feel that study should come first.' The cultural aspect of fostering will be discussed in a moment but given the high motivation towards study the question is raised, why do the wives not care for the children while their husbands pursue their studies?

The part of the wife

Three reasons may contribute to the wives' decisions not to remain at home caring for the children. First, they too may wish to gain a qualification, indeed, in the eyes of some West Africans it would be a neglect of family duty to miss the educational opportunities available in this country. Second, most of the students could not afford accommodation spacious enough for both children and study. In some cases also, the parents had been subject to pressure from their landlord to get rid of the child or had been offered accommodation – within their price range – only if they had no children. One couple, living in one room with a combined income of £700 per annum, said, 'We don't want to bring children up in squalor, rather that they were fostered.' In these circumstances the woman thought it best that she earned some money to put her child in a 'decent' environment while her husband was studying.

Third, and probably decisively, the West African couples needed a source of income. Some had come to Britain backed by grants from their own country or families but a number of factors could make these insufficient. The grants could prove to be unrealistically low in the face of the high cost of living in Britain. In other cases they dried up altogether as the students found that it took far longer to qualify than they had anticipated. The civil war in Nigeria meant that Biafran students lost the source of their income, that is their government ceased paying or their families found it impossible to send money out of Nigeria. Whatever the reasons, the West African couples tended to lack a financial income sufficient to allow one spouse to study full-time and the other to mind their child. Consequently, the mother usually worked in order to raise the money for the husband to study and if she worked care had to be sought for their child.

West African fostering

Even if mothers work, however, it does not necessarily follow that their children are fostered. Many working mothers place their off-spring in some form of daily care, taking them back when they return from work. Why did the West Africans not do this? The usual explanation is that fostering is so much a part of life in West Africa that it is natural for West Africans to continue its practice when abroad. It is also implied that their background means that West Africans are not aware of the risks of emotional deprivation arising from parental separation. June Ellis (1971) after describing some adverse private foster homes asks, 'Why is it that presumably intelligent parents put their children at risk in this way?' Yudkin queries whether they so take substitute care for granted that the concept of parental deprivation has little meaning to them (1967, p. 51).

The cultural explanation of the readiness to foster does not, however, stand up to close examination. It is true that fostering is a widespread although by no means universal practice amongst some West African tribes.[8] However, there are three major differences between British and West African fostering. First, West African fostering is by relatives or kinfolk. The anthropologist Goody states: 'The institutionalised pattern is for a daughter of the marriage to go to a father's sister and a son to the mother's brother' (1970, p. 53). Second, fostering in West Africa does not usually occur in the child's early years but later. Thus amongst the Gonja tribe a boy would go to his relatives at about the age of six to eight and remain with them until his marriage (Goody, 1970, p. 53). Third, it is frequently voluntary not 'need' fostering. That is, the parents choose to send the child to foster parents because he will benefit from their training not because *they* need to be free of him. By contrast, fostering in Britain is with non-relatives, is in the early years of a child's life with the intention of returning to the natural parents, and is of a need nature, the parents needing to be free to study.

The interviews with the twenty-one West Africans gave further grounds for doubting the view that they automatically turn to fostering. Thus twelve of the couples stated that if they had remained in their own country, their child would not have been fostered. Further, when asked if given a free choice, in which way they would like their child cared for, twelve of the twenty-one indicated they wanted the child at home all the time with them. 'I was forced to place in a foster home', said one West African, 'but I don't want to, all Nigerians are very fond of their children.' When asked if they thought separation from parents harmed a child, eight replied that it did, eleven said it depended on the quality of the foster parents and the amount of parental contact, and only two thought it did no harm. One parent replied, 'Yes definitely ... a child may be harmed psychologically but it depends on the type of foster home. We feel he [their child] hasn't been harmed. . . . The child could be harmed if he has a lot of different foster homes. The parents should look after the child if possible.'

Amongst the twenty-one West Africans, then, fostering was by no means a practice entered upon as part of a normal life routine. Neither were they unaware of the dangers inherent in fostering. Taken in conjunction with the established differences between fostering in West Africa and Britain, it can be concluded that the placing of children by West African students in British foster homes is not just an extension of a practice common in their home culture. This is not to say that familiarity with fostering does not influence the West African students. Probably their knowledge of it makes them more ready to consider using it when they find themselves needing help. But if cultural overlag is not the sole explanation why they turn to foster homes then clearly some other reasons must be given.

Other forms of care

The question remains, if the West African mothers had to work why did they not choose some other form of care apart from private fostering? Two alternatives must be considered. First, day care for instance by relatives, by day nurseries, or by daily-minders. Day care involves the children being cared for by a person other than the mother and father for a part of the day but returning to the parents for the evening and night. Second, other forms of full-time care such as fostering or residential care provided by the local authority or voluntary children's societies.

The section on availability of relatives pointed out that in Britain, a couple's own parents often provide help for their children. It also showed that the interviewed natural parents often lived far away from and saw little of relatives. None the less, the West Africans were further asked why the husband or wife's relatives had not helped. Most said their relatives lived at least one hundred miles away (in most cases being abroad). Of the few relatives who were within a hundred miles, two reasons were given why they could not help, the relatives were usually students who were also seeking care for their children or they were in poor housing conditions having no room for extra children. It can be concluded, therefore, that relatives could not be a source of help for most of the students.

Local authority day nurseries are a popular means of caring for the children of working mothers. My own study of unsupported mothers found them the primary choice of most of those who needed or wanted to work (1970a, p. 25). Yet they are unlikely to be of help to the children of West African students. The distribution of day nurseries varies from local authority to local authority in some there being none at all.[9] Even in those places where there is a comparatively large number, the demand still tends to be greater than supply with the consequent development of a system of 'priority' places for the children of unsupported parents. Children whose parents are living together and able to work are likely to be classed as non-priority cases hence having even less chance of securing a place. However, even if the West African students did obtain a place they might find that day nurseries close too early so that some working mothers cannot get to them in time. In fact, of the twenty-one interviewed couples, only three had approached a day nursery. One found the hours unsuitable and did not apply for a vacancy, one was told they were not eligible and one was still on the waiting list after two years. However, it was obvious that many of the students were ignorant of the existence of day nurseries.

If day nursery places are hard to obtain, daily-minders, as the Yudkin report shows, are not. They are defined by the Health Service and Public Health Act (1968) as women who look after a child for more than two hours a day for money. Research by Gregory (1969) supports the allegation of Yudkin that many minders are of poor quality, providing overcrowded conditions and unstimulating experiences. Some of the interviewed parents did mention unhappy experiences with minders but they were not used for two major reasons. First, and this applies equally to other forms of day care, they entail the children returning in the evening to the same housing deprivations and serving to distract parents in the hours they wish to study. Second, daily-minding tends to be more expensive than private fostering, despite the fact that the former involves care only in the day time while the latter gives full-time care. In chapter 5, it was shown that the weekly fee for most private foster children was between £1 10s. and £3, the same range which Yudkin states is charged for the daily-minded (1967, p. 5). But in addition the parents of the latter provide the cost of keeping their children in the evenings and weekends as well as supplying all the clothes. To West African students, who are short of cash, daily-minding may thus prove too expensive as well as more inconvenient.

Failing day care, the West African students could consider three other types of full-time care – private children's homes or schools, care provided by the local authority children's departments and that by voluntary societies. Private schools and homes would be not only far too expensive but usually do not provide care in the long school holidays. What of the local authority children's departments? Ten of the twenty-one interviewed West Africans had approached their local department. Of these, three had definitely asked for their children to be received into public care and had been refused. The others had gone to the departments more tentatively and were mostly given advice on how to advertise for private foster homes or even given the address of what the child care officer considered reliable private foster parents. The file records confirmed that the practice of advising West Africans to advertise for private foster parents was not uncommon. Similarly, it was clear that the departments as a policy refused to regard West African studentship as a reason for receiving into care. Thus the two departments in the study had received no children into care for this reason, while the *Summary of Local Authorities' Returns of Children in Care* does not even accord it a category. Clearly, children's officers do not interpret the Children Act (1948) as covering the need to study. Again, the main voluntary children's societies such as Dr Barnardo's and the National Children's Home will not take children in order to free parents to study.

To conclude: West African parents wishing to study found that day care was unsuitable while they did not qualify to be helped (by the provision of care) by either the statutory or voluntary children's bodies. Therefore, regardless of their cultural experience of fostering, the circumstances of the parents meant that private fostering was the only alternative available to them. The relevant hypothesis was upheld. Even finding a private foster home, however, was by no means easy, indeed, 42 per cent of the West African student parents had London addresses at the time of placement and the impression given is that difficulties in finding foster homes had forced them to look much further afield.

The influence of cultural background

It has been argued that experiences of fostering in their homeland do not fully explain why West African students turned to private fostering. However, this is not to say that attitudes and values brought from their homes did not influence them in regard to the children and fostering.[10] Three examples are offered to show the influence. First, the readiness of the wives to take paid employment to support the student husbands may reflect the common practice, which Ellis (1971) notes, of women working in much of West Africa. Second, the values of the home society explain why couples were prepared to have children while students. This practice is sometimes said, it was even conveyed by child care officers, to be irresponsible. Yudkin even wondered if the students were failing to use contraceptives (1967, p. 51). In fact, children are so valued, convey such social prestige, that to most West Africans studentship is not considered a reason for not having them. Kaye's study of Ghana (1962) noted, 'Childless adults have little or no social status; they are not invited nor expected to comment on public affairs.' In the light of this back-ground, it is hardly surprising that nineteen of the twenty-one inter-viewed West Africans declared themselves pleased at the birth of their child while only two regretted the difficulties it might entail. Again of the twenty-one, only four had used any form of birth control. To most the very idea was offensive: 'The Yorubas have no planning a family,' said one, 'Sex is for reproduction so no birth control is practised.' Statements of this nature serve to illustrate Ellis's con-clusion that West Africans consider it a duty to carry on their line and regard deliberate refusal to have children as 'immoral'. She continued: 'Considerations like these may be more important for the parents of a student and may lead them to urge their son or daughter to start a family even when studying abroad.'

Third, although fostering is by no means automatic in West Africa, is within kinfolk and occurs at a later age than in Britain, it con-stitutes the students' frame of reference about the subject. It seems likely, therefore, that their expectations of fostering will stem from the very different type of fostering practised in their own country. These expectations may well differ from those of the British foster parents and hence be a source of conflict. For instance, Goody points out that in West Africa the purpose of fostering is the training or education of the child rather than the provision of substitute parents (1970, p. 60). At least some of the West African students regarded fostering in Britain in the same light. On the other hand, most foster parents saw their role as parental or substitute parental in which they emphasised love and affection rather than training. Similarly, in West Africa, foster parents are expected to be 'strict' with their charges; spoiling, as Ellis says, is looked upon with disfavour and is the prerogative of the natural parents not the foster parents. Thus, as Goody explains, the fostering relationship is 'an additive one, not replacing that between parents and children, but experienced as something different and additional to it'. It follows that natural parents train the children and have the right 'to interfere should things not go well' (1970, p. 72). The case records showed a number of instances where the West African natural parents were transferring these patterns into their concept of private fostering, were 'supervising' the placements, and evaluated them in terms of training, being particularly critical of 'soft' foster parents. The foster parents resented the 'advice', regarding themselves as quite capable of raising the child as part of their family.

Case examples

Two case examples will conclude the section on West African students:

a   The grant of a Nigerian accountancy student in London had long since run out following a number of examination failures. His wife earned £10 a week as a typist and studied in the evening. This low income meant they lived in one room with a shared kitchen. Following the birth of their first child they tried various forms of care. A daily-minder had provided poor quality care while the child's presence in the evenings hindered study. They looked for a day nursery but the nearest one, two miles distant, was too far away. The parents then approached the local children's department who said there were no reasons why they should take the child. Relatives could not help as they were in Nigeria. Consequently, they turned to private fostering, placing their child in a foster home in the Midlands to which they were recommended. Their second child was also placed in a foster home in the same area.

b   Following the outbreak of the Nigerian civil war, a student husband returned there leaving his wife and three children in Britain. Presumably he was killed: she never heard of him again. Without any income, the wife took the children from their foster homes into her single room. She approached the children's department where she was directed to the Ministry of Social Security. An official gave her £8 and told her to find work. The mother then returned to the children's department for help with caring for the children. The office sent her to the health department but officials here could not find her a day nursery place or a daily-minder. Her studies were at an early stage and she was able only to obtain a low waged unskilled job while she changed to evening studies. She sought and found three foster homes prepared to accept her children at very low rates of payment. Even so, having paid for them and her accommodation she had almost no money remaining at the end of the week. She was friendless, facing many years of study to gain a qualification, with little chance of increasing her income and without any prospect of saving sufficient money to take her family back to Nigeria.

Unmarried mothers

Unmarried mothers appear to arrange for the care of their children in four main ways. First, by placing them for adoption. In 1967, 18,313 of 22,802 legally adopted children were illegitimate. Not all were the children of unmarried mothers and, in some cases, married couples were adopting the extra-marital child of one of the partners. None the less, it is certain that many were the children of unmarried mothers being taken by other couples.[11] Second, by the children being received into public care. In the year ending 31 March 1968, 3,157 children were so received because 'child illegitimate, mother unable to provide'. Third, by retaining the child within the mother's family. Some unmarried mothers marry, co-habit or return to live with their own parents and incorporate the child into the new family unit. Fourth, by caring for the child on their own. The Plowden Report showed that amongst children of primary school-age, 4 per cent were living with their natural mother only (Central Advisory Council for Education, 1967, vol. 2, p. 105). Not all of these children were illegitimate, some were the legitimate offspring of broken marriages. Amongst the unmarried mothers, some go to work leaving their child, if under five, in some form of daily care. Others remain at home living on social security benefits.

If most unmarried mothers use one of the above ways, it is clear that few turn to private fostering. My own studies (1970a) and those of Wimperis found very small percentages using it. In the present study, eighteen parents, 15·3 per cent of the total, were unmarried mothers who, having never received support from the putative father, placed their illegitimate children in private foster homes while they went to work. Remembering that this form of care is not usually chosen by unmarried mothers, the present study will attempt to investigate why they used it rather than other alternatives.

G

Why use private foster homes?

Given that the eighteen mothers did not want to place their children for adoption, that is, they wanted to retain their legal rights over them, they could have drawn social security and remained at home with their children. It is not known why they decided instead to go out to work but previous studies of unmarried mothers suggest three reasons. First, their income from state benefits would have been so low as to make life hardly tolerable. Second, my researches and also those of Marsden found that unmarried mothers tend to live in overcrowded conditions with poor amenities which serve as an additional inducement to spend much of the day out of them. Third, their need for social intercourse, in contrast to being cooped up with a child all day, constitutes another powerful reason.

Unmarried mothers who go out to work will usually require some form of day care for their children. However, some mothers find it is not as available or convenient as might be thought. The shortage and erratic distribution of local authority day nurseries has already been mentioned. The same situation applies to nursery schools, the Seebohm Report pointing out that less than 6 per cent of children under five in England and Wales received nursery education. Unsupported mothers can probably expect priority treatment in getting places from day nurseries and nursery schools, yet it appears that even the number of priority cases exceeds supply. Like West African students, unmarried mothers do not find it easy to find day care and it is worth recording that Davies's study of a number of local authorities found a relationship between high numbers of private foster children and low numbers of day nurseries (1968, p. 244). Of course, daily-minders are frequently available but they prove expensive while some of the unmarried mothers in the study had clearly themselves been unimpressed by the quality of their care. Next, day care amenities may be difficult to reach and open for only limited hours. My own study of unsupported mothers revealed that over 15 per cent of those working had to spend over an hour a day travelling to and from the day care amenity. Not only did such travel involve extra costs in fare, it could make for great difficulties in reaching – after work – nursery schools which closed at 3.30 p.m. or day nurseries at 6 p.m. Similarly, some of the unmarried mothers in the study commented on the inconvenient hours of day nurseries. For women whose occupation involved shift or evening work, the chances of finding suitable day care were even more remote. In fact, a majority of the eighteen unmarried mothers were in jobs requiring shift work, night work, or long hours – bus conductress, auxiliary nurse, nurse, health visitor, being examples.

Finally, in regard to day care, why did the unmarried mothers not receive help from the relatives? They were mostly born in the United Kingdom and unlike the West Africans would not have most of their relatives abroad. Four reasons are postulated why relatives were not used. First, a number of the mothers came from broken homes and had never known or had lost contact with their relatives. Second, some had never had any contact with the relatives of the putative fathers. Third, some mothers had been disowned by their families following the illegitimate birth. In one case, the girl's parents urged her to take out a court order on the putative father and, when she refused, cut off their contact with her. Fourth, a few mothers wished to hide the fact of the birth from their relatives.

Some unmarried mothers either cannot find day care or else find it unsuitable to their needs. Accordingly they turn to full-time care. But why did they not seek reception into care by the children's department? Packman discovered that some children's officers were reluctant to take illegitimate children but the Home Office figures already quoted show that large numbers are received into care. Only one of the unmarried mothers had asked for reception into care. It seemed that most mothers had been ignorant of the role of the children's department while others had feared that officials would take away their parental rights over their children. They turned, therefore, to private fostering. The hypothesis that a number of children would be placed by unmarried mothers who wanted to work and had no choice but a private foster home, was upheld.

Case examples

a The mother in question came from a broken home and was brought up by a relative. She was doing intermittent work as a film extra, when her child was born. Her landlord was not willing to accommodate the child and for the first three weeks of the baby's life she tried daily-minders who proved inadequate. Finally she left the accommodation and, in desperate straits, spent the night with her baby in a launderette. Here a person she met gave her the name of a woman who might foster the baby.

b A nursing orderly had an illegitimate daughter by a professional man who was staying temporarily in Britain. Determined to qualify as a nurse she found difficulty in caring for her child. Her mother and only sibling lived over a hundred miles away and little contact was maintained. The father's relatives were all abroad. She managed to find a daily-minder but could pay only the lowest fees out of her wage of £12 a month. The minder proved unsatisfactory as she was unwilling to care in the evenings (when the mother was on shifts) or when the baby was ill. The mother also explained how exhausting it was to return home after a day's work and have both to cope with a child and try to study. She enquired about a day nursery but decided its hours were too limited. Eventually she placed the daughter in a private foster home. At the time of the research the child had reached her teens. The now qualified nurse said how satisfied she was with the foster parents yet, at the same time, was saddened that she was now referred to as 'auntie' with her daughter calling the foster parents 'mummy' and 'daddy'. 'I'm now only the piggy bank' she commented ruefully. Having achieved a position where she could afford to have the girl back, she found her daughter opted to stay with the foster parents.

   c   A clerical worker, pregnant by a married man, had wanted to keep the child. This proved financially impossible. Unwilling to pursue an affiliation order in case it broke up the man's marriage and unable to bear the 'shame' of national assistance, she looked for day care while she went out to work. Her relatives were too elderly or too disapproving to help and other day care was not accessible. Knowing nothing of the children's department, she tramped the streets for a foster home commenting, 'I couldn't live through it again. I had to find a foster home, look after my parents who had had a stroke, and find a new job.' Eventually she obtained foster parents who gave the child affection for many years. Acknowledging this, the mother, who possessed artistic skills, still regretted that the foster home did not develop the child's abilities. 'The child is well fed, gets love', she said, 'but it's not the background I want for her. I've been there two hundred and fifty times and the TV has never gone off while I've been there. There are no books, it's not the culture I want.' Even more poignantly, she admitted she had lost her daughter. 'She accepts me but not as a mother. . . . At some date I would like to have her with me but I know in my heart this will not happen.'

Deserted mothers

Ten mothers, with eleven children in the sample, had been deserted by their husbands (or co-habitees) following a period of living together. The mothers subsequently went out to work placing their children in private foster homes.

Studies of deserted wives usually compare and contrast their position with unmarried mothers. Like unmarried mothers they have to decide whether to stay at home living from social security income or to go out to work with the associated problem of finding day care if their children are under five. Marsden's study of unsupported mothers (1969) reveals that usually the deserted wife is in a better material position than the unmarried mother. The chances of receiving voluntary payments are greater from deserting husbands than putative fathers while court orders usually fix a higher rate for husbands with some years in an established job than young putative fathers (if they are known). Further, the years spent with the husband have probably resulted in better accommodation than that of a young woman who has not co-habited as well as leading to the development of relationships between the children and relatives who might help in a time of need. Not least, at the moment of desertion, the wife's children may be above school age and less of a problem in terms of day care. By contrast, the unmarried mother deserted by the putative father is faced with the demands of a pre-school child.

The more advantageous position of the deserted wife leads to the expectation that they would have less recourse to private foster homes. But the deserted mothers in the present study were not typical, in fact, they possessed similar characteristics to the unmarried mothers. First, they were in the same age-range. Most of the unmarried mothers in this study, as in Marsden's, were under thirty when placing their child. Amongst the deserted wives, all but one were also under thirty whereas in Marsden's work they were spread over a much wider age-range, namely twenty-one to forty years. It follows that the deserted wives in the present study tended not to have the material advantages, in terms of accommodation and higher income, which usually accrue from a longer relationship with a husband. Second, they had young children. All the unmarried mothers using private foster homes had children under five at the time of placement. Similarly, all but one of those placed by the deserted wives were in the pre-school age-range. Marsden found that his unmarried mothers largely had pre-school children but that other categories of 'mother alone' had more chance of older children. Thus the deserted wives in the present study faced the extra difficulty of arranging care for the under-fives if they wanted to work. Third, the deserted wives like the unmarried mothers appeared to have few contacts with their relatives. The build-up of relationships with parents and in-laws that marks the development of many marriages had not occurred. Fourth, they also tended to have occupations – such as entertainers and nurses – which did not fit in with the hours of most day care agencies.

The deserted wives needing to work and unable to find suitable day care did, in some cases, approach the children's departments. But, as shown in the Home Office figures, 'desertion by the father' is not a major category under which children come into public care. Once a relationship has existed with the father, children's departments expect the mother to go on caring even if the father leaves and even if she feels that her occupation or other circumstances require full-time care. The unwillingness of authorities to give help does not remove the intention of the mothers to find that care. They therefore turned to private fostering.

Case examples

a   A young woman was deserted by her co-habitee at the birth of their child. She recounted that the National Assistance Board turned her away: 'They said I looked too smart to need help.' With work a necessity, she needed care for the baby; her family was in Eire, she had never met the father's folks, and she knew nobody in the town, having lived there under a year. As no landlord would rent her a room she applied for the child to be received into public care. The children's department refused and advised a private foster home. The mother managed to find one and an unskilled job for herself. Sixteen years later the child was still in the same foster home. The mother had kept regular contact and commented that she wished she had known about day nurseries before she parted with her girl.

b   One of the interviewed natural mothers, a dancer, married a man successful in the field of entertainment. He deserted shortly before the birth of their son, leaving his wife in an area she had lived in for only six months. She had, she said, 'no money, no job, and nowhere to live.' Her own mother was in a mental hospital, her father refused to help. She had no siblings and had never met her husband's family. She wanted to continue her career which was one which would not fit in with the limited hours of day care amenities. She approached the children's department who found her a private foster home, so enabling her to resume and succeed in her career.

Deserted fathers

Ten of the fathers who had placed thirteen of the private foster children, were men whose wives had deserted (or died). In general their initial reaction was to find daily care for their children, most of whom were under five, in order to preserve as much of the family life as possible. Probably many men in this predicament would receive help from relatives but a notable characteristic of these men – most of whom were born in the United Kingdom – was the absence of relatives. Some then considered day care by non-relatives and were faced with its difficulties or non-availability as already described. Indeed, the fact that men often work longer hours and have jobs which involve travelling made it even harder to find day care agencies or minders with hours flexible enough for their wants.

A few fathers then contemplated staying at home to care for their children. Those who did experienced not only a drop in income but the disapproval of social security officials. The attitude of the latter reinforced the men's own uneasiness at not having paid employment which, coupled with the inability of some to fulfil a domestic role, meant that none persisted. Consequently the ten fathers, usually reluctantly, turned to full-time care.

Given that the fathers determined on full-time care, the question is raised why the children's department did not help them. Indeed, in the year ending 31 March 1968, local authorities in England and Wales received 5,188 children because the mother had deserted and the father was unable to care, and 838 because of the death of the mother. In the present study, two fathers wanted to make their own arrangements, strongly resenting any notion of official help. Three fathers found that arrangements were made around them by friends, but in any case, were probably ignorant of the role of the children's departments. But five of the fathers had asked that their seven children be taken into care. The reason usually given for refusing the application was that the fathers were capable of making their own arrangements. These fathers, also, then had no choice but to use private foster homes.

It cannot be denied that the fathers were able to find foster homes themselves. Indeed the situation of the deserted husband often appeared to provoke a response in neighbours and friends who either offered to look after his children or else did not like to refuse when asked. The danger is that their response was an emotional reaction to the father's distressing circumstances with the foster parents having no real need or desire to take a child. With the passage of time the lack of motivation becomes evident; thus a child care officer commented in her file on a private foster home, 'the foster parents knew the father when the mother died and took the child out of sympathy' and 'do not wish to keep him permanently.' The insecurity of the situation was perceived by and affected the foster child. Again, it can be seen in the following foster mother's account of why she fostered that the motive was not strong:

> 'We didn't like to have a foster child. We happened to get to know her parents socially. The children asked to come for weekends which became routine and when the mother went the children asked to come. We just accepted it as something that had got to be done.'

Paradoxically, another difficulty of the circumstances placement is that the foster parents' affection for the child grows to the extent that they want to exclude the natural father. In one case, the father wanted the foster parents – his friends – to provide care until the boy was old enough to attend school at which point he would have him back. The foster parents agreed but in time found they wanted him as a permanent member of their family. The father, genuinely fearful of losing his child's affection, at the same time began to play upon the foster parents' fears by paying irregularly and threatening to remove the boy if they objected. It can be readily perceived that although the fathers were able to find private placements they were not necessarily ones which proved capable of meeting the needs of themselves or their children.

Case examples

a   Following his wife's desertion, a husband stayed at home to care for his children. The condemnation of officials of the National Assistance Board, who threatened to cut off his benefits, forced him back to work. He placed one child with a private foster mother with seven children of her own and well known to the NSPCC, and the other with a family he knew. At the same time a request to the children's department to help was refused on the grounds that the father could make his own arrangements. Within three months he had to move the first child to another foster home. This arrangement broke down within a week while another request to the children's department was again rebuffed. The girl was then put with private foster parents whose application to become foster parents for the local authority had been turned down as 'highly undesirable'. The girl now displayed such behavioural problems that the children's department did receive her into a children's home. Within six months the problems diminished and the department discharged her to the father who promptly placed her with the same foster mother. Next the foster mother decided to emigrate and herself placed the girl with another foster home. Meanwhile the other child had remained with her original foster parents.

   b   A struggling musician and a stripper/hostess married and agreed to find different occupations. The wife's return to the world of entertainment provoked conflict and eventually she left to live with another man. The husband sought care for their son in his locality. His relatives, including his mother, lived in the town but would not help as they were in paid employment. The mother's relatives, the father said, were unwilling to help. Daily-minding proved unsatisfactory as the father's hours in a shop were from eight in the morning to six in the evening while, when the minder was ill or on holiday, he had to take time off work to cope. A search for a day nursery was abortive, the town not possessing one. The father then turned to the children's department who refused to help, the father reporting the officer as saying: 'The child has two parents who are both all right and earning.' Eventually the boy was placed in a private foster home.

The study has demonstrated, first, that the natural parents of private foster children experienced the circumstances which precipitate family break-ups at least as much as those of local authority foster children and, second, that many turned to private fostering only because there was no alternative. The overriding question to emerge is why the children's departments did not act either to prevent the children leaving their parents or to receive them into public care, as they did with the children of other parents. Obviously, some of the parents had not known of the existence of the children's departments. Others preferred to make their own arrangements. Yet the case clearly showed that others had approached and been rebuffed by the departments.

   The Children and Young Persons Act (1963) and the Children Act (1948) are the main determinants of the work of the children's departments. The former authorises aid to families where a child is in danger of being brought before a court or taken into care. Throughout the study no examples were found of departments using the Act to prevent a child going to a private foster home even where the home seemed highly unsuitable and unlikely to last long. In other words, it was not children in danger of being separated from their parents who qualified for preventive work but only those whose separation was likely to result in their being taken into public care or brought before a court.

The Children Act (1948) stipulates certain conditions which have to be fulfilled before parents can voluntarily agree to their child being taken into care under Section 1 of the Act. These are:

> *a* that he [child under seventeen] has neither parent nor guardian or has been and remains abandoned by his parents or guardian or is lost; or
>
> *b* that his parents or guardian are, for the time being or permanently, prevented by reason of mental or bodily disease or infirmity or other incapacity or any other circumstances from providing for his proper accommodation, maintenance and upbringing; and
>
> *c* in either case, that the intervention of the local authority under this section is necessary in the interests of the welfare of the child, it shall be the duty of the local authority to receive the child into care under this section.

The two children's departments in the study areas, and others to whom the natural parents had applied, interpreted the above wording to exclude those whose reason for wanting their children taken into public care was a wish to study or desertion by their husband. They appeared to argue that such parents were not 'prevented . . . from providing for his proper accommodation, maintenance and upbringing'. The implication was that a couple living together or a woman who had previously cared for her children could provide for their own either by staying with them or by finding a private foster home. In the case of one student's child, the children's officer had written: 'I do not feel that this type of child should be a burden on the ratepayers, and do not feel prepared to take these children into care if it is not absolutely necessary.' It could have been argued on the other side, although it was never done, that the parents found themselves in circumstances which compelled them to seek full-time care for their children and that the kind of foster homes available were not always 'in the interests of the welfare of the child'.

As well as excluding students and deserted mothers, departments also sometimes refused to receive the children of unmarried mothers and deserted fathers. Yet very similar cases were taken into care and appeared in the contrast group. Two factors seemed to influence the decisions. They were very ready to accept the child of an unmarried mother when he was the product of a racially mixed union. Possibly they considered that such a child had little chance of being helped by the relatives of the mother or father. Then again, the decision could hinge on the officer's assessment of whether the parents could provide alternative care. The capacity to seek out a private foster home was sometimes taken as an indication that they were able to provide it. In some cases the fact that the parents had, on a previous occasion, used a private foster home was regarded as proof of the parents' ability, even where it had been proved unsuitable and broke down.

To conclude: the majority of natural parents of the private foster children were West African students, unmarried mothers, deserted fathers and deserted mothers. They did not wish to lose their children permanently or they would have placed them for adoption. However, needing to find some form of substitute care they turned to private fostering. In a number of cases, the children's department had expressed unwillingness to receive the children into public care, a response which highlighted the ambivalent attitudes and policies the departments took towards private fostering. On the one hand they frequently condemned it and regretted their lack of powers for dealing with it. On the other hand they encouraged the use of private foster homes by advising applicants to use private placements and by offering to vet replies to advertisements. The refusal to receive into care, however, did not end the department's responsibilities towards the private foster children. The way in which these were exercised will be explored in a later chapter. But their refusal did mean that the natural parents had to find their own foster homes. It is their relationship with the private foster homes that the next chapter will study.

9   The private foster home and the natural parents

Child care research of the last two decades is almost unanimous in emphasising the value of natural parents maintaining contact with their children in care. Even before the war, Cowan and Stout (1939) demonstrated from their research that children's adjustment to foster homes was made easier if they maintained some contact with the natural parents (or previous substitute parents). Bowlby, in his famous 1951 monograph, drew upon their research, and that of others, to attack the view that when children came into care a clean break should be made with their old environment in order to give them a fresh start (1951, pp. 112–13).[1] Lewis, in her follow-up of children who had been through a reception centre, showed that two years later those who had experienced regular contact with parents or other relatives were in 'good' condition compared with those who had not (1954, p. 102).[2] She also made the point, one increasingly taken up by children's departments, that children in touch with parents were much more likely to return to them.

Trasler's research, which was concerned only with fostering, also refuted the claim that 'children who maintain some kind of contact with their natural parents will fail in placement more frequently than those for whom contact would be impossible' (1960, p. 233). He argued that a foster child could use the parental visits 'to construct a picture of them' which 'will help him to understand more fully the events of separation' (1960, p. 234). As shown in an earlier chapter, Trasler considered that understanding was essential to the child being able to adapt to and feel secure with the fostering situation. Weinstein's work, published in the same year as Trasler's but in the USA, constructed a means of measuring the 'well-being of the foster children' and then established that 'the average well-being of children whose natural parents visit them regularly was significantly higher than children who did not have contact with their natural parents. This was the case even when the children had been in foster homes most of their lives and identified predominantly with the foster parents' (1960, p. 87).

186

The research drawn upon so far has examined contacts with the natural parents as they influenced the foster child's relationships with his foster home both in regard to the degree of adaptation made and whether a breakdown resulted. Pringle extended the range of study to take in intellectual and social effects. Although drawing her subjects mainly from children in children's homes, her findings are usually taken to apply to children in fostering situations. In one study she concluded: 'our results support the hypothesis that intellectual backwardness is more marked where the child has no contact with his family' (1965, p. 26), adding that the relationship with backwardness in language development was particularly strong (p. 51). And in a study of maladjusted children she wrote: 'Among the most stable children in care, a significantly higher proportion have regular and frequent contact with parents or parent-substitutes than those considered to be most maladjusted' (1965, p. 89).

Finally, the most recent piece of research on fostering, that by George (1970), lends its support to the value of contact between parents and children in foster homes. First, he says, 'since the function of fostering to-day is not to provide a substitute home but rather to enable the child wherever possible to return to his own parents, it is essential that the child maintains close contacts with his parents to make his return easier and smoother.' He continues, 'even if no rehabilitation is planned, visits by natural parents are considered conducive to the child's emotional health. If the foster child re-members his parents he may feel rejected if they do not visit him or he may even feel that his foster parents are trying to take the place of his parents' (1970, pp. 183–4).

The various pieces of research are not easily comparable. Some deal with fostering, others with children in institutions. The modes of measuring contact differ, while the definitions given to 'frequent' or 'regular' contact are sometimes vague. None the less, virtually all the findings are in the same direction: all stress the desirability of maintaining contact between the natural parents and the foster home. To particularise, six main benefits are claimed from contact: it causes the child to feel less rejected by his parents; it promotes his adaptation to and feeling of security with the foster home; it gives him a greater understanding of why he was separated; it promotes his intellectual and emotional development; it facilitates his eventual return home; and, finally, it encourages the foster parents to have a realistic view of the placement and not to regard themselves as natural parents.

The value of contact has not blinded writers and workers in the child care field to the problems that can arise. John Stroud (1965) refers to 'aggressive visiting' in which the natural parents are critical of the foster parents, with consequent arguments and difficulties. The visits can also cause the child to experience divided loyalties, feeling that he can only please one set of adults by rejecting the others. Most seriously, the visits can provoke the end of the placement. On the one hand, the foster parents may decide they are not willing to continue if they have to endure the visits. On the other hand, the parents may remove the child or hold the threat of removing him over the foster home. However, the usual view is that the potential problems can be prevented or modified by the child care officer who may, for instance, enable the foster and natural parents to more fully understand each other's position, or who may act as a 'buffer', softening the natural parents' intention to remove. Even where conflict occurs, it would be argued that usually it is necessary in the long term interest of the child. None the less, child care writers do admit that in occasional cases it is best for contact between child and parent to cease temporarily or permanently.

The importance attached to the relationship between foster homes and natural parents has prompted child care personnel to express concern about that between private foster homes and natural parents. As mentioned in chapter 1, it was feared that such parents, lacking the encouragement child care officers might give to parents of children in care, would visit infrequently. The same lack of contact with official-dom, it was felt, might allow parents to provoke difficulties with and to cause insecurities for the foster parents. These fears were formulated into three hypotheses:

a   That the natural parents would not maintain frequent contacts with the private foster children.

b   That the private foster parents would feel insecure in their relationship with the natural parents.

c   That visits would result in difficulties between the natural parents and the private foster parents and the private foster children.

Methodology

The testing of the hypotheses required the design of means of measurement of contacts, security and difficulties. The methods used will now be expounded and presented against the findings for the local authority contrast group as a means of comparison and evaluation.

Amount of contact

Contacts – which were taken to mean face-to-face meetings not just contact by letter or telephone – between the foster children and parents could not be calculated from the children's departments' files as they did not necessarily record them. The only sources of information were the foster mothers who were therefore questioned concerning the number of contacts (or visits).

Previous studies have tended to use very broad categories to measure contacts. Weinstein (1960) distinguished only between visiting 'yearly' or 'less'. However, it was considered that important differences might stem from different amounts of visiting – for instance those seen once a week and those once a month; hence the categories shown in Table 9.1 were devised. Again, previous research usually fails to distinguish between which parent was in contact, and whether other relatives were. The questions were thus expanded to discover this.

Security of the foster parents

The pilot study led to the conclusion that there were two aspects of security which worried foster parents. The first was the time element, that is when the child would be removed. Security stemmed not just from the knowledge of if the child would be removed, but from knowing when it would happen. Stroud points out, in his discussion of foster and natural parents, that the easy situations are when a child is taken on a definite short-term basis or a *de facto* adoption. In these cases the future is relatively sure and the foster parents can make plans and sort out their role. He adds that it is the 'indefinite cases which cause the trouble' (1965, p. 122). Again, Dinnage and Pringle, in their review of child care research, point out that, 'A great deal can be borne if a definite time is agreed upon' (1967a, p. 23). To discover the foster parents' security in regard to time they were asked how long they expected the child to stay with them. Their replies were categorised in order of sureness of expectancy, as follows:

a   Definitely expected to stay on long-term basis. A common reply fitting into this category was 'until he gets married'.

b   Definitely expected to stay, but on a more limited time span. For instance, students might place a child saying they would take him back at the end of their three years' course.

c   Definite that the child would leave at some stage, but not sure when. A typical reply was, 'he'll stay until his parents claim him'.

d   Not sure whether the child would stay or not, or how long he would stay.

The second aspect of security revolved around the parents' rights to remove the child at will. The foster parents were asked whether they thought natural parents could remove too easily and their responses placed into carefully defined categories.[3]

Difficulties arising from parental contact

The third hypothesis required information about the difficulties experienced between foster homes and the natural parents. As part of a larger study, which is not recorded here, the foster parents were asked, 'What are the main difficulties you have met in fostering this child?'[4] The results showed a large number of difficulties amongst the private fosterings and a lesser amount amongst the local authority ones. Amongst the difficulties identified were those occurring in the 'relationship between the foster parents and the natural parents' and 'between the foster children and natural parents'. The former happened in forty-eight of the private and twenty of the local authority fosterings, the latter in fifty and eight respectively. As data on frequency of contacts was also obtained it became possible to examine the relationship between contacts and difficulties.

Contact between natural parents and foster homes

Table 9.1   Frequency of contact between private foster children and their mothers and fathers

	Mothers		Fathers	
	No.	%	No.	%
At least once a week	35	24·5	28	19·6
At least once a month	53	37·1	45	31·5
At least once a year	23	16·1	23	16·1
Less than once a year	8	5·6	10	7·0
Never seen:				
parent alive	18 ⎫24	16·8	37 ⎫37	25·9
parent dead	6 ⎭		0 ⎭	
Totals	143	100·0	143	100·0

Thirty-five of the private foster children, that is 24·5 per cent, were seeing their mothers at least once a week, while twenty-eight, 19·6 per cent, saw their fathers at this frequency. Including these, over half the children had contact with their mother at least once a month, while over half saw their father. Yet thirty-two children, 22·4 per cent, met their mothers less often than yearly or never, and the same applied to forty-seven, 32·9 per cent, in respect of their fathers.

Of course, those not seeing their fathers frequently may have had the compensation of seeing their mothers, and vice versa. Hence figures relating to contact with either the father or the mother are required. These show (Table not given) that ninety-five, 66·4 per cent, of the private foster children saw at least one of their parents at least once a month, leaving forty-eight, 33·6 per cent, who saw neither. To take another cut off point, 120, that is 83·9 per cent, had contact with at least one parent at least once a year, while twenty-three, 16·1 per cent, saw one less often than a year or never.

Parents are not the only relatives whom children might meet; they may also have siblings, aunts and uncles and grandparents. Only forty-five, 31·5 per cent, of the private foster children had any contact whatsoever with these relatives, but this number included some who had no contact with their parents. Thus altogether thirteen, 9·1 per cent, at the most had contact less than yearly, and at worst had no contact at all with any relatives of any kind.

If frequent contact is taken to mean 'at least once a month' then two-thirds of the private foster children were in frequent contact with at least one parent, so the hypothesis that the parents would not maintain frequent contact cannot be upheld. This finding, however, should not be used to overlook the disadvantages which might accrue to the sizeable minority having little or no contact with their parents.

Which children?

Which children were prone to have frequent or infrequent parental contact? Those children categorised as grouping (a), that is the legitimate children of West African students, were significantly more likely to have frequent contact than other groupings (dividing groupings $a/b–d/e$, $\chi^2 = 17·014$, d.f. $= 2$, P $= <0·001$). The test of significance given relates to seeing at least one parent at least once a month but significant results were found when testing the parents separately or testing for other relatives or whatever the frequency rate. Not unexpectedly, when isolating the reason for placement from other factors, those placed because their parents wished to study had more contact. But, more interestingly those placed by their fathers because of the death or desertion of the mother, or by their mothers, the father never having been present or deserted, had significantly less chance of being visited (dividing death or desertion of mother, father deserted or never present/students/others, $\chi^2 = 18\cdot433$, d.f. $= 2$, P $= <0\cdot001$).

Two reasons can be offered to explain why the children of West African students saw more of their parents and relatives than those of unmarried mothers, deserted mothers and deserted or deceased fathers. First, they were not placed for reason of a family break-up. They were the legitimate offspring of a married couple who acted together in making the placement. Hence both partners knew where the children were. Most of the other children were placed by one parent for some reason connected with the other parent's absence. The missing parent, if alive, might not even have known where the child was placed. Hence the chances of that person maintaining regular contact were correspondingly reduced. Second, the West African students, usually living together, would have plans and prospects of making a home into which the children later could be incorporated. The prospects for mothers or fathers living alone were much more bleak. The near certainty that the former would be able to take over the care of their children no doubt motivated them to visit more regularly to maintain contact. The latter, often with no future certainty, could become dispirited so that their visits tailed off. In turn, their children would develop more closely with their foster parents which, when observed by the natural parents, could reinforce their disinclination to visit.

Effects of contact

A further point of importance concerns the effects of contact. The findings confirm in three main spheres what previous writers have affirmed, namely that a lack of contact is associated with adverse features. First, the less the contact with natural parents, the less chance did a child have of knowing the truth about his relationships with them (dividing contact with at least one parent at least once a month/once a year/less, $\chi^2 = 7\cdot0253$, d.f. $= 2$, P $= <0\cdot010$). Second, the less the contact the more the retardation in developmental stages. For instance, children with least contact were more likely to soil after the age of four ($\chi^2 = 7\cdot5371$, d.f. $= 2$, P $= <0\cdot010$). Third, the less contact the more the chance of ill-health. For instance such children were more likely to have experienced pneumonia ($\chi^2 = 6\cdot5485$, d.f. $= 2$, P $= <0\cdot010$). Although not quite statistically significant, clear trends showed that the children's educational achievements with regard to writing, reading and arithmetic were adversely associated with a lack of contact with a natural parent. Interestingly, too, the children whose foster fathers participated least had less contact with their parents (dividing highly/moderately/non-participant foster fathers, $\chi^2 = 11 \cdot 001$, d.f. $= 4$, P $= <0 \cdot 050$). In other words, they suffered doubly, having a lack of contact with their own parents and with their male substitute parent.

Comparison with local authority children

Usually throughout the study, the private foster children have emerged in a more disadvantageous position than the local authority ones. The reverse was true concerning contact with relatives. Only twenty-four, 16·8 per cent, of the local authority children saw their mothers at least once a month, a further nineteen, 13·2 per cent, saw them at least once a year, while as many as a hundred, 69·9 per cent, saw them less often than yearly or never. The corresponding figures for their fathers were: fifteen, that is 10·5 per cent; nine, 6·3 per cent; and 119, 83·2 per cent. Only thirty-one, 21·7 per cent, saw at least one of their parents at least once a month and so were significantly less likely to be in this position than their private counterparts ($\chi^2 = 14 \cdot 222$, d.f. $= 1$, P $= <0 \cdot 001$).

One reason that springs to mind to explain the difference in visiting frequency is that the local authority sample contained no children from the West African-legitimate-student grouping (who received most visits) and more from those whose placement was precipitated by the absence of one parent. However, even when the West African grouping was removed from the private fostering sample, it still remained significantly more likely to have contact although not to the same extent. A further explanation is required, and it is suggested that the involvement of at least one natural parent in the actual placement of the private children creates a link which is not easily broken. By contrast, the parents of the local authority children who usually initially placed their children with the child care officers were not themselves identified with the choice of foster parents, and hence had no direct link with them and so visited less. Thus the essence of private fostering, the freedom of parents to choose their foster parents, can result in the use of people with unsuitable fostering characteristics yet also appears to encourage increased parental contact – an illustration of the complex nature of private fostering.

Security of the foster parents

Expectancy of tenure

The second aspect of the relationship between the private foster homes and the natural parents concerned the foster parents' feelings of security. Their sense of how long the children would remain with them was sought by a straightforward question which rested on two main assumptions. First, that they correctly perceived the natural parents' intent (or lack of it) about the future of the child. A similar question to the interviewed natural parents suggests that they tended to make an accurate perception.[5] Second, that the feeling associated with their expectancy was that of 'security' or 'insecurity'. Accepting these assumptions, the findings can now be presented.

Table 9.2   Expectancy of tenure of private foster children as expressed by private foster mothers

	No.	%
Definitely long-term	32	22·4
Definitely short-term	43	30·1
Child will definitely leave, not sure when	5	3·5
Unsure of future	63	44·0
Totals	143	100·0

It can be seen from Table 9.2 that the private foster mothers were unsure of the future in regard to sixty-three, or 44 per cent, of the private foster children (forty-three foster mothers expressed this expectation). These mothers had no idea if or how long the child would stay, or had received conflicting messages from the natural parents. But which type of children were subject to such insecurity? The answer was sought by examining the expectancy of tenure against the groupings. Table 9.3 shows that the groupings (*b, c, d*) made up of United Kingdom children placed because of the absence of one parent, were mainly divided between the two extremes of expectancy – 'definitely long-term' and 'unsure of future'. The lone parents appeared to take one of two opposing courses. Some found their circumstances so difficult that they gave up hope of having their children back and allowed the foster parents to know the children would stay long-term. Others strove to form a new home for their children, so giving the foster parents no security. The children in grouping (*a*), the legitimate offspring of West African students,

Table 9.3   Expectancy of tenure of private foster children as expressed by private foster mothers according to groupings of the children

	a	b	c	d	e
Definitely long-term	3	8	3	4	14
Definitely short-term	37	1	0	0	5
Child will definitely leave, not sure when	1	1	2	0	1
Unsure of future	42	5	4	4	8

Total no. of private foster children = 143.

were mostly divided between 'definitely short-term' and 'unsure of the future'. It might have been anticipated that nearly all would have been in the former category, on the grounds that most students would know how long their courses last and would convey this to the foster parents. True, nearly half the children of the West African students were in this position, a higher proportion than for any other group, but over half were categorised as 'unsure of the future'. Why were so many private foster parents given such insecurity of tenure by students? One reason is that the students did not always know exactly how long their studies would last. Some failed their examinations, and had to study further. Others deferred taking their finals while they worked to earn enough to resume their courses. Others were studying part-time and took their examinations when they felt ready, rather than according to a set date as occurs within full-time courses. Yet others had to decide whether to go for additional qualifications once passing their basic examinations. Thus it was not a straightforward matter of all students embarking on a course whose length they knew and which could be conveyed to the foster parents. Second, even where the students did know the length of their stay, they did not necessarily tell the foster parents. Some West African natural parents did not perceive the foster parents' wish to take on the role of parent, and thus did not appreciate their need for assurance concerning the child's length of stay. The lack of communication was reinforced when the foster parents could not raise the subject. One foster mother said she dare not ask the natural parents how long they would let her West African foster child stay, for fear they would think she was getting too possessive and remove him. Third, some students, although intending their child to be fostered for a definite short-term, were not prepared to commit him to one foster home for that period. In order to save money they might intend to take the child themselves during their holidays, or even look for a cheaper foster home. They could not, therefore, give assurances to one set of foster parents.

Ease of removal

Table 9.4   Private foster mothers' opinion whether child can be too easily removed by natural parents

	No.	%
Can be removed too easily	95	66·4
Not	43	30·1
Not sure	5	3·5
Totals	143	100·0

From Table 9.4 it can be seen that ninety-five fosterings gave rise to the opinion of sixty-five foster mothers that the natural parents could remove the child too easily. They usually explained that they felt they had no rights over the children, while recounting past experiences of removals or threats to remove in the face of which they were powerless. Forty-three of the fosterings were accompanied by the thirty-two foster mothers who did not feel that removal could occur too easily. This was not to say that they were unaware of the natural parents' legal right to remove the child at any time, but that they acknowledged it should exist. The first group believed the rights should be limited in some way.

Which fosterings were associated with the opinion that the child could be removed too easily? Only one significant relationship was found. The grouping (*b*) containing the illegitimate children of unmarried mothers was associated with the view that the children could not be removed too easily ($\chi^2 = 4·5243$, d.f. $= 1$, P $= <0·050$). Interestingly, the amount of contact with natural parents was not significantly related to the opinions, nor to the expectations of tenure.

Comparison with local authority children

The local authority fosterings were much less likely than the private ones to be associated with feelings of insecurity of tenure or that the children could be removed too easily. Only fourteen of these fosterings had foster mothers, ten in all, who were completely unsure of the future of their child. The difference between the two groups was statistically significant (dividing unsure/other, $\chi^2 = 39·371$, d.f. $= 1$,

P = <0·001). Similarly, far fewer local authority fosterings, 48·3 per cent, as compared with 66·4 per cent, felt the natural parents could remove too easily. Again the difference was statistically significant ($\chi^2 = 9\cdot941$, d.f. = 1, P = <0·010). The difference between the two types of fostering was not related to differing amounts of contact with the natural parents. Instead an alternative explanation will be offered at the end of the chapter. Meantime, it is enough to conclude that as 44 per cent of the private fosterings gave the foster mothers feelings of complete unsureness about the future, as 66·4 per cent were associated with the foster parents feeling the child could be removed too easily, and as on both counts the insecurity was significantly higher in the private fosterings, the hypothesis that the private foster parents would feel insecure in their relationships with the natural parents can be considered upheld.

Case examples

The private foster mothers had not been specifically asked to illustrate the nature of their insecurities but so many did so that not only was the importance of the subject underlined but their examples can be used to portray the kind of insecurities they suffered and how they were affected by them. First, a number described how natural parents had actually removed their previous or present foster children, experiences which made them fear the same would happen again:

a One foster mother had been caring for a West African child for some months when the parents called to take her out, saying that they were going to have her photographed. They returned the next day, and took her cot saying that they had decided to have her home for a fortnight. The foster mother never saw them or the child again.

b A foster mother obtained her child from meeting a young unmarried mother in a cafe. She explained: 'A few weeks later the mother suddenly rang up and said "I want the child back." I had to agree, and she collected the child, saying that she needed another child in order to get some money back from the National Assistance, but if he cried a lot I could have him back. The same evening, she rang up again, saying he would not do a thing for her and I could have him back.' The child was returned to the foster mother, but within one week the natural mother took him again. She placed him in three further, different foster homes, repeating the same pattern of placing and sudden withdrawal. Finally the natural mother telephoned the foster mother again, who this time replied that she would only take the child if the mother made a 'legal' agreement signed over a stamp. In fact it had no legal validity, but the mother agreed and left him.

Second, many foster parents had experienced not an actual removal of their child, but the threat of removal:

a   An elderly mother formed a very close relationship with her foster child, the illegitimate daughter of a West African nurse. So strong was the relationship and the corresponding fear that the child would be removed, that the natural mother was able to use it – to quote the child care officer involved – 'as a lever' to manipulate the foster mother. The officer wrote: 'Mrs X is extremely frightened of displeasing the mother as she wants very badly to keep the child and is afraid that if she does not do everything the mother wants the child will be removed.' Using this threat, the mother was able to get the foster mother to send the child to nursery school and then to a private school, and forced her to arrange her own accommodation when she came to visit. The mother was recorded as saying, 'She is mine to do with as I like.'

b   More than one foster mother said that the natural parents had threatened to remove the child unless she agreed to take as well the child's sibling, usually a newborn baby.

c   Two foster mothers mentioned that they had actually seen their present foster child advertised in the paper. Presumably the natural parents were seeking cheaper rates.

Third, and fortunately rarely, foster parents could be caught between the struggles of estranged parents who had different plans for the child's future. Not surprisingly, the foster parents in the following case were revealing severe signs of anxiety and tension in a situation which began to adversely affect the foster girl concerned:

a   A girl of a few months old had been placed by her parents during a period when the mother was mentally unstable. Later the parents separated but continued to visit the girl for many years, although arguments did occur between the foster and natural mother. When the girl was in her teens she went to tea with the mother. The natural father happened to call at this time, was considerably annoyed that his daughter had been entrusted to his wife, found them and provoked a major argument. To avoid such situations the foster mother then tried to prevent the natural mother from taking her daughter out, but the latter countered by meeting her from school.

The child was warned not to go with her mother and, on hearing this, the latter 'stampeded' to the foster home, created a scene and had to be driven out with a broom. Two years later the mother again began meeting the girl at school. She then demanded that the foster mother send the girl to tea with her. The foster mother by this time was actively siding with the natural father, even running the mother down in front of the daughter, but felt she had no choice but to allow her to go despite the father's opposition. By this stage he was about to remarry, and it was clear that both parents were going to demand the child back on a permanent basis.

In such cases, the foster parents' insecurity about if and when the child would leave was increased by having to arbitrate between the natural parents and by not knowing what legally was the correct way of responding to conflicting demands from the parents.

The above cases breathe life into the statistics showing how many private foster mothers experienced insecurity and give explanations of why so many thought the children could be removed too easily. The possibility, even probability, of a sudden removal hung like a sword of Damocles over many of the foster parents and, no doubt, in turn over the foster children. Some foster parents confessed to 'sleepless nights', 'a living dread', and 'removal always in our minds'. They admitted that they considered how they could persuade or prevent the natural parents taking the child. One mother described how she actually did stop a removal:

'I did something awful when she was two. She [the natural mother] wrote and said she was going to put her on the plane to Nigeria – like a parcel. I couldn't let her go. I took her away in the country when she came. I didn't mind what they did to me.'

Another foster mother was prepared to offer a large sum of money to keep the child. No doubt such drastic actions were rare but equally without doubt the private foster mothers were prone to emotional suffering. It may be remembered that the chapter on the treatment of the foster children showed that most of the foster mothers regarded their private foster children as their own, would like to adopt them, and had a high keeping score. Of the seventy-one fosterings where foster parents regarded the child as their own, twenty-six had foster mothers who were unsure of the child's future. Of the ninety-one with the highest keeping scores, thirty-six were unsure. Of the ninety-three where the foster parents wanted to adopt, forty-three had foster mothers who had no certainty about the future. These foster mothers were thus in the unenviable position of needing or wanting the nearest of relationships with their children, yet having no assurance of the future, even having to face the prospect that a knock on the door could mean the end of their relationship.

Lastly, although many foster parents were prone to insecurity in that the natural parents had the legal right to remove their child at will, it must be interjected that occasionally a foster mother reversed the situation. The private fostering market, being one where demand exceeded supply, gave some foster parents a hold over natural parents who would find difficulty in finding another placement if their child was ejected. Most foster mothers would not dare try such a tactic for fear that the parents actually would remove the child to whom they had grown attached but there were cases of it being used. Occasionally, too, the foster mothers' personality appeared to dominate the parents and operated to squeeze them out of the picture, as in the following example:

> The foster mother did not actually tell the natural father, a deserted husband, not to visit, but made him feel very unwelcome. She would make it clear that the times he chose to call were inconvenient, did not communicate with him when he came, and would not allow the child to go out of her sight.
> The father was in no position to form a home of his own, and realising the child was settled with the foster mother, had to choose between not visiting or enduring very uncomfortable experiences.

Examples of foster parents acting in these ways were rare, and usually operated against a single parent, whose lack of a partner's support and the need to work put them in a particularly vulnerable position.

Difficulties and parental contact

The relationship between parental contact and difficulties in the fosterings was examined in three ways. First, by testing the hypothesis that visits would result in difficulties between the natural parents and the private foster parents and the private foster children. Second, by comparison with the number of difficulties in the local authority fosterings. Third, by looking at the nature of the difficulties.

In general, Tables 9.5 and 9.6 show that the less the amount of contact with natural parents the greater the likelihood of difficulties.

Table 9.5 *Difficulties in private fosterings* between foster parents and natural parents according to amount of contact*

	A parent seen at least once a month	Seen at least once a year	Less often than a year	Never
Difficulties	22	13	8	5
No difficulties	73	12	0	10

*No. of private fosterings = 143.

Table 9.6 *Difficulties in private fosterings* between foster children and natural parents according to amount of contact*

	A parent seen at least once a month	Seen at least once a year	Less often than a year	Never
Difficulties	27	10	7	6
No difficulties	68	15	1	9

*No. of private foster children = 143.

However, when the amount of contact is broken down more closely it is observed that difficulties occurred least not only when a parent visited at least once a month, but also when there was no contact at all. They occurred most when the visiting was existent but infrequent. These differences were statistically significant, concerning the difficulties between foster parents and natural parents (dividing at least one parent seen at least once a month and never/at least once a year and less often than a year, $\chi^2 = 17 \cdot 395$, d.f. $= 1$, P $= <0 \cdot 001$) and concerning those between the foster children and natural parents ($\chi^2 = 5 \cdot 1674$, d.f. $= 1$, P $= <0 \cdot 025$). It appears that either regular or no contact gave the stability which allowed children and foster parents to work out their attitudes towards the parents in a satisfactory manner; it was infrequent contact which proved unsettling and provided fertile soil where differences could grow. Thus the hypothesis cannot be considered upheld although a relationship between parental contact and the incidence of difficulties was established.

Comparison with local authority fosterings

From Tables 9.7 and 9.8 it can be seen that the private fosterings were significantly more likely than the local authority ones to have difficulties between the foster and natural parents ($\chi^2 = 14 \cdot 523$,

Table 9.7   Difficulties in fosterings between foster parents and natural parents

	Private		Local authority	
	No.	%	No.	%
Difficulties	48	33·6	20	14·0
No difficulties	95	66·4	123	86·0
Totals	143	100·0	143	100·0

Table 9.8   Difficulties in fosterings between foster children and natural parents

	Private		Local authority	
	No.	%	No.	%
Difficulties	50	35·0	8	5·6
No difficulties	93	65·0	135	94·4
Totals	143	100·0	143	100·0

d.f. $=1$, P $=<0·001$). Similarly, they were more likely to have difficulties between the foster children and natural parents ($\chi^2 = 38·341$, d.f. $=1$, P $=<0·001$). If the relationship between frequency of contact and incidence of difficulties had been a straightforward one with incidence increasing consistently with a lack of contact, then the local authority fosterings (having less contact) could have been anticipated to have far more difficulties than the private ones. But, as with the private fosterings, they showed the same association, with those in most regular contact or no contact having the least difficulties. With regard to the foster parent/natural parent difficulty this was statistically significant ($\chi^2 = 5·7792$, d.f. $=1$, P $=<0·025$). With regard to the foster child/natural parent difficulties the trend was clear, although not quite statistically significant.

The nature of the difficulties

The difficulties experienced between the private foster parents and the natural parents could be subdivided. On the one hand were disagreements during visits especially concerning the amount of visiting, the child-rearing practices used, the question of removing the child and the language used. On the other hand were difficulties which could occur inside or outside of visits, for instance, disagreements over payments. The difficulties between the children and their parents could similarly be subdivided. First, difficulties experienced during visits which disturbed the children. Second, difficulties aroused in the children because their parents did not visit. Some examples will now be presented to convey more vividly the kind of difficulties which arose:

a The foster parents of a Nigerian foster child resented the natural parents' persistent questioning of the way they treated her and telling them what to do. The foster mother said, 'They would inquire about the slightest scratch on the child. They expect too much of the child, they think she should be putting on her shoes at two-and-a-half. They also bring lots of friends when they call. On one occasion they had been drinking, and asked my husband if we wanted to adopt her. When he said "yes" they flew at him and the police had to be called.'

b 'It's difficult to understand them, they do talk in their own language. They are £20 in debt, and when we argued about it they threatened to remove her so I didn't press it. She [mother] examines the child's ears and hair. When they come they stay for one hour and then go to the pictures. They never offer to baby-sit while I go.'

c The mother of a five-year-old girl never visited the foster home but still made her influence felt. To use the foster mother's words, 'I had a bust-up with her on the 'phone. She'd had a row with her husband and threatened me with a solicitor's letter. She criticised the way I did her [foster child's] hair. She said she was coming to get her. I said, "You can't because the father handed her over." But later I found I was wrong. She [foster child] cries and says she doesn't want to go with her mother. She told her teacher she hasn't got a mummy now ... I feel uncomfortable when the father comes. He never speaks, he's only just started saying "Hallo". He watches the T.V. The only thing he ever says is, "I'm going soon".'

d 'They just call without notice. I'm out and they get annoyed when they have to wait.'

e Several children showed distress when parents visited. One child cried, 'I'm not coming to you, mummy – she's my mummy', pointing to the foster mother. A young girl was suddenly confronted with her father after an absence of several years: 'She became very distressed and refused to look at him ... she became hysterical, begging us not to let her go.'

f Other children were disturbed that their parents did not visit. Two siblings were placed in a foster home when their parents' marriage split up. The foster mother said of visiting, 'They should come regular or leave them alone completely. The father used to visit monthly and lived near. So the children lived two lives. When they went home they did as they liked and told me I wasn't their mum. When they became demanding the father agreed to stay away. It worked out fine for two and a half years, then the mother turned up. Then she stayed away for another two years.' The boy, in particular, was hit by the lack of contact. The foster mother recorded him as saying, 'I went to church and said my prayers for mummy and daddy but now I'm not, there's nothing to pray to.'

   g   Some foster mothers felt the natural parents did not visit enough. One attributed her foster child's behavioural problems to the lack of contact. 'He feels they do not want him and I persuaded them to take him for week-ends. Now he fears Fridays when sometimes he goes home. He screams and hangs on to my husband, his stutter gets worse, he's miserable.' Another added, 'When they do come they don't kiss or cuddle her like we do, they never take her out for a walk to show they feel for her. She was singing to herself, "My mummy doesn't want me".'

The above cases serve to illustrate the nature of difficulties but it must be emphasised that a majority of the private fosterings revealed no difficulties in the relationships between the fostering participants. Although not specifically asked, a number of private foster parents spoke of their good relationships. Interestingly, some likened their relationship to the West African student parents as that of parents to child while a few of the students openly said that they had left their mothers in West Africa and looked upon the foster mother to take over the mother role. Clearly, a number of foster mothers went to great pains to help parents, giving them accommodation, encouraging contact, teaching young mothers how to handle their babies and even reducing payments. As one put it, 'You've got to be interested in the parents as much as the children so that you understand both.'

The foster home, natural parents and the local authority

The study, the first one of the relationship between private foster homes and natural parents, has made some interesting and possibly unexpected findings. Two-thirds of the private foster homes received a visit from a parent at least once a month although another 16·1 per cent had little or no contact. The private foster mothers tended to feel insecure in their relationships with the natural parents. In two-thirds of the fosterings they believed the child could be removed too easily, while in 44 per cent they had no idea how long the parents would allow the fostering to continue. Lastly, some light was thrown on the kind of difficulties occurring between private foster homes and the natural parents.

Two factors emerged as of special importance to the relationships. First, the foster child grouping made up of the legitimate children of West African students took on a pattern quite distinct from the other groupings. They tended to have the most frequent contact with parents while their expectancy of tenure was divided between being definitely short-term and unsure. On the other hand the groupings made up of children placed by a lone parent tended to have fewer visits from the parents while the expectancy of tenure was divided between definitely long-term and unsure of the future. It appeared that the interested parent of these children had less chance of making a home to which a child could return and so had a tendency to leave them longer in the foster home, during which period the visits could tail off. These children, being visited less, were in the greatest danger of suffering the ill-effects of infrequent parental contact. Second, the amount of contact between the private fosterings and the parents was found to be related to other factors. Those fosterings with very frequent or no visits were less likely to experience difficulties between the natural parents and the foster parents and children. Moreover, as mentioned, the low contact rate was associated with the children's adverse conditions in the fields of ill-health, developmental stages, and a lack of self-knowledge. Clearly, the amount of contact is central to the dynamics and consequences of fostering and it can be postulated that child care officers can play an important part in encouraging and regulating natural parent visitation. Whether they do so will be examined in the next chapter.

In one area, however, frequency of contact was not obviously related to the factor studied, namely the insecurity of the private foster parents. As their feelings of security are likely to affect the children as well as the happiness of the private foster parents themselves, the chapter will close with a discussion of the reasons for their insecurity in comparison with that of the local authority foster mothers.

An examination of the cases leads to the suggestion that the difference in security was linked to the essential difference in the types of fostering, namely with the private placements resting on the initiative of the natural parents and the local authority ones on the child care officers. To enlarge, the making of a foster home placement for children in public care has the following elements. First, the selection of the foster parents and the placing of the child is executed by the children's department. Second, the natural parents enter into a signed agreement and relationship with the department and agree to follow certain procedures. They supply their addresses, give details of relatives and of the child's background, provide details of their financial position, and agree to inform the local authority if they change their address. From this the officers can gain some indication of the natural parents' plans and hopes for the child's future. Third, the child is usually removed from the foster home by the children's department even if he is returning to his parents.

Private placements are made by the natural parents. They enter into no formal agreement with the foster parents and are under no obligation to provide any details or information whatsoever. The method has one major advantage, the involvement of the natural parents in choosing the foster home appears to motivate them towards regular visitation. On the other hand, the loose, informal and undefined nature of the process has certain disadvantages for the foster parents. Because no information need be exchanged, the foster parents may gain no idea of the natural parents' intentions for the child's future. As little discussion appears to take place about the child, the way is left open for future disagreements about the manner in which the child is being raised. Above all, the date and way in which the child will be removed may not be mentioned. Consequently, the parents can take him without giving any notice at all. With no hold over the foster child and possibly no information about future intentions, the foster parents' insecurity is multiplied.

It is not denied that local authority foster parents can also feel insecure about the possible actions of natural parents. Unless the parents have had their parental rights removed from them by a legal process – and this applied to only 11·2 per cent of the local authority contrast group – they are free to claim their children. Indeed, cases of parents, who for years had no contact, demanding the return of children in care have enjoyed much publicity,[6] one result of which was the setting up by the Home Secretary in 1969 of the Houghton Committee to consider, *inter alia*, 'the position of long-term foster parents who wish to keep a child permanently by adoption or otherwise against the wishes of the natural parents'. However, the special relationship of the local authority foster parents to the children's departments served to minimise their insecurities compared with those of their private counterparts. First, the parents of children in care depend upon the child care officers to find them a new foster home and so have less scope for suddenly swooping the child off to another placement. Second, even if the parents did insist on a removal, the child care officers could temper the effect by giving the foster home plenty of warning and making the change a slow and gradual operation. Third, the officers could, and did, undertake work with the parents to persuade them to leave the child in the foster home. Fourth, if the parents were creating tensions and insecurities by their visits, the officers could attempt to act as a 'buffer' between them, drawing the parents' aggression and fears on to themselves. As the child care officers had much less contact with the private foster homes and the natural parents of the private foster children, the private foster parents were much more open to situations which provoked and emphasised their feelings of insecurity. Obviously, the work of the child care officers was of influence within the fostering field. It is to a study of the officers that attention will now be given.

H

10   The children's departments and private fostering

Local authorities have certain statutory duties in regard to private fosterings which are exercised through their children's departments.[1] Within the framework laid down by statute, the child care officers have some scope to develop their work with the fostering participants. The extent and manner in which they can and do render service to the private fosterings, in comparison with the local authority ones, is the subject of the present chapter. It will be necessary, first, to discuss how officers should work with the foster parents, children and natural parents. Then, second, to analyse the obligations and limitations placed on them by statute. The way will thus be cleared to state objectives and to consider the means of measuring the officers' contributions.

The work of child care officers with the fostering participants

A large number of child care text books were studied in order to assess the recommended ways in which officers should work with the fostering participants. These devoted a large part of their volumes to such subjects and, although terminology varied, revealed a remarkable consensus of opinion.

Child care officers and foster parents

The view of Balls that officers should rely on the foster parents 'to make a success of the job with the minimum of interference from the visitor' (1958, p. 144) has now been firmly rejected. Trasler (1960, p. 235) and Timms (1962, pp. 148–9) reflect the prevailing opinion when they argue succinctly that officers should relate closely with both foster parents to further the well-being of the child. Within this relationship, as Pugh explains, officers are expected to perform three main roles, the supervisory (or inspectoral), the supportive and the educative (1968, pp. 60–3).

Supervision (or inspection) is expressed in checks on the children's physical, material and emotional condition. Stroud makes the point

208

that such activities are welcomed, not resented, by foster parents as they reassure them that their responsibilities are being shared by the children's departments (1965, p. 116). It is also displayed when officers enforce the sanctions of inspection, that is they use or threaten to use their official powers to force the foster parents to accord with the wishes of the children's department.

The supportive role of the officers involves all the means they can employ to encourage and aid the foster parents in their task. Three means can be mentioned. First, the conveyance to the foster parents that their work is valued and valuable (Pugh, 1968, p. 62). Second, the capacity to enable foster parents to 'ventilate' their negative feelings about the fostering situation. Charnley describes it as an 'escape valve' through which the foster parents can 'pour out their irritations and frustrations on the officer rather than on the child or parents' (1955, p. 157). Third, support is given through material and physical help which includes not only the foster parents' financial allowance but also specific material goods such as beds and bedding, and services such as baby-sitting.

'The educational aspects . . . involve helping the foster parents to understand both the needs of the foster child and their own feelings about the demands he makes on them' (Pugh, 1968, p. 62). At one level these ends can be achieved by passing on information about the child and his family. The officer will also give advice concerning some of the specific problems met by the foster parents such as enabling them to answer the foster child's questions (Trasler, 1960, p. 235). At another level, some writers like Gordon and Charnley say that the officer can enable the foster parents to understand and control their own modes of behaviour and so learn how to relate more effectively to the foster children.

Child care officers and the foster children

Nearly all text books recommend officers to form a direct and close relationship with foster children. They state that the child, when old enough, should be seen alone, as well as with the foster parents, and that 'visits must be frequent enough to permit her [the officer] to observe what is happening, and to permit the child to know her interest in him' (Gordon, 1956, p. 113).

During visits child care officers are expected to work towards two main objectives: to maintain the child's links with his parents and to make his placement a positive experience. The link is most obviously formed as the officer achieves meetings between a child and his parents. But even if this is not possible he is advised to enable the child to build up a positive picture of the parents in order that he might respect them (Gordon, 1956, p. 116) and understand the continuity between past and present (Timms, 1962, p. 41). In order to ensure that the child obtains the maximum benefit from a fostering experience, the officer is exhorted to minimise feelings of hostility towards the foster parents by explaining to the child why he is with them (Bowlby, 1951, p. 119) and to aid them resolve any problems of relationships. Indeed, the officer is expected to promote any and all aspects of a child's capacities (Pugh, 1968, p. 47).

Child care officers and the natural parents

'Skilful work with parents is, I believe, the most important part of the child placement worker's job', wrote Charnley, 'I believe no social worker may ever abandon a parent' (1955, p. 123). Modern child care literature unanimously agrees with Charnley that officers should maintain contact with the parents of children, even in the apparently few number of cases where they think that no contact between them and the child should occur.

As with the child, the officer is expected to work with the natural parents before and at the point of separation. This apart, three main objectives are put forward. First, the officer works with them to preserve the fostering placement. By minimising differences between the natural and foster parents, the chance of a fostering breakdown is reduced. Second, the natural parents' help needs to be enlisted in enabling the child to make the most of the foster home. Gordon claimed that children accept fostering more easily when they see that their parents are in favour of it. In addition, Gordon (1956, p. 87) and Charnley (1955, p. 81) believe that children without parental contact may develop such fantasies about their parents that they are unable to relate to their foster parents. Third, and stressed above all, the child care officers are encouraged to work towards reuniting the child with his natural parents. This is also pre-eminently achieved by facilitating parental visits so that the child does not 'die' in the life of the parents. Heinicke and Westheimer, in their study of short-term placements, concluded that the longer the separation the harder the parents found it to express concern for the child (1966, p. 236). It follows that officers should attempt to get parents to visit as soon as possible after the separation. They also found that the child's immediate reaction to seeing the parent again was a negative one, and that a social worker was needed to prevent the parents interpreting this as a rejection of themselves (pp. 215 and 309). Charnley points out that parents may require considerable casework help before they can visit. Some are riddled with guilt about rejecting their child, and contact only serves to fan such feelings (1955, p. 107). The officer's task becomes that of dealing with the guilt, which is partially achieved as the worker concentrates on and builds up the positive strengths of the parents, showing them what they can offer the child. Lastly, the child care workers may command physical resources such as financial grants or help in obtaining accommodation which may lead to the parents being able to have their child back.

The statutory relationship between children's departments and private fostering

The child care texts, which have been used to describe the ways in which officers are recommended to deal with fosterings, usually have been written with children in public care in mind. It is assumed that their child care principles and precepts apply to private fostering as well. In addition to the recommended practice, the services given by officers will depend on their legal duties and powers. Therefore, attention must now be focused on the local authorities' statutory rights and obligations in regard to private and then local authority fosterings.

The major piece of legislation pertaining to private fostering is the Children Act (1958) which, apart from defining the meaning of private foster children, can be divided into five main parts:

1 Notification by the private foster parents

The major duties laid upon private foster parents are to notify the children's department concerning the reception and departure of private foster children. The Act states that a person proposing to maintain a foster child must give written notice to the local authority of his intention not less than two weeks before the child is received. In the case of an emergency the notification should be not later than one week after the placement is made (Section 3). Upon the removal of the child to another foster home the foster parents are obliged to notify the local authority within forty-eight hours, giving the address to which he has gone.

2 Duties of the local authority

Section 1 of the Act places a duty upon the children's departments to visit private foster children 'from time to time' to 'satisfy themselves as to the well-being of the children and give such advice as to their care and maintenance as may appear to be needed'.

3 Information

The local authority has the power to require the private foster parents to give particulars of the name, age, sex, date and place of birth, and the name and address of the parents of the foster child.

4 Powers to prohibit placements

a   Section 6 lists five types of persons who are disqualified from taking private foster children unless the local authority gives its consent. These are: persons from whom a child had been removed under the 1958 Act; persons from whom a child had been removed having been found to be in need of care and protection under the Children and Young Persons Act (1933); a person convicted of any offence specified in the First Schedule of the 1933 Act; a person whose parental rights over a child had been vested in a local authority under Section 2 of the Children Act (1948); a person whose registration to take daily-minded children had been refused or cancelled under the Nurseries and Child Minders Regulation Act (1948).

b   Apart from disqualified persons, the Act allows local authorities to prohibit the making of placements where they are of the 'opinion that it would be detrimental to that child to be kept by him [foster parent] in those premises' (Section 4).

These words have generally been interpreted – for instance by the Association of Children's Officers, the Association of Child Care Officers, and Yudkin (1967, p. 42) – to mean that prohibition cannot be applied to persons but only to premises. Moreover, the Act makes clear that the prohibition can only be applied before a child is taken, not while he is there. Foster parents whose premises are so prohibited have the right of appeal to a juvenile court (Section 5).

5 Powers to remove private foster children

Under Section 7, a local authority can complain to a juvenile court that a foster child is being kept by a person 'unfit to have his care' or in premises detrimental to him. The court can then, the case being proved, make an order to remove the child to a place of safety. In cases of imminent danger the order can be made by a Justice of the Peace. Further, children so removed can be received into the care of the local authority under Section 1 of the Children Act (1948). Appeals by the foster parents against such decisions can be made to a higher court (Section 11).

Other provisions of the Children Act (1958) relate to the taking out of insurance on foster children, to various requirements, such as the medical and staff arrangements, which can be imposed on premises used 'wholly or mainly' for fostering (Leeding explains (1966, pp. 67-8) that this does not apply to couples in a normal sized house, but to establishments used exclusively for fostering and maintaining a staff), and to notifications on the death of foster children. However, the above paragraphs describe all the major sections of the Act. A study of them can only lead to the conclusion that the duties and powers of children's departments in regard to private foster children are very limited. Their powers to stop a placement taking place appear restricted to cases where premises rather than persons can be shown to be detrimental. Once a placement is made they have no direct powers of removal, but have to go via a juvenile court. They are given no duties at all in regard to natural parents, except to inform them should the child be removed under a place of safety order (Section 7). It is interesting to note that regulations are stricter for children minded daily than for those who live with foster parents. The Nurseries and Child Minders Act (1948), now amended by the Health Service and Public Health Act (1968), requires women to be registered with the local authority before they can take more than two children. Women taking two or fewer can register voluntarily, receiving a Certificate of Registration from the authority. No such provisions apply to private foster parents.

The statutory relationship between children's departments and local authority fostering

The main piece of legislation defining the relationship between children's departments and children taken into their care and placed in their foster homes is the Children Act (1948). Contained in the Act was the power for the appropriate minister to issue regulations. Hence there followed the *Boarding-Out of Children Regulations* published by the Government in 1955. In addition, the Children and Young Persons Act (1963) contained measures which could be interpreted to help the natural parents of children in local authority foster homes.

Duties towards children in care

Local authorities are obliged, if practically possible and if desirable, to put children into foster homes (1948 Act, Section 13). But whether fostered or not their duty to all children in care is to 'exercise their powers with respect to him so as to further his best interests, and to afford him opportunity for the proper development of his character and abilities' (1948 Act, Section 12). As will be shown below, they are also instructed to try to return children to their parents where it is in the interests of their welfare.

Powers over foster home placements

All children fostered by the children's departments are placed with foster parents who are initially chosen or approved by the departments themselves. Their means of selection have already been examined in a previous chapter.

Duties of the foster parents

Local authority foster parents are required under Regulation 20 of the Boarding-Out Regulations to sign an undertaking. The form is given in full in the Appendix of Leeding's work (1966, pp 118–19) and here it is sufficient to note that the foster parents agree to bring the child up as 'we would a child of our own'; to encourage him to practise his religion; to look after his health, and to allow him to be medically examined as the local authority requires; to inform the authority of any serious occurrence affecting the child; to permit officers to visit the home and the child; to allow him to be removed by officers; and to inform the local authority of any change of address.

Duties towards the foster children

The Regulations lay compulsory duties upon the local authority in respect of medical examinations, visits and administration:

   a   Children must be medically examined within one month of being placed in a foster home for those under two years old. Thereafter examinations must be six-monthly while under two years, and annually after that (Regulation 7).

b A child has to be visited by the officer within one month of a placement in a foster home. Thereafter, children under five must be visited at a minimum of once every six weeks in the first two years, and then every three months. A child over five years has to be seen every two months for the first two years and then every three months (Regulation 6).[2] In addition, the officer must visit the home or see the child within one month of a change of address, and immediately if any complaint is made about or from the child.

c Child care officers are obliged to make written reports on the child's welfare, health, conduct and progress after each visit (Regulation 9). Further, reviews of the child's situation have to be made at least every six months by persons other than the visiting child care officer (Regulations 17 and 22).

Powers of removal

The children's department has the power to remove any child in its care from any foster home if it thinks the placement is no longer in the child's interests (Regulation 4).

Duties and powers towards natural parents

Section 3 of the 1948 Act gives a clear duty to return children to the parents when in their interests. Although statute does not explicitly state that child care officers should encourage natural parents to visit their children in foster homes, the department's general duty to rehabilitate children where in the interests of their welfare, to quote Leeding, makes it 'obvious that in many cases they have the right to see their child who is boarded out' (1966, p. 34). Moreover, in order to facilitate such contact the 1948 Act gives powers to pay the expenses of parents to visit children (Section 22). Lastly, the Children and Young Persons Act (1963) makes it a duty upon local authorities 'to make available such advice, guidance and assistance as may promote the welfare of children by diminishing the need to receive children into or keep them in care' (Section 1). The section goes on to specify that the assistance can be 'in kind or, in exceptional circumstances, in cash'. This provision can be, and is, interpreted to mean that material and other help can be given to the parents of children already in care in order to enable them to receive their children back.

Even a cursory comparison makes it evident that the duties and powers of children's departments towards private fosterings are far less than towards local authority ones. The most obvious differences are nine-fold. First, the local authority has no comparable duty towards private foster children with that of its general duty to work to return children in care to their natural parents. Second, it has very little power by which it can influence the making of private placements. It has no obligation to see either foster parents or child beforehand and extremely limited powers to stop an intended placement. On the other hand, the children's department selects both child and foster parents for local authority fosterings. Third, the private foster parents take on no obligations as to the way in which a child should be raised, whereas local authority foster parents must sign an undertaking. Fourth, the number of visits child care officers should make to private foster children is not laid down in any detail, but rests on the words 'from time to time'. The Children Act (1948) gave the appropriate minister power (which the 1958 Act did not give him) to make regulations, including the minimum number of visits, in respect of local authority children. Fifth, the children's department is not obliged to keep records of visits or to have a review procedure for private foster children as it must for local authority foster children. Sixth, children's departments have no duty to ensure that private foster children are regularly medically examined as it must for their local authority counterparts. Seventh, the local authority has no obvious power to give financial or material aid to the private foster parents and children. Possibly Section 1 of the 1963 Act could be construed to give help on the grounds of preventing children from coming into care, but children's departments are unlikely to do this as they appear to regard private fostering as an alternative means of care. By contrast, the local authority not only pays its foster parents a weekly remuneration but can give additional allowances and, indeed, can pay to further the child's interests in almost any way it wishes. Eighth, the local authority has no obligation to help or even see the natural parents of private foster children. It has a duty both to keep in touch with the parents of children in local authority foster homes, and the power to give them material or other aid to help them receive back their children. Lastly, the children's department can only enforce the removal of a private foster child by going via a juvenile court. On the other hand, it can directly remove from a local authority foster home.

Two assumptions implicit in the Children Act (1958) are that private foster children do not merit the same amount of supervision and help as their local authority counterparts, and that the legal machinery it installs will operate to effectively safeguard them. Both these assumptions can be challenged. The present research has already demonstrated that the condition of the private foster children and their treatment by their foster parents is, in many ways, inferior to that of local authority foster children. The present chapter will examine if and how the machinery does safeguard them in practice. However, it must be added that the 1958 Act leaves much to the interpretation of children's departments. The words 'time to time' could be interpreted by child care officers to visit private foster children more frequently than they do local authority ones. Thus it is important to establish how often officers do visit, and indeed how they conceptualise their role towards private fostering – which is equally open to interpretation – in comparison with local authority fostering.

The review of the child care texts and of the legal framework of fostering combined with opinions voiced about private fostering gave rise to six hypotheses:

a that the legal requirements of private foster parents to notify children's departments of their intention to take foster children would generally not be observed;

b that the children's departments would not prohibit the placement of some children in private foster homes which they consider unsuitable;

c that child care officers would perceive their role towards private fostering differently from that towards local authority fostering;

d that the private foster mothers would have a different opinion of and perceive the child care officer's role differently from local authority foster mothers;

e that in terms of visiting the foster parents, children and natural parents, of the nature of help given, and of the administrative arrangements, the children's departments would give an inferior service to private as compared with local authority fostering;

f that the children's departments would not remove some private foster children from fosterings of which they disapprove.

Consideration must now be given to devising means of obtaining the information necessary to explore the claims of these hypotheses.

Obtaining the information

Not only does there exist no previous research on private fostering but that focused on local authority fostering has paid little attention to the relationship between officers and participants. Therefore new approaches and measures had to be devised.

Notification

The date on which the private foster child was placed and the date upon which the local authority was notified by the foster parents could easily be ascertained from the files of the children's department. It was also considered useful to discern how the foster parents discovered that they were obliged to notify the local authority. They were thus asked, 'How did you discover that you had to inform the children's department about the arrival of a foster child?'

Prohibition of placements

In a previous chapter the measures used to ascertain the unsuitability of foster parents were explained. The information collected was considered sufficient to lead to a discussion about prohibition.

The role of the child care officer

Articles in child care journals have pointed out that the officers' and foster parents' conception of the formers' role[3] will shape the service that is actually given. Unfortunately, the articles are not based on research and in Britain, only George (1970) has made an empirical investigation of the subject.[4] He asked officers and foster parents which of a number of listed alternatives most closely described the relationship between them. He does not explain how the alternatives – 'colleagues', 'supervisors', 'inspectors', 'teachers', 'friends' – were arrived at and so the danger existed that respondents were not given the fullest opportunity to use their own definitions.

Open-ended questions were employed for the present research in order to allow the interviewees full scope for their responses. Thus the foster parents were asked why they considered the officers visited and the officers what they considered to be their role towards private foster homes. The replies were categorised and coded by independent judges in the manner used throughout the research. Reliance on a single question was avoided by asking the foster parents how helpful they found the visits, it being assumed that helpfulness (or unhelpfulness) was related to the officers' role. Next, Thurstone's method was used to compile a number of statements which described the relationship between officers and foster parents as follows:[5]

'She is really concerned about the child and me'
'She is a friend of our family'
'She is interesting to talk to'
'Somebody has got to see what is going on'
'She isn't very interested in us'
'My business is nothing to do with her'
'She's always looking for trouble'

The foster parents were asked whether or not they agreed with the statements and their replies scored to give a measure of their opinion towards the child care officers. The officers were also asked supplementary questions concerning the difference between their role to private and local authority fostering. From the replies as a whole, it was hoped both to compare how the various fostering participants perceived the activities of the officers and to assess them besides the roles recommended by the child care literature.

Work of the officers with the fostering participants

A review of child care literature suggested four directions in which the work could be assessed:

1 *Number of contacts.* The number of contacts made by the officers to the fostering participants could easily be ascertained from the files.[6] Therefore a count was made of the number of contacts between the officer and the foster home in the preceding twelve months. However, this was not considered sufficient as it has already been emphasised that both the foster father and the child were important partners in the fostering situation. Therefore, with regard to the foster home, four kinds of count were made:

a the number of times the foster home was visited (this almost invariably meant that the foster mother was seen);
b the number of times the foster child was seen;
c the number of times the foster child was seen alone;
d the number of times the foster father was seen.

As some fosterings had not been in existence for twelve months, some form of average had to be worked out for that period. Therefore, as well as a total count of number of visits in the preceding twelve months, an average for visits per twelve months was also calculated.

Similarly, the number of contacts between the officer and the natural parents could also be counted. Information was collected on the number of times the natural mother was seen, the number of times the natural father was seen, and the number of times at least one was seen in the preceding twelve months.

2   *Practical help.* The practical help offered to foster parents or natural parents could be divided into, first, the direct provision of a commodity, such as money, blankets, bed, pram, etc.; and second, a referral to another agency which might provide help, for instance the National Assistance Board or the Youth Employment Office. A question was constructed for the file schedule in order to record the practical help given.

3   *Nature of interview work.* Child care writers stress that the most valuable part of an officer's work occurs during interviews with the fostering participants. The files, which contained written records of the interviews, were examined in respect of all interviews during the preceding twelve months. Before doing so, however, a framework around which the information could be collated had to be devised. To this end the views of the child care experts gave some indication of the kind of subjects, objectives and techniques officers may use, although the researcher had to be careful not to read these into the material when they were not present. In addition, Hollis's (1968) analysis in the USA of recorded interviews between social case-workers and clients and Goldberg's study[7] of the interaction between social workers and elderly clients were also used in order to find guidelines. From these sources a means of classifying the interview work of officers was formulated and then tested in the pilot study. The pilot indicated that child care officers so rarely saw foster children on their own that there was little point in preparing a recording schedule for them. And so it proved, as the figures for the number of contacts between officers and children alone will show. However, the research went ahead with preparing schedules to assess the interaction between the officers and the foster parents, and between the officers and the natural parents. The pilot study further confirmed that the breakdown of interview work between the officers and foster parents into 'supervisory', 'supportive' and 'educative' with their various subheadings, was a workable basis for collating material. However, it showed that the child care officers and natural parents rarely if ever touched upon the subject which the child care experts call 'helping the child to make the most of the fostering experience'. The schedule therefore omitted this classification, but included two others which the textbooks emphasise,

namely 'to preserve the fostering' and 're-uniting child and natural parents'. The full framework which was devised will appear later in the Tables in the text.

4   *Administrative arrangements.* The administrative arrangements made by the children's departments for both private and local authority fosterings were obtained by observing the forms collected on the files, by examining procedure instructions given to child care officers, and by talking to the administrative staff of the departments.

Removal of private foster children

As described in chapter 4, child care officers were asked which private foster parents they considered unsuitable. They were further asked which children they approved or disapproved of being with their foster parents. For children for whom they expressed disapproval they were further asked whether they were prepared to go to court to effect a removal. If they replied in the negative, the reasons for their answers were further elicited.

The research methods having been outlined, the results can now be presented.

Notification

Private foster parents have a statutory responsibility to notify their local authority of an intending placement fourteen days before it occurs. The times by which the private foster parents of the children in the study gave notification are shown in Table 10.1.

Table 10.1   Time taken by private foster parents to notify local authority of intention to take the foster child

	No.	%
On time (14 days before placement)	3	2·1
0–13 days before placement	5	3·5
Up to one month after placement	69	48·3
1 to 3 months after placement	34	23·8
3 to 6 months after placement	18	12·6
6 to 12 months after placement	2	1·4
More than 12 months after placement	7	4·9
Notice never given*	5	3·5
Totals	143	100·0

*In these cases the officer discovered the placement more than a year after it started and, presumably, thought it too late to get the foster parents to complete a notification form.

This Table shows that only three, 2·1 per cent, of the private fosterings were notified to the children's departments fourteen days before the placement. Another five, 3·5 per cent, of the total, did get the notification in before the child arrived. The remaining 94·4 per cent did not come to the notice of the departments until after the placements started. For twelve children, 8·4 per cent, the notification came at least twelve months too late or never came.

As far as the private foster children in the present study were concerned, the system of notification generally did not work. It was presumably written into legislation in order to give children's departments the opportunity to take action against any forthcoming unsuitable placements. Pugh comments, 'The two weeks statutory notice of placement is rarely long enough for her (child care officer) to do more than exclude the most obviously unsuitable homes' (1968, p. 69). In fact, the situation is worse than Pugh believes. The officers in the present study in most cases did not even have the fourteen days. The children were placed before they could take any preventive action. The hypothesis that the legal requirement to notify children's departments would not generally be observed can be considered upheld.

With so few private foster parents observing the notification requirement, it is of interest to know through what means they did become aware of it (see Table 10.2). This Table refers to the number of private foster parents, whereas Table 10.1 refers to notifications in

Table 10.2   Means through which private foster parents first became aware of a duty to notify the local authority of intention to take a foster child

Health visitor told foster parents	22
Child care officer was informed child was there, and called*	20
Child care officer discovered child while calling for another purpose	15
Friends told foster parents	14
Foster mothers 'felt' they would have to notify	10
Natural parents told foster parents	5
Doctor told foster parents	2
Foster parents saw notice in a newspaper	2
Foster parents saw notice in a post office	1
Other	9
Total	100

*The meaning is that the officer was informed by someone other than the foster parents. In seven cases the natural parents were the informants.

relation to each child. It shows that the methods employed by children's departments to advertise the duty to notify, by notices in public places, in newspapers, and occasionally on television, were largely ineffective. In passing, it must be said that the small size of the notices, their legalistic language and, in post offices, their tendency to be covered with other posters, hardly attracts the attention of passers-by.

Prohibiting placements

A previous chapter explained how the private foster parents were assessed regarding their suitability to foster. Taking the criteria used to assess applicants for local authority parenthood, it was established from the file material that 55 per cent of the private foster parents were unsuitable. Further, the child care officers judged that they would not approve or would be doubtful of approving 52 per cent of them to act for the local authority. The case material given also showed that some foster parents were grossly unsuitable. Yet all these foster parents were allowed to foster. In not one instance did the children's departments attempt to use their powers under the Children Act (1958) to prohibit them. Neither could the departments concerned find any instances outside the research samples where action had been taken. Thus the hypothesis that the children's departments would fail to prohibit the placement of some children in private foster homes which they considered unsuitable, was upheld.

Why were the children's departments so reluctant to prohibit? A major answer is that most placements were made before they knew of them, and hence could not be prohibited. However, although official notification of only 5·6 per cent of the fosterings was received before the placements were made, in other cases the children's departments were aware of the prospect of certain placements. On the one hand, they were sometimes in touch with natural parents who were seeking foster homes. These could be parents who had sought reception into public care but the officers had advised them to use the private fostering market. Although the departments were prepared to vet any replies the natural parents received from advertisements they inserted, they did not appear to follow up the cases to see where exactly the children were to be placed and whether the placement should be prohibited. Similarly, they sometimes knew of unsuitable foster mothers who were seeking new children yet were not prepared to take action against them.

Clearly, ignorance about forthcoming placements was not the sole reason for the children's departments' reluctance to prohibit placements. No doubt another reason was the difficulty of establishing the grounds for such a prohibition. As explained earlier, unless the foster parents were disqualified persons, an intended placement could only be prohibited if the local authority was of the opinion that the keeping of a child 'in a particular premises' would be detrimental to the child. As the foster parents had the right to appeal to a court the evidence had to be easily demonstrated, and both the Association of Children's Officers and the Association of Child Care Officers have voiced the difficulty of compiling evidence relating to premises. Even so, the departments had not even used their powers of prohibiting disqualified persons from fostering. Some officers said there was little use in prohibiting one placement when the natural parents would promptly put the child somewhere even worse. This reluctance to prohibit private placements stands in contrast to local authority placements. Once a child is taken by the children's department he is placed with people of its choice. If necessary he can be put in a reception centre or children's home while suitable foster parents are sought.

The role of the child care officer to the private foster home

The foster parents' view

It will be remembered that Thurstone's technique was used to devise a question whereby the private foster mothers could express their opinion of the child care officer. Scores were given according to the

Table 10.3   Scores of private foster mothers' opinions of child care officer, according to number of private foster mothers*

Positive opinion (score 0·8–2·64)	36
Middling opinion (2·65–6·4)	56
Negative opinion (6·5 and above)	8
Total	100

*In a similar question to assess the foster parents' opinion of the natural parents in the preceding chapter the Table was given in terms of numbers of private foster children, because some foster mothers had more than one foster child and might hold different views towards their parents. No matter how many foster children they had, the foster mother only received visits from one officer at a time, so the calculations are made according to the number of foster mothers, that is the number of foster homes.

statements about the child care officers with which the foster parents agreed or disagreed. Their median score represented the intensity of their attitude towards the officers. The results are shown in Table 10.3.

The question which elicits the foster parent's view of what kind of person the officer was, shows that very few private foster mothers regarded them in a negative way. Over a third thought very positively of them, regarding them as friendly persons genuinely concerned about themselves and the foster children. Over half had what can be termed a middling opinion: they thought the officers were interesting and doing a job that had to be done. Only eight of the private foster mothers saw the officers in an entirely negative light, their views corresponding with the statements, 'She isn't very interested in us', 'My business is nothing to do with her', 'She's always looking for trouble'.

Turning to the local authority foster mothers it was found that ninety, that is 73·8 per cent, had a positive opinion of the child care officer, thirty-one, 25·4 per cent, a middling one, and only one, 0·8 per cent, a negative view. The private foster mothers were significantly less likely to have a positive view of the child care officers than their local authority counterparts ($\chi^2 = 33\cdot924$, d.f. $= 2$, P $= <0\cdot001$).

The foster parents' opinion of the officers need not necessarily imply that they found them helpful. A foster mother might describe her officer as interested and considerate, yet regard her as unhelpful because she lacked the power to help. The findings for the private and local authority foster mothers' opinions on the helpfulness of the officers are given in Table 10.4.

Although thirty-six of the private foster mothers possessed a positive opinion of the child care officers, only seven found their

Table 10.4   Foster mothers' opinion on helpfulness of the visits of child care officers

	Private foster mothers		Local authority foster mothers	
	No.	%	No.	%
Very helpful	7	7	42	34·7
Sometimes	29	29	34	28·1
Hardly	36	36	27	22·3
Not at all	28	28	18	14·9
Totals	100	100	121*	100·0

*One local authority foster mother did not answer this question, so their total was 121, not 122.

visits very helpful. Twenty-nine thought the visits were sometimes helpful but the majority, sixty-four of the one hundred, found them hardly or not at all helpful. By contrast, 34·7 per cent of the local authority foster mothers found the visits very helpful, 28·1 per cent sometimes helpful, and only 37·2 per cent hardly or not at all helpful. The local authority foster mothers were thus significantly more likely to find the officers' visits helpful (dividing, very helpful, sometimes/ hardly, not at all, $\chi^2 = 15\cdot744$, d.f. $= 1$, P $= <0\cdot001$).

In order to portray some idea of what the foster mothers had meant by being or not being helpful, the following quotations from their replies are given. The few private foster mothers finding visits very helpful usually found the officers consistently helpful. One said:

'They are behind you in case they [natural parents] disappear.
She makes me feel I am doing alright. I've no complaints.
Advised me to get a mirror on the pram so she can see
she is coloured. She often advises you – you need it with children
who are not your own. When I was worried about their tempers
she told me it was usual in Nigerians, so I didn't worry so much.'

The private foster mothers who thought the officers' visits were sometimes helpful usually quoted examples of the officer being helpful but mentioning their limitations:

'They know you are doing your best and they reassure you. But as soon as you get used to one she goes.'

The replies categorised as 'hardly' typically mentioned the good intent of the officer's visits, but added it was unusual to receive much help:

'Very nice and understanding, but no help. I do it all myself.'

'She's pleasant, but they never give me cots or beds or anything like that.'

Those regarding the visits as of no help at all generally expressed themselves in strong terms:

'I asked for some clothes for him [foster child]. She was rude, saying the child was not her responsibility. I got nothing.'

'It doesn't matter to me if they come or not. There is nothing they can help me in.'

The private foster mothers' opinions of the officers and their assessment of the helpfulness of their visits throw some light on the way they expected them to behave. This information was more directly sought by asking them why they thought the officers visited (see Table 10.5).

Table 10.5 Reasons given by private foster mothers for visits of child care officer

To inspect the foster parents	75
To inspect the foster child	27
To help (either child or foster parents) with any problems	8
To fulfil their legal duty	3
Other	9

Note: The total does not make 100 as foster mothers could give more than one reason.
Number of private foster mothers = 100.

Three-quarters of the private foster mothers perceived the role of the child care officer as inspectoral with regard to themselves. Indeed, over half gave this as their sole answer. Some examples follow:

'There are good and bad foster parents, they see if they are good, bad or indifferent.'

'To keep an eye on me.'

Twenty-seven defined the role in terms of inspecting the child rather than inspecting the foster mother, for instance:

'To see that the child is looked after and is happy.'

'To keep tabs on where children are and see if grossly neglected.'

Very few of the private foster mothers saw the role in any other terms than inspectoral. However, eight considered they came in order to help either them or the child with any problems:

'They come to see if I have any worries.'

Another three said the officers came because it was their duty, 'It's the law.' Lastly, nine gave replies which could not be classified separately. They included the cryptic statement, 'She's only come once.'

The local authority foster mothers also largely saw the officer's role in inspectoral terms. Seventy-three, that is 59·8 per cent, stated that the officer came to inspect them (Table not given). However, they were still significantly less likely to name the inspectoral role than the private foster parents ($\chi^2 = 5.6864$, d.f. $= 1$, P $= <0.025$). Forty-three, that is 35·2 per cent, saw the officer as inspecting the condition of the child. The major difference, however, was that twenty-seven, 22·1 per cent, of the local authority foster mothers specified the officers as having a role to help them or the child with problems, whereas only 8 per cent of the private ones did so. The difference is statistically significant ($\chi^2 = 8.2633$, d.f. $= 1$, P $= <0.010$). Further, ten of the local authority foster mothers saw the officer visiting because it was their duty, and eight gave answers which were classified as 'other'. Among the latter were three which could be called 'educational' in that the foster mother saw the officer as having a role in giving her or the foster child information about the natural parents. The local authority foster mothers gave less emphasis to the role of inspecting themselves, more to the officer's role towards the foster child, and much more to the role of dealing with problems.

To summarise: the private foster parents did not generally possess a negative opinion of the officers as persons; indeed, with some exceptions, a certain predisposition of good will towards them could be discerned. Their positive opinion did not mean, however, that the visits of the child care staff were considered helpful; on the contrary, only 7 per cent regarded them as 'very helpful'. Most perceived the officer's role only in terms of inspection, few as having a 'problem-helping' role. Few mentioned the possibility of officers talking directly to the foster children, and none regarded them as acting as a link between the natural parents and the foster home. Of the three roles which child care literature stipulates for child care officers – supervisory (or inspectoral), supportive and educational – only the first was appreciated by the private foster parents. Consequently, they were not geared towards accepting from the officers the kind of help which the child care literature says is necessary if foster children are to receive the maximum help from their foster homes. Certainly they would not benefit to the same extent as their local authority counterparts, for the statistical findings served to confirm the hypotheses that the private foster mothers would have a different opinion of and perceive the child care officer's role differently from the local authority ones.

Why did the private foster mothers tend to regard the officers as not helpful and having only an inspectoral role? The reasons were sought, first, by a statistical analysis of the data, and second, by examining the comments of the foster mothers. From the former, three factors emerged as important. Foster parents who had received practical aid were more likely to regard the officers as helpful (dividing at very, sometimes helpful/other, $\chi^2 = 4 \cdot 1005$, d.f. $= 1$, P $= <0 \cdot 025$). The longer the children had been in the placement the less likely the foster mothers were to see the officers as inspectors (dividing at up to 4 years/more, $\chi^2 = 6 \cdot 0289$, d.f. $= 1$, P $= <0 \cdot 025$). Foster parents who were childless or had only one natural child were more likely to perceive the officers as being helpful (dividing at very helpful, sometimes/other, $\chi^2 = 3 \cdot 3800$, d.f. $= 1$, P $= <0 \cdot 050$) and having a 'problem-solving' role ($\chi^2 = 8 \cdot 8451$, d.f. $= 1$, P $= <0 \cdot 010$). It appeared that the receipt of practical aid could convince foster parents that the officers wanted to help while the longer the children were in the home the greater the opportunities for them to gain a broader conception of what the officers could do. Foster parents with less experience of their own children were more prepared to concede that the child care officers could help. However, most private foster parents, as will be shown, tended not to receive practical aid, most children had not been in their placements for over four years, and most of the foster mothers had more than one natural child. Thus substantial numbers did not regard the officers as helpful and few perceived them as having anything but an inspectoral role.

Turning to the comments of the private foster mothers, the most frequent was that the officers lacked the necessary powers to help:

'They can do nothing. They encourage it [private fostering] but do nothing. They can't give you money, even if the parents may not pay.'

'She [the officer] can do hardly anything. . . . The child care officer only gives sympathy. They need more powers, it must be very depressing for them.'

Clearly, these comments tie in with the statistical association found between foster parents who received practical help being more likely to regard the officers as helpful. Lacking the power to give practical help or to control the natural parents in any way, the officers were, in the private foster mothers' eyes, left with no function but to inspect.

Another not unusual complaint was that officers came so infrequently and changed so often that it was impossible for them to really know what help the foster home needed. Certainly, as a subsequent section will show, many private foster homes received a low number of visits from the officers, far fewer than those given to the local authority foster homes. An examination was also made of the turnover rate of child care officers, with the finding that over a third of the private foster mothers had experienced a change of officers on average at least once every twelve months.[8]

By contrast with the private foster parents, the local authority ones experienced the power of the officers both to place children and to provide material help. This, plus more extensive contact, appeared to give them a wider perspective of the kind of aid child care workers can offer and a greater readiness to use it.

The child care officers' view

The thirty-six care officers who were responsible for all the foster children in the study were asked to express their opinion of their role (see Table 10.6). Thirty, that is 83·3 per cent, of the officers saw them-

Table 10.6 Child care officers' opinion of their role towards private foster homes

	No.	%
To inspect and supervise foster parents	30	83·3
To support foster parents	9	25·0
To advise (educate) foster parents	9	25·0
To be a link between foster and natural parents	4	11·1
Same as towards local authority foster children	3	8·3
Other	1	2·8
Totals*	56	—

*Totals do not make 36 or 100 as officers could give more than one opinion. Number of child care officers=36.

selves in an inspectoral or supervisory role towards the private foster homes. Remembering that the child care experts defined work towards fostering as embracing supervision, education and support, it is of note that only a quarter of the officers felt they had the latter two roles towards the private foster homes. It is also of interest that only four mentioned the natural parents while none commented on a direct role with the foster children.

Of the thirty-six officers, thirty-three thought there was a difference between their roles towards the two types of fosterings. Their reasons are given in Table 10.7.

Table 10.7 Reasons child care officers considered their role towards private foster homes different from local authority ones

	No.	%
C.C.O. arranges local authority placements but not private ones	14	42·4
C.C.O. feels she works with local authority foster parents but not private ones	7	21·2
Effective action cannot be taken with private placements	13	39·4
C.C.O. feels she has less responsibility towards private foster homes	5	15·2
C.C.O. has less contact with the natural parents of private foster children	7	21·2
Role towards private foster homes not clearly defined	4	12·2
Other	2	6·1
Totals*	52	—

*Totals do not make 36 and 100 as officers could give more than one reason. Number of child care officers = 36.

The main reasons offered for the different role adopted towards the two kinds of fostering centred around the officers' lack of involvement in, powers towards, and duties in respect of private fosterings.[9] Some officers argued that as, in contrast to local authority fosterings, the natural parents selected the foster homes and placed the children themselves, they tended to have less involvement with both the natural and foster parents. This disengagement was reinforced by the fact that they could not financially help private foster parents or natural parents as they did local authority ones. On top of this they felt they had no clearly defined duties and role towards private fosterings, no guidelines on how to treat the children, no regulations on how often to visit. What were they to make of an Act which told them to visit 'from time to time' and what was meant by 'to satisfy themselves as to the well-being of the children and give such advice as to their care and maintenance as may appear to be needed'? As some officers pointed out, the imprecise nature of these statements was made the more glaring when contrasted with the precise directions applicable to children in public care. Further, even if they were not satisfied, the officers had no powers comparable with those for local authority fostering to prohibit, stop or influence the private placements. Feeling uninvolved, unable to take effective action, having no defined position towards the foster parents, the officers could formulate no role but an inspectoral one towards private fostering. As many considered, in addition, that their social work skills could not be fully utilized in this setting, it is not surprising if private foster homes are accorded low priority by officers always busy with other cases for which they have a clear statutory responsibility. Thus no matter what the child care literature declared the roles of officers towards the fostering participants should be, in practice the officers found that the above factors worked to exclude the roles of education and support.

If the views of the child care literature are valid – namely that officers should accept three roles towards foster homes, supervisory, supportive and educational, and in addition should undertake direct work with foster children and natural parents – then clearly a satisfactory situation does not exist in regard to private fostering. Yet interestingly, there was no clash of expectation between the officers and private foster parents with one side anticipating the giving of a special service or attitude and being rebuffed. Thus both sides emphasised the inspectoral aspect of the officer's work. Hardly any of the private foster mothers and only a minority of the officers regarded the latter as playing supportive or educational roles, and barely any from either side saw them as having direct contact with the foster child or natural parents. Indeed, although the private foster parents found the officers generally unhelpful, they did not display great animosity towards them. Pugh's assertion that private foster parents 'Will not at the outset be aware of the department's interest in the arrangement and the child care officer will appear as an unwelcome inspector' (1968, p. 68), is correct in emphasising the inspector role, but false in calling it 'unwelcome'.

The hypothesis that the child care officers would perceive their role towards private fostering differently from that towards local authority fostering can be considered upheld. Consequently, it appeared that the officers regarded themselves as giving private foster children inferior treatment than their local authority counterparts even if their needs were similar. This situation would seem unlikely to change until children's departments have more definite duties and powers towards the participants of private fostering.

The service given to the private fostering participants

Attention will now be given to the service provided by the children's departments to the private fostering participants in terms of numbers of visits, practical help, content of interviews, and administrative arrangements. In each case comparison will be made with the local authority contrast group.

Numbers of visits[10]

Table 10.8 Average number of visits by child care officers to fosterings in preceding twelve months

No. of visits	Private No.	Private %	Local authority No.	Local authority %
0	21	14·7	5	3·5
1 to under 5	74	51·7	34	23·8
5 to under 10	44	30·8	56	39·2
10 and over	4	2·8	48	33·6
Totals	143	100·0	143	100·0

Only four, 2·8 per cent, of the private fosterings (that is the unit of foster child and foster parent) had received an average of ten or more visits during the twelve months investigated (see Table 10.8). Forty-four, that is 30·8 per cent, were visited between five to under ten times. Seventy-four, over half the private fosterings, were seen between one and under five times, which is at the very most less than once every eight weeks. At the bottom end of the scale, twenty-one, that is 14·7 per cent, were not visited at all. Of course, some of the fosterings came under the same foster mother, so it is as well to point out that 3 per cent of the private foster mothers had ten or more visits, 30 per cent had five to under ten visits, 50 per cent had one to under five visits, and 17 per cent had no visits.

How do these figures compare with those for the local authority contrast group? Forty-eight, over a third, of the local authority fosterings received an average of ten or more visits (against the 2·8 per cent of private fosterings). Fifty-six, 39·2 per cent, had five to under ten visits. Thirty-four, 23·8 per cent, had one to under five visits. Only five, 3·5 per cent, received no visits. The corresponding figures for the local authority foster mothers were 29·5, 42·6, 24·6 and 3·2 per cent. There can be no doubt that the local authority fosterings received far more visits, the difference being highly significant (dividing 0 to under 5/5 and over, $\chi^2 = 48·991$, d.f. $= 1$, P $= <0·001$). Certainly the findings refute Packman's assumption that private fosterings would be visited at a similar rate to local authority ones (1968, p. 178).

The records revealed that the foster mothers were invariably seen on visits. The same could not be said for the foster children who, for instance, might have been at school when the officer visited. Thus it was necessary to calculate separately how often the foster children were seen. The figures are now presented not as an average but for the total number of contacts in the twelve months.

Table 10.9 Number of times foster children were seen during visits by child care officers in preceding twelve months (or in period child had been in foster home if less than twelve months)

No. of visits	Private		Local authority	
	No.	%	No.	%
0	25	17·5	5	3·5
1	31	21·7	9	6·3
2	20	14·0	21	14·7
3–5	47	32·9	58	40·6
6–10	20	14·0	44	30·8
More	0	0·0	6	4·2
Totals	143	100·0	143	100·0

It can be observed from Table 10.9 that twenty-five, 17·5 per cent, of the private foster children had not been seen by the child care officer in the previous twelve months (or since their placement started). In all, seventy-six, that is over half, were seen as little as twice or less. Forty-seven, just over a third, were contacted three to five times, and only twenty, 14 per cent, seen six to ten times. No private foster children were seen more than this. By contrast, only thirty-five, 24·5 per cent, of the local authority foster children were contacted as few times as twice or less (compared with 53·2 per cent). Fifty-eight, 40·6 per cent, were seen three to five times and forty-four, 30·8 per cent, six to ten times. For six, 4·2 per cent, of the local authority children it was over ten times compared with none of the private children. Thus the private foster children were significantly more likely to be seen fewer times by the child care officer than their local authority counterparts (dividing at 0–5/over 5 visits, $\chi^2 = 16·663$, d.f. $= 1$, P $= <0·001$).

The child care texts suggest that officers should see children apart from their foster parents in order to create an environment where they would feel free to talk. Of the private foster children aged two and over, ninety-six, that is 95·1 per cent, were not seen alone in the preceding twelve months while the remainder were seen but once. Of the 105 local authority children, 23·9 per cent were spoken to alone, several of them on a number of occasions each. Thus the private foster children were significantly less likely to see their officer without other persons being present ($\chi^2 = 14·714$, d.f. $= 1$, P $= <0·001$).

As has been mentioned several times, modern child care writers have placed great stress on the importance of the foster father in the fostering situation. Accordingly, a count was made of the number of times they were seen (see Table 10.10).

Table 10.10   Average number of times foster fathers* were seen by child care officers in preceding twelve months

| | Private | | Local authority | |
	No.	%	No.	%
0	66	72·5	47	42·3
1 to under 5	22	24·2	47	42·3
5 to under 10	3	3·3	11	9·9
10 and over	0	0·0	6	5·4
Totals	91	100·0	111	100·0

*The number of foster fathers does not equal the number of foster mothers as some fosterings were conducted by single, separated, divorced or widowed women.

Sixty-six, 72·5 per cent, of the private foster fathers did not see the child care officer in the preceding year. The sixty-six were foster fathers to ninety-four of the private foster children. Forty-seven, 42·3 per cent, of the local authority foster fathers, serving fifty-nine children, were likewise not seen. Clearly, the local authority foster fathers were significantly more likely to receive a visit ($\chi^2 = 18·485$, d.f. $= 1$, P $= <0·001$).

The third party of the fostering triumvirate who can be visited by the child care staff are the natural parents (see Table 10.11). It will be noticed that the Table has been presented in terms of the number of fosterings or foster children. This does involve some double counting, for some children were the offspring of the same parent. As pointed out previously, the 143 private foster children belonged to 118 pairs of natural parents; the 143 local authority ones to 127 pairs. Working the calculations in terms of the actual number of parents made no substantial difference to the result, and the figures are not presented.

Table 10.11 shows that 129, 92·1 per cent, of the private foster children never had a visit paid to their mother in the preceding year. By contrast, sixty-one, 45·5 per cent, of the mothers of local authority

Table 10.11. Average number of visits by child care officers to natural mothers of foster children in preceding twelve months (by number of fosterings)

No. of visits	Private		Local authority	
	No.	%	No.	%
0	129	92·1	73	54·5
1 to under 2	7	5·0	20	14·9
2 to under 3	2	1·4	17	12·7
3 and over	2	1·4	24	17·9
Totals	140	100·0	134	100·0

Note: The mothers of three private foster children and nine local authority foster children were deceased. Where the parent died within the preceding twelve months she was excluded from the Table.

foster children received at least one visit. In twenty-four of these cases (which actually involved twenty-three natural mothers) an average of at least three visits per year were made. The natural mothers in private fosterings were significantly less likely to receive a visit than the local authority ones ($\chi^2 = 50\cdot139$, d.f. $= 1$, P $= <0\cdot001$).

Natural fathers were seen even less. Only eleven of the fathers of the private, and twenty of the local authority fosterings were seen at all in the preceding year. Using material for both mothers and fathers, it became possible to calculate whether at least one parent had been visited (see Table 10.12).

Table 10.12   Visits by child care officers to at least one natural parent in preceding twelve months (according to number of fosterings)

	Private		Local authority	
	No.	%	No.	%
A parent not seen	129	90·2	78	54·5
A parent seen	14	9·8	65	45·5
Totals	143	100·0	143	100·0

Over half the local authority fosterings had not had a parent visited in the preceding twelve months, but for the private fosterings the figure was 90·2 per cent. The difference was clearly statistically significant ($\chi^2 = 45\cdot489$, d.f. $= 1$, P $= <0\cdot001$). Further, the file records showed that not only, in most cases, were natural parents of private foster children not seen in the preceding year, but frequently had never been seen at all.

Given that the officers gave only limited attention to private foster homes, attention was directed towards detecting whether they visited any particular types of private foster parents or children more than others. Very few significant results were found. Thus the most unsuitable private foster mothers, the least participant foster fathers, the children displaying the most adverse conditions, the single natural parents with no support of a partner, were not given compensatory help through extra visits. With regard to children in public care, officers do possess official stipulations on how often to visit. In the absence of such a guide for private fosterings, officers do not appear to have devised alternative criteria to determine their pattern of visits. The consequent paucity of and haphazard nature of visiting, it seems safe to assert, will therefore increase the risk situation of private foster children. Beyond doubt, many were subject to unsatisfactory treatment, conditions and foster parents. Such children were liable to traumatic experiences – a change of foster home, emotional bewilderment wondering why parents have left them, disappointments about parents who fail to turn up, and so on. Most of the children could have gone through such experiences for months before the officer called. For twenty-one they could have continued for twelve months or more without the officer knowing. It can be concluded that the children's departments were not visiting frequently enough to fulfil adequately their inspectoral duties, let alone the comprehensive services advocated by the child care literature.

Practical help

The distinction between help in interviews, taken to be verbal help, and practical help is to a certain extent a false one. Practical help, or the prospect of it, is discussed during interviews and may be seen as a solution to the problems discussed. None the less, it was felt that foster parents would make the distinction, and indeed it has already been shown that the experience of such a service influenced the foster parents' conception of the child care officer's work.

The practical services given to the local authority fosterings (see Table 10.13) did not take into account the regular services like payments or allowances which the children's department rendered them. Even so, the thirty-two local authority fosterings, involving thirty-one foster mothers, exceed the twelve private fosterings involving seven private foster mothers. The difference was statistically significant ($\chi^2 = 11 \cdot 110$, d.f. $= 1$, P $= <0 \cdot 001$).

Table 10.13   Practical services given by child care officers to fosterings in preceding twelve months

| | Private | | Local authority | |
	No.	%	No.	%
Service given	12	8·4	32	22·4
Not given	131	91·6	111	77·6
Totals	143	100·0	143	100·0

A closer examination of the practical services given the private fosterings shows that only on three occasions was material help given directly. Once the officer managed to contribute a second-hand pram, another time a present for the private foster child, and third, an officer gave one foster mother a personal loan of a small amount. The other practical aid was of a more indirect nature. Five times the officers, at the foster parents' request, contacted the natural parents to persuade them to pay more or more regularly. One foster mother was offered support in her application for a council house, and another was referred to legal advice.

Practical help towards the parents of private foster children was even more sparse. In fact, the only practical service offered in the preceding twelve months was when an officer arranged a holiday for another child of one of the natural parents. Practical help towards the natural parents of children in care could hardly be called a frequent occurrence, but in the preceding twelve months it was given on twenty occasions to seventeen natural parents. Again, the most common form of help was the provision of some material item, such as a pram or cot. Only once was cash given directly. The other most frequent form of aid was that directed towards the obtaining of accommodation.

Content of interviews

As explained, an analysis was made of the content of the child care officers' interviews with the foster parents as recorded on the files. The results can be seen in Table 10.14.

This Table reveals very forcibly that inspection and assessment was the predominant item reported upon by the officers with regard to their visits to private foster homes. It was noted 408 times in 433 interviews, covering 123, that is 86 per cent, of the fosterings and 84 per cent of the foster parents. Moreover, it was frequently the only item in the reports and one which tended to have a stereotyped form.

Table 10.14 Content of interviews between child care officers and foster parents in preceding twelve months

	Private			Local authority		
	Items	No. of foster-ings	No. of foster parents	Items	No. of foster-ings	No. of foster parents
Supervisory inspection and assessment	408	123	84	702	138	117
use of authority	2	2	2	3	1	1
Supportive discussion of problems	27	22	14	90	51	43
ventilation	7	6	5	29	26	22
reassurance and encouragement	7	4	4	31	30	21
Educative advice and information	30	23	15	67	39	34
understanding of self	0	0	0	1	1	1
Other	22	13	9	74	68	42

Note: This Table shows in the first column the total number of times the item was found in all the interviews. Some items would occur more than once in the same interview or be repeated with the same fosterings, so column two gives the number of fosterings and column three the number of foster parents who experienced the item at least once.

Number of private fosterings=143.
Number of private fosterings for which at least one interview recorded=122.
Number of private foster parents=100.
Number of private foster parents for whom at least one interview recorded=83.
Total number of interviews with private fosterings=433.
Number of local authority fosterings=143.
Number of local authority fosterings for which at least one interview recorded=138.
Number of local authority foster parents=122.
Number of local authority foster parents for whom at least one interview recorded=118.
Total number of interviews with local authority fosterings=708.

An actual and typical example of a whole report on a private fostering is: 'Called to see Mrs K. As usual the home seemed full of children and toys. All the foster children looked fit and well, and there is nothing unusual to report.'

Such reports contain a quick description of the situation, plus an evaluative comment. Even where a problem was observed it was rare

I

to find the officers doing more than make a note of it. The predominance they gave to inspection and assessment ties in with the opinions of most officers that such functions made up their major role towards private foster homes.

Assuming that the reports accurately reflect what the officers did, it is clear that supportive work was rarely undertaken with the private foster parents. Discussion of specific problems occurred only twenty-seven times, and concentrated on three main subjects – the foster parents' fears about losing a specific child, the disturbing effect of visits from natural parents, and behaviour difficulties of particular children. Interestingly, on only one occasion did an officer discuss a problem relating to the child's colour, and again, only in one interview was a child's problem of not knowing about his real relationship explored. The two other aspects of support, namely ventilation and reassurance, were noted only seven times each.

Educative work was recorded only thirty times, involving 16·1 per cent of the fosterings and 15 per cent of the private foster parents. Helping foster parents to understand themselves occurred not at all, the educative interaction consisted only of giving advice and information. The most frequent items of information passed on concerned explaining the Children Act (1958). The most common piece of advice involved what fees the foster parents should charge. Only four times did an officer directly advise them how to handle their foster children.

The twenty-two 'other' items ranged over a wide variety of subjects. Several times discussion centred on the private foster parents' wish to foster on behalf of the local authority – usually with the officer trying to put off the possibility of the application. Other items included the foster parents' natural children, their health, and, on one occasion, the foster mother's marriage plans.

Overall, it is fair to say that for many of the private fosterings the visits of the officers served little other purpose than to allow them to keep an eye on the situation. The work undertaken during the interviews bore little resemblance to that recommended by the child care texts. The supervisory role was carried out, howbeit only very occasionally in many cases, but the various aspects of the supportive and educative roles were found in only a minority of fosterings. One aspect, help directed towards allowing the foster parents to understand how their own experiences and feelings influenced the fostering, was observed not at all.

The local authority fosterings received 708 interviews during the preceding twelve months. As with the private ones, nearly all the local authority fosterings, 96·5 per cent in all, had been subject to supervision. The amount of supportive and educative work with the local authority fosterings may seem surprisingly low. Not one of the particular items occurred with more than half of the fosterings. This finding would appear to support a major theme of George's research, that a large gap exists between theory and practice in children's departments. A similar finding was noted in Jarrett's study of the work of four other children's departments in 1959.[11]

It is worth noting that even with the local authority foster parents, the officers rarely attempted what is called interpretation or insight giving by casework text books. Lastly, 74 items did not fit into the defined categories. The most common subjects here were discussions about the foster mother's own family, and efforts by the officer to persuade the mothers to take more foster children.

Whatever the gap between the ideal and the actual with regard to the local authority fosterings, there is no doubt that the officers gave supportive and educative help to them far more often than to the private ones. Thus specific problems connected with the fostering were discussed ninety times in the local authority interviews, compared with twenty-two in the private ones. Again, the local authority fosterings and mothers were more likely to receive help in ventilating their anxieties and in receiving reassurance and encouragement. Taking the three aspects of supportive work together, 44 per cent of the local fosterings, involving 43·4 per cent of their foster parents, received help. The comparative private figures were 22·4 and 23 per cent (the difference is statistically significant, for the foster parents, $\chi^2 = 9\cdot1698$, d.f. $= 1$, P $= <010$). Educative help was offered to a total of 28 per cent of the local authority fosterings and 24·5 per cent of the foster parents. The private figures were 16·1 per cent and 15 per cent (the difference was not quite statistically significant).

The findings of the different sections of this chapter interlock. Generally speaking the private foster mothers saw the officers' role as inspectional and did not expect help. The officers similarly perceived an inspectoral role, not seeing what else they could do to help. Consequently, the actual interviews between the two reveal little more than inspection and assessment. Yet the research interviews with the foster mothers revealed a number who badly needed help which they were not receiving. The following examples are presented to illustrate different types of aid required, but which was not given:

a   Providing information. A West African private foster child was somewhat disturbed about his relationship with his foster parents. Both the foster parents and the child were ignorant of the facts that the child had siblings who were in Nigeria, and that the natural father was alive, not dead as they had been led to believe. Probably the foster family as a whole would have been helped had the officer ascertained their lack of knowledge and informed them of the truth.

b   Coping with natural parents. Several private foster parents felt puzzled as to how to handle the natural parents. One foster mother, who believed the child should see her parents, found the latter frequently quarrelled between themselves during visits, much to the bewilderment of the child. The foster mother could not decide whether she should ask them not to visit. Similarly, other foster mothers needed information in order to understand the behaviour patterns displayed by parents from another culture on their visits to the foster home. Another frequent aspect of the relationship with the natural parents concerned the foster parents' fears that they would suddenly take the child. The foster parents were torn between trying to get the parents to state categorically how long they intended leaving the child, and fearing that such an attempt would actually provoke them to remove the child. The child care officers could have helped by mediating between the foster and natural parents.

c   Dealing with child's behavioural problems. More than anything else, private foster parents could be at a loss in coping with difficult children. A foster mother who had persevered with two extremely deprived school-age youngsters said,

> 'When the child is difficult you don't know whether it's because it's not happy with you, or whether it has suffered previously and is not sure of you. When you know more you can understand the child. When he came he used to soil himself, and I never knew why.'

Another foster mother had had her five-year-old foster boy for nearly three years. His condition has already been mentioned in a previous chapter. Unable to communicate with adults, unusually withdrawn and anxious, backward in his motor and speech functions, the foster mother desperately needed help. She complained that the hospital had been unco-operative. She managed to get an appointment with the local child guidance clinic, but was told the child was all right. Her general practitioner merely advised that she return the child. No child care officer had called in the previous twelve months, while she said that those from the year before had offered no help. She remarked in bitter fashion, 'They must know more than they offer.' Thus a woman highly motivated to persevere with a disturbed child felt she was near breaking-point because she could not get help.

d Reassurance re-adequacy. A number of private foster mothers, feeling unsupported in their role and probably knowing no other foster mothers, appeared to want reassurance that they were treating the foster children properly.

e Answering questions. Several private foster mothers expressed the need for advice on how to answer questions put to them by the foster children about their illegitimacy and colour. The officers, who would have given similar advice to local authority foster mothers, could thus have been of use to the private ones.

To summarise. Compared with the kind of help which the literature claims fosterings are likely to need, the range and amount of help via interviews given to the private foster parents was remarkably limited. It did not approach that given to the local authority fosterings although, as the private ones had more unsuitable fosterings and displayed more adverse conditions, a case could be made for giving them the greater amount and range of service.

A similar content analysis was carried out on the reports of the interviews between the child care officers and the natural parents. The findings are given in Table 10.15.

The paucity of the officers' visits to the natural parents of the private foster children is reflected in the small number of items which could be counted in the interviews. Only eight times was the officer observed trying to preserve the fostering. Only with six parents did the officers verbally move towards reuniting child and parent. In no record was there evidence of the parent being encouraged to visit the child more often. Neither in amount nor in content did the work with them approximate to the great stress which the child care literature places on work with natural parents.

Turning to the local authority situation, it was found that although the work with natural parents of children in care could not be described as extensive, it covered significantly more parents and more subjects than those of the private foster children. Thus with the objective of preserving the fostering in mind, eleven natural parents covering thirteen local authority fosterings were encouraged to leave their child in the foster home, whereas this happened with only one of the parents of a private child. The most common item was the encouragement to visit more often, occurring fifty-four times amongst

Table 10.15   Content of interviews between child care officers and natural parents in preceding twelve months

	Private			Local authority		
	Items	No. of foster-ings	No. of foster parents	Items	No. of foster-ings	No. of foster parents
To preserve fostering						
encourage to pay regularly/pay more	5	4	3	—	---	—
encourage to modify behaviour on visits	1	1	1	—	—	—
encourage to leave child in foster home	1	1	1	16	13	11
discuss fears that child is ill-treated	1	1	1	6	6	6
To reunite						
encourage to visit more	—	—	—	54	33	30
encourage to have child back	8	7	5	18	11	11
discuss feelings (guilt, rejection) concerning loss of child	1	1	1	3	2	2
Other						
parents request reception into care	1	1	1	—	—	—
parents advised to change foster home	2	2	2	—	—	—
other	5	5	3	42	23	19

Note: Total number of private fosterings = 143.
Number of private fosterings for which at least one visit to natural parents recorded = 14.
Total number of pairs of natural parents of private foster children = 118.
Number of pairs of parents for whom at least one visit recorded = 10.
Number of local authority fosterings = 143.
Number of local authority fosterings for which at least one visit to natural parents recorded = 65.
Total number of pairs of natural parents of local authority foster children = 127.
Number of pairs of parents for whom at least one visit recorded = 61.

thirty natural parents. Further, the child care officers took far greater interest in the natural parents, a large proportion of the items marked 'other' being where they had discussed their personal situation and problems. Such discussion rarely happened between the officers and parents of the private foster children.

The lack of contact between officers and natural parents of private foster children might lead to the impression that effective interaction never occurred between them. This would be a false impression, for the few cases found in the preceding twelve months, plus the records which often stretched back beyond that period, gave some examples – howbeit few in number – of valuable work. However, these were the exception. The files and the interviews with natural parents revealed many more examples of those who needed some form of social work help but did not receive it.

a Encouragement to visit. A number of parents had stopped visiting or reduced their visiting because their children had not seemed to welcome them, or because the sight of their children intensified their feelings of guilt at having placed them. Thus the visits of a natural father dropped off sharply when his son failed to address him as 'Daddy'. A few natural parents had actually taken their children home for weekends with a view to reunification, only to find their behaviour so difficult and rejecting that they concluded they could not cope. These reactions of guilt or initial rejection by children are well-known to child care officers, and it is within their capacities to explain to parents that they constitute normal behaviour elements in cases of separation. However, these parents lacked the casework aid which could have caused them to persist, and instead their visits and contact tailed off.

b The experience of separation. The interviews with the natural parents indicated that unmarried and separated parents in particular went through agonies as to whether they should part with their children and, having so decided, agonies of worrying if the child was all right. Many would have appreciated help at this time.

c Relationship with the natural child. Even where natural parents continued to visit, they could still experience problems in relating to their own children. Some parents found it difficult to get their children to talk to them. An unmarried mother who had faithfully visited her daughter's foster home for fifteen years asked the girl to spend the weekends at her flat, not with a view to permanently rejoining her but in order to increase communication between them, and 'because I'm lonely'. The teenage daughter bluntly replied, 'No, get married', much to the hurt of the mother.

d Ignorance about rights and services. Regular contact between child care officers and natural parents at least could have saved many from mistaken ideas. Not only were some parents unaware of the existence of useful services, such as day nurseries, but they were confused as to their relationship with the private foster parents. A minority believed they had handed their parental rights over to the foster parents. Others were not sure of their right to visit. In the case of a broken marriage, the parent who had not placed the child could think he had lost custody.

e   Personal problems. The placement of a child might well be only one expression of parents' complex problems which could also have benefited from the concern and skills of a social worker. One parent, friendless, despondent, and with the loss of her child perceived as the last straw, tried to commit suicide. She was never, at any time, seen by a child care officer.

The duty of local authorities to rehabilitate children in their care gives them a responsibility to work with the children's natural parents. They have no such obligation towards the parents of private foster children. Hence child care officers may not know about the parents' problems or, if knowing, may feel they are outside their scope. The local authority does possess duties – howbeit very limited ones – towards private foster children, and it can be argued that to have this without a corresponding duty towards their parents is to make an unreal distinction. For instance, a teenage private foster child wrote to the child care officer:

'I called to see my mother Wednesday last and found her, as I expected, in a terrible state. I've never seen anyone let themselves go so much. . . . If you have a spare moment call to see my mother, would you? I think she is very unhappy.'

The child in this case could only have had her pain alleviated through her mother. In other words, the conditions of child and mother were intertwined, yet the children's department had no duty to help the latter. She, like so many parents of the private foster children, was in need but received no aid.

As only five private foster children were seen alone by the child care officers in the preceding twelve months, there is little point in statistically comparing the content of the interviews with those of the local authority foster children. None the less, these five, and work done in periods before the twelve-month period, made it clear that valuable results could come from contacts between officers and children. In one case the officer, assessing a private foster child to be unhappy because she had lost contact with her brother, arranged for them to spend some time together. Another officer, perturbed by the extreme anxiety symptoms displayed by a boy, had a long talk with him and established that they became most severe when he wondered if his mother still loved him, and if he would have to leave the foster home.

Although the occasional case demonstrated how private foster children could be directly helped, far more revealed those who needed such help but did not obtain it. Very common were the children who wanted knowledge of (or contact with) their siblings and parents. In some cases children did not know that their siblings were living only a few miles away in another foster home. In other cases children were clearly in need of help to deal with fears and insecurities. Thus one illegitimate teenage girl was concerned that she would 'inherit' the promiscuous behaviour pattern of her mother; another her mother's alcoholism. The chapter on the condition of the children gave ample evidence of how many displayed extreme emotional traits. Yet it was the exception to find the child care officers directly helping them with these problems.

Administrative arrangements

It seems a reasonable assumption that an agency's sense of responsibility for its clients will be reflected in the extent and type of administrative arrangements it makes for them. A comparison was thus made of the children's departments' arrangements to collect information, to regulate visits, and to review local authority and private fosterings.

Children's departments collect information on the local authority fostering participants in order to aid their understanding of them and, thereby, to plan more adequately for their future. They usually seek out details of significant events in the children's histories which may have influenced their development, as well as knowledge of the existence and whereabouts of relatives who may be able to help them. Similarly, they will aim to collect information about the foster and natural parents. To take the foster parents: the children's departments 'vet' foster parents and so collate information about them before they start to foster. Both departments used forms which specified a minimum amount of items to be sought. These included the age, religion and previous history of the prospective foster parents, their income and outgoings, their type of accommodation, their previous mobility, and their health record with particular reference to disabilities and mental illness. In addition, references were taken up from a doctor and two others, while the child care officer also submitted further details under a 'general report' heading. After the foster child was placed, the officers' reports would continue to build up an even fuller picture. By contrast, details about the private foster parents were taken after the children were placed. The ineffectiveness of the notification system made an earlier collation virtually impossible. A special form was used for the first interview and, interestingly, the minimum number of items to be sought was smaller in number and given less space than those for the local authority foster parents. Information was not sought on the private foster parents' financial position, their type of housing or their mobility. Instead of specifying which aspect of health to explore, the form merely left one line for 'health'. A similar space was left for the officer to describe 'general suitability'.

The same contrast appeared concerning information about the foster children and natural parents. At the point of reception into public care, the department assembled a great amount about their history and present situation. With regard to private fostering, however, the only details the officer had to compile were the name, age, legitimacy, religion and place of birth of the children, along with the name and address of the parents and the amount they paid the foster parents. There was no obligation to record the children's histories, whether they had siblings, or the addresses of other relatives.

Following the collection of information, attention was turned to the departments' systems of regulating visits. As explained, the Boarding-Out Regulations stipulate the minimum number of visits to local authority foster children. In both the children's departments investigated the child care officers were supervised by seniors who tried to ensure that no fostering was under-visited. No Boarding-Out Regulations apply to private foster children, and hence any supervision of visit regularity depended on the individual senior child care officer concerned. The paucity of contact with private foster children suggests that most officers chose not to enforce a system of strict supervision.

It is also in accordance with the Boarding-Out Regulations that local authority foster children are subjected to regular reviews. Their form consists of a review report written by the child care officer, which is then examined by persons other than the officer himself. Both children's departments employed special schedules for review purposes. The one used by the county children's department, for instance, included a section headed 'Summary of progress, behaviour and personality' followed by specific items relating to the child's contact with his own family, his health, progress at school or work, the condition of the foster home and plans for the future. In both departments the review was seen not only by the children's officer but by a lay committee, to which the officer reported. No such review took place for the private foster children.

The collection of information, the supervision of visits and the review system are just parts of the administrative machinery created to help children in care. Mention could also be made of less structured supervision, such as the comments of senior child care officers about their handling of cases, of the financial machinery which ensured that payments, allowances, etc., were paid to the local authority foster homes, and of the provision for regular health and educational reports. All were focused primarily on the children in care, while the private foster children were hardly touched by the system.

Overall contact

The method of examining separately the child care officers' number of visits and content of interviews with each of the fostering participants, although necessary, does fail to give an overall view of the work with the foster family as a whole. To rectify this, two cases will be presented to contrast the service rendered to private and local authority fostering. In both cases the child concerned had periods in the care of the children's department and in a private foster home:

a Following the desertion of his wife, a lorry driver's three-year-old daughter was received into the care of the children's department. After three months he took her back, stayed at home a while, and then placed her in a private foster home. This and a subsequent home broke down before a third was found. The girl, now six, displayed such severe behavioural symptoms that the foster mother informed the children's department about them. The child care officer concerned assessed the foster mother as extremely unsuitable, and the child was received into care again. During the following six months in a children's home she received much attention from the child care officer and treatment from the child guidance clinic. The clinic reported, 'demanding and attention-seeking. ... The sexual difficulties are yet another symptom of her general disturbance. .... The most urgent need is the stability and security of a long-term placement with accepting parent figures.' Despite the recommendation, the girl was discharged to the same private foster parents from whom she was received and they, within six months, passed her on to another couple. At the time of the research the girl's private foster home had been visited twice by the officer, the girl seen alone not at all, and the contact with child guidance dropped altogether. This is to be contrasted with the close contact and encouragement to attend the clinic while she was in care.

b   The second example is even more interesting in that the child was fostered from the local authority and then privately in the *same* foster home, and supervised by the same officer. The child concerned, then a four-month-old baby girl, was received into care by the children's department when her family was homeless following an eviction. She was placed with local authority foster parents, remaining there for two years and ten days. During this period the child care officer made eleven visits to the foster home, arranged for the girl to be medically examined three times, saw the natural mother on thirteen occasions and the natural father four times. The interviews with the natural mother were lengthy and with much content: the officer encouraged her to co-operate with the foster mother and began to work towards the time when she could have her daughter home; together they explored the natural mother's marital situation and moved on to examine how her childhood experiences had contributed to her present problems; help was given to enable the mother to pay off her debts and to put her in line for a council house. Partially as a result of the casework, the mother began to plan definitely to resume the care of her child and, having obtained suitable accommodation, the girl was discharged to her care. The reunion did not work out well. The mother, finding that she and the girl were not relating, wanted the children's department to take her back. The department refused, arguing that the cause for the original reception had now disappeared. Consequently, within two days of taking the child, the mother placed her privately with the same foster parents. In the ensuing four years and five months the officer visited the foster home only eight times, never saw the natural parents, and of course provided no administrative services such as arrangements for medical examinations.

In both cases the children's and natural parents' problems, needs and symptoms appeared similar at all stages. Yet the range and number of services dropped dramatically once they passed from local authority to private fostering. These two cases merely serve to illustrate in a compact way that which has been shown throughout this section: children in similar conditions receive help not according to need but according to their designation – private or local authority. The findings uphold the hypothesis that in terms of visiting, of the nature of help given, and of the administrative arrangements made, the participants in private fostering received an inferior service compared with local authority fosterings.

The enforced removal of private foster children

To establish, as was done earlier, that the child care officers did not consider certain private foster parents as suitable is not quite the same as saying they disapproved of a placement which was in operation. For instance, they might consider it best for a child to stay with unsuitable foster parents with whom he had a relationship rather than risk a move to anywhere else. Thus, in addition, the officers were asked about present placements with the result that they showed disapproval of thirty-six fosterings actually continuing. They were then asked if they would be prepared to take court action to effect the removal of the children. Not one officer was so prepared.[12]

Two main reasons were offered for not taking action. The most common, applying to twenty-one of the children, being that evidence would not be strong enough to obtain a court order. The officers argued that it was virtually impossible to prove 'emotional neglect' to a court. For example, an officer described one foster mother – whose application to the local authority had been rejected – as 'ill and neurotic' and the foster child as 'frightened and backward and showing extreme anxiety symptoms'. He declared the foster mother was 'unable to deal with the child's emotional needs', but added that 'the physical care is adequate – difficult to establish a [court] case on other grounds'.

The officers, then, complained that a case against private foster parents sufficient to win a removal under Section 7 of the Children Act (1958) demanded evidence of physical neglect or cruelty. However, there was no history of the departments trying to win cases where the evidence presented on the files appeared so strong that the courts would have had difficulty in dismissing them on either physical or emotional grounds. Moreover, advantage was not taken of cases of physical neglect. For instance, several private foster children were in overcrowded conditions by any standards. In one case, where seven children and two adults were living in a small dwelling, the outbreak of an infectious disease caused the housing department to complain of the overcrowding to the children's department. Although the officer disapproved of the placements, she still was not willing to concede that a case could be made before the juvenile court. It is difficult not to draw the conclusion that the child care officers were reluctant to use the courts. Possibly some felt uncomfortable about giving evidence in the judicial situation, while others, as the second reason shows, felt there was little point in removing children when it was difficult to see where they would go.

In eight cases, the child care officers explicitly stated that removal via a court was pointless because of the unlikelihood of providing anywhere better. If the court entrusted the child to the care of the children's department, the officers were given the task of finding a placement in a situation where foster homes acceptable to their standards were in short supply. If he was returned to his natural parents they might place him in another equally unsuitable private foster home.

The hypothesis that the children's departments would not remove some children from private fosterings of which they disapproved was upheld. Clearly, local authorities have greater powers to remove children who are in their care from foster homes. Here removals can be the result of the officers' professional judgment concerning the interests of the children, they do not depend upon proving a case to a court. Not only do the children's departments lack similar powers for private foster children, they are also reluctant to use the limited method of enforced removal via the courts. Consequently, children with similar needs, similar symptoms of deprivation or similarly unsuitable foster parents, are likely to be subjected to different treatment from the children's departments according to their status as private or local authority foster children. A final example makes the point: the children's department removed a local authority foster child from foster parents whom they considered could no longer cope with fostering. No action was taken when the same foster mother immediately took a private foster child, the officer commenting that no removal action could be taken because there was 'no concrete evidence for court purposes. The child is not neglected or ill-treated'.

The legislation relating to local authority and private fostering appears based on the assumption that they require different kinds of supervision and help. The assumption may spring from the view – which the research demonstrates to be false – that private foster children have fewer problems and difficulties than local authority ones, or from a belief that to impinge too closely on private arrangements is an infringement on personal freedom. Whatever the reasons, statute gives local authority children's departments definite duties, precise regulations and strong powers in relation to children received into public care. For those taken into private foster homes it gives them a vague duty, no regulations and extremely limited powers.

The differing legislative emphasis is reflected in the interpretation, made by both private foster parents and child care officers, that the latter can give but little help to the former. The acting out of this interpretation resulted in only minimal involvement of the officers in the private fostering situation. In terms of contacts with the private foster homes, foster fathers, foster children and natural parents, in terms of giving practical help and of the content of interviews with the fostering participants, the service given to private fostering was small compared with local authority fostering. Certainly the work did not approximate to that recommended by the child care texts.

The contrasting legislation, the differing roles fulfilled by the officers towards the two types of fosterings, and the different levels of service given, leads to the conclusion that, at least in the areas studied, there are two nations in fostering. Local authority foster children were assured of regular supervision; the children's department had a duty to try to reunite them with their parents; their foster parents were guaranteed certain financial and material aid; and if the foster home did not attain standards of child care which satisfied the children's department it had sufficient powers to end the placement. The private foster children were not assured of regular supervision; the local authority was not obliged to work towards reunification with their parents; their foster parents were not guaranteed a regular income; and however low the standards of child care the children's department was not likely to effect a removal. Throughout this study the private foster children have been shown to be in adverse material, emotional and educational conditions in comparison with the local authority foster children, to receive inferior treatment and to be less likely to have their needs met. Instead of being compensated by extra attention and services from the children's departments, the reverse occurred, so reinforcing their position.

Two factors recurred as important influences in determining the relationship between the officers and the fostering participants. First, the lack of a financial relationship between the children's departments and the private fostering participants. Neither the private foster parents nor the natural parents were likely to receive material help from them. Consequently, both they and the child care officers considered the latter's hands were tied in offering help. Second, the children's departments' limited powers to prohibit and end placements was also perceived as nullifying any effective role the officers could play. Examples were found of relatives (not the parents) 'snatching' a child from foster parents, and of natural parents shuttle-cocking children between placements, as well as of children being left with unsuitable foster parents. In such cases the officers stood hopelessly by, becoming more reluctant to be involved where they could do so little to help. If the situation of the private foster children, foster parents and natural parents is to alter, then changes will have to occur in their relationship with the children's department. The final chapter will discuss the feasibility of change.

11   The future of private fostering

The study, which comprises the first research project on private fostering in this country, has ranged over all the participants in the fostering process. The findings can now be summarised, the main characteristics identified, and some proposals for changes be put forward.

The private foster children

Two major characteristics distinguished private foster children not only from the child population as a whole but from children in the care of local authorities. First, private fostering was shown to be very largely a phenomenon of the under-fives. Over two-thirds of the children were of pre-school age at the time of the research, while over 90 per cent had been in this age-group when placed in their foster homes. The local authority contrast group had been matched for age but comparison with other children in public care revealed that their proportions in the lower age-ranges were far less. These early years, all writers are agreed, have a vital influence on children's social, emotional, physical and intellectual development. It would seem equally vital, therefore, that particular attention be paid to the quality of care given to a group of children characterised by separation from their own family before the age of five.

Second, the nationality, legal status and reasons for placement of the private foster children were further distinguishing features in comparison with the local authority foster children. Four main groupings of private foster children were identified, the legitimate children of West African students, the illegitimate children of unmarried mothers from the United Kingdom, the legitimate children of fathers from the United Kingdom whose wives had deserted, the children of mothers from the United Kingdom whose husbands had deserted. The fact that some 60 per cent of the children were in the first grouping confirmed the belief that West African children made up a substantial part of private fostering. The differences between the private and local authority children were such that it was difficult to draw up similar groupings. The local authority sector had few West African children but much higher proportions of illegitimate children, of those with a racially mixed background, and of those separated from their parents because of accommodation problems and the illness of mothers.

West African children

The number of West African children in the private fostering sample, taken in conjunction with the accusations that they are particularly neglected, makes it necessary to draw together the findings about them.

In comparison with other private foster children the West Africans were more likely to find their foster homes via the advertising system with less adequate preparation being made for their placements. They experienced greater overcrowding with regard to bedroom density and a higher incidence of some respiratory illnesses although not other kinds of illness or handicap. Their foster parents tended to show slightly less determination to retain care of them in face of difficulties although this was associated with the shorter duration of their placements which gave less time for the relationship between them to develop.

If the above factors revealed the West African children in a more disadvantaged light, other findings showed the reverse. Their foster parents were more likely to regard them as and to treat them as foster and not as natural children. Perhaps as a consequence the West African children were less likely to be deceived about the nature of their relationship to the foster parents. The greater frequency of contact with their parents, combined with the fact that most West African children had two interested parents, leads to the reasonable deduction that such children have a more definite prospect of rejoining their parents than those whose only interested parent visited infrequently. In addition, the West African children were not significantly different from others in their number of moves, in their chance of being with unsuitable foster parents, in having non-participating foster fathers, or in the display of signs of deprivation. Of course, it must be stressed that the West African children, as part of the private fostering group, tended to show more adverse conditions and inferior treatment than the local authority counterparts but not more than other private foster children.

These findings do not mean that all bodes well for the future of the West African children. It is anticipated that most will return to their parents, hence it is necessary to speculate on the effects of their fostering experiences on their future functioning. A possible difficulty is that their fostering experiences may have socialised them into educational patterns which are not acceptable to the parents to whom they return. Many of the West African children's foster parents were from social classes IV and V, the very classes who, Wilson claims, tend to instil the least educational aspirations and whose children tend to under-achieve (1970, pp. 125–8). As most of the children were placed under the age of one year and stayed during the years considered crucial in forming a child's pattern of development, they could be expected to incorporate the educational aspirations and attitudes of their foster parents. However, the same children will return to natural parents whose own periods of study show them to have high educational hopes and who will expect much from their children. If the latter are unable to achieve, parental disappointment and family conflict is to be anticipated.

Educational problems can be expected whether the West African families remain in Britain or return to their homeland. Other problems will be intensified if the children are taken back to a West African society. It is true that the parents will probably settle in urbanised districts and will themselves have been influenced by their stay in western society. None the less, they will retain West African ways of thought and behaviour very different from their children who have been socialised within working-class British homes. Oyerinde, in his comparison of the Yoruba people and western society, highlights two major differences. First, Nigerian children have a far greater respect for age whereas western youth tends to admire youth. Second, sex roles, that is the 'culturally approved characteristics for males and females' are more clearly defined in West Africa, with the father being more authoritarian and the child 'used to seeing his mother treat his father like a lord and head of the house' (1967, p. 47). Children raised in Britain, especially in foster homes where the woman may have dominated, will find it hard to accept attitudes and behaviour so different from their immediate past. Their confusion will be increased if, having been used to a close relationship with one mother figure, they enter a wider West African kin group where a number of women interact closely with the children. Lastly, children who speak only the English language will have problems in relating to a society which has an additional tongue.

The condition of the private foster children

Both private and local authority foster children tended to display adverse emotional, physical and educational conditions. Certainly, as far as other studies allowed comparison, they appeared in worse condition than children not separated from their parents. Moreover, the private foster children could be distinguished from the local authority children by showing significantly worse conditions in the following – possessing the traits of aggression and anxiety, having suffered from bronchitis and persistent colds, being daily enuretic, performing poorly at school in attainment and behaviour, and having a more hurtful explanation for the separation from their parents. Similarly, although it is worthy of concern that the child care officers were at the best doubtful that the material, emotional, and intellectual needs of 0·7, 9·8 and 4·9 per cent respectively of the local authority children were being met, the corresponding percentages for the private children were 4·2, 24·5 and 26·6.

Child care services

Despite the generally disadvantageous position of the private foster children, they received little help from the children's departments. In a twelve-month period, 17·5 per cent were not seen at all by an officer while an additional 35·7 per cent were seen only once or twice. Similarly, the officers rarely made contact with the children's parents, indeed, less than 10 per cent had been seen in the twelve months. It might have been expected that the illegitimate private foster children, who made up 22·4 per cent of the total, and their parents would have received extra attention from the officers. Such children have to face and deal with the fact of their legal status while their parent, usually an unmarried mother, would find it difficult to maintain contact and even more difficult to work towards receiving them back. But the illegitimate received no more attention than the other fosterings. The local authority foster children received a far more regular and extensive service. The hypothesis that the private foster children would reveal conditions and difficulties at least similar to those of their local authority counterparts without receiving a similar level of service from the children's departments was convincingly upheld.

The private foster parents

Private foster parents have been accused of 'baby-farming', of crowding in large numbers of children for financial gain. However, it was found that only eight had three or more foster children at the time of the research while most received less even than the low fees paid to their local authority counterparts. After invalidating the view about 'baby-farming', the study proceeded to identify ways in which the private foster parents were similar and dissimilar to those of the local authority.

Similarities

In many ways, the women who cared for private foster children seemed like any other foster mothers. Their place of birth, marital status and size of their natural family were rarely distinguishable from those selected to take children for the children's departments. Like them, most had already had previous experience of caring for other people's children. Most of both kinds appeared motivated by a desire to create or extend their own families or an altruistic wish to help children. They possessed attitudes of affection and wanted to promote the happiness of their charges. Around two-thirds of both types of foster parents would have liked to adopt them. By using the above data only, a typical private or local authority foster mother could be described as middle-aged, married, born in her present area of residence, with three natural children, expressive of great concern for deprived children and already experienced in looking after other people's children. However, the use of further data reveals important differences.

Distinguishing features

Although both private and local authority foster parents were disproportionately drawn from the lower social classes, the former were even more likely to come from social classes IV and V. More important was the finding that private foster parents were significantly more likely to be unsuitable to act in the fostering role. Indeed, nearly two-thirds were so assessed. In addition, the private rather than the local authority foster parents were those whose treatment of the children in terms of preparing them for the placement, handling explanations about fostering, perceiving the need to tell the truth about relationships, and providing adequate accommodation, was likely to be wanting. Particularly worth attention was the fact that over a quarter of the private foster fathers, but very few local authority fathers, were graded as non-participant in relation to the fostering. Foster father non-participation proved to be one of the key factors being significantly associated with children who displayed adverse conditions and whose emotional and intellectual needs were not met.

Thus it was not motivation, age, marital status or family structure which distinguished private foster parents but rather the capacity to carry out in a satisfactory manner the task of fostering. However, the study should not be used to give the impression that *all* private foster parents are unsuitable. One of the uses of the present research is to invalidate false generalisations and myths. It has demonstrated that private foster mothers tend not to take large numbers, that West African children make up a substantial but not total part of the private fostering population, and that alongside the unsuitable foster parents are a number of suitable ones. The latter are an essential social service providing capable care for children whose parents cannot do so. Emphasis must be placed on the important findings about the unsuitable but not to the point of tarring all foster parents with the same brush.

Lack of help

On top of the high number of unsuitable private foster parents must be added the further findings which tended to increase the magnitude of their task. First, they were significantly more likely than the local authority foster mothers to feel insecure in their relationship with the children. Nearly half just did not know when the fostering would end. Clearly many lived in fear as to the time and manner in which the children would be taken, a fear which could be conveyed to the children. Second, a number of private foster mothers received low or irregular payments from the natural parents. Some declined to ask for more knowing the parents could not afford it, and being more concerned about the children than money. Others feared that such a request might provoke parents to end the placement. Consequently, some private foster parents appeared in financial difficulties. One foster mother, her husband was a milkman earning under £16 per week, with two foster children of secondary school-age, was paying 15s. a week school-dinner money and had to provide school uniforms as well as other clothing and all other care from under £5 a week received for both the children. She 'felt the pinch' when paying for extra items like school-outings and remarked bitterly that they could not afford holidays or to allow the children to choose their own birthday presents. Unlike the local authority foster parents, the private ones could experience irregularity of payment, tended to receive lower levels of payment, and lacked the built-in perks – such as extra allowances for school uniforms, birthdays and holidays – which are part of the children's departments' system.

A picture thus builds up of private foster parents, with some considered unsuitable, coping with foster children, many of whom presented fostering difficulties and displayed adverse emotional and other traits, being not only insecure in their relationships but often without financial security. In addition, of course, they shared the problems of all foster parents – how to explain to the child why he was fostered, trying to love him yet being prepared to part with him, worrying as to whether the natural parents would criticise their ways of child-rearing. It appears obvious that such private foster parents stood in great need of help from the children's departments. Yet I found that in a twelve-month period, the child care officers visited 66·4 per cent of the private foster homes less than five times, and 14·7 per cent not at all: 72·5 per cent of the private foster fathers were not seen at all: only 8·4 per cent of the private foster homes received any practical aid. The analysis of the interviews between officers and foster parents revealed that little supportive or educative help was offered. Not surprisingly the private foster parents considered the officers to be of little help, saying they had insufficient powers to give material help or to influence the fostering process in any way. On all points, the service given them was significantly inferior to that for the local authority foster parents.

The private fostering market

The private fostering system can fairly be described as a market. Parents require a service, foster parents offer a service, the two sides contact each other, negotiate the terms, and the goods (the children) change hands. The market is remarkably free from restraints as can be shown in three major areas.

The private market allows children to be placed and received almost at will. The placers, the parents, can approach and use almost any persons who want a child. Foster parents were found through friends 'who knew somebody who wanted a baby', through chance meetings in a shop or at a bus-stop, as well as by advertising. In one case, an unmarried mother made a contact in a launderette and placed the baby the same night. A tradesman, calling to repair a housewife's electrical appliance, got into a conversation which ended with her taking his child. One child was dumped by flitting lodgers on a landlady who then took over his care. Demand tended to exceed supply of foster homes, so natural parents were sometimes so relieved to find somewhere that they hardly considered the quality of the foster parents. A foster mother who answered an advertisement said:

> 'The father called and just said, "it's alright". He didn't even want to see round the house. I said, "don't your wife want to come?" He said, "no".'

Foster mothers suddenly faced with a request to take a child may agree on the spot without consulting their husbands. As one foster mother put it:

> 'It was a bit of a bombshell for my husband. He'd just gone round the shops and when he came back we'd got another one.'

It is perhaps not surprising that many of the private foster fathers were found not to be fully committed towards and not fully involved in the fosterings.

Of course, the private foster mothers were not obliged to say 'yes' to the pleas of parents. Similarly, if they lost one child they could easily obtain another. As one explained, 'I can always get another tomorrow.' If it is considered what elaborate procedures, negotiations and planning permission is demanded by local authorities of house-holders who wish to structurally improve their property, then it is true to say that in Britain it is easier to get a child than an extension on one's garage.

The selection of foster parents and foster children is not the only aspect of private fostering which is open to free and easy trading. The manner in which placements are made also lacks restraints. Often the fostering participants do not appear to have taken into account the age, condition, feelings and needs of children when making moves. The child care texts are agreed that children should be moved to a foster home gradually and over a period of time in which they have opportunities to meet and get to know their new parent sub-stitutes. The suddenness with which private foster children could be moved is well illustrated by a woman who arranged, through a friend at work, to take a five-year-old girl without knowing either her or her parents. She stated:

> 'I went to the school and met the child, her hair was full of nits,

because I'd never met her I asked if she'd like to come with me and she said "yes", and I took her.'

An earlier chapter showed that the private foster children were likely to be placed without any preparatory work in the form of meetings beforehand or the passing on of information about the children to the foster parents.

Once placements are made there is no guarantee that they will continue or that they will only be ended if considered to suit the welfare of the children. The study was of ongoing placements so obviously, the children had not been removed from their present foster parents. Nevertheless, it was evident from the private foster parents' previous experiences, and from the histories of the children, that the private fostering market was open to placements being abruptly brought to a close. The private fostering contract is unwritten and binding on no party, hence any sudden decision and action by either the foster or natural parents could result in the end of a placement. Usually the foster mothers were keen to retain care but there were instances of those who, without any warning, informed the parents that the child must go. A casual attitude towards such decisions was revealed in a private foster mother who had had eight previous foster children. When her husband entered a mental hospital she explained:

'I had to work so I sent him [foster child] back. But I missed him so much I decided to have him back. But I'll have to work again so I'm sending him back on Sunday. I'll have him back when things are better.'

More often the initiative for removal came from the natural parents. A disagreement between them and the foster parents or the opportunity to move the child to another foster home which was less expensive or which they considered more satisfactory prompted them to remove their children in an abrupt manner.

Considering the ease with which private fosterings can be ended, it was not altogether surprising to discover that of the 320 children previously cared for by the private foster mothers, 172 had stayed for less than a year. Of the private foster children in the study, only 16·1 per cent were in placements which had continued for five years or more. A comparison with the lengths of time completed by children in public care makes it clear that local authority placements are likely to be of longer duration. Of course, the fact that private placements were likely to be shorter does not necessarily mean that they were abruptly closed or that the removal was against the interests of the children. The higher proportion of married couples using private foster homes indicated that private foster children had a greater prospect of returning to a settled natural home. However, if the local authority foster parents determined to finish a fostering, they would contact the child care officer who might persuade them to continue it or, at least, would ensure that any change was gradual rather than sudden. The private foster parents, by contrast, would announce their decision directly to the natural parents. Again, should the natural parents decide on a removal from a local authority home, the child care officer could act as a 'buffer' between them and the foster parents in order to smooth out any disagreements or hasty decisions. The minimal involvement of the officers in the private fosterings made it unlikely that a similar brake would be applied. The private foster children, therefore, were much more liable to sudden removals, shorter placements and more numerous foster homes. Consequently, the foster parents, fearing abrupt removals, could be insecure in their relationships with the children. The children might not be given time to settle down even in one home. The private foster child who suffered eight moves in nine years was the exception, but his experience illustrates what is possible in a market so open to abuse.

Thus in three spheres – the placement at will of children, the manner of the placement and the ending of the placement – the private fostering market could operate with virtually no controls on it. The children's departments had negligible powers to effect any intervention but, at least in the areas studied, did not even use these to influence the market.

Freedom, uncertainty and choice

Private fostering is not only characterised by a lack of restraints but also by participants being unable to exercise choice in certain areas of their lives. Indeed, if a model of private fostering is constructed from the evidence of the present research, it would show an interaction of wide-ranging freedoms, uncertainty of role performances and a lack of choices. The freedoms arise from the virtual non-existence or ineffectiveness of legal regulations. The role uncertainties spring from the fostering participants' lack of knowledge about how they should behave within the fostering situation. The lack of choice relates to the non-availability of alternative ways of caring for children.

Natural parents have freedom, it might even be called licence, to place their children as they please. The law stipulates very few conditions concerning the kind of homes or persons with whom they can be put. Yet, paradoxically, the natural parents in the study had little choice whereby that freedom could be exercised. They turned to private fostering because alternative forms of care did not exist, were denied or were unknown to them. Even within the private fostering market, the excess of demand over supply could mean that they had little or no choice about the foster parents for their child. In law, having complete freedom to place their child where they liked, the natural parents could be left with a 'take it or leave it' decision regarding the one available but possibly unsuitable private foster home. Having placed their children, the natural parents could then be puzzled as to how to behave towards the children in their new environment and towards the foster parents. The placing of children in foster homes is not a common experience and no established social norms and expectations make it clear how the natural parents should behave. The role of the parent who has placed a child is not defined or understood as is, say, the role of a natural mother towards her child or of a policeman towards an offender. Having almost no contact with the child care officers, the parents of the private foster children do not even receive guidance from that informed source. None the less, they have to take decisions as to how often to visit the foster homes, how to speak to and treat their children, and what kind of relationship to develop with the foster parents. The way is open for uncertain, inconsistent behaviour and for difficulties between the natural parents and the foster homes.

The private foster mothers express a desire or need to look after other people's children. Many are not acceptable to the local authority children's departments or voluntary agencies and in order to foster they must do so privately. With very few exceptions, any woman is free to take in private foster children. Moreover, she has complete freedom to take in whom she likes. Yet for all this freedom, the private foster mothers were short of social instructions determining how they should perform the role of private foster mother. As with the natural parents of foster children, there is no generally perceived and recognised manner in which foster mothers should behave. It is true to say that certain general values are associated with fostering. Few would quibble with the judgment that foster mothers do a worthwhile task. But society has not laid down prescriptive norms which spell out precisely how foster mothers should behave in the fostering situation. It is also true that child care texts and child care officers have definitive views on how foster mothers should behave, namely that they should not try to play the role of a natural mother but, while giving love and affection, should ensure that the child knew the details of his real relationship, should give him a positive explanation for his separation from his parents and, in short, never pretend that he is anything but a foster child. Unfortunately, these views were rarely conveyed to the private foster mothers, for the officers tended only to inspect and not to educate or support them. With society in general and the officers in particular not applying constraints to their behaviour, the private foster mothers were likely to follow the role they knew best – that of a natural mother. Those who did not consciously try to regard the child as a natural one were, however, unlikely to perceive the importance of him knowing fully and positively why he was not living with his real parents. Those who did regard themselves in the role of natural mothers had to live with the evidence that this was not true. Payments are not received for natural children and their parents do not visit. Consequently, the private foster mothers, unable to perceive how they should treat foster children, could find that the role they did adopt promoted conflicts within themselves as they tried to resolve the behaviour of a natural parent with situations which demanded responses which natural mothers do not have to make. Thus, on the one hand, free to foster, on the other hand uncertain of the role of how to foster, the imprecision of the fostering situation is completed by the private foster mothers' lack of choice in one vital area – whether the fostering will continue. Private foster mothers have no rights over the foster children. They are free to take them but not free to keep them if the parents decide otherwise. Consequently, their behaviour towards both children and natural parents could be shaped by the constant fear of a sudden removal.

The child care officers, the agents of the children's departments, have no choice but to be concerned with private fosterings. The Children Act (1958) gave them a legal duty to visit private foster homes. At the same time, they possess few legal constraints which can be applied. As explained, their powers to prohibit, to render material aid, and to end placements are extremely limited. These legal limitations on prohibition and removal are reinforced by a scarcity of alternative provision. The children's departments were reluctant to take steps leading to private foster children coming into public care when local authority foster homes were so hard to find. Thus, in practice, some officers felt they had no choice but to let unsuitable foster homes continue. The officers are free to interpret the Act in order to visit and to undertake casework with the private fostering participants as they wished. However, their lack of powers meant that the officers tended to regard their role as restricted to inspection with the educative and supportive aspects, which are stressed by the child care texts, deemed as inapplicable. Feeling of little use, many officers withdrew from the private fosterings, so offering the private foster mothers even less guidance on how to perform their role towards the foster children and the natural parents.

The natural parents, private foster mothers and child care officers all experienced the private fostering characteristics of freedom, role uncertainty and a lack of choice. In turn, these factors shaped the way they functioned in the fostering process. All were forced into the private fostering field, yet once there they were unsure how to behave. Their insecurity and the uncertainty of the situation resulted in disadvantages for the children. They were the ones who could be placed with the unsuitable foster parents or removed without a moment's notice. They were the ones who felt the foster parents' and natural parents' uncertainty and the treatment associated with it. And no matter how they were treated, they were unlikely to be helped by the child care officers imposing constraints or giving help. Consequently, in contrast to the local authority foster children, they experienced the maximum risk of disturbing or damaging situations, but the minimum chance of being helped.

The Children and Young Persons Act (1969)

The present study was carried out at a time when the Children Act (1958) governed the position of private fostering. This Act was amended by the Children and Young Persons Act (1969), its provisions coming into force on 1 January 1970. The 1969 Act is mainly concerned with the reception of children into public care especially through the courts. Only six of its seventy-three sections deal with private fostering, but it is necessary to consider the likely effects they will have.

Before describing and evaluating the Act, it is worth re-stating the findings of the present research which indicate weaknesses in the statutory relationships between children's departments and private fostering:

1 The notification system worked satisfactorily in only 2·1 per cent of the fosterings.

2   The departments found it extremely difficult to prohibit intended unsatisfactory placements, partly because they were not informed of the intention and partly because of their limited powers.

3   The departments had no powers by which they could control the manner in which children were placed.

4   Their powers of removal from unsatisfactory placements were also extremely limited.

5   The departments could do nothing to prevent natural parents suddenly removing children and placing them in a succession of foster homes.

6   The departments had no clearly defined statutory responsibility towards the private foster parents, children or natural parents. Hence child care officers found it difficult to formulate a positive role towards them while departments did not fit them into their administrative system.

7   The departments lacked the powers to aid the fostering participants in practical ways which, combined with their lack of other powers, meant the private foster parents did not perceive the officers as helpful.

While reviewing the 1969 Act, it will be worth while considering if it remedies any of these weaknesses.

Definition of private foster children

The Children and Young Persons Act (Section 52) extends the definition of private foster children in two directions. First, it includes those for whom 'reward' (payment in cash or kind) is not made. Second, it takes in those who are kept for under one month. The basic definition thus becomes: 'a child below the upper limit of compulsory school age whose care and maintenance are undertaken by a person who is not a relative or guardian of his' (Section 52 (1)). However, the definition is hedged with a number of qualifications. The care and maintenance has to be undertaken for more than six days while persons who are not regular foster parents are exempted if the stay is less than a month (Section 51 (3) (3A)).

The overall effect of the amendment will probably be to increase the total number of private foster children throughout the country for those previously regarded as *de facto* adoptions – long-term placements where no payment is made – will now fall within the definition. Had the 1969 Act been operational at the time of the research, the sample size would probably have been only slightly increased for the number of *de facto* adoptions are considered to be small.

Notification

The 1969 Act amends Section 3 of the Children Act (1958) which required any persons maintaining private foster children to notify the local authority on each occasion they received a child. After a minor change in the wording of the period in which notice must be given (Section 53 (2)), the Act causes the notification to refer to the intent of a person to foster and not to the reception of each child.[1] Thus notification is not required in respect of a child if, 'he [foster parent] has on a previous occasion given notice under that subsection in respect of that *or any other child* . . . and he has not, at any time since that notice was given, ceased to maintain at least one foster child' (Section 53 (4)) (my italics). Similarly, according to the new Act the foster parent does not have to notify for each child that leaves but only when she ceases to be a foster parent. The Home Office Circular No. 251/1969, which provides a commentary on the Act, says, 'The objective is to relieve local authorities and foster parents of some of the work of giving and dealing with notifications in cases where the authority is satisfied with the general quality of care foster parents provide.'

Far from strengthening the notification provisions, the Act actually weakens them. The amendments to the private fostering law provoked hardly any comment from the national or social work press, but in April 1969, *Child Care News* described the relaxation of the requirement to notify in advance for every child as 'most alarming', fearing that children would come and go without the local authority knowing. The change was certainly a far cry from the proposal of the Association of Child Care Officers that natural parents as well as foster parents should be obliged to notify in advance for every child.

The new legislation appears based on two assumptions. First, that child care officers visited private foster homes so frequently that any child staying for a length of time was sure to come to notice. But the research demonstrated that many homes might not be visited for a year. Unless the local authorities make extensive use of their reserve powers to require notification for every child, it seems that many will be placed and removed without the authorities ever being aware. Second, it assumes that a notification system dependent upon foster parents taking the initiative to contact the children's department's actually works. The research revealed this as an unjustified assumption.

Powers to prohibit placements

The 1969 Act increases the powers of local authorities to prohibit placements in two directions. The first, and most important, allows this if they are of the opinion that the premises are not suitable or the foster parent is not suitable, or 'it would be detrimental to that child to be kept by that person in those premises' (Section 55). Whereas the 1958 Act was generally interpreted as giving the authorities power to prohibit premises not persons, the new Act makes it quite clear that unsuitability of person is sufficient grounds. However, it must be added that the research indicated that children's departments failed to prohibit not just because of lack of powers but also because placements were made before they knew of them and because it was difficult to find other accommodation for the children.

In the second place, the same Section amends the 1958 Act to allow the requirements, which a local authority could impose on foster parents using premises 'wholly or mainly' for fostering, to be placed on any foster home whatsoever. Two further requirements – relating to fire precautions and supplying information about the foster children – are added to the six stipulated in the 1958 Act.

Duties towards private fostering

The duty placed upon local authorities by the 1958 Act to visit private foster homes 'from time to time' is changed by the new Act to visit from time to time where they think it 'appropriate' (Section 51). The Home Office Circular explains that the amendment is designed to 'make the duties of local authorities more flexible'.

The change is hard to understand. The situation was already flexible in that departments could visit once or a hundred times a year. Moreover, the research, demonstrating that the children were under-visited in proportion to their needs, led to the conclusion that, as with children in care, a minimum number of visits should be regulated allowing the flexibility to proceed from this safeguard. By failing to make such a reform, the new Act also fails to provide child care officers with a defined statutory obligation towards private fostering.

Other changes

The new Act makes it clear that an official of a local authority may inspect the whole of the premises in which private foster children are kept, and empowers Justices of the Peace to issue a warrant to authorise an official to enter premises (Section 54). Finally, the number of grounds under which a person may be disqualified from fostering is increased. In particular, a person placed on probation or given an absolute or conditional discharge in respect of an offence against children can be disqualified.

Had the 1969 Act been operational at the time of the research, it seems that the results obtained would have been little different. The size of the sample of private foster children may have been slightly increased due to the extension of their definition to take in those placed without reward and for under one month. On the other hand, the weakening of the notification system may have served to reduce numbers. The greater powers to prohibit placements would have been little used in a situation where the children's departments rarely knew they were going to take place. It follows that the Act is unlikely to have much effect on the future relationships between children's departments and private fostering.

The 1969 Act is most notable for its omissions. The local authorities are given no powers to control the manner of placements, no increased powers to effect removals nor to limit the constant moving of children. It includes no system of regulating visits, no clear definition of duties and no provision to materially aid the fostering participants. Consequently, the Act will not result in the child care officers and private foster parents formulating a definite role for the former. Like the Children Act (1958), the new Act appears to rest on the assumption that private fostering does not require the same kind and extent of help as local authority fostering.

The future

The study has not claimed to be representative of private fostering as a whole. However, the initial chapter explained that the two local authorities chosen were not greatly different from others in regard to their child care and other social features. Thus it is not unreasonable if the final section of the study proceeds on the assumption that the findings concerning the relationship between the local authorities and private fostering are relevant to private fostering in general. Attention will therefore be turned to ways in which the care of private

K

foster children could be improved. The discussion is necessary for three reasons. First, because the research findings prompt grave concern for the children involved. Second, it is assumed that ways should be found to give sufficient help to children in need whatever its cause. In other words, it is not satisfactory that services should be held back from private foster children simply because the reasons they were separated from their parents do not, at present, fit into the eligibility categories which qualify for help from statutory bodies. Third, there is no reason to suppose that the demand for private foster homes will decrease. The reduction in the rate of immigration into the United Kingdom, due to successive Immigration Acts, does not affect the entry of students who constitute a large section of the source of private foster children. The number of deserted spouses and un-married mothers who need care for their children reveals little decline. The situation of a demand which exceeds the supply of foster homes appears likely to continue.

The under-fives problem

Before examining various proposals for change, it is necessary to emphasise that the needs of private foster children, who are mainly under five years of age, are related to the general lack of provision for pre-school children. No doubt some children would not go to private foster homes if adequate day care amenities were available. A previous chapter has already instanced the general shortage and erratic distribution of such facilities which, combined with an inflexibility of opening times and sometimes quite high charges, makes them of limited use to some parents. The Yudkin Report (1967) has already called for a government enquiry on the care of pre-school children, and the present study of one sector of that care lends support to that call.

Hopefully, the availability of day care and other amenities will increase. Already some local authorities, often backed by the government's urban aid programme, are developing pre-school facilities. For example, at Kirkby in Lancashire, the local authority has opened a day care centre where deserted fathers and overburdened parents may leave their children daily in a stimulating environment instead of putting them in foster homes. Other children's departments, including Cornwall, Lewisham and Camden, have employed 'mobile' foster mothers who look after the children in their own homes until their parent returns. Children looked after at home or in their own districts can more easily maintain contact with friends and other relatives as well as with their parent(s). However, the local authorities have restricted these services to children who were at risk as defined by the Children and Young Persons Act (1963). They would not take children whose parents wished to study. Here voluntary bodies have made some progress. The Handsworth Day Care Centre in Birmingham was established to provide adequate day care with hours tailored to parents' needs. Valuable as these advances are, they barely touch the problem. The era when the needs or desires of all who want adequate day care amenities will be met is still not in sight. Daily-minders, although the most unsatisfactory form of day care, are, as Yudkin shows, still the largest source of day care places (1967, p. 16). Further, day care would not meet the needs of many parents who use private foster homes. Therefore, attention must be given to improving the private fostering system.

Just as private foster homes are sometimes used because of the general lack of day care provisions for the under-fives, so the reasons why parents decide to part with their children can be partially a reflection of the continued existence of socially depriving conditions in society. In particular, poverty, inadequate housing and a lack of access to amenities which promote healthy child socialisation can provoke situations which result in separation. The pressures resulting from such deprivation can lead not only to homelessness but to tensions in marital relationships, mental ill-health and difficult child behaviour. In turn, the parents may feel they have no solution to their problems but to seek substitute parents. The removal of these conditions awaits political and social changes within society (this is not to say that many parents will not still require placements even after conditions do improve). However, within the context of the present study, the discussion will concentrate on changes which would promote their better care in foster homes.

Suggestions for change

The Association of Children's Officers and the Legal Sub-Committee of the Association of Child Care Officers have made several suggestions to tighten up the laws relating to private fostering. Some of the proposals were incorporated into the Children and Young Persons Act (1969) but others can now be mentioned.

a Both associations called for reforms of the notification system.

The Association of Child Care Officers stated, 'It would be an additional safeguard if the person who yields up the child (usually the parents) were also required to give notice' (1965, p. 3) as well as the foster parents. It added that the term 'emergency' should be defined in the text of the 1958 Act where provision is made for foster parents to notify local authorities one week after placement in cases of emergency. Both associations further suggested that both foster and natural parents should furnish the local authorities with more information than is at present given about the children. These proposals appear eminently sensible, particularly in the light of the research findings of the inefficiency of the workings of the notification system. The notification by natural parents as well should serve to increase the number of placements which come to the notice of the children's departments before they commence. Of course, many parents would be as ignorant as foster parents of the requirement to notify, but once they did know of their obligation they might well be keen to observe it in future placements in order to involve the children's departments as an additional safeguard for the welfare of their children.

b The Association of Children's Officers considered that the frequency of visits by child care officers to private foster homes 'should be laid down by statutory regulation and should be the same as is required for boarded out children' (p. 1). If implemented, the reform would not only help reduce the neglect of visitation to private foster homes which was detected but, equally important, would give officers the definite statutory responsibility they felt they lacked.

c The Association of Child Care Officers proposed a system of registration of private foster parents similar to that in force for daily-minders. Foster parents whom the children's departments considered suitable would be recorded on a register and natural parents could be referred to them. Two drawbacks stand out. First, the register would cover only foster parents taking children for 'an indefinite length of time' (1965, p. 5). Yet the research showed that a high proportion of children are placed for definite and short durations. Long, indefinite placements are not the only ones in which emotional harm could be done to a child. Second, the registration of suitable foster parents would do nothing to exclude the unsuitable. In a situation of demand exceeding supply, foster parents can easily obtain children without recourse to receiving a stamp of approval from the authorities.

Apart from the register question, the proposals of the two associations would lead to improvements in the present system. However, even if implemented, they would not touch upon the local authorities' lack of powers to prohibit placements, to make removals, to reduce child turnover, to improve the manner of placements and to give practical help to the fostering participants.

More radical changes in child care legislation have been hinted at by E. P. Brown, a former president of the Association of Child Care Officers and children's officer for Wiltshire. In 1965 he stated:

> A tightening up of our child protection law is very overdue.
> The rights of a parent should not extend to fostering her child
> in dubious circumstances, still less should the traffic in private
> adoption be permitted. The powers of the local authorities
> need to be strengthened in these fields.

A year later in another speech he added:

> It may be necessary to subject the prospective foster parents of
> such children to a similar process of investigation and supervision,
> however short or long the fostering is to be, as the local
> authority uses for the children who are in its care.

Unfortunately, he did not enlarge on his ideas, but it is noteworthy that a children's officer should consider measures involving severe limitations on the rights of natural parents to place their children with whom they please, and on foster parents to foster as they please, to be necessary.

The matters mooted by the associations and Mr Brown would require legislative changes. Two further suggestions advocate the greater use of existing legislation and resources. It has been argued that the Children and Young Persons Act (1963) should be used to give material aid to enable parents to keep their children at home rather than in private foster homes, and to enable them to make a reasonable payment to suitable private foster parents. Fitzherbert provides an example of the Act being used to help a natural father pay a private foster mother (1967, p. 107). However, as already has been shown, the two departments studied would not concur with the interpretation of the Act to this end. They would argue that the wording of Section 1 of the Act to allow authorities to give material aid to diminish 'the need to receive children into or to keep them in care ... or to bring children before a juvenile court' means that such help can be given only to prevent receptions into public care and not into private homes. Official reports issued by the Home Office suggest that most departments have not used the 1963 Act in relation to private fostering. Even if the broad interpretation is accepted, local authorities would still not be obliged to materially help private fostering under the Act, they would merely be allowed so to do if they thought fit.

New legislation would not be required for voluntary bodies to orientate themselves towards private fostering. One society, the Commonwealth Students' Children Society, has been established specifically to help students who tend to use private foster homes. The society has drawn up a list of some reliable foster parents and tried to encourage the promotion of more day care facilities. It is noticeable that voluntary children's societies care for a decreasing number of children (Home Office, 1970a, p. 6). Some are seeking new ways of helping children and may find an outlet in the needs of children described in this research. Probably small children's homes would be preferable to very unsuitable private foster homes or to constant changing between homes. The latest venture of the Commonwealth Students' Children Society has been to open just such a home which takes up to twenty-five children. Of course, it is not envisaged that voluntary societies could or should cope with the whole of the needs of private foster children. Most children will continue to be placed in foster homes, and the safeguarding of them will require further responsibilities to be shouldered by the statutory authorities.

Fostering guardianship

The adverse conditions and risk situations to which the private foster children were exposed justifies, in the writer's view, an extension of the powers of the local authorities to protect and aid them. These powers can be termed 'foster guardianship'.

In the United Kingdom, a guardian usually means a person other than a natural parent who has charge or control over a child or young person. The term 'legal guardian' is used when a person is appointed as guardian by a legal deed or will or by an order of a court.[2] Under the Guardianship of Infants Act (1952), a court can appoint any person as the legal guardian of a child who has no parents of his own. Usually, a guardian acts in every way towards a child as would his natural parents. Abroad, the term 'guardianship' has sometimes been used to express the powers and duties of the state towards certain groups of children. The meaning is not that after hearing a case about individual children, a court makes an order giving parental rights to the state or local authority as happens with a Fit Person Order in Britain. Rather, the guardianship is automatically extended towards children in certain categories, in particular those not living within the normal natural family structure. For instance, in Denmark, until recently, a local body, the child care committee, shared with the parents the rights over daily-minded children, foster children and illegitimate children living with their natural parents. Although the parents were free to make their own arrangements for the children's care, the committee could prevent them needlessly removing their children from a suitable private foster home. The Care of Children and Young Persons Act (1964) made some changes in Denmark. The re-designated child and youth welfare committees (elected by the local councils for four-year terms) were given general powers to aid children under the age of eighteen where it appeared in the interests of the child concerned. If necessary, help can be given without the consent of the parents, although every effort is made to work with them. Thus, for example, its far-reaching powers allow a committee to intervene on behalf of a child whose parent is unsupported or whose substitute parents do not provide adequate care. The aid can be direct financial assistance, the provision of a mobile foster mother, or help with paying for day care or other private forms of care. In particular, a committee can resolve that a private foster child must not be removed from a foster home without reasonable cause, and may even resolve that a child be not returned to his parents if contrary to his welfare.[3] Denmark is not alone in such arrangements and Wimperis provides a wide-ranging account of forms of guardianship in European countries (1960, ch. 15). It is not proposed that replicas of the European committees or boards be established in Britain. However, the concept of a guardianship covering a category of children and the generalised powers to help children who are not in public care do suggest useful approaches.

A proposal, here put forward for consideration and discussion, is the creation of a new legal responsibility, called foster guardianship, which should be discharged by local authorities through their children's departments (social service departments as from 1971) in respect of all children coming within the definition of private foster children. In brief, foster guardianship should bestow upon local authorities the powers to prevent the placement of the children, to influence the manner of placements, to make and to prevent removals, to arrange for adequate supervision and help, and to materially aid the children, their foster and natural parents.

Private foster children will only be fully protected from unsuitable foster parents when the local authorities have the right to directly and immediately prohibit a potential placement and to remove from a foster home when they consider such action to be in the interests of the welfare of the child. It is proposed that they be given these powers with the foster parents having the right of appeal to a juvenile court. Further, any child so removed should be eligible for reception into public care in much the same way as children removed by a court order can be received under the 1958 Act (Section 7). Powers of this nature would enable authorities to remove speedily, whereas now they act slowly via a court. The increased control over private foster homes would bring the private foster children nearer the careful selection processes involved in placing children who are in care.

Three major objections can be made against the proposals: that they impinge too greatly on the freedom of parents and private foster parents: that they will either lead to more children being received into public care or that the shortage of local authority foster homes will continue to make the officers reluctant to use their powers of removal: that the prohibition aspects will be rendered ineffective as the children's departments usually do not have prior warning of placements. That restrictions would be imposed on natural and foster parents is not denied. The justification for them is that the present system has failed to protect children from damaging environments. The numbers received into care and the officers' readiness to undertake removals would be affected by the greater involvement of the officers with the private foster homes which would be regularised as a statutory obligation. Hopefully the involvement would lead to an improvement in the standards of the private foster homes, so lessening the need for compulsory removals and possible reception into care. At the same time, the officer's visits would be so regular that, where necessary, they would feel obliged to take action and would be unable to withdraw from the situation. If the children's emotional, physical and intellectual needs could only be met by taking into public care, then it could be forcibly argued that this should occur whatever the pressure it places upon the departments. If the children cannot be placed in foster homes they may well benefit more from a stable children's home (community home) than a grossly unsuitable private fostering or a succession of private foster mothers. However, the increase in the number of child care officers, which will be spelt out in a later section, should enable extra local authority foster parents to be sought out. The officers, therefore, could be expected to use their new powers. The prohibition of unsuitable intended placements is dependent upon the departments being informed of them. This does not nullify the desirability of departments having such powers. The fact that they can remove a child immediately they learn of the placement will convince some foster parents that there is little to be gained from deliberately failing to notify while the proposals in the following paragraphs should serve to increase the number of notifications.

The proposal of the child care associations that natural parents, as well as foster parents, be required to give notification would not only improve the chance of local authorities learning about intended placements, but would enable the child care officers to influence the parents about the way placement is executed. Once in touch with the parents, equipped both with powers to remove and, as will be shown, by help in other ways, the officers should be able to enter into a relationship which encourages the placers to introduce their children gradually into their new foster homes while, at the same time, supplying the foster parents with full information. It is not considered that the children's departments should actually make the placements, for the research suggested that the involvement of the parents in selection and placement forged a link which encouraged them to maintain contact afterwards.

A further and basic part of foster guardianship should be the requirement that the private foster children be supervised and helped in a manner comparable with that of children in local authority foster homes. Not only should visits be regularised in accordance with the Boarding-Out Regulations but the children should be subjected to regular reviews and medical inspections. The purposeful and humane exercise of a defined and regulated responsibility is the only way to avoid cases where, to give one example, a misunderstanding between two officers combined with the lack of reviews and checks meant that a private foster child was forgotten for well over a year. In addition, it would give officers that sense of commitment and statutory obligation which they felt was necessary to develop a relationship with the private foster parents.

The negative powers of prohibition and removal will need to be balanced by more positive ones to allow the provision of material aid to private foster children and foster parents. Three kinds of help can be envisaged. First, the payment of fees to encourage the attendance of some private foster children at pre-school play groups. A host of special reports, including the Plowden and Yudkin Reports, has stressed the benefits which socially disadvantaged children can receive from pre-school communal experiences. The present study showed that intellectually and physically, as well as emotionally, many private foster children compared unfavourably with the local authority children as well as with children not separated from their parents. They therefore constitute the very children who appear most in need of extra stimulating experiences at an early age. Second, the private foster parents would benefit from occasional extras or supplements much as do local authority foster parents. The pram, the extra cot, a contribution towards the foster child's holiday, are necessary extras for foster parents, most of whom were from occupations which suggested low incomes. Third, the direct payment of fostering fees to the private foster parents by the children's departments. It is proposed that after the natural and private foster parents have agreed terms, the natural parents should pay the children's departments which would then pay, and guarantee to pay, the foster parents. The department would be responsible for obtaining the parents' fees much as it collects contributions from the parents of children in care.

The guarantee of regular income plus occasional extras would entail fewer private foster parents and children suffering financial hardship. It must be recalled that nearly a third of the private foster homes had received only irregular payments. Some fostering breakdowns would be avoided for it was shown that some of the foster mothers had previously returned children when payments were missed. A bone of contention between the foster participants would have been removed. The financial powers combined with the proposed powers to prohibit and remove, the regulated visitation system, and the positive attitude which private foster parents already hold towards the officers, would open the way for the development of a relationship between officers and foster parents akin to that in the local authority situation.

Lastly, fostering guardianship should involve statutory duties and powers towards the natural parents of private foster children. Child care texts have already been cited showing that it is considered wise policy for children in care to keep in touch with their parents and, in most cases, to be returned to them if possible. The same applies to private foster children. Indeed, one of the strongest findings of the study concerned the importance of frequent parental contact. It follows that local authorities should have a duty to work towards private foster children returning to their parents and that they should be empowered to financially assist the parents in order to achieve this end. The duty and power should cause more frequent and regular contact between child care officers and the natural parents. Through these contacts, the parents, it is hoped, would be encouraged not only to visit regularly but to help their children obtain maximum benefit from the fostering experience, not to remove them needlessly from home to home, and, eventually, to receive them back into their own care.

The establishment of foster guardianship, through the extensive expansion of the local authorities' duties and powers towards private foster children, would serve to decrease many of the risks inherent in the present private fostering market. At the same time, the private foster parents, natural parents and child care officers would be able to define and accept a role for the officers. The officers would not only inspect but also give help of a supportive, educational and practical nature to the participants, so maximising the many strengths of the foster and natural parents. In many ways they would be rendering the same services as they do to participants in local authority fostering, but a clear distinction between the two types would remain. Children taken into care are eligible for a whole range of residential services, including children's homes as well as foster homes, which are selected by the children's departments. The private foster children, even under the new proposals, would only have available foster homes selected by the parents. Local authority foster parents are paid according to scales devised by the departments, private foster parents according to terms agreed with the parents. Most important, in cases of children taken into care under Section 2 of the Children Act (1948) or committed by a court order to public care, the parental rights are transferred from the parents to the local authorities who can retain care even against the wishes of the parents. All private foster children are and would remain under the direct recall of their own parents.

The foster guardianship proposals could achieve a compromise between controlling (in order to protect private foster children) and retaining the involvement and freedom of their parents. But it may be objected that the extra work entailed for the local authorities makes the cost too high in terms of manpower and finance. The study will, therefore, close with a rough calculation of the costs of the proposals. They will be based on the assumption that the number of private foster children in England and Wales is 12,000. The Home Office reported that on 31 March 1969, there were 10,907 notified private foster children. During the course of a year, some cease to be privately fostered while others become so, but the figures will be taken to be constant. The total is upgraded to 12,000 to take into account any increase due to the widening of the definition of private foster children under the Children and Young Persons Act (1969).

It is taken that in the future child care officers would devote nearly as much time to a private fostering case as to that of a child in care. To calculate the number of extra officers required, therefore, involves having a figure of how many cases an officer deals with in a year. It was assumed that an officer would carry about fifty cases.[4]

It follows that 12,000 private foster children would require 240 new officers, which works out at an average of less than one and a half per existing children's departments. These calculations do ignore, on the one hand, existing work officers do with the private foster children and, on the other, any extra staff required for supervision and administration.

The question of costs can be approached in two ways. First, it can be assumed that children under foster guardianship wlil cost local anthorities the same as a boarded-out child in care. In 1969–70, a boarded-out child cost a weekly average of £3 11s. 3d.[5] On this basis, 12,000 private foster children would mean an extra expenditure of £42,750, an average of just under £246 per each children's department. This would be £2,223,000 per year, an average of under £13,000 per department. Of course, the figures do not take into account the extra increases in costs since 1969–70, neither is it possible to incorporate estimates of how many private children would be received into care under the new proposals, a process which will decrease the numbers and costs of private foster children but increase those of children in care.

The second approach is to estimate the amounts children's departments are likely to have to spend on private fostering under the new proposals. The research found that most natural parents paid the private foster parents between two and three pounds per child. Using the higher figure as an average for all payments, again erring on the side of over-estimating, the children's departments would pay the foster parents £36,000 per week. Of course, the natural parents would be expected to pay the full amount to the departments, but for the purposes of the discussion it can be assumed that their contributions would only make up the costs of the departments in paying for play-groups and extras on behalf of the private foster children. The yearly expenditure would be £1,872,000 per year, or an average under £11,000 per department.

Taking the first and higher calculation, the cost to the average children's department to implement foster guardianship would be £246 per week plus not more than one and a half extra officers. Averages conceal much. Some local authorities have very few private foster children. At the other extreme, an authority such as Kent, which had 1,180 in March 1968, would require for, say 1,400 private foster children, an additional £5,000 per week and about twenty-eight extra officers. Overall, the increased financial outlay of nearly £2½ million pounds seems small for departments spending annually nearly forty-six million pounds (Home Office, 1970b, p. 12).

The extra staff would be more serious, 240 being a substantial addendum to a total field staff which for the year ending 31 March 1969, totalled the equivalent of 3,222 officers.[6] None the less, the investment must be considered worthwhile if it serves to counter some of the adverse conditions, poor treatment and vulnerable situations to which, as the study showed, many private foster children are subject. As the Seebohm Report (Home Department, 1968, para. 191) succinctly put it:

Expenditure of time, effort, talent and money on children in need of social care is, above all, an investment in the future. It makes no sense to us, either on humanitarian grounds or in terms of sheer economics, to allow young children to be neglected physically, emotionally or intellectually. By doing so, we not only mortgage the happiness of thousands of children, and the children they in turn will have, but also pile up future problems and expense for society into the bargain.

Appendix

I. Construction of the interview recording schedules

The success of the research was dependent upon the respondents or interviewees giving forth information which was both truthful and full. Therefore, particular attention was given to the overall shape of the interview recording schedules used for the foster parents, the natural parents, and the child care officers.

Design of the schedules

Two main guidelines determined the shape of the recording schedules. The first was that the questions should, generally speaking, move from straightforward, easy-to-answer, 'factual' questions, to the more complex, attitudinal and emotive ones. Thus the foster parent recording schedule started with questions about the foster mother's birthplace, number of children, and so on, it being reasoned that her answering them would increase her confidence, lessen any fears and establish rapport with the interviewer. More emotionally-laden questions, such as concerning fears of losing her foster child, and ones which might appear offensive to some people, such as asking about her marital status (which might imply she was co-habiting) were held back for later in the schedule. However, the design was not quite as simple as this, for an 'offensive' question was followed by a more neutralising one. Thus the marital question was followed by one about the foster father's occupation.

The second guideline was that the questions should develop logically, should be sequential, should – as Goode and Hatt put it – carry the interview forward (1952, p. 195). It was reasoned that such a sequence would allow the foster parent's contributions to develop in what would seem a natural way to her, thus continuing to keep her interest and co-operation. The pattern of the foster parent recording schedule therefore develops in the following manner: the foster mother's previous child care experiences, reasons for fostering, present housing conditions, manner of meeting present foster child,

285

payment for this child, attitudes to this child, child-rearing methods employed with this child, the involvement of the foster father with the child, the physical, mental and emotional development and condition of the child, difficulties in the fostering, relations with and attitudes to the natural parents, relations with and attitudes to the child care officer.[1] Similar plans were worked out for the recording schedules for the natural parents and child care officers.

The recording schedules were of a structured nature. The questions and order were decided in advance and precisely kept to in each interview. Such an approach was necessary to allow the collection of comparable data from each interview. The disadvantage of the structured schedule is that, unlike the unstructured one where the interviewer has a subject but no set questions, the interviewee may be constrained by the interviewer to stick so rigidly to the exact point of the question that she feels inhibited. To counter this, the interviewer allowed the respondents to go where they wished for some time before tactfully bringing them back to the schedule. The fact that a tape recorder was used meant that the researcher was not forced to write down rapidly all that was said. Thus a balance was retained which enabled the schedules to be completed in a comparable manner, did not inhibit the interviewees, and produced some valuable extra material as they developed subjects about which they felt strongly.

II. Question construction

If the questions in a research project do not clearly convey to and obtain from the interviewee precisely the kind of information which is relevant to the testing of the hypotheses or purpose of the study, then all the interviewing in the world is to little avail.

The questions for the present research were initially designed to obtain the necessary information while avoiding four major pitfalls in question construction, which are as follows: first, there are questions where the meaning is unclear or ambiguous. Second, 'loaded' questions which provoke a socially acceptable answer. For instance, mothers asked about smacking might feel it socially unacceptable to admit to an interviewer that they chastise their children. Third, questions which compel the interviewee to give an opinion on a subject about which he has none. This may well happen in a Gallup poll where persons are pressed for a view on some political issue. Fourth, questions which offer too little choice in the form of their answers. Thus a person might be asked whether abortions should be made illegal, 'Yes', or 'No'. Yet he might think that abortions should be illegal in most cases but legal in certain circumstances.

In any interview, two major types of questions are employed – the closed or pre-coded question, and the open or free question. These will now be briefly described along with some indications of the steps taken to avoid some of the dangers of faulty question construction.

Closed questions

A closed question presents a number of alternative answers – either printed on a card or read out by the interviewer – instead of leaving the word content of the answer in the interviewee's hands. For instance, instead of asking 'How old are you?' a person is asked 'In which of the following age groups do you belong?', is presented with a card containing

> 0–20 years
> 21–40 years
> 41 and over,

and responds by indicating his group. Frequently, but not always, closed questions are used when the replies are 'factual'. As Oppenheim says, the adjective 'factual' is 'used to distinguish this type of question from others thought to be more difficult to design, that may deal with knowledge, motives or attitudes' (1966, p. 253).

The closed question has the advantage of encouraging an unambiguous response, the respondent choosing one category. Further, as the replies are already coded, the task of coding them by independent judges is not required. But closed questions are particularly prone to the dangers of forcing interviewees to give an answer from amongst too few alternatives and of giving an opinion where they hold none. How can these be countered? The latter danger was not generally applicable to this particular piece of research, for the questions focused on fostering and were applied to persons closely involved with this activity in some way. They were not asked for their opinions on the government or some other subject which they may not have considered. None the less, on questions where there was a possibility of ignorance, the category 'don't know' was offered as an option. The 'too few alternatives' danger could only be met by careful selection of the answer categories which were offered. These had to cover the 'universe of content' of the subject, that is they had to enclose the whole range of possible answers and they had to be inclusive, not overlapping with each other. In some cases, such as a person's kind of dwelling, the alternatives were already established by previous research or custom; in others they had to be compiled from answers given in the pilot study.

Although closed questions frequently involve pre-coded replies in the form of 'concrete' items, such as the number of children or the type of dwelling, they are still liable to be misunderstood. The interviewee may look at his card and wonder what is the difference between a 'flat' and 'rooms'. The interviewer, therefore, was equipped with instructions which defined the terms, and which could be used to explain to the interviewee.

Open questions

Open-ended questions can be answered by respondents in any way they like. Their replies are recorded in full and have to be categorised and coded after the interview. It is sometimes assumed that closed questions are limited to 'factual' replies, leaving open questions to elicit information about opinions or attitudes. However, attitudes can be pre-coded and thus dealt with by the former type where the number of alternative answers is fairly small and the field of content established. But where the question might provoke the respondent to hypothesise over a wide range of feeling or behaviour, or where the researcher wants to use the person's own words, then an open question is employed.[2]

Open-ended questions, like closed ones, need to be unambiguous with their terms easily understood or defined. Unlike them, they do not present the danger of offering too few alternatives but, precisely because they do not constrain replies into categories which cover a range of content, they may cause respondents to give a socially acceptable answer. For instance a person faced with 'Do you think children should stay on at school after fifteen years of age?' may well feel that an acceptable answer can only be in the affirmative. But if pre-coded replies indicated that some people disagree or disagreed only in certain circumstances, he might feel more free to say the view that was his own. In fact, the problem has less force in relation to the present research, as fostering is a subject about which socially acceptable ideas are not clearly established. Thus the foster parents and natural parents probably felt free to put forward their own views on fostering. However, there are established views on whether children should leave their parents and on the way parents or parent substitutes treat children, and both foster and natural parents may have felt that their views should accord with these. The child care officers were aware of literature on child care, and may similarly have felt they should voice the expected, not their actual view. The researcher can tackle this danger in two ways. First, and most important, he must establish in the interview an atmosphere which enables the interviewee to speak freely, convincing him that his own opinions are valuable and necessary to the research, and assuring him that his identity will not be revealed to others. Second, questions can be inserted which assume that the interviewee's view is not the socially acceptable one, and leave him to contradict it. For instance, a foster mother could be asked how she punishes her child. She may not feel free to say she smacks him, so another question could ask, 'For what kind of naughtiness would you smack him?' the assumption being that smacking does occur. The foster mother could then feel free to say why she smacks, or to deny that she ever does.

The information gained from closed and open questions can therefore be received with more confidence when they are constructed with due regard to the safeguards described above. However, their construction becomes more complex when the objective becomes not just to record and tabulate replies but to measure their content. For instance, it is not enough to ask and record what a child care officer thinks of a private foster parent; the desired information is to know how strongly the officer approves or disapproves of them in comparison with others. One approach is to scale the alternative answers from which interviewees choose, or for judges to rank their replies. For instance, the child care officers were asked whether they would have approved the private foster parents for taking local authority foster children on the following scale: 'yes', 'probably', 'doubtful', 'no', 'don't know' and 'other'. The officers were used to grading persons who applied to foster and hence a scale could be formed which was within their understanding and practice. In cases where the scale was adjudged not by the interviewee but external judges, it was necessary to define closely the meaning and limits of each category so that no overlap occurred between them, and so that the judges evaluated each case in the same way. A second approach is to allocate numerical values to replies and simply compare totals. Thus, for instance, the system devised by the Newsons for assessing father participation was adopted. A series of questions discovered the extent to which foster fathers undertook certain activities with the children, and a score was given according to whether this was 'often', 'sometimes' or 'never' (these being closely defined). The different totals were then taken to represent 'high', 'moderate' or 'non'-participation.

The normal use of the scales described above is sufficient when a ranking order is established or accepted. Clearly, in assessing applications to foster 'yes' ranks above 'doubtful'. Further, the issue is comparatively focused on a single factor – whether to accept or reject an application. The matter becomes more complicated when it is desired to rank, say, a foster mother's opinion towards the child care officer when it is not obvious which opinion gives most approval. Does the foster mother who says 'the officer is nice' have a more positive view than the one who says 'she is helpful'? Again, the allocation of an arbitrary mark to each item, as happened in the Newsons' method, does not really show the amount of difference between the foster fathers; it just shows there are differences. In the classical ranking order 'strongly agree', 'agree', 'disagree', 'strongly disagree', the direction of the intensity of feeling is obvious but there is no way of knowing the 'spacing' between each item. 'Strongly agree' and 'agree' may be very close, while 'disagree' and 'strongly disagree' may be very far apart in intensity. Lastly, the methods discussed so far do not distinguish between the different conditions or circumstances under which attitudes or opinions are expressed. A foster parent may have a very positive opinion of a parent who visits the foster home once a month and is very polite. The same foster parent may change to a negative opinion towards the same parent when circumstances change and he visits once a day and is very impolite.

Attention was therefore turned towards methods which measured the intensity of opinions or attitudes, the distinction between them, and the differing circumstances under which they existed. The two used in the research were those devised by Thurstone and Guttman, as will now be explained.

Questions based on Thurstone's method

Thurstone's method is an attempt to provide a measure of the intensity of different opinions or attitudes within boundaries (of approval and disapproval) determined by something more than the subjective guess of the researcher. In the present study the procedure used was as follows. Some sixty statements about the subject under examination (opinions towards child care officers or foster child) were collected during the pilot study. Twenty judges were then asked to sort the statements into three and then nine piles, according to their opinion of the favourability expressed in the statement. Thus pile one expressed strongest approval, and pile nine the least. The next stage was to score a scale-value for each statement. Each statement was then taken individually and scored according to the piles it had been allocated, thus giving their frequency distribution. The frequencies were then converted into percentages of the total number of frequencies. The distribution percentages were then added up *cumulatively*. Thus for each pile number there was a cumulative percentage which was converted into a graph noting that the pile number was plotted as a *mid-point*. Lines were then drawn across the graph for the median and the two quartiles, and the corresponding pile-value read off. The semi-interquartile range Q is then calculated by $\frac{1}{2}$ (third quartile-first quartile). The next step was to select some of the items or statements for use in the question. Those chosen were ones whose scores provided an equal distance between them and the one next to it, and yet which covered the whole range of statements as evenly as possible.

The chosen statements were then presented through a question to the interviewee who was asked to agree or disagree with each one. His score was taken as the mean of the scale-values of the items he endorsed. It was then possible, in order to simplify presentation, to differentiate between scores which made up a 'positive', 'neutral' (or 'middling') or 'negative' attitude.

The advantage of the Thurstone method is mainly two-fold. First, it provides a means of knowing that an equal distance or score exists between the statements or attitudes which are presented to the respondent. There is no longer any doubt whether a certain statement should be regarded as 'positive' or 'negative'. Second, the method of using statements originally made by foster parents and then graded by judges meant that the former were not presented with statements outside their frame of reference, while the intensity or ranking order was not dependent upon the subjective views of the researcher.[3]

Questions based on Guttman's scales

The Thurstone method, being a measure of an attitude or opinion towards a person at a specific time, was not useful for exploring the ways subjects would think or act in differing circumstances. It was desirable to assess under which conditions the foster parents would keep or cease to keep the foster children, and to this end use was made of the methods devised by Guttman.[4] Guttman's scales emphasise cumulativity, so that a person agreeing (or disagreeing) with one item is likely (or not likely) to agree with another. For instance, Oppenheim gives the example of addition, multiplication and the extraction of square roots, which are arithmetical operations ordered according to their cumulative degree of difficulty. Anyone answering that they can multiply is also likely to answer that they can add. If the items are indeed cumulative a total score given for each the respondent can do, will allow one to infer precisely which items he answered. Similarly, a person willing to keep a child under one condition of difficulty is likely to keep him under a condition of less difficulty.

The pilot study allowed scales to be drawn up for the subject mentioned above. It was assumed that few foster parents would stop keeping the child if payments ceased, that more would do so if the natural parents 'were a nuisance', and even more if the foster child was 'a bad influence on your own children'. It follows that foster parents who would not keep them for the first reason would not do so for the succeeding reasons. By giving a score to each item a measure of 'keeping' is devised. A foster parent with the highest score thus would keep the children under all the postulated circumstances, a foster parent scoring none would stop them if any of the circumstances were encountered.

The success or reliability of a Guttman scale depends on whether the interviewee's replies really are cumulative. A check can be made by calculating the coefficient of reproducibility, which involves examining the pattern of replies in every case. This done, the formula applied is

$$r = 1 - \frac{\text{No. of errors}}{\text{No. of responses}}$$

Guttman regarded a score of below $0 \cdot 9$ as unsatisfactory. In the case of the question applied to keeping the foster child, $r = 0 \cdot 99$ for the private foster cases and $0 \cdot 96$ for the local authority ones.

III. Reliability and truthfulness

The information upon which the research depended was obtained, in the main, from the file records of the children's departments and from the opinions and assessments of foster parents and child care officers. Was this information reliable? Did the interviewees give accurate and truthful replies?

Reliability

The methods used in a research project can be considered reliable if (i) they produce similar results when employed in subsequent research, if (ii) the researcher, who is research variable, treats each case in the same way, and if (iii) different people engaged in the same project come to similar conclusions when making the same assessment or engaged on the same operation. The testing of a research project at a later stage in exactly the same form as its initial manner rarely occurs. The researcher is enabled to treat each case alike by the careful design of recording schedules, accompanied by instructions and guides, which are rigorously applied on every occasion. The design of the schedule, its questions and instructions, has been described earlier. Here some account will be made of the reliability of the persons who recorded or gave the information, the file recorder (the researcher), the child care officers and the foster parents. The method of testing their reliability was to ask other persons to provide the same information. For instance, the same information was sought from the following pairs:

child care officers and senior child care officers

the foster parents and the child care officers.

The assessments or opinions of the pairs were examined to discover their percentage agreement and disagreement, and from this a product-moment correlation was calculated.

The child care and senior child care officers

Both the child care officers and the senior officers who supervised them were asked whether they would approve the private foster parents for taking local authority foster children. As the seniors had access to the same records and the file reports of the officers, it was assumed that a comparison of their replies would show whether they evaluated and interpreted the material in the same way, and whether they drew upon similar criteria to make their judgments. If the officer and his senior would both 'approve' or 'probably approve' the foster parents, they were recorded as in agreement. Similarly, if they both 'disapproved' or were 'doubtful'. All other combinations were taken as disagreements. They agreed with regard to 90 per cent of the private foster parents, the coefficient (r) of the product-moment correlation being a satisfactory $+0.78$.

The child care officers and their seniors were also asked to assess the private and local authority foster homes according to their adequacy to meet the children's material, intellectual and emotional needs. The percentage agreement, high for both types of fostering, tended to be highest for the local authority homes. As officers were in more frequent contact with these homes than with private placements, it is likely that they had more information on which to make their judgments which led to more agreement.

The foster parents and the child care officers

The foster parents and child care officers were asked to assess the extent to which the foster children aged two and over displayed the traits of aggression, anxiety, difficulties in making relationships, and withdrawal. Where both parties considered the trait to be shown 'persistently' or 'often', agreement was recorded. Similarly where both recorded 'occasionally' or 'never'. All other combinations were assigned as disagreement. The results are seen in Table A.1.

Table A.1   Percentage agreement between foster parents and child care officers regarding the extent to which foster children displayed traits

	Private foster children %	Local authority foster children %
Aggression	51·5	59·8
Anxiety	48·9	49·5
Relationship difficulties	72·7	55·9
Withdrawal	75·8	68·9

No. of private foster children=101.
No. of local authority foster children=105.

The high rate of agreement found between child care officers and their seniors was not totally unexpected, for both were likely to be trained observers using the same frame of reference. A similar percentage rate could not be expected between officers and foster parents, especially as the latter might regard the admittance of a trait as a criticism of their own handling of the children. None the less, except with regard to the trait of anxiety, the percentage of agreement was above fifty in every case, with the coefficient ranging from $+0·17$ to $+0·80$ with a median of $+0·51$.

Truthfulness

What reason is there to suppose that the persons interviewed gave truthful answers? It is assumed that the child care officers, who were not asked questions about their personal lives, were professionally aware of the need to provide accurate information for a research project. But what of the foster mothers, who were asked for such personal details as their age and marital status? Two techniques were employed to check the veracity of their replies. First, it was possible to check some items of information they supplied to the interviewer with answers previously given to the child care officers and recorded on the file records. These items were: the foster mother's age, her marital status, whether her foster child had been convicted of an offence or referred to a child guidance clinic, if the foster mother had applied to foster for the local authority, the number of private foster children she had and the payments received from the natural parents. The last three items applied to the private foster mothers but not to the local authority ones. The check revealed a very high rate of agreement, two examples of which are given in Tables A.2 and A.3.

Table A.2   Whether foster child had been referred to a child guidance clinic or not

	Private foster children %	Local authority foster children %
Agreement between file and interview	97	100
Disagreement	3	—
Totals	100	100

No. of private foster children to whom question applied = 101.
No. of local authority foster children to whom question applied = 105.

Table A.3   Whether private foster mothers had applied or not to foster for the local authority

	%
Agreement between file and interview	96
Disagreement	4
Total	100

No. of private foster mothers = 100.

In no item did the amount of disagreement rise above 7 per cent. Even here, disagreements could have been due to a time lag. For instance, the child care officer may have recorded the amount the foster parent said she was paid by the natural parent. After a while the amount was raised without the officer's knowledge, but the new level was told to the interviewer. Bearing in mind discrepancies of this kind, which are not due to deliberate intent, there is reason to believe that the foster mothers gave truthful replies.[5] Certainly, some made no attempt to hide such matters as their own co-habitation or the rejection of the application to foster for the local authority.

A second check on truthfulness was to examine the consistency of the foster mothers' replies within the interview. It would not have been useful to ask the same factual question twice over, but it was possible to ask different questions to which similar answers could be expected. For instance, it is reasonable to expect that foster mothers who expressed a wish to adopt their foster child would also give answers indicating a strong desire to keep him whatever the circumstances they met. Although a few foster mothers might truthfully wish to adopt and yet record a low 'keeping' intent, the assumption is that most would not take up this position. Thus internal consistency checks were made on the following assumptions:

a that foster fathers, whom the foster mothers said were involved in the decision to foster, would also be said not to try to persuade them to give up fostering;

b that foster mothers who fostered to 'have or enlarge' a family would want to adopt the foster child;

c that foster mothers who said they received under two pounds a week for their foster child would also say that the income they received was not sufficient to keep the child;

d that foster mothers who regarded their foster child as their 'own child' would want to adopt him;

e that those who wanted to adopt would have a high 'keeping' score;

f that foster mothers who said their husbands tried to persuade them to give up fostering would not record them as being highly participant;

g that foster mothers who found the child care officers' visits 'very' or 'sometimes' helpful would also have a positive opinion of them.

In all the above cases the results were in the expected direction, and in each case proved statistically significant. To give one instance, those foster parents saying they would adopt the foster child were significantly more likely (than those who would not or did not know whether they wished to adopt) to have the highest 'keeping' score ($x^2 = 19 \cdot 008$, d.f. $= 2$, P $= <0 \cdot 001$). It can be concluded that the truthfulness of the foster mothers in the items tested and the consistency in the general trend of their replies suggests that they were not deliberately trying to give false answers.

IV. Categorising and coding

In order to quantify the information collected on the recording schedules, categories had to be formed, the material allocated to them, a code number given to each category, and the numbers transferred to the IBM punch cards ready for analysis.

The formation of categories and their coding was quite straightforward in some cases especially where previous research had resulted in well-established categories. For instance, tenure types are usually divided into 'owner-occupied flat', 'owner-occupied house', etc. In such cases the placing of the replies into the various categories, that is the coding process, was also straightforward, leaving virtually no room for error, and could be left to the interviewer working on his own. Other more complex categories and coding frames were also adapted where they had proved valuable to previous researchers, for their use facilitated comparison with the findings of this research. But in many cases the categorising was not straightforward, and careful techniques had to be chosen.

The formation of categories (or classifications) and the coding of material in all but the straightforward cases introduces the possibility of error and bias in three main directions. First, the categories which are formed may not accurately fit the information which has been collected. Second, the coding process, that is the allocation of the material to the categories, may be inaccurately completed. Material belonging to one category may be placed in another. Third, the coder may be inconsistent in his interpretations of material, so that on different cases he may allocate the same kind of material to different categories.

Inevitably, a coding and categorising procedure loses some information because it is basically a means of compressing it. However, the following steps were taken to minimise error and bias. It was determined that the categories formed would aim to be (i) exhaustive, that is they would cover all the kinds of information that was collected, and (ii) exclusive, that is one category should not overlap with another. A practical consideration was that the number of categories had to be restricted to the number of code numbers in a column on a punch card. To form the categories, two categorisers or judges, working independently, studied the replies to the questions (which had been written out from the tape recordings) and formulated them into categories. They then compared their findings, ironed out some differences and submitted remaining disagreements (which, in fact, were few) to the arbitration of a third judge. Code numbers were then given the categories.

The allocation of the material to the categories, the coding process, was carried out by a further pair of judges or coders, again working independently. They were assisted by the definitions of categories which promoted consistency of interpretation between the coders. Again, where disagreement occurred, a third person was brought in to arbitrate. The use of two coders combined with explicit instructions appeared successful in promoting consistency of practice.

It is possible to calculate the measure of agreement between the two coders. Using the system devised by David (1967, p. 59) and considering questions where the information had to be placed in one category only, the following procedure was applied. Agreement on all cases was $=100$ per cent. For each disagreement a penalty of $100\frac{1}{n}$ was subtracted. Thus in the case of one question 222 foster mothers gave replies. The coders disagreed in eight cases, so the reliability percentage was 100 minus $100 \times \frac{1}{222} \times 8 = 96\cdot4$ per cent. In other questions the respondents could give multiple answers, that is, the replies could be coded into more than one category. For instance, the question 'Why does the child care officer visit a foster home?' had five categories, all of which might have been involved in the answer. In such questions, where the coders had complete disagreement, that is there was no overlap at all in the categories they chose, then a penalty was subtracted in the same way as mentioned above. Where partial disagreement occurred, that is they might agree on one category but disagree on another, a penalty of $50\frac{1}{n}$ was subtracted. With regard to the above question, there were ten total and twenty-one partial disagreements. The reliability percentage was therefore 100 minus $4\cdot5 + 4\cdot83 = 90\cdot67$ per cent.

The percentages for the above two questions were particularly high. However, the agreement percentage rarely fell below seventy. Interestingly, they were, on the whole, higher than those achieved and considered satisfactory by David in his work (1967, pp. 271–2).

V. The foster parent recording schedule

A lack of space does not allow the reproduction of all the schedules used in the research. These comprised the foster parent interview recording schedule (private and local authority), the file schedule (private and local authority), the natural parent interview schedule, the child care officer interview recording schedule (senior and child care officer), and the school postal questionnaire. However, it is possible to give one, the private foster parent interviewing schedule.

Form F.1.

Private foster parent interview

Name of child
Foster child number
Fostering number
Name of foster parents
Address
Foster parent number
Date and time of interview

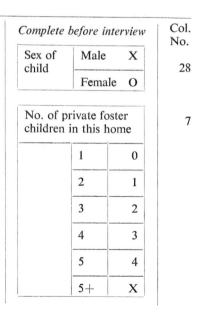

Complete before interview			Col. No.
Sex of child	Male	X	28
	Female	O	
No. of private foster children in this home			7
	1	0	
	2	1	
	3	2	
	4	3	
	5	4	
	5+	X	

1. Where were you born?
2. Where was your husband born?

	Foster mother	Foster father
U.K.		
Eire		
West Indies		
Africa		

Complete before interview

	Foster mother	Foster father
Asia (Specify)		
Elsewhere in Europe (specify)		
Other (specify)		

(if in U.K. complete)

Northern		
Ridings		
Midlands		
Eastern		
London & S.E.		
Southern		
S.W.		

Wales		
N.W.		
Scotland		
Other		

Col.
No.

3. (If from Midlands) were you born in [name of town]?

Yes	
No	

Code after interview

Area of birth of foster mother	
[Name of town]	0
Elsewhere in Midlands	1

1

Complete after interview

Area of birth of foster mother

Elsewhere in U.K.	2
Eire	3
West Indies	4
Africa	5
Asia	6
Elsewhere in Europe	7
Other	8

4. Which age group: (hand card)
(a) are you in now?
(b) were you in when you took your first ever foster child?
(c) were you in when you took your present foster child?

2, 3, 4

	a	b	c
Under 25 years	0	0	0
25–30	1	1	1
31–35	2	2	2
36–40	3	3	3
41–45	4	4	4
46–50	5	5	5
51–55	6	6	6
56–60	7	7	7

	a	b	c
61–65	8	8	8
66+	9	9	9

Code after interview

5. How many natural children (include adopted) have you?

0
1
2
3
4
5
6
7
8
More

0	X
1	0
2–4	1
5–6	2
7–9	3
More	4

6

. Including your natural
children who are still at
home, how many other
children do you now look
after?

No. of natural children at home		Col. No. 6
0	5	
1	6	
2	7	
3	8	
4	9	
5 and more	X	

		0	1	2	3	4	5	if more, specify
vate foster nildren	Sex							
	Age							
cal Authority oster children	Sex							
	Age							
atural hildren	Sex							
	Age							
aily inding	Sex							
	Age							
her pecify)	Sex							
	Age							

Total no. of children cared for		
1	5	7
2	6	
3–4	7	

Code after interview

Total no. of children cared for		
5–6	8	5
7–9	9	
More	X	

. Apart from the children
you look after at present,
have you previously had:

	Yes	No
private foster children	0	X
Local Authority foster children	1	X
daily minded children	2	X
others not your own (specify)	3	X

[for those who have
previously fostered privately]

. Would you give me some
details about your previous
private foster children?

1   *Code after interview*

No. of private foster children previously cared for	
0	4
1–2	5
3–5	6
6–10	7
11–20	8
More	9

No. of previous private foster children	Age on arrival			Time he stayed				Whether Local Authority Informed		To whom the child went			Reason the child left					
	under one year	1 year & under 5 years	5 years and over	under one year	1 year & under 2 years	2 years & under 5 years	5 years and over	Yes	No	Parents	Foster parents	Others	Child misbehaved	Child ill	Parents found accommodation	Parents completed studies	Parents nuisance	Other (specify)
0																		
1																		
2																		
3																		
4																		
5																		
6																		
7																		
8																		
9																		
10																		
10+ specify																		

9. What made you, and your
husband, think you would
like to have foster children?

*Categorise and code after
interview*

Col.
No.

Primary

8

Have or enlarge family	0
Circumstances	1
Fondness and concern for children	2
Fill vacuum in foster mother's life	3
Other	4

Multiple

Have or enlarge family Lost own child	
Couldn't have children	
Adoption substitute	
Wanted more	
Wanted child of particular sex	
Circumstances Related to child	
Particular child	
Developed from other form of care	

Developed from temporary to permanent	
Fondness and concern for children	
Fond of children	
Want to help/ feel sorry	
Contact with unhappy children	
Related to own childhood experiences	
Give others what had themselves	
Need to fill vacuum in foster mother's life	
Need to work	
Loneliness	
Fill place of own children	
A plaything	
Other	
Financial	
Needs of own child	
Influenced by neighbours	

Influenced by advert		

10. What kind of dwelling is this? (hand card)

Owner occupied flat	X
Owner occupied house	0
Private rented house	1
Private rented flat	2
Private rented rooms	3
Council house	4
Council flat	5
Other	6

49

Complete immediately after interview

49

Approximate date of house	
Pre-1914	7
1914-1939	8
Post-1939	9

L*

11. How many bedrooms, other rooms (excluding toilet and bathrooms) and occupants are there here in your household?

Number of bedrooms								
0	1	2	3	4	5	6	6+	

Number of other rooms								
0	1	2	3	4	5	6	6+	

Occupants											
0	1	2	3	4	5	6	7	8	9	10	10+

12. With how many other people does the foster child share a bed?

0	4
1	5
2	6
3 & more	7

13. Has your household got, or does it share:

	Sole use	share	none
piped water			
cooking stove			
sink			
water toilet			

Code after interview

Room density	
Up to 1·5 per room	7
Over 1·5 and up to 2 per room	8
Over 2 per room	9

Bedroom density	
Up to 1 per room	2
Over 1 and up to 2	3
Over 2	X

No. of basic amenities			
Shared		Lacking	
0	X	0	X
1	0	1	5
2	1	2	6

Col. No.

53

50

50

51

					Col. No.
fixed bath					
garden					

3	2	3	7
4	3	4	8
5–6	4	5–6	9

14. Which school does he go to?

Name of school	Type	
	Below or over school age	3
	Infant or Junior	4
	Grammar	5
	Secondary Modern	6
	Comprehensive	7
	Special (specify)	8
	Other (specify)	9

66

15. How did you come into
contact with this child?

Code after interview

16. How many times did you
meet the child before he came
to live with you?

			Answered advert	0	
			Inserted advert	1	37
			Via a friend or relative	2	
			Knew parents beforehand	3	
			Other (specify)	X	

0	4
1	5
2–4	6
5	7
more	8

37

17. What information did his parents give you about him?

Food	
Sleeping habits	
Behaviour	
Previous experience of care away from parents	
Child rearing methods used	
Other	

Barest details (0–1 topics)	9	37
More (2 or more topics)	X	

18. How much money per week do you get for this child from:

The Parents	
Family Allowance	
Other	
Children's Dept.	

Code after interview   36

Under 30/-	0
30/- but under £2	1
£2 but under £3	2
£3 but under £4	3
£4 but under £5	4
£5 and over	5

19. How often is clothing provided as well?

Categorise and code after interview   36

Regularly	6
Occasionally	7
Never	X

Col.
No.

20. Do you find this income sufficient to keep the child?

Yes	8
No	X

36

21. Are payments from the parents made regularly?

Yes	9
No	X

36

22. Which of these statements, if any, sums up your attitude towards the child? (hand card)

'I regard him as my own child'	0
'I know he's not mine but I treat him the same'	1
'he is a means of making money while at the same time doing something worthwhile'	2
Other (specify)	3
Don't know	x

38

23. For how long do you expect the child to stay with you?

Categorise and code after interview

38

definitely leave, not sure when	6
definitely short-term	7
definitely long-term	8
unsure of future	9
other	X

24. Do you think a private foster child can be removed from the foster home too easily by his parents?

Yes	0
No	X
Don't know	1

39

25. Would you keep your foster child even if:

	Yes	No
Payments stopped altogether	2	X
The parents were a nuisance	3	X
His behaviour was very difficult	4	X
He was a bad influence on your own children	5	X

39

Calculate score after interview

39

Keeping score (1 for yes, 0 for no)	
0 points	6
1	7
2	8
3	9
4	X

26. If his parents consented, would you adopt this foster child?

Code after interview

Yes	4
No	X
Don't know	5

Col. No.

38

Questions 27 to 32 applicable to children below 5 years old [applicable to this child]

Yes	0
No	X

27. If he falls over and cries what do you do?

Categorise and code after interview

Love it better	1
Pick up	2
Investigate	3
Ignore	4
Other	X

40

28. How long will you leave him to cry if you thought there was nothing wrong with him?

Not at all	5
Up to 5 mins.	6
5–15 mins.	7
15–30 mins.	8
Over 30 mins.	9
Other	X

40

29. How do you punish him when he's been naughty?

None	0
Smack	1
Warning, then smack	2
Verbal	3
Other	X

41

30. What do you do when you prepare something for him and he won't eat it?

41

anxious about it	4
mildly concerned	5
unconcerned	6

Col. No.

31. For what kind of naughtiness would you smack him?

Categorise and code after interview

never	7
for danger only	8
for other reasons	9

41

42

32. How many times do you think you have visited the Welfare Clinic on behalf of your foster child in the last six months?

Code after interview

Average no. visits per last 6 mths.	
0	X
Under 1	0
1 and under 2	1
2 and under 6	2
more	3

43

33. With whom did the idea of
fostering start?

Foster mother	0
Foster father	1
Both	X
Not applicable	2

34. Has your husband ever tried
to persuade you to give up
fostering?

Yes	3
No	X
Not applicable	4

35. How many evenings is your
husband away each week?

0	5
1	6
2–4	7
5–7	8
Not applicable	9

36. How many weekends per
month is he away?

0	X
1	0
2–4	1
Not applicable	2

I will now mention some things some fathers do with their children and I should like to know how often your husband does them.

Question 37 applicable to children under 5 and where a foster father present
[applicable to this child]

Yes	3
No	X

37. For instance, how often does he:

44 &
45

	Change the nappy	Feed him	Bath him	Get him to sleep	Attend to him at night	Play with him	Take him out without you
Often	4	7	0	2	4	6	8
Sometimes	5	8	1	3	5	7	9
Never	X	X	X	X	X	X	X
Not applicable	6						

Question 38 applicable to children 5 years and over and where a foster father present
[applicable to this child]

46

Yes	0
No	X

38. How much does your husband have to do with him? For instance how often does he:

	Take him out alone	Play with him or Do hobbies with him or Take an interest in his hobbies	Talk with him
Often	1	3	5
Sometimes	2	4	6
Never	X	X	X

Degree of participation of foster father	
Highly	0
Moderate	1
None	2
Not applicable	X

47

Questions 39–41 applicable to children of 11 years and over, providing a foster father is present
[applicable to this child]

Yes	0
No	X

48

39. With whom does your foster child spend most of his time when indoors?

Foster mother	1
Foster father	2
Foster sibling	3
Natural sibling	4
Self	5
Other (specify)	X

48

40. If he is in trouble, with whom will he usually consult?

Foster mother	6
Foster father	7
Nobody	8
Child Care Officer	9
Other (specify)	X

48

41. If he wants advice, to whom
    will he usually turn?

Foster mother	6
Foster father	7
Nobody	8
Child Care Officer	9
Other (specify)	X

15

*Calculate and code after
interview*

Communication with f. father	
Fully with f. father	3
Mainly or some f. father	4
None f. father	5
Not applicable	X

47

Communication	
None outside self	6
Mainly with f. father	7
Mainly with f. mother	8
Mixed re f. parents	9
Other	X

47

*Questions 42–45 applicable to
children aged 2 years and
under 7 years*
  [applicable to this child]

Yes	0
No	X

54

42. By 1½ years of age was the
    child walking alone? (a few
    yards without support)

No	1
Yes	2
Don't know	X

54

43. If No, at what age?

Col.
No.

44. By 2 years of age was the
    child talking (joining 2
    words?)

No	3
Yes	4
Don't know	X

54

45. If No, at what age?

*Question 46 applicable to
children aged 4 and over*
[applicable to this child]

Yes	5
No	x

54

46. Has he wet by day after 3
    years of age? (ignore
    occasional mishaps).

Yes	6
No	7
Don't know	X

54

*Question 47 applicable to
children aged 5 and over*
[applicable to this child]

Yes	0
No	X

55

47. Has he soiled by day after 4
    years of age? (ignore
    occasional mishaps).

Yes	1
No	2
Don't know	X

55

Question 48 applicable to children aged 6 and over [applicable to this child]

Yes	3
No	X

48. Has he wet by night after 5 years of age? (ignore occasional mishaps).

Yes	4
No	5
Don't know	X

55

All Children

49. How many colds has he had in the last 3 months?

0–1	6
2–4	7
More	8
Don't know	X

55

50. While with you has he had:

	Yes	No
bronchitis	0	X
asthma	1	X
pneumonia	2	X
whooping cough	3	X

56

51. While with you has he had an accident for which you had to get hospital or a doctor's treatment?

Yes	4
No	X

52. If YES, please give details:

No of Acci-dents	Type of Accident					
	burn	scald	broken bone	cut	bruise	other (specify)
1						
2						
3						
4						
5						
5+						

Calculate and code after interview

Average no. of accidents per 12 months	
0	5
Under 1	6
1 under 2	7
2 under 3	8
more	9

56

53. Has the child any physical handicap or disabling condition for which he receives or has received medical treatment?

Yes	X
No	0

56

54. If YES, please give details

visual	1
epilepsy	2
motor	3
cardiac	4
t.b.	5
speech	6
deafness or impaired hearing	7

57

57

| mental deficiency or sub-normality | 8 |
| other (specify) | 9 |

Questions 55–57 applicable to children aged 2 years and over
[applicable to this child]

| Yes | 0 |
| No | X |

55. To what extent does he display more than normal: (give card)

	Persis-tently above normal	Often above normal	Occasion-ally above normal	Never or normal	Don't know
Aggression	1	2	3	4	X
Anxiety	5	6	7	8	X
Difficulties in making relation-ships	0	1	2	3	X
Withdrawal	4	5	6	7	X

58

59

56. To your knowledge has he ever been advised to attend the Child Guidance Clinic?

| Yes | 8 |
| No | X |

58

57. If YES, please give details.

Calculate and code after interview

Gradings of Emotional Traits	
no trait persistently or often	0

59

		Col. No.
one	1	
two	2	
three	3	
four	4	
other	X	

Questions 58–59 applicable to children aged 8 years and over
[applicable to this child]

60

Yes	8
No	X

58. To your knowledge has he ever appeared before the Courts? (count only appearances for offences)

Yes	9
No	X

59. If YES, please give details.

60. What are the main difficulties you have met in fostering this child?

Categorise and code after interview

68

Child's behaviour aggression anxiety relationships withdrawal		0
Relationship private foster parent and natural parents conflict re. visits		

conflict payments threat of removal		1
Relationship private foster child and natural parents child fears natural parents child wants natural parents		2
Child's physical health illness or handicap lack of development		3
Physical and material conditions		4
Educational		5
Feelings about colour and race private foster parents feelings child's feelings		6
Foster parents general insecurity about fostering		X
Problems within the foster family		Y

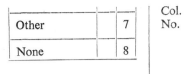

				Col. No.
Other		7		
None		8		

61. How often does the child see his mother and father? (hand card)

69

	mother	father
at least once a week	0	5
at least once a month	1	6
at least once a year	2	7
less often than a year	3	8
never	4	9
parent is dead	X	X

62. Does he have contact with any other relatives? (apart from siblings with whom he lives)

70

Yes	X
No	0

code after interview

70

relatives	last seen

Contact				
Relation not seen for 1 yr.				
	Yes	No	Not appl	D. K.
mother	1	X	2	
father	3	X	4	
sibling	5	X	6	7

63. Does the child know that you are not his real parents?

	Yes	0
	No	X
Child is under 2 years old		1

71

64. If answer is YES, how have you explained to him why he doesn't live with his own parents?

categorise and code after interview

knew before he came	2
picked it up	3
natural parents explain	4
reasonable explanation by foster parents	5
hurtful explanation by foster parents	6
reasonable and hurtful by foster parents	7
other	8

71

65. Do you think he should be encouraged to see his parents?

categorise and code after interview

66. What effect does contact with his parents have on him?

Yes	0
No	1
Depends on parents' interest	2

72

67. Would you try to stop the parents visiting if:

	Yes	No
they came without warning you	4	X
they kept criticizing you	5	X
they disturbed the child	6	X

68. Do you agree or disagree with the following statements about the child's mother (give card)

	agree	not
'Really, she is a wonderful mother'	0	x
'She's a plucky girl who does her best'	1	x
'She would prefer to look after the child herself'	2	x
'She should let me get on with looking after him'	3	x
'She doesn't deserve to have children'	4	x
'She's disgusting!'	y	x

69. How did you discover that you had to inform the Children's Department about the arrival of a foster child? (Not applicable to Local Authority foster parents)

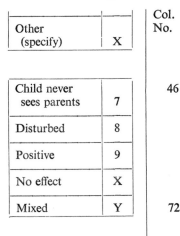

Col. No.

Other (specify)	X

Child never sees parents	7	46
Disturbed	8	
Positive	9	
No effect	X	
Mixed	Y	72

calculate score after interview

72

Parents stopping scale (1 for yes, 0 for no)		
0 points	7	
1 point	8	
2 points	9	
3 points	X	74

calculate score after interview

10

positive	0
middling	1
negative	X

code after interview

Via Health Visitor	5	74
Neighbours	6	

M

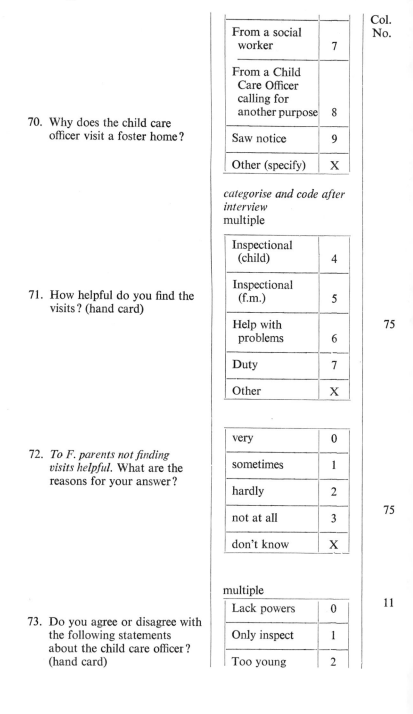

Col.
No.

70. Why does the child care officer visit a foster home?

From a social worker	7
From a Child Care Officer calling for another purpose	8
Saw notice	9
Other (specify)	X

categorise and code after interview
multiple

71. How helpful do you find the visits? (hand card)

Inspectional (child)	4
Inspectional (f.m.)	5
Help with problems	6
Duty	7
Other	X

75

72. *To F. parents not finding visits helpful.* What are the reasons for your answer?

very	0
sometimes	1
hardly	2
not at all	3
don't know	X

75

multiple

11

73. Do you agree or disagree with the following statements about the child care officer? (hand card)

Lack powers	0
Only inspect	1
Too young	2

	agree	not
'She is really concerned about the child and me'	0	X
'She is a friend of our family'	1	X
'She is interesting to talk to'	2	X
'Somebody has got to see what is going on!'	3	X
'She isn't very interested in us!'	4	X
'My business is nothing to do with her'	5	X
'She's always looking for trouble!'	Y	X
Don't know	6	X

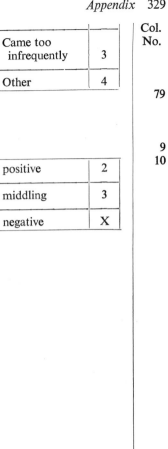

		Col. No.
Came too infrequently	3	
Other	4	
		79

		9
		10
positive	2	
middling	3	
negative	X	

74. Have you ever applied to your local Children's Department, another Children's Department or a voluntary society, to become a foster parent for them?

	Yes	No
Local Children's Department		
Other Children's Department		
Voluntary Society		
Other		

code after interview

Applied and accepted	5	77
Applied and rejected	6	
Not applied	7	
other	X	

75. If answer YES, what was the
    result of your application?

accepted
rejected
other (specify)

76. If accepted by Children's
    Department or society, why
    do you take private foster
    children?

*categorise and code after
interview*

Circumstances	4
Already a p.f.m.	5
Request of L.A.	6
L.A. stopped using	7
other	8

77. What do you gain from
    having a foster child?

*categorise and code after
interview*

Love	0
Satisfaction of helping others	1
General happiness	2
Companionship	3
Complete family	4
Other	11

78. What do you regard as your
    duty to give to your foster
    child?

multiple

Love	5
Security	6
Same as own children	7
Normal family life	8
Physical needs	9
Other	12

Col.
No.

10

9

9

79. If you were to give some advice to new private foster parents, what would you say?

categorise and code after interview

multiple

Love	4
Treat as own	5
Patience and understanding	6
Emotional detachment	7
Sacrifice	8
Consider implications	9
Other	X

Col. No.

42

80. What is your marital status (hand card)?

married	0
divorced	1
separated	2
widowed	3
co-habiting	4
single	5

22

81. What is your husband's occupation?

complete after interview

12

Foster parents'	Occupa- tional group
I	0
II	1

		Col. No.
III	2	
IV	3	
V	4	

This is a description of an actual case. We should like your views on how it should be dealt with. (hand card)

'Mrs X. was an experienced foster mother looking after 2 boys and her own daughter. Annette, aged $7\frac{1}{2}$, was placed with her. She was illegitimate, and had already been in a nursery and a previous foster home.

Mrs X. was very firm with Annette and quickly suppressed her cheekiness. She proved useful in the home, although rather a cry-baby. At school she was competent in her work but a nuisance in class because she was always seeking attention.

After 2 years the 2 boys left to get employment. Annette was very lonely. Mrs X. did not encourage her to make friends, and would not allow her to bring other children home to play, so she spent most of her time alone in her bedroom.

Annette asked Mrs X. questions about her own mother, but the foster mother thought it best to avoid them and said, 'They are no good to you – don't bother your head about them'.

Annette had occasional bouts of screaming and temper tantrums. Mrs. X. punished her by corporal punishment.'

	categorise and code after interview		Col. No.

82. What caused Annette to behave as she did?

multiple

C46

f.m. not give enough love and affection	0
f.m. not give enough attention	1
f.m. too strict	2
child testing f.m.	3
not enough friends	4
child felt unwanted	5
child felt insecure	6
child unable to express feelings	7
related to previous child care experiences	8
related to confusion about own mother	9
other	X

83. How should the foster mother have dealt with Annette?

Categorise and code after interview

multiple

47

Love and affection	0
Understood causes	1
Not corporal	2

Col.
No.

Corporal punishment if necessary	3
Coaxing	4
Friends in	5
Explain re mother	6
Other	X

84. How should the foster mother have answered Annette's questions about her mother?

Primary

Nothing	7
Whole truth	8
Partial truth to avoid pain	9
Other	X

Notes

Chapter 1   Background to the research

1 Since the research was completed, children's departments have been incorporated into the local authority social service departments.
2 *Child Care News* (82), January 1969.
3 Heywood, *Children in Care*, p. 94.
4 The Children and Young Persons Act (1969) has since slightly altered the legislation as will be explained later.
5 The Adoption Act (1958), which is very similar to the Children Act of that year, sets out the local authorities' duties towards children placed privately for adoption.
6 For a full review of the content of the sources, see R. Holman, 'Private foster homes: a study of the foster children and foster parents supervised by children's departments under the Children Act (1958)', Ph.D. thesis, University of Birmingham, 1971.
7 *Sunday Times*, 23 February 1969.
8 *Hansard*, 4 June 1964, col.1226.
9 *Report on the Work of the Children's Department of the City of Birmingham for the Three Years ending March 1967*, Birmingham, 1967.
10 I am grateful to the Home Office Research Unit for advice on this point.
11 The constraints of time and distance themselves arose from the position of a research project being carried out by one person on a small budget.
12 These are not necessarily coloured immigrants, neither do they show the number of coloured children born in the UK.
13 A. Simon, in Parker, *Decision in Child Care*, p. 23.

Chapter 2   The private foster parents

1 Tables in this study present data either according to the number of foster parents or the number of foster children. The two differ because some foster children had the same foster parents. The child in relation to his foster parents is, of course, the basic unit and can be referred to as 'a fostering'.
2 A discussion of the means of measuring social class can be found in British Sociological Association and Social Science Research Council, *Comparability in Social Research*, Heinemann, 1969, pp. 100–1.
3 As is usual with the χ^2 test, the difference was taken to be significant

when P (probability) was not greater than 0·050. Of course, such a finding does not necessarily demonstrate a causal relationship between the factors tested but shows that they are associated in some way. A clear explanation of the use – and limitations – of χ^2 tests is found in A. G. Maxwell, *Analysing Qualitative Data*, Methuen, 1964, reprinted in 1967.

4 *Fertility Tables*, Census, 1961, HMSO, 1966. The Tables did not allow comparison according to a breakdown of social class. The Fertility Tables for the sample census, 1966, were not available at the time of the research.

5 The placements measured by Gray and Parr were ongoing, so once completed the average would have been higher than 4·7 years. On the other hand, short stay placements have a high turnover rate so all the short-term cases occurring in a one-year period would not be reflected in a sample, like Gray and Parr's, which was drawn on a given date. Their sample, therefore, had its average length increased considerably by the long stay cases who would stay on the records of children's departments for long periods.

6 It must be pointed out that these numbers of children do not contain all the private foster children in the local authorities at a given time in the way that the population of ongoing cases consisted of them all on a certain date in 1968. Rather, they consisted of children previously in the homes of private foster mothers who were still fostering in 1968.

Chapter 3   The private foster children

1 A difficulty of the English language is its lack of terms which distinguish between nationality and colour. Thus to say that a child's parents were both West African usually means that not only did they originate from that part of the world but that also his pigmentation is black (or coloured) – but not invariably so. To clarify matters it can be stated that all the children in the study who were born to two parents from the United Kingdom were white, while all those whose both parents were from the West Indies or West Africa were black. The West Africans were from two countries, the majority from Nigeria, the remainder from Ghana.

2 The parents of the children who were placed in the city and county were not necessarily resident in the Midlands. Indeed, the research showed that many were placed by parents from London and the south-east. Interestingly, the county contained a greater proportion of West African children than even the city.

3 The figures issued by the societies and departments and the definitions used for 'coloured' are found in my Ph.D. thesis, op. cit., ch. 3.

4 The concern of some authorities over the number of West Indian children being received into care prompted an investigation and a project to reduce their numbers which is the subject of Fitzherbert's *West Indian Children in London*.

5 From 1922–67 the percentage of illegitimate to all live births varied from 4·07 to 9·33 (*Registrar General's Statistical Review of England and Wales, 1967*, HMSO, 1969). The highest figure recorded in 1968 by any one local authority was 18·4 illegitimate births per 1,000 births, a number still below that of the private foster children. See *Hansard*, 18 March 1970, col. 144.

6 A difficulty in presenting findings in this study is that the foster children are in matched pairs, the foster parents are not. Thus Table 3.2 could be presented as follows where the total is the number of matched pairs:

| | Private foster children | | |
	Legitimate	Illegitimate	Totals
Local authority foster children			
Legitimate	37	11	48
Illegitimate	74	21	95
Totals	111	32	143

However, such presentation would mean giving two forms of Tables, one for the foster children, one for the foster parents. Further, much of the study is concerned with the private children only. For the sake of clarity, it has been decided to present all Tables in the form of Table 3.2. But as mentioned in chapter 1, a matched-pairs Table requires the McNemar's test of significance, namely:

$$\chi^2 = \frac{(a-d)^2}{(a+d)} \text{ where a and d are the unlike pairs.}$$

Thus any statistical explanations for the matched pairs foster children use this test, that for the foster parents a normal χ^2. I am grateful to the Home Office Research Unit for advice.

7 The account of Eisenberg's research is given in Dinnage and Pringle, *Foster Home Care: Facts and Fallacies*, p. 118.

8 In addition, the study established that few children of either group had experienced residential care.

9 It is interesting that some of the local authority children's previous foster homes had been private ones. In all, eleven had been in private foster homes, eight of whom had actually been received into public care from those placements.

10 As mentioned, the classification was based on that of the Home Office which was in respect of children received into care under Section 1 of the Children Act (1948). Of the 143 local authority foster children in the contrast group, 127 were in care under a Section 1 order and were easily placed in a category. Another ten were in care under Section 2 of the same Act, but as they had first come through Section 1 they too could be easily allocated a category. Six children had been committed to care by the courts via a Fit

Person Order. However, all were non-offenders and the reasons they were brought before the courts could be inserted into the categories.

Chapter 4   The suitability of the private foster parents

1 Religion is ascertained not to gauge the applicants' general suitability to care for children but in order that foster children can be placed, where possible, with persons of the same religion as recommended by Section 14 of the Children Act (1948).
2 The full review can be found in my Ph.D. thesis, op. cit., pp. 100–6.
3 It thus was possible to avoid the mistake of regarding a factor which resulted from the practice of fostering as being in existence before the fostering. For instance, in her study of adoption, Kornitzer (1968, p. 112) states that 10 per cent of adopters had a mental or physical illness without specifying if it existed before they adopted or whether it was revealed after they adopted, possibly even being provoked by the very experience of adoption.
4 *Daily Mail*, 6 April 1966.
5 The responses are given in full in my Ph.D. thesis, op. cit., pp. 115–17.
6 It may be asked how children's departments came to approve applicants who possessed an unsuitability factor. The answer is that they considered the persons' advantages outweighed that factor. The assessments by the child care officers, as shown in Table 4.2, were overall judgments which weighed factors against each other thus serving as a balance to the single factor approach.
7 The file material showed unsuitable factors against fifty-five private foster parents, the officers were dubious or disapproving of fifty-two. The question is raised, were they the same foster parents or were the officers disapproving of those with no unsuitability factors recorded? The overlap totalled forty-five, that is forty-five foster parents appeared in the two lists.
8 The social class V foster parents were also significantly more likely to have been rejected by official bodies following applications to foster but the numbers concerned were very small.

Chapter 5   The treatment of the private foster children (1)

1 Edwards accepts Thurstone's definition of an attitude as 'the degree of positive or negative effect associated with some psychological object'. By a psychological object is meant any symbol, phrase, slogan, person, institution, ideal, or idea toward which people can differ with respect to positive or negative effect (see A. Edwards, *Techniques of Attitude Scale Construction*, Appleton-Century-Crofts, 1957).
2 A full review can be found in my Ph.D. thesis, op. cit., pp. 142–6.
3 Guardians' Allowance is paid to persons who care for a child whose own parents are dead and who were insured under the National

Insurance Acts. See the Ministry of Social Security leaflet, N.I.14, October 1968.

4 A few months after the research was completed, the rates were raised by the two children's departments by between 15*s*. and 20*s*. according to age. The research of Adamson suggests that the rates paid by these departments were neither unusually low nor high in comparison with other departments (1968, pp. 3 and 18–21).

5 In my Ph.D. thesis (op. cit., pp. 169–79), attention was given to the whole range of child-rearing practices, including those applicable to natural children, such as feeding practices, used by the foster parents. Here attention is given to situations applicable only to foster children.

6 The questions used in this section and the definition of the categories are to be found in my Ph.D. thesis, op. cit., Appendix VI.

Chapter 6   The treatment of the private foster children (2)

1 Andry's work applied only to boys. However, McCullough has observed a connection between girls sent to a probation hostel and a lack of opportunities to form a relationship with a father (see M. McCullough, 'The absent fathers', *New Society*, 19 May 1966).

2 In these figures, as in Table 6.3, homes with no foster fathers or ones of very recent addition are excluded.

3 The percentages in the Plowden findings take into account children with no father, whereas Tables 6.1–6.3 have excluded homes without foster fathers before making percentage calculations. As the latter number is small the difference has little impact on the overall percentages.

4 The definitions of each item and of the rankings are given in my Ph.D. thesis, op. cit., Appendix VI.

5 The private foster mothers who indicated that their husbands never talked with the foster children were pressed on their answers. It appeared that the foster fathers literally never spoke to them and, in fact, were deliberately ignoring them as a way of expressing resentment at the children's presence.

6 The tests of significance were as follows (d.f. $=2$ in each case):

Item	χ^2	p
Nappy change	10·370	$<0·010$
Feeding	28·571	$<0·001$
Bathing	33·507	$<0·001$
Get to sleep	46·949	$<0·001$
Attend at night	36·801	$<0·001$
Play	34·481	$<0·001$
Take out alone	32·948	$<0·001$
Take out alone ⎱ older	4·5245	Not significant
Play and hobbies ⎰ children	21·415	$<0·001$
Talks	15·445	$<0·001$

7 It is worth pointing out that in their later study of the fathers of four-year-olds, the Newsons record that father participation

becomes greater with the age of the children. Therefore, the foster fathers were being compared with natural fathers who were probably at their stage of least participation.

8 A full account of the methodology and results is given in my Ph.D. thesis, op. cit., pp. 220–4.

9 The definitions of the housing terms used and the formation of the questions used is given in my Ph.D. thesis, op. cit., pp. 229–31 and Appendix VI.

10 M. Woolf, *The Housing Survey in England and Wales*, HMSO, 1967. Woolf's age-bands differ slightly from those of the present study, for instance, he has 'Up to 1919' instead of 'Up to 1914'. But as the extra years were war years in which little building occurred, it is not likely to cause much difference in the comparison.

Chapter 7   The condition of the private foster children

1 It is fair to add that Vernon discusses the criticisms of the use of the term 'trait' and points out that some psychologists prefer the term 'trend' as used by Gregory, or 'teleonomic trend' as used by F. Allport.

2 Questions about deprivation traits were put only regarding children of two years and over. The reasons for this, the definitions used for the terms, the actual questions, and the instructions to the interviewer are located in my Ph.D. thesis, op. cit., ch. 3.

3 It is important to note that Douglas's figures refer to attendance, and those of the study to referral. Some of the seven private foster children, although referred, had not been taken to the clinic by their foster parents.

4 The review in full and the postal questionnaire used can be found in my Ph.D. thesis, op. cit., pp. 274–8 and Appendix V.

5 For a discussion of the spread of attainment, see Pringle, *Deprivation and Education*, p. 176.

6 The questions were applied only to children of two years and over as it may have been impossible to tell whether younger children knew the truth or not. The definitions of the categories used are to be found in my Ph.D. thesis, op. cit., Appendix VI.

7 A statistical analysis of the adverse conditions which were significantly likely to appear in combination is given in my Ph.D. thesis, op. cit., pp. 298–9.

8 As far as is known, no local authorities give foster children preferential treatment in regard to educational services. A suggestion worth considering is that both local authority and private foster children should be given priority treatment to compensate for any educational handicaps resulting from their separation from their natural parents. For instance, they could be given priority in obtaining places at nursery schools or in starting school at the earliest age possible.

9 The full definitions can be found in my Ph.D. thesis, op. cit., Appendix VI.

10 No calculations were made in respect of material needs as the number of those assessed with unmet needs was so low.

Chapter 8   Natural parents and their use of private foster homes

1 The natural parent interview schedule is given in my Ph.D. thesis, op. cit., Appendix V.
2 For instance, see Ministry of Housing and Local Government, Report of the Committee on Housing in Greater London (Milner Holland Report), Cmnd. 2605, HMSO, 1965.
3 For a review of the findings of Young and Willmott, Rosser and Harris, and other research into kinship ties, see my Ph.D. thesis, op. cit., pp. 364–6.
4 Parents were classified as students if studying full-time. Those in paid employment and studying in the evenings were classified according to their paid occupation.
5 It should be noted that the occupation and class of fifty-one of the local authority parents could not be ascertained.
6 Statement in House of Commons, 20 February, 1968, see *Hansard*, col. 90 (written answers).
7 Department of Employment and Productivity, *Employment and Productivity Gazette*, May 1969.
8 For a fuller account of West African fostering see my Ph.D. thesis, op. cit., pp. 376–8.
9 For studies of the incidence and distribution of day nurseries see T. Ryan, *Day Nursery Provision under Health Service, England and Wales 1948–63*, National Society of Children's Nurseries, 1964; Holman, *Socially Deprived Families in Britain*, p. 165 and Appendix A; Packman, *Child Care: Needs and Numbers*, pp. 80–3.
10 For an informed description and discussion of life in West Africa see Gibbs, ed., *Peoples of Africa*, especially the chapters by P. Ottenberg, 'The Afiko Ibo of Eastern Nigeria' and P Lloyd, 'The Yoruba of Nigeria'.
11 See Association of Child Care Officers, *Adoption – The Way Ahead*, Monograph No. 3, 1970.

Chapter 9   The private foster home and the natural parents

1 For an interesting documentation of the views of those who believed a clean break was best for the children see Middleton, *When Family Failed*, p. 193.
2 The children followed-up by Lewis were not all in foster homes; some were in institutional care, while others had returned to their families.
3 The definition of these categories is in my Ph.D. thesis, op. cit., Appendix VI.
4 The study of difficulties and a discussion of the reliability of the information, which was sought from the files as well as the foster parents, can be found in my Ph.D. thesis, op. cit., pp. 332–45.

5 The interviewed natural parents were asked how long they had intended their child to stay in the foster home. Their replies were categorised in the same way as the foster mothers' expectancy of tenure. Comparing the two, it was found that 73 per cent of the foster mothers gave the same reply as the natural parents. In other words, the majority of foster mothers had the same expectancy of tenure as that expressed by the natural parents.

6 For instance, see J. Watson, 'Tug-o'-war children', *Guardian*, 21 August 1969.

Chapter 10   The children's departments and private fostering

1 As from April 1971 the children's departments were merged into the local authority social service departments in compliance with the Local Authority Social Services Act (1970). As the present study was carried out prior to this date, the term 'children's departments' is used throughout.

2 The regulations are slightly different for children whose placement is expected to be under eight weeks (Regulation 24).

3 The term 'role' is being used in the way defined by Banton as 'a set of rights and obligations, that is an abstraction to which the behaviour of people will conform in varying degree' (1965, p. 21).

4 In the USA, Wolins (1963) and Fanshel (1966) have made studies relating to voluntary child care agencies.

5 An explanation of Thurstone's method is given in the Appendix.

6 A visit, contact or interview (the words are used interchangeably) was taken to include either the officer visiting the fostering participants or the participants seeing the officer at the children's department. An accidental encounter in the street was not counted. In other words, a contact was counted when a deliberate intention to see the other party was carried through.

7 E. M. Goldberg's work which has since been published as *Helping the Aged*, Allen & Unwin, 1971, was not published at the time, but the author kindly allowed me to see the schedules she used beforehand.

8 The examination excluded foster mothers whose child had been present for less than a year or where no officer had visited at all. Interestingly, the turnover rate for the local authority foster mothers, although not so marked, was not significantly different from that of the private ones.

9 Further questions asking why officers visited private less than local authority foster homes produced similar responses.

10 Rates of visiting was one of the few items showing a significant difference between the two children's departments studied. Both with regard to private and local authority foster homes, the county children's department visited more frequently. As shown in the first chapter, the proportion of officers to total population was, if anything, in favour of the city, but it had more children in care while its concentrated urban population, more than six times the

size of the county, appeared to put greater pressures on the child
care officers.

11 Quoted in Dinnage and Pringle, *Foster Home Care : Facts and
Fallacies*, p. 61.

12 Further, no member of the two children's departments could recall
a case in previous years of removal from a private foster home via
the court.

Chapter 11   The future of private fostering

1 However, the Act does empower local authorities to require
particulars of individual children in cases where they think it necessary.

2 For a fuller definition see L. Banwell and J. Nicol, *Clarke Hall and
Morrison on Children*, Butterworth, 7th ed., 1967, p. 112.

3 Dr P. H. Kuhl, Director of the Danish National Institute of Social
Research, kindly provided information on the position in Denmark.
See also the publication by the Danish Ministries of Labour and
Social Affairs, *Care of Children and Young People*, 1967.

4 Child care officers almost certainly carry more than fifty cases per
year. A Home Office study by E. Grey, *Workloads in Children's
Departments*, HMSO, 1969, found that nine departments, in a two
week period, had 8,025 cases on their books. This works out at just
over forty-one cases per each member of the child care staff. But
the staff included children's officers and senior officers who would
carry few if any cases. Further, over a whole year the number of
cases would be greatly multiplied. However, the low figure of fifty
cases was chosen for two reasons. Firstly, both the Home Office
and some children's officers suggest that work with immigrants,
including West Africans, takes extra skills and time (for instance,
the Home Office report for 1967–9, pp. 12–13, and the report of the
London Borough of Lambeth's Children's Officer, *Children's Service,
the Second Year*, 1967). Secondly, it was considered best to err on
the side of overestimating rather than underestimating the number
of officers needed.

5 Home Office, *Children in Care in England and Wales, March 1970*,
HMSO, 1970, p. 12. The costs exclude the amounts recouped from
parental contributions, on the one hand, and the costs of
administration on the other.

6 Figures issued by the Home Office (Home Office Circular No.
241/1969).

Appendix

1 Some writers believe that question order affects the answers given,
and that therefore the order of questions should be randomised
(see H. Cantril, *Gauging Public Opinion*, Princeton University
Press, 1947, ch. 4). However, it was thought that the advantages
gained from a sequential pattern outweighed this point. It should be
added that at the pilot stage a number of orders was tried. The one

selected seemed to best gain the involvement of the interviewees.

2 For a detailed description of closed and open questions and a discussion of when to use them see R. Kahn and C. Cannell, *The Dynamics of Interviewing*, Wiley, 2nd printing, 1958, pp. 131–43.

3 Although of many years standing, Thurstone's method, as Lovell points out, 'generally yields as equally good results' as any other measure of attitudes. For a fuller explanation of it and for a discussion of its advantages and disadvantages, see one of the following: K. Lovell, *Educational Psychology and Children*, University of London Press, 1963; Oppenheim (1966); and A. Edwards, *Techniques of Attitude Scale Construction*, Appleton–Century–Crofts, 1957.

4 For a full explanation of Guttman's work see Oppenheim (1966), especially pp. 143–51; and C. Selltiz, M. Jahoda, M. Deutsch and S. Cook, *Research Methods in Social Relations*, Methuen, 1965, pp. 344–84.

5 It is possible that the foster mothers were untruthful to the child care officers and the researcher. However, it would seem likely that inconsistencies would have appeared in their lies. Moreover, in such matters as being rejected by the local authority the child care officer's knowledge was not dependent upon the foster mother's information but on a decision by the children's department.

Bibliography

Adamson, G. (1968), 'The foster family. A study of the sociological and psychological background to foster home care with particular reference to the attitudes of foster mothers and to the relationship between child-placing agency and foster mothers', unpublished thesis, University College of South Wales.

Andry, R. (1960), *Delinquency and Parental Pathology*, Methuen.

Association of Child Care Officers, Legal Sub-Committee (1965), duplicated report, January.

Association of Children's Officers, *Child Protection*, duplicated, undated.

Balbernie, R. (1966), *Residential Work With Children*, Pergamon Press.

Balls, J. (1958), *Where Love Is*, Gollancz.

Banton, M. (1965), *Roles*, Tavistock.

(Dr) Barnardo's Homes (1966), *Racial Integration and Barnardo's*.

Baylor, E. and Monachesi, E. (1939), *Rehabilitation of Children*, Harper & Row.

Bowlby, J. (1951), *Maternal Care and Mental Health*, World Health Organisation.

Bowlby, J., *et al.* (1956), 'The effects of mother/child separation: a follow-up study', *Br. J. Med. Psych.*, 29, parts 3 and 4.

Brown, E. P. (1965), 'Change – the children's officer', in *Change and the Child in Care*, Residential Child Care Association.

Brown, E. P. (1966), 'Preventive work', in *Child Care Conference, 1966*, Association of Municipal Corporations.

Central Advisory Council for Education (1963), *Half Our Future* (Newsom Report), HMSO.

Central Advisory Council for Education (1967), *Children and their Primary Schools* (Plowden Report), vols. 1 and 2, HMSO.

Charnley, J. (1955), *The Art of Child Placement*, University of Minneapolis Press.

Child Welfare League of America (1962), *Maternal Deprivation*.

Committee on Higher Education (1963), *Higher Education* (Robbins Report), HMSO.

Cowan, E. and Stout, E. (1939), 'A comparative study of the adjustment made by foster children after complete and partial breaks in continuity of home environment', *Am. J. Orthopsychiat.*, 9, (2).

Cullingworth, J. (1965), *English Housing Trends*, Bell & Son.

David, G. (1967), *Patterns of Social Functioning in Families With Marital and Parent-Child Problems*, University of Toronto Press.

Davies, B. (1968), *Social Needs and Resources in Local Services*, Michael Joseph.

Davis, A. and Havighurst, R. (1947), *Father of the Man*, Houghton Mifflin.

345

Departmental Committee on the Adoption of Children (1970), *Adoption of Children* (Houghton Report), HMSO.

Dinnage, R. and Pringle, M. K. (1967a), *Foster Home Care: Facts and Fallacies*, Longmans.

Dinnage, R. and Pringle, M. K. (1967b), *Residential Child Care: Facts and Fallacies*, Longmans.

Douglas, J. (1964), *The Home and the School*, MacGibbon & Kee.

Douglas, J. and Blomfield, J. (1958), *Children Under Five*, Allen & Unwin.

Dyson, D. (1962), *No Two Alike*, Allen & Unwin.

Ellis, J. (1971), 'The fostering of West African children in England', *Social Work Today*, 2, (5).

Fanshel, D. (1966), *Foster Parenthood, A. Role Analysis*, University of Minnesota Press.

Ferguson, T. (1966), *Children in Care – and After*, Oxford University Press.

Fitzherbert, K. (1967), *West Indian Children in London*, Bell & Son.

Freud, A. and Burlingham, D. (1954), *Infants Without Families*, International University Press.

Gale, J. (1963), 'Non-European children in care', *Child Care*, 17, (4).

Gardner, D. (1964), *Development in Early Childhood*, Harper & Row.

Gay, M. (1969), 'The attainments of children in residential care', *Social Work*, 26, (2), April.

George, V. (1970), *Foster Care: Theory and Practice*, Routledge & Kegan Paul.

Gesell, A. (1954), *The First Five Years of Life*, Methuen.

Gibbs, J., ed. (1965), *Peoples of Africa*, Holt, Rinehart & Winston.

Glickman, E. (1957), *Child Placement Through Clinically Orientated Carework*, Columbia University Press.

Goldfarb, W. (1943), 'Infant rearing and problem behavior', *Am. J. Orthopsychiat.*, 13, (2).

Goldfarb, W. (1945), 'The effects of psychological deprivation in infancy and subsequent stimulation', *Am. J. Psychiat.*, 102.

Goodacre, I. (1966), *Adoption Policy and Practice*, Allen & Unwin.

Goode, W. and Hatt, P. (1952), *Methods in Social Research*, McGraw-Hill.

Goody, E. (1970), 'Kinship fostering in Gonja', in *Socialisation, the Approach from Social Anthropology*, Tavistock.

Gordon, H. (1956), *Casework Services for Children*, Houghton Mifflin.

Gray, P. and Parr, E. (1957), *Children in Care and the Recruitment of Foster Parents*, Government Social Survey.

Gregory, E. (1969), 'Child minding in Paddington', *Medical Officer*, 5 September.

Heinicke, C. and Westheimer, I. (1966), *Brief Separations*, Longmans.

Heraud, B. (1970), *Sociology and Social Work*, Pergamon Press.

Herstein, N. (1957), 'The replacement of children in foster homes', *Child Welfare*, 36, (7).

Hewitt, L. and Jenkins, R. (1946), *Fundamental Patterns of Maladjustment and the Dynamics of their Origin*, University of Illinois.

Heywood, J. (1959), *Children in Care*, Routledge & Kegan Paul.

Hollis, F. (1968), 'A profile of early interviews in marital counselling', *Social Casework*, 44, (1).

Holman, R. (1966), 'The foster child and self-knowledge', *Case Conference*, 12, (9).

Holman, R. (1970a), *Unsupported Mothers and the Care of their Children*, Mothers in Action.

Holman, R., ed. (1970b), *Socially Deprived Families in Britain*, Bedford Square Press.

Holman, R. (1971), 'Private foster homes: a study of the foster children and foster parents supervised by children's departments under the Children Act (1958)', Ph.D. thesis, University of Birmingham.

Home Department; Department of Education and Science; Ministry of Housing and Local Government; Ministry of Health (1968), Report on the Committee on Local Authority and Allied Personal Social Services (Seebohm Report), Cmnd. 3703, HMSO.

Home Office (1946), Report of the Committee on the Care of Children (Curtis Report), Cmd. 6922, HMSO.

Home Office (1951), *Sixth Report on the Work of the Children's Department*, HMSO.

Home Office (1968), *Summary of Local Authorities' Returns of Children in Care at 31 March, 1968*, HMSO.

Home Office (1970a), *The Home Office's Report on the Work of the Children's Department, 1967-9*, HMSO.

Home Office (1970b), *Children in Care in England & Wales, March, 1970*, HMSO.

Hopkirk, M. (1949), *Nobody Wanted Sam*, John Murray.

Howe, E. (1966), *Under 5*, Conservative Political Centre.

Hutchinson, D. (1943), *In Quest of Foster Parents*, Columbia University Press, 3rd printing, 1951.

Inner London Education Authority (1969), *The Education of Immigrant Pupils in Primary Schools*, ILEA.

Jehu, D. (1966), 'Empirical and theoretical developments in the study of discontinuous parental care', *Social Work*, 23, (1).

Jenkins, R. (1963), 'The fostering of coloured children', *Case Conference*, 10, (5).

Jenkins, R. (1965), 'The needs of foster parents', *Case Conference*, 11, (7).

Kahn, J. (1965), *Human Growth and the Development of Personality*, Pergamon Press.

Kastell, J. (1962), *Casework in Child Care*, Routledge & Kegan Paul.

Kay, N. (1966), 'A systematic approach to selecting foster parents', *Case Conference*, 13, (2).

Kaye, B. (1962), *Bringing up Children in Ghana*, Allen & Unwin.

Kerr, M. (1958), *The People of Ship Street*, Routledge & Kegan Paul.

Kornitzer, M. (1968), *Adoption and Family Life*, Putnam.

Leeding, A. (1966), *Child Care Manual*, Butterworth.

Levy, D. (1943), *Maternal Overprotection*, Columbia University Press.

Lewis, H. (1954), *Deprived Children*, Oxford University Press.

McWhinnie, A. (1967), *Adopted Children. How they Grow Up*, Routledge & Kegan Paul.

Marsden, D. (1969), *Mothers Alone*, Allen Lane: Penguin Press.

Middleton, N. (1971), *When Family Failed*, Gollancz.

Ministry of Education (1955), *Report of the Committee on Maladjusted Children* (Underwood Report), HMSO.

Ministry of Social Security (1967), *Circumstances of Families*, HMSO.

Moss, S. (1966), 'How children feel about being placed away from home', *Children* (USA), 13, (4).

Newson, J. and E. (1963), *Infant Care in an Urban Community*, Allen & Unwin.

Newson, J. and E. (1968), *Four Years Old in an Urban Community*, Allen & Unwin.

Oppenheim, A. (1966), *Questionnaire Design and Attitude Measurement*, Heinemann.

Oyerinde, D. (1967), 'The development of age and sex role preferences in American and Nigerian children', unpublished senior thesis, Lake Forest College, USA.

Packman, J. (1968), *Child Care: Needs and Numbers*, Allen & Unwin.

Parker, R. (1966), *Decision in Child Care*, Allen & Unwin.

Philp, A. (1963), *Family Failure*, Faber & Faber.

Pringle, M. K. (1965), *Deprivation and Education*, Longmans.

Pringle, M. K., Butler, N. and Davie, R. (1966), *11,000 Seven Year Olds*, Longmans.

Pugh, E. (1968), *Social Work In Child Care*, Routledge & Kegan Paul.

Raynor, L. (1970), *Adoption of Non-White Children*, Allen & Unwin.

Report on the Work of the Children's Department of the City of Birmingham for the Three Years ending March 1967, City of Birmingham, 1967.

Ribble, M. (1943), *The Rights of Infants*, Columbia University Press.

Roberts, V. (1962), 'An experiment in group work with foster parents', *Case Conference*, 9, (6).

Rosser, C. and Harris, C. (1965), *The Family and Social Change*, Routledge & Kegan Paul.

Schaffer, H. and E. (1968), *Child Care and the Family*, Bell & Son.

Schorr, A. (1964), *Slums and Social Insecurity*, Nelson.

Shaw, L. (1954), 'Impressions of family life in a London suburb', *Sociological Review*, 2.

Sheridan, M. (1960), *The Developmental Progress of Infants and Young Children*, HMSO.

Spence, J., *et al.* (1954), *A Thousand Families in Newcastle-upon-Tyne*, Oxford University Press.

Spencer, K. (1970), 'Housing and socially deprived families', in R. Holman, ed. (1970b).

Spinley, B. (1954), *The Deprived and the Privileged*, Routledge & Kegan Paul.

Spitz, R. (1954), 'Unhappy and fatal outcomes of emotional deprivation and stress in infancy' in I. Galdston, ed., *Beyond the Germ Theory*, Health Education Council.

Spitz, R. and Wolf, K. (1946), 'Analytical depression; an enquiry into the genesis of psychiatric conditions in early childhood', in *Psycho-analytic Study of the Child*, 2, Imago Publishing Co.

Stott, D. (1957), 'The reliability of data in early life', *Case Conference*, 4, (3).

Stott, D. (1965), *33 Troublesome Children*, National Children's Home.

Stroud, J. (1965), *An Introduction to the Child Care Service*, Longmans.

Tarachow, S. (1937), 'The disclosure of foster parentage to a boy', *Am. J. Psychiat.*, 94.

Timms, N. (1962), *Casework in the Child Care Service*, Butterworth.

Trasler, G. (1955), *A Study of Success and Failure of Foster Home Placements*, Ph.D. thesis, University of London.

Trasler, G. (1960), *In Place of Parents*, Routledge & Kegan Paul.

Vernon, P. (1964), *Personality Assessment*, Methuen.

Wakeford, J. (1963), 'Fostering, a sociological perspective', *British Journal of Sociology*, 14, (4).

Weinstein, E. (1960), *The Self-Image of the Foster Child*, Russell Sage Foundation.

Williams, J. (1961), 'Children who break down in foster homes: a psychological study of patterns of personality growth in grossly deprived children', *J. Child Psychol. & Psychiat.*, 2, (1).

Wilson, H. (1962), *Delinquency and Child Neglect*, Allen & Unwin.

Wilson, H. (1970), 'The socialisation of children', in R. Holman, ed. (1970b).

Wimperis, V. (1960), *The Unmarried Mother and her Child*, Allen & Unwin.

Winnicott, C. (1964), *Child Care and Social Work*, Codicot Press.

Witmer, M., *et al.* (1963), *Independent Adoptions*, Russell Sage Foundation.

Wolins, M. (1963), *Selecting Foster Parents*, Columbia University Press.

World Health Organisation (1960), *Child Guidance Clinics*.

World Health Organisation (1962), *Deprivation of Maternal Care*.

Young, M. and Willmott, P. (1957), *Family and Kinship in East London*, Routledge & Kegan Paul.

Yudkin, S. (1967), *0–5, a Report on the Care of Pre-School Children*, National Society of Children's Nurseries.

Yudkin, S. and Holme, A. (1963), *Working Mothers and Their Children*, Allen & Unwin.

Index

International Library of Sociology

Edited by
John Rex
University of Warwick

Founded by
Karl Mannheim

as The International Library of Sociology
and Social Reconstruction

*This Catalogue also contains other Social Science
series published by Routledge*

Routledge & Kegan Paul   London and Boston

68-74 Carter Lane London EC4V 5EL
9 Park Street Boston Mass 02108

Contents

● *Books so marked are available in paperback*
All books are in Metric Demy 8vo format (216 × 138mm approx.)

GENERAL SOCIOLOGY

Belshaw, Cyril. The Conditions of Social Performance. *An Exploratory Theory. 144 pp.*

Brown, Robert. Explanation in Social Science. *208 pp.*

Cain, Maureen E. Society and the Policeman's Role. *About 300 pp.*

Gibson, Quentin. The Logic of Social Enquiry. *240 pp.*

Homans, George C. Sentiments and Activities: *Essays in Social Science. 336 pp.*

Isajiw, Wsevold W. Causation and Functionalism in Sociology. *165 pp.*

Johnson, Harry M. Sociology: *a Systematic Introduction. Foreword by Robert K. Merton. 710 pp.*

Mannheim, Karl. Essays on Sociology and Social Psychology. *Edited by Paul Keckskemeti. With Editorial Note by Adolph Lowe. 344 pp.*

Systematic Sociology: *An Introduction to the Study of Society. Edited by J. S. Erös and Professor W. A. C. Stewart. 220 pp.*

Martindale, Don. The Nature and Types of Sociological Theory. *292 pp.*

● **Maus, Heinz.** A Short History of Sociology. *234 pp.*

Mey, Harald. Field-Theory. *A Study of its Application in the Social Sciences. 352 pp.*

Myrdal, Gunnar. Value in Social Theory: *A Collection of Essays on Methodology. Edited by Paul Streeten. 332 pp.*

Ogburn, William F., and **Nimkoff, Meyer F.** A Handbook of Sociology. *Preface by Karl Mannheim. 656 pp. 46 figures. 35 tables.*

Parsons, Talcott, and **Smelser, Neil J.** Economy and Society: *A Study in the Integration of Economic and Social Theory. 362 pp.*

● **Rex, John.** Key Problems of Sociological Theory. *220 pp.*

Stark, Werner. The Fundamental Forms of Social Thought. *280 pp.*

FOREIGN CLASSICS OF SOCIOLOGY

● **Durkheim, Emile.** Suicide. *A Study in Sociology. Edited and with an Introduction by George Simpson. 404 pp.*

Professional Ethics and Civic Morals. *Translated by Cornelia Brookfield. 288 pp.*

● **Gerth, H. H.,** and **Mills, C. Wright.** From Max Weber: *Essays in Sociology. 502 pp.*

Tönnies, Ferdinand. Community and Association. *(Gemeinschaft und Gesellschaft.) Translated and Supplemented by Charles P. Loomis. Foreword by Pitirim A. Sorokin. 334 pp.*

SOCIAL STRUCTURE

Andreski, Stanislav. Military Organization and Society. *Foreword by Professor A. R. Radcliffe-Brown. 226 pp. 1 folder.*

● **Cole, G. D. H.** Studies in Class Structure. *220 p.*

Coontz, Sydney H. Population Theories and the Economic Interpretation. *202 pp.*

Coser, Lewis. The Functions of Social Conflict. *204 pp.*

Dickie-Clark, H. F. Marginal Situation: *A Sociological Study of a Coloured Group. 240 pp. 11 tables.*

Glass, D. V. (Ed.). Social Mobility in Britain. *Contributions by J. Berent, T. Bottomore, R. C. Chambers, J. Floud, D. V. Glass, J. R. Hall, H. T. Himmelweit, R. K. Kelsall, F. M. Martin, C. A. Moser, R. Mukherjee, and W. Ziegel. 420 pp.*

Glaser, Barney, and **Strauss, Anselm L.** Status Passage. *A Formal Theory. 208 pp.*

Jones, Garth N. Planned Organizational Change: *An Exploratory Study Using an Empirical Approach. 268 pp.*

Kelsall, R. K. Higher Civil Servants in Britain: *From 1870 to the Present Day. 268 pp. 31 tables.*

König, René. The Community. *232 pp. Illustrated.*

● **Lawton, Denis.** Social Class, Language and Education. *192 pp.*

McLeish, John. The Theory of Social Change: *Four Views Considered. 128 pp.*

Marsh, David C. The Changing Social Structure in England and Wales, 1871-1961. *272 pp.*

Mouzelis, Nicos. Organization and Bureaucracy. *An Analysis of Modern Theories. 240 pp.*

Mulkay, M. J. Functionalism, Exchange and Theoretical Strategy. *272 pp.*

Ossowski, Stanislaw. Class Structure in the Social Consciousness. *210 pp.*

SOCIOLOGY AND POLITICS

Crick, Bernard. The American Science of Politics: *Its Origins and Conditions. 284 pp.*

Hertz, Frederick. Nationality in History and Politics: *A Psychology and Sociology of National Sentiment and Nationalism. 432 pp.*

Kornhauser, William. The Politics of Mass Society. *272 pp. 20 tables.*

Laidler, Harry W. History of Socialism. *Social-Economic Movements: An Historical and Comparative Survey of Socialism, Communism, Co-operation, Utopianism; and other Systems of Reform and Reconstruction. 992 pp.*

Mannheim, Karl. Freedom, Power and Democratic Planning. *Edited by Hans Gerth and Ernest K. Bramstedt. 424 pp.*

Mansur, Fatma. Process of Independence. *Foreword by A. H. Hanson. 208 pp.*

Martin, David A. Pacificism: *an Historical and Sociological Study. 262 pp.*

Myrdal, Gunnar. The Political Element in the Development of Economic Theory. *Translated from the German by Paul Streeten. 282 pp.*

Verney, Douglas V. The Analysis of Political Systems. *264 pp.*

Wootton, Graham. Workers, Unions and the State. *188 pp.*

FOREIGN AFFAIRS: THEIR SOCIAL, POLITICAL AND ECONOMIC FOUNDATIONS

Bonné, Alfred. State and Economics in the Middle East: *A Society in Transition. 482 pp.*
 Studies in Economic Development: *with special reference to Conditions in the Under-developed Areas of Western Asia and India. 322 pp. 84 tables.*
Mayer, J. P. Political Thought in France from the Revolution to the Fifth Republic. *164 pp.*

CRIMINOLOGY

Ancel, Marc. Social Defence: *A Modern Approach to Criminal Problems. Foreword by Leon Radzinowicz. 240 pp.*
Cloward, Richard A., and **Ohlin, Lloyd E.** Delinquency and Opportunity: *A Theory of Delinquent Gangs. 248 pp.*
Downes, David M. The Delinquent Solution. *A Study in Subcultural Theory. 296 pp.*
Dunlop, A. B., and **McCabe, S.** Young Men in Detention Centres. *192 pp.*
Friedlander, Kate. The Psycho-Analytical Approach to Juvenile Delinquency: *Theory, Case Studies, Treatment. 320 pp.*
Glueck, Sheldon, and **Eleanor.** Family Environment and Delinquency. *With the statistical assistance of Rose W. Kneznek. 340 pp.*
Lopez-Rey, Manuel. Crime. *An Analytical Appraisal. 288 pp.*
Mannheim, Hermann. Comparative Criminology: *a Text Book. Two volumes. 442 pp. and 380 pp.*
Morris, Terence. The Criminal Area: *A Study in Social Ecology. Foreword by Hermann Mannheim. 232 pp. 25 tables. 4 maps.*
Trasler, Gordon. The Explanation of Criminality. *144 pp.*

SOCIAL PSYCHOLOGY

Bagley, Christopher. The Social Psychology of the Child with Epilepsy. *320 pp.*
Barbu, Zevedei. Problems of Historical Psychology. *248 pp.*
Blackburn, Julian. Psychology and the Social Pattern. *184 pp.*
● **Fleming, C. M.** Adolescence: *Its Social Psychology: With an Introduction to recent findings from the fields of Anthropology, Physiology, Medicine, Psychometrics and Sociometry. 288 pp.*
● The Social Psychology of Education: *An Introduction and Guide to Its Study. 136 pp.*
Homans, George C. The Human Group. *Foreword by Bernard DeVoto. Introduction by Robert K. Merton. 526 pp.*
 Social Behaviour: *its Elementary Forms. 416 pp.*

Klein, Josephine. The Study of Groups. *226 pp. 31 figures. 5 tables.*
Linton, Ralph. The Cultural Background of Personality. *132 pp.*
Mayo, Elton. The Social Problems of an Industrial Civilization. *With an appendix on the Political Problem. 180 pp.*
Ottaway, A. K. C. Learning Through Group Experience. *176 pp.*
Ridder, J. C. de. The Personality of the Urban African in South Africa. *A Thematic Apperception Test Study. 196 pp. 12 plates.*
● **Rose, Arnold M.** (Ed.). Human Behaviour and Social Processes: *an Interactionist Approach. Contributions by Arnold M. Rose, Ralph H. Turner, Anselm Strauss, Everett C. Hughes, E. Franklin Frazier, Howard S. Becker, et al. 696 pp.*
Smelser, Neil J. Theory of Collective Behaviour. *448 pp.*
Stephenson, Geoffrey M. The Development of Conscience. *128 pp.*
Young, Kimball. Handbook of Social Psychology. *658 pp. 16 figures. 10 tables.*

SOCIOLOGY OF THE FAMILY

Banks, J. A. Prosperity and Parenthood: *A Study of Family Planning among The Victorian Middle Classes. 262 pp.*
Bell, Colin R. Middle Class Families: *Social and Geographical Mobility. 224 pp.*
Burton, Lindy. Vulnerable Children. *272 pp.*
Gavron, Hannah. The Captive Wife: *Conflicts of Household Mothers. 190 pp.*
George, Victor, and **Wilding, Paul.** Motherless Families. *220 pp.*
Klein, Josephine. Samples from English Cultures.
  1. Three Preliminary Studies and Aspects of Adult Life in England. *447 pp.*
  2. Child-Rearing Practices and Index. *247 pp.*
Klein, Viola. Britain's Married Women Workers. *180 pp.*
  The Feminine Character. *History of an Ideology. 244 pp.*
McWhinnie, Alexina M. Adopted Children. *How They Grow Up. 304 pp.*
Myrdal, Alva, and **Klein, Viola.** Women's Two Roles: *Home and Work. 238 pp. 27 tables.*
Parsons, Talcott, and **Bales, Robert F.** Family: *Socialization and Interaction Process. In collaboration with James Olds, Morris Zelditch and Philip E. Slater. 456 pp. 50 figures and tables.*

SOCIAL SERVICES

Bastide, Roger. The Sociology of Mental Disorder. *Translated from the French by Jean McNeil. 264 pp.*
Carlebach, Julius. Caring For Children in Trouble. *266 pp.*
Forder, R. A. (Ed.). Penelope Hall's Social Services of Modern England. *352 pp.*
George, Victor. Foster Care. *Theory and Practice. 234 pp.*
  Social Security: *Beveridge and After. 258 pp.*

● **Goetschius, George W.** Working with Community Groups. *256 pp.*

Goetschius, George W., and **Tash, Joan.** Working with Unattached Youth. *416 pp.*

Hall, M. P., and **Howes, I. V.** The Church in Social Work. *A Study of Moral Welfare Work undertaken by the Church of England. 320 pp.*

Heywood, Jean S. Children in Care: *the Development of the Service for the Deprived Child. 264 pp.*

Hoenig, J., and **Hamilton, Marian W.** The De-Segration of the Mentally Ill. *284 pp.*

Jones, Kathleen. Lunacy, Law and Conscience, *1744-1845: the Social History of the Care of the Insane. 268 pp.*

Mental Health and Social Policy, 1845-1959. *264 pp.*

King, Roy D., Raynes, Norma V., and **Tizard, Jack.** Patterns of Residential Care. *356 pp.*

Leigh, John. Young People and Leisure. *256 pp.*

Morris, Pauline. Put Away: *A Sociological Study of Institutions for the Mentally Retarded. 364 pp.*

Nokes, P. L. The Professional Task in Welfare Practice. *152 pp.*

Timms, Noel. Psychiatric Social Work in Great Britain (1939-1962). *280 pp.*

● Social Casework: *Principles and Practice. 256 pp.*

Trasler, Gordon. In Place of Parents: *A Study in Foster Care. 272 pp.*

Young, A. F., and **Ashton, E. T.** British Social Work in the Nineteenth Century. *288 pp.*

Young, A. F. Social Services in British Industry. *272 pp.*

SOCIOLOGY OF EDUCATION

Banks, Olive. Parity and Prestige in English Secondary Education: a Study in Educational Sociology. *272 pp.*

Bentwich, Joseph. Education in Israel. *224 pp. 8 pp. plates.*

● **Blyth, W. A. L.** English Primary Education. *A Sociological Description.*
1. Schools. *232 pp.*
2. Background. *168 pp.*

Collier, K. G. The Social Purposes of Education: *Personal and Social Values in Education. 268 pp.*

Dale, R. R., and **Griffith, S.** Down Stream: *Failure in the Grammar School. 108 pp.*

Dore, R. P. Education in Tokugawa Japan. *356 pp. 9 pp. plates*

Evans, K. M. Sociometry and Education. *158 pp.*

Foster, P. J. Education and Social Change in Ghana. *336 pp. 3 maps.*

Fraser, W. R. Education and Society in Modern France. *150 pp.*

Grace, Gerald R. Role Conflict and the Teacher. *About 200 pp.*

Hans, Nicholas. New Trends in Education in the Eighteenth Century. *278 pp. 19 tables.*

● Comparative Education: *A Study of Educational Factors and Traditions. 360 pp.*

Hargreaves, David. Interpersonal Relations and Education. *432 pp.*
● Social Relations in a Secondary School. *240 pp.*
Holmes, Brian. Problems in Education. *A Comparative Approach. 336 pp.*
King, Ronald. Values and Involvement in a Grammar School. *164 pp.*
● **Mannheim, Karl,** and **Stewart, W. A. C.** An Introduction to the Sociology of Education. *206 pp.*
Morris, Raymond N. The Sixth Form and College Entrance. *231 pp.*
● **Musgrove, F.** Youth and the Social Order. *176 pp.*
● **Ottaway, A. K. C.** Education and Society: *An Introduction to the Sociology of Education. With an Introduction by W. O. Lester Smith. 212 pp.*
Peers, Robert. Adult Education: *A Comparative Study. 398 pp.*
Pritchard, D. G. Education and the Handicapped: *1760 to 1960. 258 pp.*
Richardson, Helen. Adolescent Girls in Approved Schools. *308 pp.*
Simon, Brian, and **Joan** (Eds.). Educational Psychology in the U.S.S.R. *Introduction by Brian and Joan Simon. Translation by Joan Simon. Papers by D. N. Bogoiavlenski and N. A. Menchinskaia, D. B. Elkonin, E. A. Fleshner, Z. I. Kalmykova, G. S. Kostiuk, V. A. Krutetski, A. N. Leontiev, A. R. Luria, E. A. Milerian, R. G. Natadze, B. M. Teplov, L. S. Vygotski, L. V. Zankov. 296 pp.*
Stratta, Erica. The Education of Borstal Boys. *A Study of their Educational Experiences prior to, and during Borstal Training. 256 pp.*

SOCIOLOGY OF CULTURE

Eppel, E. M., and **M.** Adolescents and Morality: *A Study of some Moral Values and Dilemmas of Working Adolescents in the Context of a changing Climate of Opinion. Foreword by W. J. H. Sprott. 268 pp. 39 tables.*
● **Fromm, Erich.** The Fear of Freedom. *286 pp.*
The Sane Society. *400 pp.*
● **Mannheim, Karl.** Diagnosis of Our Time: *Wartime Essays of a Sociologist. 208 pp.*
Essays on the Sociology of Culture. *Edited by Ernst Mannheim in co-operation with Paul Kecskemeti. Editorial Note by Adolph Lowe. 280 pp.*
Weber, Alfred. Farewell to European History: *or The Conquest of Nihilism. Translated from the German by R. F. C. Hull. 224 pp.*

SOCIOLOGY OF RELIGION

Argyle, Michael. Religious Behaviour. *224 pp. 8 figures. 41 tables.*
Nelson, G. K. Spiritualism and Society. *313 pp.*

Stark, Werner. The Sociology of Religion. *A Study of Christendom.*
  Volume I. *Established Religion. 248 pp.*
  Volume II. *Sectarian Religion. 368 pp.*
  Volume III. *The Universal Church. 464 pp.*
  Volume IV. *Types of Religious Man. 352 pp.*
  Volume V. *Types of Religious Culture. 464 pp.*
Watt, W. Montgomery. Islam and the Integration of Society. *320 pp.*

SOCIOLOGY OF ART AND LITERATURE

Beljame, Alexandre. Men of Letters and the English Public in the Eighteenth
  Century: *1660-1744, Dryden, Addison, Pope. Edited with an Introduction
  and Notes by Bonamy Dobrée. Translated by E. O. Lorimer. 532 pp.*
Jarvie, Ian C. Towards a Sociology of the Cinema. *A Comparative Essay
  on the Structure and Functioning of a Major Entertainment Industry.
  405 pp.*
Rust, Frances S. Dance in Society. *An Analysis of the Relationships between
  the Social Dance and Society in England from the Middle Ages to the
  Present Day. 256 pp. 8 pp. of plates.*
Schücking, L. L. The Sociology of Literary Taste. *112 pp.*
Silbermann, Alphons. The Sociology of Music. *Translated from the German
  by Corbet Stewart. 222 pp.*

SOCIOLOGY OF KNOWLEDGE

Mannheim, Karl. Essays on the Sociology of Knowledge. *Edited by Paul
  Kecskemeti. Editorial note by Adolph Lowe. 353 pp.*
Stark, Werner. The Sociology of Knowledge: *An Essay in Aid of a Deeper
  Understanding of the History of Ideas. 384 pp.*

URBAN SOCIOLOGY

Ashworth, William. The Genesis of Modern British Town Planning: *A Study
  in Economic and Social History of the Nineteenth and Twentieth Centuries.
  288 pp.*
Cullingworth, J. B. Housing Needs and Planning Policy: *A Restatement of
  the Problems of Housing Need and 'Overspill' in England and Wales.
  232 pp. 44 tables. 8 maps.*
Dickinson, Robert E. City and Region: *A Geographical Interpretation.
  608 pp. 125 figures.*
  The West European City: *A Geographical Interpretation. 600 pp. 129 maps.
  29 plates.*
● The City Region in Western Europe. *320 pp. Maps.*

9

Humphreys, Alexander J. New Dubliners: *Urbanization and the Irish Family.* *Foreword by George C. Homans. 304 pp.*

Jackson, Brian. Working Class Community: *Some General Notions raised by a Series of Studies in Northern England. 192 pp.*

Jennings, Hilda. Societies in the Making: *a Study of Development and Redevelopment within a County Borough. Foreword by D. A. Clark. 286 pp.*

Kerr, Madeline. The People of Ship Street. *240 pp.*

● **Mann, P. H.** An Approach to Urban Sociology. *240 pp.*

Morris, R. N., and **Mogey, J.** The Sociology of Housing. *Studies at Berinsfield. 232 pp. 4 pp. plates.*

Rosser, C., and **Harris, C.** The Family and Social Change. *A Study of Family and Kinship in a South Wales Town. 352 pp. 8 maps.*

RURAL SOCIOLOGY

Chambers, R. J. H. Settlement Schemes in Africa: *A Selective Study. 268 pp.*

Haswell, M. R. The Economics of Development in Village India. *120 pp.*

Littlejohn, James. Westrigg: *the Sociology of a Cheviot Parish. 172 pp. 5 figures.*

Williams, W. M. The Country Craftsman: *A Study of Some Rural Crafts and the Rural Industries Organization in England. 248 pp. 9 figures. (Dartington Hall Studies in Rural Sociology.)*

The Sociology of an English Village: *Gosforth. 272 pp. 12 figures. 13 tables.*

SOCIOLOGY OF INDUSTRY AND DISTRIBUTION

Anderson, Nels. Work and Leisure. *280 pp.*

● **Blau, Peter M.,** and **Scott, W. Richard.** Formal Organizations: *a Comparative approach. Introduction and Additional Bibliography by J. H. Smith. 326 pp.*

Eldridge, J. E. T. Industrial Disputes. *Essays in the Sociology of Industrial Relations. 288 pp.*

Hetzler, Stanley. Technological Growth and Social Change. *Achieving Modernization. 269 pp.*

Hollowell, Peter G. The Lorry Driver. *272 pp.*

Jefferys, Margot, *with the assistance of Winifred Moss.* Mobility in the Labour Market: *Employment Changes in Battersea and Dagenham. Preface by Barbara Wootton. 186 pp. 51 tables.*

Millerson, Geoffrey. The Qualifying Associations: *a Study in Professionalization. 320 pp.*

Smelser, Neil J. Social Change in the Industrial Revolution: *An Application of Theory to the Lancashire Cotton Industry, 1770-1840. 468 pp. 12 figures. 14 tables.*

Williams, Gertrude. Recruitment to Skilled Trades. *240 pp.*

Young, A. F. Industrial Injuries Insurance: *an Examination of British Policy. 192 pp.*

ANTHROPOLOGY

Ammar, Hamed. Growing up in an Egyptian Village: *Silwa, Province of Aswan. 336 pp.*

Brandel-Syrier, Mia. Reeftown Elite. *A Study of Social Mobility in a Modern African Community on the Reef. 376 pp.*

Crook, David, and **Isabel.** Revolution in a Chinese Village: *Ten Mile Inn. 230 pp. 8 plates. 1 map.*

The First Years of Yangyi Commune. *302 pp. 12 plates.*

Dickie-Clark, H. F. The Marginal Situation. *A Sociological Study of a Coloured Group. 236 pp.*

Dube, S. C. Indian Village. *Foreword by Morris Edward Opler. 276 pp. 4 plates.*

India's Changing Villages: *Human Factors in Community Development. 260 pp. 8 plates. 1 map.*

Firth, Raymond. Malay Fishermen. *Their Peasant Economy. 420 pp. 17 pp. plates.*

Gulliver, P. H. Social Control in an African Society: a Study of the Arusha, Agricultural Masai of Northern Tanganyika. *320 pp. 8 plates. 10 figures.*

Ishwaran, K. Shivapur. *A South Indian Village. 216 pp.*

Tradition and Economy in Village India: *An Interactionist Approach. Foreword by Conrad Arensburg. 176 pp.*

Jarvie, Ian C. The Revolution in Anthropology. *268 pp.*

Jarvie, Ian C., and **Agassi, Joseph.** Hong Kong. *A Society in Transition. 396 pp. Illustrated with plates and maps.*

Little, Kenneth L. Mende of Sierra Leone. *308 pp. and folder.*

Negroes in Britain. *With a New Introduction and Contemporary Study by Leonard Bloom. 320 pp.*

Lowie, Robert H. Social Organization. *494 pp.*

Mayer, Adrian C. Caste and Kinship in Central India: *A Village and its Region. 328 pp. 16 plates. 15 figures. 16 tables.*

Smith, Raymond T. The Negro Family in British Guiana: *Family Structure and Social Status in the Villages. With a Foreword by Meyer Fortes. 314 pp. 8 plates. 1 figure. 4 maps.*

DOCUMENTARY

Meek, Dorothea L. (Ed.). Soviet Youth: *Some Achievements and Problems. Excerpts from the Soviet Press, translated by the editor. 280 pp.*

Schlesinger, Rudolf (Ed.). Changing Attitudes in Soviet Russia.

2. *The Nationalities Problem and Soviet Administration. Selected Readings on the Development of Soviet Nationalities Policies. Introduced by the editor. Translated by W. W. Gottlieb. 324 pp.*

SOCIOLOGY AND PHILOSOPHY

Barnsley, John H. The Social Reality of Ethics. *A Comparative Analysis of Moral Codes. 448 pp.*

Douglas, Jack D. (Ed.). Understanding Everyday Life. *Toward the Reconstruction of Sociological Knowledge. Contributions by Alan F. Blum. Aaron W. Cicourel, Norman K. Denzin, Jack D. Douglas, John Heeren, Peter McHugh, Peter K. Manning, Melvin Power, Matthew Speier, Roy Turner, D. Lawrence Wieder, Thomas P. Wilson and Don H. Zimmerman. 358 pp.*

Jarvie, Ian C. Concepts and Society. *216 pp.*

Roche, Maurice. Phenomenology, Language and the Social Sciences. *About 400 pp.*

Sklair, Leslie. The Sociology of Progress. *320 pp.*

International Library of Social Policy

General Editor   Kathleen Janes

Jones, Kathleen. Mental Health Services. *A history, 1744-1971. About 500 pp.*

Thomas, J. E. The English Prison Officer since 1850: *A Study in Conflict. 258 pp.*

Primary Socialization, Language and Education

General Editor   Basil Bernstein

Bernstein, Basil. Class, Codes and Control. *2 volumes.*
  1. *Theoretical Studies Towards a Sociology of Language. 254 pp.*
  2. *Applied Studies Towards a Sociology of Language. About 400 pp.*

Brandis, Walter, and **Henderson, Dorothy.** Social Class, Language and Communication. *288 pp.*

Cook, Jenny. Socialization and Social Control. *About 300 pp.*

Gahagan, D. M., and **G. A.** Talk Reform. *Exploration in Language for Infant School Children. 160 pp.*

Robinson, W. P., and **Rackstraw, Susan, D. A.** A Question of Answers. *2 volumes. 192 pp. and 180 pp.*

Turner, Geoffrey, J., and **Mohan, Bernard, A.** A Linguistic Description and Computer Programme for Children's Speech. *208 pp.*

Reports of the Institute of Community Studies and the Institute of Social Studies in Medical Care

Cartwright, Ann. Human Relations and Hospital Care. *272 pp.*
Parents and Family Planning Services. *306 pp.*
Patients and their Doctors. *A Study of General Practice. 304 pp.*
Dunnell, Karen, and **Cartwright, Ann.** Medicine Takers, Prescribers and Hoarders. *About 140 pp.*
● **Jackson, Brian.** Streaming: *an Education System in Miniature. 168 pp.*
Jackson, Brian, and **Marsden, Dennis.** Education and the Working Class: *Some General Themes raised by a Study of 88 Working-class Children in a Northern Industrial City. 268 pp. 2 folders.*
Marris, Peter. Widows and their Families. *Foreword by Dr. John Bowlby. 184 pp. 18 tables. Statistical Summary.*
Family and Social Change in an African City. *A Study of Rehousing in Lagos. 196 pp. 1 map. 4 plates. 53 tables.*
The Experience of Higher Education. *232 pp. 27 tables.*
Marris, Peter, and **Rein, Martin.** Dilemmas of Social Reform. *Poverty and Community Action in the United States. 256 pp.*
Marris, Peter, and **Somerset, Anthony.** African Businessmen. *A Study of Entrepreneurship and Development in Kenya. 256 pp.*
Runciman, W. G. Relative Deprivation and Social Justice. *A Study of Attitudes to Social Inequality in Twentieth Century England. 352 pp.*
Townsend, Peter. The Family Life of Old People: *An Inquiry in East London. Foreword by J. H. Sheldon. 300 pp. 3 figures. 63 tables.*
Willmott, Peter. Adolescent Boys in East London. *230 pp.*
The Evolution of a Community: *a study of Dagenham after forty years. 168 pp. 2 maps.*
Willmott, Peter, and **Young, Michael.** Family and Class in a London Suburb. *202 pp. 47 tables.*
Young, Michael. Innovation and Research in Education. *192 pp.*
● **Young, Michael,** and **McGeeney, Patrick.** Learning Begins at Home. *A Study of a Junior School and its Parents. 128 pp.*
Young, Michael, and **Willmott, Peter.** Family and Kinship in East London. *Foreword by Richard M. Titmuss. 252 pp. 39 tables.*

Medicine, Illness and Society
General Editor W. M. Williams

Robinson, David. The Process of Becoming Ill.
Stacey, Margaret. *et al.* Hospitals, Children and Their Families. *The Report of a Pilot Study. 202 pp.*

13

Routledge Social Science Journals

The British Journal of Sociology. *Edited by Terence P. Morris. Vol. 1, No. 1, March 1950 and Quarterly. Roy. 8vo. Back numbers available. An international journal with articles on all aspects of sociology.*

Economy and Society. *Vol. 1, No. 1. February 1972 and Quarterly. Metric Roy. 8vo. A journal for all social scientists covering sociology, philosophy, anthropology, economics and history.*

Printed in Great Britain by Lewis Reprints Limited
Brown Knight & Truscott Group, London and Tonbridge   21972